TALES FROM THE AMERICAN FRONTIER

Pantheon Books   New York

TALES FROM THE AMERICAN FRONTIER

EDITED, TOLD, RETOLD, AND ILLUSTRATED BY RICHARD ERDOES

LIBRARY OF CONGRESS CATALOGING-IN-PUBLICATION DATA

Tales from the American frontier/edited, told, retold, and illustrated
by Richard Erdoes.
    p.   cm.—(The Pantheon fairy tale and folklore library)
   ISBN 0-394-51682-6
   1. Tales—West (U.S.)   2. Frontier and pioneer life—West (U.S.)
—Folklore. I. Erdoes, Richard. II. Series: Pantheon fairy tale &
folklore library.

GR109.T35   1991   90-53436

398.2'0978—dc20

Grateful acknowledgment is made to the following for permission to
reprint previously published material:

Alfred A. Knopf, Inc.: "Thunder Bay" from *The Saginaw Paul Bunyan*
by James Stevens. Copyright 1925, 1947 by Alfred A. Knopf, Inc., and
renewed 1953 by James Stevens. "Good for Our Assets" from *Saloons
of the Old West* by Richard Erdoes. Copyright © 1979 by Richard
Erdoes. Reprinted by permission of the publisher.

American Folklore Society: "The Two Witches" from "A New Mexico
Village" by Helen Zunser, from *Journal of American Folklore* 48:188,
1935. Reprinted by permission. Not for further reproduction.

The Richmond Organization: Excerpts from *Billy the Kid* collected,
adapted, and arranged by John A. Lomax and Alan Lomax. TRO –
copyright © 1938 (renewed) Ludlow Music, Inc., New York, N.Y.
Reprinted by permission.

Book Design by Anne Scatto

Manufactured in the United States of America

First Edition

To Jean, my favorite storyteller

Contents

It Ain't Necessarily So

Reader beware! This is a book of legends and fairy tales, not a work of cold, factual history. Sagas of the American West differ from those of other countries insofar as they often deal with real, historical personalities made into fairy-tale characters. Some events had hardly occurred when mythmakers were already at work to *corriger la vérité,* as the French put it, making poetical mountains out of historical molehills.

Davy Crockett and Jim Bowie did not fight to the death at the Alamo, but surrendered and were later butchered. John Colter did not hide himself inside a beaver hut in company with its furry tenants, but under floating driftwood. Wild Bill Hickok, "King of the Pistoleers," could not shoot straight. Pegleg Pete did not amputate his own leg, but let Bill Sublette do it for him. Calamity Jane did not acquire her name because she rescued a soldier from dire calamity, but because gentlemen, after spending a night with her, were struck by a "venereal calamity." Deadwood Dick, Paul Bunyan, and Pecos Bill existed only in some writers' vivid imaginations. All true, but when faced with a choice between sober fact and beguiling poesy, I have chosen poesy every time. Damn the debunkers!

These tales are all well over one hundred years old. They reflect the language, foibles, and prejudices of their time. The settlers who despoiled the Indians of their land called them "fiends," "heathens," or "red devils." They were themselves often considerably more savage than those they called savages. Scalping, after all, was a white man's invention. And of course, you hate most those whom you have injured and robbed. On the other hand, there was much intermarriage, legal or illegal, between whites and Native Americans, some of the pathfinders and trappers becoming more Indian than the Indians themselves in the process. White America could never make up its mind whether to look upon the Indians as noble savages, unspoiled children of nature—morally superior to their white conquerors—or "fiendish redskins." The Indians, for their part, had their own choice epithets for the palefaces—"fat-takers," "hairy fools," or "evil spidermen," in their respective languages. We should not forget that white bounty hunters going after human game, "to make room for civilization," received ten dollars for every scalp from an Indian male and five dollars for those from women and children.

In the Southwest, those called Anglos and Norteamericanos called the Hispanics "greasers." The locals retaliated by calling the invaders "gringos." However, it was the Hispanic vaquero who taught the newcomers how to become cowboys, enriching the American language with such words as "lasso," "rodeo," "corral," "remuda," "bronco," and innumerable others.

Some of the stories that struck the nineteenth-century frontiersman as funny seem outrageous to us now, yet are an unerasable part of our folklore. The Frontier West was macho country, in which, sometimes, women played a conspicuous part. It was a violent land in which folks went to see a hanging as nowadays they would go to a movie or a county fair. And yet, reading today's newspapers or watching the news on the idiot box, one might come to the conclusion that the Old West was a comparatively peaceable place. Colorful, raunchy, violent, lyrical, tragic, or funny, these tales are not always—to use a modern term—"politically correct." Enjoy them in a spirit of innocence.

Richard Erdoes

Foreword

Myths are indications of people's soul and character. We carry within us the memories of age-old ancestral tales, transmitted by mouth from generation to generation until the arrival of the myth-killing boobtube. In the words of Joseph Campbell, "Myths are clues to the spiritual potentialities of human life."

Legends become a nation's fate. The Odyssey embodies not only the poetry of the ancient Greeks, but also their restless, adventurous nature, which urged them to sail their frail oared crafts from the Black Sea to the Pillars of Hercules and beyond, to the Land of Amber on the Baltic shores.

The Saga of the Nibelungs epitomizes the German's lust for war —war for its own sake, waged not to win, but to die.

In the stories of Gargantua and Pantagruel shines forth the spirit of France—*l'esprit, élan vital,* humor, ribaldry, the love of women and the good things in life.

The essence of American legends, particularly of western tales, is exaggeration. Nowhere else in the world can one find boastful grandiloquence like this. It is an exaggeration born of space—tales as big as the continent, stretching from sea to sea, stories evolving from a background of mighty rivers, endless plains, and shining mountains. It is this penchant for exaggeration which, in our own days, gave rise to a John Wayne, a Rambo, or a Batman. In western tales everything is larger than life, blown up out of all proportions as super-trappers fight super-Indians, super-ghosts, and super-bears. Lies are super-lies, as big as the proverbial Ocean of Grass.

Heroic tales rise out of a people on the move, discovering what is unknown, possessing themselves of new, strange lands, leaving history behind, pushing into a barely perceived future. Bragging is elevated into a novel, uniquely American art. Strangers introduce themselves: "I'm a rip-tail roarer! I can whip my weight in wildcats and tackle a grizzly without flinchin'! I was suckled by a she-bear and the click of a six-shooter is music to my ears. I'm from Texas, gentlemen. They call me the Great-Rip-tailed Roarer!"

The answer to this brag might be: "I'm the double-jawed hyena of the West. I got two rows of nipples and holes bored for more. I pull up trees by the roots an' if a mountin gits in my way, I jest kick her to one side. I'm a rarin', tearin' tornado of chain lightning, the idol of all wimmin and bad news to their men. I hail from Missouri, gentlemen. I'm half horse and half alligator!"

Fellows such as these had women to match. A toughened "soiled dove of the prairie" might announce herself: "I'm the human wildcat! I can lick a mountain lion with one hand tied behind my back! My bonnet is a hornets' nest garnished with bear claws. My dress is all wolfskin. I can scream like a panther and outdance any gal from here to Californy. I have a baked horny toad for breakfast and can take on ten gentlemen in a single hour and leave 'em limp with exhaustion! They call me Deadwood Dolly!"

The legends of the Old World go back to the dawn of history. They are peopled with gods and heroes of Ancient Greece, Egypt, and Babylon. They carry the traces of deeds of Thor, Odin, and Celtic faeries. By contrast, tales of the American West are newborn, a product of, at most, a measly two hundred years. They deal, therefore, in many cases with real people and real events, with such backwoods characters and mountain men as Mike Fink, Davy Crockett, Paul Bunyan, Kit Carson, or Killbuck. Some of these men became legends in their own lifetime thanks to the fertile imagination of eastern journalists and writers of penny dreadfuls who had Daniel Boone or Davy Crockett kill three Indians with one bullet, subdue ferocious grizzlies with their fists, swing Tarzan-like from vines and branches to save themselves from savage pursuers. A fanciful article in *Harper's Weekly* made Wild Bill Hickok, the King of the Pistoleers, into a culture hero overnight. Other writers manufactured out of whole cloth a love affair between him and an outrageously romanticized Calamity Jane, in reality a horse-faced, alcoholic sometime prostitute. In reality, Wild Bill could not hit the side of a barn at five paces according to those who really knew him.

Buffalo Bill was, 90 percent of him, an invention of Nat Buntline's creative mind. Deadwood Dick never existed except in the pages of a New York city slicker called Ed Wheeler.

David Crockett pretended to be annoyed with the writer who had made him into a living legend, so annoyed that he decided to write his own autobiography. Crockett complained that the author of his spurious "autobiography" "professed to give my narrative (as he often does) in my own language, and then puts in my mouth such language as would disgrace even an outlandish African. He must himself be sensible of the injustice he has done me, and the trick he has played off on the public. I have met with hundreds, if not thousands of people who have almost in every instance expressed the most profound astonishment at finding me in human shape, and with the countenance, appearance, and common feelings of a human being. It is to correct all these false notions, and to do justice to myself, that I have written." Thus the irrepressible backwoodsman made his own myths, "full of lies as a dog has fleas," in the opinion of one contemporary.

The men out of whose lives fairy tales were created did indeed exist. Their legends are history turned upside down; for the overwhelming part they are fiction, but with a microscopic dash of fact to give them verisimilitude. Many of these folk heros were less than imposing in real life. Kit Carson was a diminutive fellow weighing 135 pounds with his boots on. Brooklyn-born Billy the Kid was a buck-toothed juvenile delinquent, Calamity Jane ugly as sin. Many of these supermen and superwomen, by modern standards, were not very attractive personalities. One nineteenth-century author wrote, somewhat apologetically: "If it be objected that many of these worthies seem to lack a sufficient respect for the sacredness of human life, their surroundings should be remembered. If they were apparently too ready with the knife or the trigger it was because their own lives were felt to be held cheaply by many about them who were unrestrained by the law." The writer added piously: "At least we have glorified no gory outlaws, nor have we painted in alluring colors the road to the penitentiary and the scaffold."

Western legends tell not only of semihistorical heroes and badmen but also of witches, ghosts, devils, and fabulous beasts. They speak of buried treasures and lost mines. Some are known, pure and simple, as "lying stories," and here again the lies are the biggest and most unbelievable in the world. Many tales recur again and again in many guises, involving different people in a variety of places and situations.

Tales of the Hispanic Southwest have an altogether different flavor of pride and honor, of saints and Penitentes, of haughty caballeros and seductive señoritas.

The well has not dried up. The West abounds in modern legends, tales of ghostly trains, planes, and automobiles, even of bewitched computers. Tabloids on display in western supermarkets scream at us with strange headlines, such as I CARRY THE BABY OF ELVIS PRESLEY'S GHOST or JOHN WAYNE IS ALIVE ON THE PLANET ZENOBIA!

"West" is a word of many meanings. To the western Viking it meant first Greenland and then Vinland, that is, North America. From the very beginning the first white men who stepped upon the shores of the New World steeped their stories in myth. Thorgisl, sailing westward for weeks on end, cut his nipple and let his starving baby son tug on it until, at first, blood flowed from it. He made the infant suck and suck until the blood turned into milk. Thus, a father's love nourished the son.

The Vikings came ashore in the land of "One-Footers" *(Einfoetingr)*.

This is true, us men pursued
a One-Footer who came to the strand.
This One-Footer ran swiftly over hills.
This we tell you.

Thorvald, son of Eric the Red, was killed by such a One-Footer. And there was "Freydis, big with child, whetting her sword on her bare breasts," facing the Skraelings with blade and blood-ax until they fled in terror.

The border advanced bit by bit. To the pilgrims and the settlers of New Amsterdam, the West was the land beyond the Alleghenies. "Kaintuck," the country beyond the Cumberland Gap, was the Far West. To the early keelboatmen, the Ohio country was the wilderness eventually called The Old Northwest. As that region became the Midwest, the West meant the prairies beyond the Mississippi and Missouri rivers, the playground of Indians, buffalo, and the mountain men or beaver trappers. The area slightly beyond that became the home of gold-seekers, cowboys, gunfighters, and vigilantes; in time it came to be known as the Wild West. The last barrier to be pierced was the Rockies, Zebulon Pike's "Shining Mountains." Once the great range had been conquered, the way lay open to the Sierras and, finally, the Pacific, the Farthest West. After 1847, the vast region won as the result of the War with Mexico became the Southwest.

Each of these clearly marked geographical areas gave birth to a special sort of men and women, to a particular form of speech, and to a distinct form of mythology and folklore, to the legends of back-woodsmen and pathfinders, of pioneers and keelboatmen, prospectors and farmers, cowboys and shootists, gamblers, painted cats and railroaders. Thus were born a thousand wild and untamed tales told around a thousand campfires, expressive of William Blake's heartfelt "Oh, how I dreamed of things impossible!"

TALES
FROM THE
AMERICAN FRONTIER

CHAPTER 1

Ohio Fever

*Disowned in an age of scepticism, there was once—and the time is not
so far removed, no part of the body politic over which what we now
vaguely term the legendary did not exercise the strongest influence, so
that far from being merely a record of amusing fables, these tales,
which are mostly founded in fact, disclose the secret springs by which
society was moved and history made.*

SAMUEL ADAMS DRAKE

The colonists called it "the West." What they meant by this was the
Pennsylvania wilderness beyond York and Lancaster, a country teeming
with bears, catamounts, wolves, and deer, as well as with hostile Indians.
On its farthest border an occasional buffalo could be met with. Here the
French barred the advance of English-speaking settlers pressing forever
westward, consumed by "Ohio fever."

It has been said that the wilderness was conquered by the ax, the long
rifle, the canoe, and the Conestoga wagon. Emerson Hough, a man inspired
by dreams of empire and manifest destiny, waxed lyrical in his paeans to
these four articles by which, in his opinion, the West was won.

I ask you to look at this splendid tool, the American ax. . . . If you cannot use it, you are not American. If you do not understand it, you cannot understand America.

This tool is so simple and so perfect that it has scarcely seen change in the course of a hundred years. It lacks decoration, as do the tools and weapons of all strong peoples. . . . It is simple, severe, perfect. . . . It is a tremendous thing, this ax of early Americans.

Over the second article Hough exulted:

Witness this sweet ancient weapon of our fathers, the American rifle, maker of states, empire builder. . . . This is no belonging of a weak or savage man. It is the weapon of the Anglo-Saxon, that is the Anglo-Saxon in America, who invented it because he had need of it.

Of the third article he remarked:

Here is the fairy ship of the wilderness, the birchbark canoe, the first craft of America. . . . It is the ship of adventure, belonging by right to him that goes far and travels light, who is careless of his home coming. . . . It is a great-hearted craft.

As to the Conestoga wagon, it became the "inland ship," the "frigate of commerce," and, ultimately, the "prairie schooner."

Stripped of its John Wayne verbiage, there is some truth in Emerson Hough, but he was a chauvinist, even a racist, otherwise he would have known that his "American rifle" was the creation of German gunsmiths who first wrought this wonder weapon at the town of Hickory, later known as Lancaster. Known as the Kentucky rifle, it should rather be called the Pennsylvania rifle. By 1750 thousands of them were in use all along the border. The birchbark canoe was invented by American Indians and mightily improved upon by French voyageurs. The Conestoga wagon was first knocked together by Pennsylvania Dutchmen of the Conestoga Valley in Lancaster County. So much for that.

The early Pennsylvania border was a place where peaceful sectarians found their utopias, but also a region of massacres, abductions, and hairbreadth escapes. Here young Major George Washington founded Fort Necessity and was forced to surrender it to the French. Here General Braddock and a large British and colonial army was defeated by a force of French regulars, Canadian coureurs de bois and their Indian allies. Here was the country of the homespun heroes whom some historians have called the "first westerners."

The Devil and Major Stobo

This story appears in many versions, taking place in different locales with different characters. Only one of the protagonists remains always the same.

Major Stobo, a hero in war as in love, had grown old. His hair had turned white, his skin to parched leather. He was suffering from gout and, worse, John Thomas was no longer answering all the demands the major made upon him. Favors, once granted willingly, nay, with enthusiasm, had now to be paid for. Worst of all, he had finally run through his fortune—no great surprise considering his lifestyle. He was reduced to one tottering manservant who worked, unsatisfactorily, for room and board. An ancient cackling crone prepared his meals, no longer dainty and mouth-watering but, in Stobo's opinion, unpalatable. He was sitting hunched over before his fireplace, a plaid over his shoulders, his suffering, throbbing foot swathed in bandages, resting on a padded footstool. Stobo was grumbling to himself: "Old age be damned! I'd sell my soul to the devil to be rid of this confounded gout, to be able to roger Belette, that saucy wench, to have John Thomas do his duty again, to have some money to spend!"

No sooner said than there was a deep rumbling in the chimney. The crows on the tree before the window broke into a diabolic cackling. Screeching with terror, the old tomcat leaped down from the major's lap to hide himself, his fur setting off sparks. The elderly hound dog howled mournfully, cowering in a corner. A shower of sparks came down the chimney, followed by great clouds of choking ashes, followed, in turn, by a smiling stranger of endearing manners. The decidedly odd fellow was dressed in red velvet. His white ruffled shirt and white laced cuffs were clean and unsmudged. Not a speck of soot could be discerned on his face, quite remarkable in view of the path by which he had entered the house. The stranger was swarthy. He had a pointed nose, a pointed stylish goatee, oddly pointed shoes, and a towering, old-fashioned wig with two points at each side at the top.

Stobo perceived at once that he was in the presence of his satanic majesty. The wig, he had realized at once, was intended to hide the horns. Yet the devil was clearly a gentleman, something Stobo had always suspected.

"At your service," said Old Nick, making a courtly bow.

"Are you always in such a devilish hurry?" asked the major.

"My dear sir. I am ever prompt in giving satisfaction to my customers, especially men of quality like yourself. Also you are an old soldier. I am partial to them."

"The devil you are."

"Indeed. I chanced to overhear your monologue, my dear major. All your wants shall be taken care of. I am entirely at your command. Your gout—but it has already vanished, I trust. The fair Belette shall swoon tonight in your arms. Rest assured John Thomas will do his soldierly duty. Me thinks he is already bestirring himself. As to the wherewithal, the money, behold the pewter tankard yonder on the mantelpiece, a good-sized mug. You will find it full to the brim with specie—louis d'or, golden Georges, écus, thalers, escudos, doubloons, crowns, pieces of eight. And no matter how much you take out, esteemed Major Stobo, you shall find this most excellent bumper always filled to overflowing."

"God's fish! Doubloons, louis d'or you say?"

"Full to the brim, always and forever. There remains the small matter of price. A mere trifle, a superfluity you'll never miss. I have prepared a document"—and here the devil drew from his ample sleeve a parchment scroll—"pray, peruse it. You will remark a blank space, left blank to insert the number of years after which this note shall be due. Shall we say three years?"

"Shall we say seven?"

"I can refuse nothing to you, sir. I ever indulge the wishes of an old hero. Seven it is." And at once, as if by magic, the words "seven years" appeared in the open space. "It awaits only your signature."

"Of course, but see here, old fellow, my eyes are not what they used to be. I will fetch my spectacles to study this agreement before appending my name. Also I shall apply my seal to make it official. I shall be back anon."

The major went into an adjoining chamber, absentmindedly taking the scroll, closing the door behind him. Once alone, the major
put on his spectacles and quickly scrutinized the document, which
read:

"For services rendered Major Rbt. Stobo hereby bequeathes his
body and soul to myself. This promissory note to fall due seven years
from signing. Apollyon Mephisto, Esqu."

Now the major had been many things in his life—soldier, Indian
fighter, duelist, womanizer, and cardsharp. But these were not the
total sums of his accomplishments. Stobo had also served as spy in
the service of his royal master, King George, and was adept in the
ways of this craft. He took from a drawer a phial of invisible ink and
inserted between the words body and soul the sentence "in no wise
my immortal." He then heated sealing wax in the flame of a candle
imprinting his signet ring with the Stobo coat of arms upon it. He
then joined his guest by the fire.

"Ah, here you are, Major. I trust you found everything in order."

"I did indeed, good sir. I shall now sign this agreement before
your eyes." Stobo was about to dip quill into inkwell, but the devil
stayed his hand: "No, no, no, my dear major, my notes must be
signed in blood." Deftly, Lucifer pricked Stobo's index finger with
the tip of what looked like a lady's jeweled hatpin and drew a little
blood. Stobo took up a few drops on the nib of his goose quill and
signed with a flourish: Major Robert Stobo, Knight. This done, he
turned to his guest, saying, "This calls for a drink, my dear fellow."

"I must decline, Major," protested the devil, "I am abstemious.
Never touch the stuff. Besides, I have pressing business elsewhere.
I bid you adieu, my friend. I shall see you again seven years hence."
With this Lucifer took his departure by the usual route, up the chim-
ney, not without making a great din of rattling and rumbling.

The rest of the night the major spent agreeably in the bed of a
cooperative Belette, John Thomas putting on a sterling performance.
Soon the major's table was again covered with gleaming silver plate.
Instead of mean rushes dipped in pitch, ornate candelabra with innumerable tapers now illuminated his splendidly refurbished home.
He took on a French cook and a dozen new servants. Instead of one
poor sorry nag, he now had blooded, high-spirited horses in his stable,
and, beside his ancient half-blind dog, a fine pack of pedigreed
hounds in his kennel. His cellar was filled with the choicest tipple—
port, claret, sherry, madeira, sack, brandy, cognac, and Barbados
rum, as well as the robust local applejack and Monongahela rye. He

bought new gold-embroidered, brocaded clothes, shoes with silver buckles, and a dozen of the latest fashionable wigs. Also a brace of French pistols inlaid with ivory and silver wire. Best of all, he had regained a decidedly youthful appearance and a certain spring to his step so that his astonished friends assured him that he seemed to have come fresh from the Fountain of Youth. Thus the good major lived right merrily.

As the seventh year after the signing of the aforementioned document drew near, the major began to feel poorly. He seemed to have aged greatly, almost overnight. His last remaining teeth fell out. His neck became scrawny like that of a plucked chicken. His limbs grew stiff and feeble. His whole system was riddled with the pox, a gift of the fair Belette. His much-swollen liver was rotten from excessive imbibing of usquebaugh. His kidneys refused to function. He had trouble making water. He was, however, free from gout and John Thomas performed as before. As the seventh year ended, Stobo caught a chill. His spare, shaking frame was racked by a hacking cough. He was spitting blood. At last he heard once again the familiar rumbling in the chimney, preceded by sparks and clouds of ashes. Dressed as before in red velvet and unsmudged, brilliantly white lace, Old Nick approached Stobo's sickbed.

"You seem to be unwell, Major," said the devil, smiling pleasantly. "You are aware, I trust, that payment is due. I have come to collect it. You can have no objections. Here is the original document. You can see that everything is in order."

"My eyesight is almost gone, sirrah, please hand me a candle."
"With pleasure."

The major passed the flame close to the parchment. Instantly, the heat made the invisible ink visible. "Pray note that my soul is expressly exempt from the deal. Remark the words in this brownish color 'in no wise my immortal soul.'"

The devil took it badly. His satanic majesty was outraged. "Cods and bollocks! Perdition and damnation! I'm bubbled and buggered! I am deeply hurt, major. I took you for a gentleman. You have cheated me! I knew that you cheated the hangman, cheated at love, cheated at cards—but cheating me, me, me! It has never happened before!"

"You are welcome to the body, dear fellow. My skin and bones may bring a few pennies."

"Your pox-ridden carcass is of not the slightest use to me," said the fiend with indignation, uttering foul curses, breaking wind for emphasis, filling the hall with clouds of yellow sulphur. Then, quick as lightning, he shot up the chimney never to return.

"I foxed him," said the major with a toothless grin, "my soul is saved. I yearn to be reunited with my old comrades in arms." Thus, the hero of many battles shuffled off his moral coils. His soul, sinful but repentant, was wafted up to heaven where brave General Wolfe's ghost welcomed it with a brimmer of celestial ambrosia. Stobo's spectre took a mighty swig: "Not bad, not bad at all, but Scottish usquebaugh is better."

The Cheater Cheated

Traders to the Indians are part of the early West's folklore. On the whole they were a sorry lot. As an eighteenth-century writer put it:

> The English manner of carrying on the Indian trade is this: the regular traders undertake twice or oftener each year journeys to the Indian villages, their Packhorses laden with Strowds, match coats, hats, looking-glasses, beads and bracelets of glass, knives, and all manner of Gawdy Toys and Knacks for children, as well as guns,

flint, Powder, and Lead, and cags of potent Rum to be watered when they arrive to the Indian country. When there these Traders live with the Indians, selling them goods in prospect of the season's fur catch and often keeping one or more squaws as wives and are trusted by their neighbours for they are content of two or three centum profit. . . .

Other Traders there are who frequently creep into the Woods with spirituous liquor and cheating trifles, after the Indian hunting camps, in the Winter season, and putting down several Cags before them, make them drunk selling their liquor at ten times its value, as the Indians will sell even their wearing shirt for inebriating liquors. . . . These Traders are the most vicious and abandoned Wretches of our Nation, a set of Mean Dishonest mercenary Fellows . . they even debauch the Indians' young women, and even their wives, when the husbands are from home or drunk.

But here is a tale of the cheater cheated.

♦   ♦   ♦

There was a Nipissing chief called the Red Owl, a mighty hunter and trapper, who brought enough meat to his wigwam to support several wives. His abode was always filled with the choicest pelts of otter, beaver, fox, mink, and weasel.

There also was a trader, Smith, or Miller, or, possibly, Cooper. Well, whatever his name, he was a mean liar and cheat who would have sold his own mother's soul to the devil for two pieces of eight. One day this thieving swindler came to the Red Owl's wigwam, pointing to a stack of prime beaver plews, saying, "I'll have those."

"What you gimme for them?"

"How about this keg of whiskey, Chief? Strong as lightning."

"No whiskey," said the Red Owl, who could not be bamboozled by an offer of rattlesnake piss.

"Tell you what I'll do for you, Chief," said the trader, handing the Red Owl a small bag of coarse-grained powder. "I'm in a giving mood today. I'll swap this for your beavers."

"This little powder for big heap pelts?"

"These are seed grains, Chief. You plant 'em in the soil and grow bushels of grains like these. You'll never need to swap for powder again."

"Let's smoke calumet. You smoke'um calumet, you cannot tell a lie."

"Sure, Chief, let's smoke."

They smoked the pipe and this Smith, or Miller, or Cooper, went off with the furs whistling a merry tune.

The Red Owl planted the powder grains. He cared for them tenderly. He watered them every day. But no plants heavy with powder grains ever came up.

A year later the same trader came to the Red Owl's wigwam. He had so many tricks up his sleeve that he had forgotten the one he had played on this chief. He spread his wares.

"I take'um gun, lead, looking glass, two bags of beads, bolt red stuff, bolt blue stuff, coat with gold lace."

"Fine, fine, Chief," said the trader rubbing his hands. "Now for all that stuff I want so and so much beaver, silver fox, red fox, ermine, otter, and musquash."

"Me not have'um pelts. Took on one more wife. Young, plump, very active. No time for trapping. Come back in twelve moons. The Red Owl give mighty heap of pelts, beaver, silver fox, red fox, ermine, otter, and musquash."

"Let's smoke the calumet, Chief. When you smoke the calumet, you can't lie. Right?"

"Let's smoke," said the Red Owl.

Another year went by. Again this Smith, or Miller, or, possibly, Cooper appeared at the lodge: "Here I am, Chief, let's have those furs you promised me."

"No furs for you!"

"What, you cheating, thieving red devil? No furs?"

"No furs!"

"You miserable red varmint, you helliferous savage, you promised. We smoked the calumet!"

"No furs!"

"Damn you, you painted godless heathen! Hand over the furs! Hellfire and brimstone! You promised!"

"White man," said the Red Owl grinning broadly, "you gave me bag of black powder, bag so little, like this. Told me to plant'um grain. Watch powder bushes grow. Tell chief never again gottum swap pelts for powder. Grains grow slow. Very slow. Come back sometime when bushes heavy with powder grains. Then chief pay with big heap beaver, silver fox, red fox, ermine and musquash."

"Damn your eyes!" said the trader.

The Wild Hunt

This story of English origin occurs in many American versions.

There was a gentleman whom everybody called Squire Jack. He had the air of a lord and was the wealthiest man in the colony. He owned the biggest estate between York and Somerset. He also owned the most imposing house, the finest horses, and the keenest hunting dogs. He dressed most elegantly and could be very polite to the ladies, but was strong-willed and much given to cursing and swearing. He kept a good table and even better cellar. His home was always open to his many boon companions and hangers-on.

A confirmed bachelor, he never spoke of his past. Some said that he had left England on account of a tragic love affair. Others were sure that he had fled a debtor's prison or had escaped the hangman after having killed his rival for a lady's favors in a duel. Still others maintained that he had been a gentlemanly highwayman getting away to America with all his loot. Nobody knew for certain and nobody asked because Squire Jack was rich, powerful, and dangerous when crossed. His passion was for woman flesh and horseflesh, but his greatest obsession was riding to the hounds.

One fine Sunday morning the church bells were ringing, but Squire Jack and his friends—no churchgoers they—were off to the chase. Merry fellows all, they blew their horns, hollered, and huzzahed, jumping their horses over fences and ditches. A buck or two fell victims to their hunt. The day was hot. Frequently, the young bloods stopped to take a swig from their flasks, drinking a toast to the chase, to their ladyloves, to the health of good King George. The day wore on. Squire Jack felt for his flask, but it was empty. He shook it. Not a drop was left. He called to his friends for a swig, but their flagons were empty too.

"Dammee," said Squire Jack, "I'd go to hell for a quaff!"

Instantly, there was at his side a newcomer, a horseman nobody had noticed before, certainly no acquaintance to any of them. The stranger, obviously a gentleman, was attired in a suit of black velvet with large silver buttons. His pale, sharply etched face was adorned with a black mustache and Vandyke beard, which had been the rage in the long-ago days of the Second Charles. His curly black wig hailed from the same period. His horse also was raven black. The strange gentleman was accompanied by a blackamoor servant, dressed like his master, but wearing a turban on his head instead of a wig.

The decidedly odd cavalier doffed his hat and proffered Squire Jack a foaming brimmer, saying, "Allow me, sir, this small offering."

"God's wounds," said the astonished squire, "where in hell have you come from?"

"From the place you just mentioned," answered the smiling stranger.

"Harroomph, Sir, you are an odd fish, but your liquor is exceedingly good. Let me have another swig."

"With the greatest of pleasure."

The chase continued. Squire Jack's hounds brought a stag to bay. The squire shot it, but instantly the strange hunter claimed it for himself, ordering his servant to throw it over his horse's crupper.

"What is the meaning of this, sirrah!" shouted the squire angrily. "Would you cheat me of my meat, sirrah?"

"Is a brimmer of the choicest liquor not worth a little venison?"

"You provoke me, sirrah! Hand the deer over at once!"

"You shall not have it!"

"Damnation, you rogue. I'll go to hell to get my meat back!"

"And so you shall!"

With these words the strange cavalier snatched Squire Jack from his mount and sat the surprised hunter before him on his black horse. Off they went, at breakneck speed, ventre-à-terre, over stick and stone, tearing through the countryside, followed by the squire's yelping hounds and, at a distance, by his companions trying in vain to catch up. On and on went the wild hunt. They came to a wide, swift-flowing stream and without the least hesitation the horse with its two riders plunged right into the middle of the swirling waters, followed by the howling dogs. When the squire's friends reached the stream, its waters were boiling and all was covered with white-hot steam while a foul odor of sulphur pervaded the air. When the steam evaporated, the waters were seen flowing as before. Squire Jack, the strange cavalier, the dogs, all had been swallowed up without a trace. They looked for the stranger's servant who, they thought, had ridden among their midst, but he, too, had vanished. They rode their horses into the water up to their saddles, hoping to bring the squire to the surface, if not alive, then dead, to give his body a Christian burial, but find it they could not. They rode downstream on both sides of the river, searching for a long time, but not a wig, not a button, not a hair turned up.

"The devil take it all," cursed one of Squire Jack's companions.

"I fear he has done so," was another's comment.

Dreams

Among most Indian tribes dreams are considered sacred and their fulfillment an equally sacred obligation.

Soon after Sir William Johnson had been appointed superintendent of Indian affairs in America he wrote to England for some suits of clothes richly laced. When they arrived, Hendrick, king of the Mohawk nation, was present and particularly admired them. In a few succeeding days Hendrick called on Sir William and acquainted him that he had had a dream. On Sir William's enquiring what it was, he told him that he had dreamed that he had given him one of those fine suits he had lately received. Sir William took the hint and immediately presented him with one of the richest suits. The Indian chief, highly pleased with the generosity of Sir William, retired. Some time after this, Sir William happening to be in company with Hendrick, told him that he had also had a dream. Hendrick being very solicitous to know what it was, Sir William informed him that he had dreamed that he (Hendrick) had made him a present of a particular tract of land (the most valuable on the Mohawk river, of about five thousand acres). Hendrick presented him with the land immediately, but not without making this shrewd remark: "Now, Sir William, I will never dream with you again, you dream too hard for me."

The Skeleton Hand

Jacob Schutz probably never existed in the flesh, but he lives on in a saga of the earliest "Far West," namely the Pennsylvania wilderness, battleground of Indians, settlers, Canadian coureurs de bois, and British and French soldiers. The name Schütz, in German, means "shooter" or "marksman"—a fitting name, as Jacob's overmastering passion was the hunt. No ordinary huntsman was he. Small game was not for him. Only the fabulous and supernatural drew him on. He had no use for a woman and children of his own, who would have been in the way of his one and only passion. He shunned the company of men and lived the solitary life of a badger. If any pioneer settled closer than ten miles from his one-room log cabin, he at once felt crowded and abandoned his hovel to move deeper into the primeval forest. He suffered only two living beings to share his hermit life—a huge, black, shaggy dog called Wacker, that is, "bold," and an equally huge, black, and ornery stallion named Rabe, meaning "raven." His cabin was made of rough, untrimmed logs, carelessly chinked, so that the wind whistled through it whenever a storm arose. The floor was dirt trampled into metallic hardness. The chimney and fireplace was indifferently cobbled together with rocks of various sizes and colors. Acrid smoke filled the single room whenever a fire was lit. A bearskin served as bed, a rolled-up deer hide as pillow, two sewn-together timber wolf skins as blanket. Of possessions there was an iron kettle, blackened with soot; a knife and fork; a wooden spoon, plate, and cup, artlessly carved by Schutz himself; an ax and a saw—that was all. At night the chimney fire shed the only light.

As the house, so the man. Jacob's lean, muscular frame was encased in dirty gray homespun pants and a fringed rawhide shirt, made by a long-departed squaw who had also fashioned for him a pair of beaded moccasins, now worn with age, the beads mostly gone. A coon cap and a sort of woolen poncho completed the huntsman's wardrobe, everything mended and remended, yet full of holes. Of visage this Schutz was severe, hollow-eyed, sharp-nosed and beetle-browed. His hair was matted, his shaggy beard unkempt, his body scarred. His eyes were compelling, piercing, and steely blue—the eyes of a fanatic, a madman even. By contrast, his weapons were fine and lovingly cared for—an ancient jager, a snaphaunce-type weapon his father had brought over from the old country, artfully inlaid with figures of men and animals, done in ivory, paired with a recently made Lancaster rifle, unadorned, yet beautiful in its perfection. An incised powder horn, the fruit of much labor on its owner's part, and an old German hirschfänger completed the armament. The latter was wicked, outlandish, more sword than hunting knife, designed to give a wounded beast the coup de grace.

Jacob's nourishment consisted almost entirely of meat—fowl and venison. He was not finicky. If he could not feast on deer or wild turkey, a muskrat, possum, or gopher would do. He eked out this monotonous diet with dried berries, nuts, and wild roots. Twice a year he would ride sixty miles to the nearest settlement to swap his furs for powder and lead, flour, salt, tobacco, and a keg of Mononga-hela rye. If someone had asked him how a Christian could live in this appalling manner, he would have answered that this kind of life suited him perfectly. He had, however, few occasions to philoso-phize. Only rarely did white men venture into his forbidding realm, which swarmed with dangerous beasts and hostile Indians. The latter avoided Schutz, thinking him mad. Madmen had strange powers. Their persons were sacred and inviolate. White folks, too, were afraid of him though he did them no harm. Jacob's speech was a mixture of German, English, and Indian, including a few French words thrown in for good measure, almost unintelligible for lack of practice. Surprisingly, he was pious and God-fearing. The son of a Moravian Dutchman who had fled his native land to seek freedom of religion in the New World, Jacob prayed long and often, mostly for a successful hunt. A rare backwoodsman stumbling upon his cabin was given shelter for the night, a meal, a dram of whiskey, and then was speedily sent on his way. Fellow hunters were eyed with suspicion. They might have a hankering for what Jacob was after.

And what was Jacob after? First of all, he lusted after the Great Fanged Death, a giant catamount, bigger than a tiger, with huge curved fangs, emitting a fearful, ear-splitting scream that turned men's blood to ice.

Second, he wished to possess as a trophy the pelt of the Loup-Éclair, the supernaturally swift wolf of eight legs, four of them in their usual place, and four more on its back. When one set of legs got tired, the Loup-Éclair simply flipped itself over to run with redoubled speed on four fresh legs.

Third, Jacob had in mind to capture a fantastic creature the Indians called the Gormagunt. It was said to be almost as big as an elephant, with enormous flapping ears, a porcine snout, and warty skin, equipped with two male members and three female pudenda.

Finally, Jacob's supreme quest was for the Great White Hart, the fabled Lord of the Mountains, an animal majestic and unblemished, with a royal set of antlers, its snow white body glowing like burnished silver in the moonlight.

Jacob Schutz first came upon the Great Fanged Death, the gigantic man-eating catamount. The terrifying beast leapt down upon its pursuer from a cliff, digging its enormous claws and fangs into Jacob's back, inflicting fearful wounds. Commending his soul to God, and with the help of his ferocious black dog, Jacob got the better of the panther, thrusting his hirschfänger through its gaping maw deep into its heart. The Fanged Death's oversized pelt henceforth replaced the twin wolfskins as Jacob's blanket. For a while the huntsman rested content.

As soon as Jacob's wounds were healed, he was seized with restlessness once more, resolved to hunt down the Loup-Éclair. It had been seen far beyond the outermost English settlement in country claimed by the French. There, in the most inaccessible fens, the strange beast made its home. A whole summer long Jacob searched for the speedy wolf's tracks, living himself like a wild animal, sleeping under overhanging rocks or in caves. Sometimes, like a burrowing rodent, he dug a hole into the side of a hill to serve as shelter.

At last, he saw signs that the wolf was nearby. The Loup-Éclair could not be outrun, or outridden, but it could be outfoxed. The lone hunter used a live fawn as bait, tying it to a tree, waiting for the Loup-Éclair to appear. For two days and nights he waited in vain. The eight-legged beast moved only at night, but Jacob had his long rifle loaded with a silver bullet, prayed over by pious Moravian elders and subjected to a spell by an ancient crone rumored to be a Hexe, that is, a witch. The silver bullet never failed to find its target, even in total darkness. During the third night the hunter sensed the wolf's presence. The fawn bleated anxiously, straining at the rope. At last, Jacob's sharp eyes discerned movement, a shape darker than the dark, moonless night. Swiftly, he aimed his rifle at his nearly invisible prey and fired. The silver bullet found its target, slamming into the wolf's vitals. Jacob had slain the Loup-Éclair. Soon the eight-legged skin adorned the hunter's cabin. And again Schutz felt calm and fulfilled, staying close to his log hut, hunting only for his own and Wacker's daily meal. During the winter he hibernated in his cabin like a bear, well supplied with smoked and salted meat, not infrequently taking a nip of brandywine. At night the black dog shared his blanket while the stallion munched hay in his lean-to. On the rare occasions Jacob felt lonely, he took up his jew's-harp, drawing from it melancholy wailing sounds, like laments for the dead.

Winter cold gave way to warmer weather and, with the thaw, spring fever seized the solitary hunter. He woke up one morning, his eyes glowing with excitement.

"Ja, ja, jetzt geht's hinter dem Gormagunt hier," Jacob muttered to himself. "Now for the Gormagunt!"

Mounted on his snorting stallion, his shaggy dog by his side, his rifle primed and loaded, the hunter set out for the strangest beast ever seen by human eyes. His search carried him farther than ever before into the untamed wilderness beyond the Ohio. In the mud of an evil-smelling swamp, "ein dreckich, schtinkich Loch." And there, in its farthest recesses, Jacob found the Gormagunt. The creature was even more fantastic and misshapen than rumor had described it, but it was a sluggish, slow-moving, harmless plant eater. Jacob decided to take it alive and bring it back with him among people as proof of his prowess. But the Gormagunt was so huge. How was it to be moved?

Jacob sought out a band of Erie Indians. In a mixture of German and English, sprinkled with a few French and Indian words, he indicated what he wanted. Gesturing and waving his arms, he commanded them to do his bidding.

"This is a sacred fool seized by holy madness," said the chief. "His powers are great, his anger terrifying. We must humor him and do as he says."

The Indians furnished horses and ropes. They followed Jacob into the swamp. Their wonder and awe were great when they beheld the Gormagunt. Three heads, two male members, and three female pudenda! This was a beast beyond their wildest imagination. They prostrated themselves before the one who had found it. Twelve horses were harnessed to the Gormagunt. The huge beast was at first unwilling to cooperate, but it was docile and let itself be dragged along. It took over two months and the labor of the whole tribe to pull the creature to the nearest settlement and beyond to the town of Lancaster, where Jacob swapped some of his store of pelts for beads, mirrors, vermilion paint, and much brandy, which he handed over to the Eries as their well-earned reward. To the townspeople Jacob said, "Feed this Gormagunt, feed it water plants and swamp plants, and things that grow along streams and ponds. Give him lots of it!"

He left the bewildered Gormagunt standing in the marketplace. The good Dutch folk did not know what to do. Two enterprising Yankees took the beast off their hands, exhibiting it across the land, at the Crown and Eagle, at the Bull's Head, at the Royal George, at the Red Lion, for one shilling per spectator. They printed and distributed handbills:

> Whereas a surprizing MONSTER was caught in the wilds of NEW FRANCE, and has with great difficulty been tamed, this is to inform the discerning, scientifick PUBLICK that it will be exhibited in this towne. The Monster is of uncommon Shape, having three Heads, six Legs, three fundaments, two male and three female genitories. It is of various Colours, very beautiful, and makes a noise like the conjunction of three or four different noises. Nobody knew its name until an old Indian SACHEM said HE remembered that, when he was a boy, his Father told him that it was called a GORMAGUNT!

The exhibitors got rich. Jacob Schutz took no interest in the matter but went on living in his usual hermit way. "The Gormagunt was nothing," he was heard to say, "now for the Great White Hart, the Weisse Hirsch!" Winter was near. It was too late to start on another expedition. Again the huntsman hibernated. But this time he was fidgety, talking to himself: "The Hart is mine! Mein, mein!

Der Hirsch gehört mir. Lieber Gott, please let no one else have him. Das Geweih, those big antlers. I must have them. For the Great White Hart I would give my soul to the devil, dem Teufel. No, no, no, I did not mean that. But I must have him. Blitz und Donner!"

Thus he kept muttering, scratching himself, pacing to and fro, drinking more branntwein than he was used to.

Spring came, eagerly awaited. Jacob could only think of the Hart and nothing else. But first he had to get provisions for a long journey. Again he brought his furs to town.

The preacher hailed him: "How goes it, Jacob?"

"I am after the White Hart this time. After the big antlers. I must have them."

"No, no, Jacob," said the parson, "do not wallow in sinful pride. The White Hart is for no man. God does not mean you to have it. It is sure death to chase after him."

"Und solls mein Leben kosten! Even at the cost of my life!" exclaimed the hunter.

This time he traveled where no white man had been before. Everywhere among the tribes he inquired in word and sign language: "Where is the White Hart? Who has seen him?"

Indians did not answer him. To speak about the White Hart was bad medicine, very bad.

He chanced upon a half-breed voyageur: "Où est le Grand Cerf Blanc?"

"Speak not of him, mon vieux, it is sure death. C'est la mort."

After months of wandering, man, horse, and dog had been reduced to skin and bones, worn out by their exertions. Still Jacob doggedly pursued his quest. At last, he fell in with a French coureur de bois, a man not unlike himself.

"Tell me, where can I find the White Hart? You must tell me!"

"I once thought to run him down myself, mon ami. I was young and foolish then. I know better now. None who have hunted the White Hart ever returned."

"Verdammter Franzose! Damn frog-eater! Villain! Tell me, tell me!"

"Eh bien," sighed the coureur de bois, "if nothing will persuade you, I will show you the way, or rather the spot where the path begins. Naturellement, I will not go with you farther than that, as I intend to live a little while longer."

He led Jacob to a seemingly endless rock ledge, stretching as far as the eye could see along the side of a forbidding mountain of black granite, devoid of vegetation except for some lichens and a few tufts of moss here and there. On one side of the ledge rose a sheer rock wall, on the other yawned a dreadful, seemingly bottomless abyss. The ledge was barely wide enough for a horse and rider.

"Voilà, mon pauvre chasseur," said the voyageur, pointing ahead, "there it is. Ride on as your evil genius bids you. I shall never see you again."

At the sight of the dreadful ledge Raven reared up. His eyes rolled in fright. With whip and curses Jacob forced him along. Once on the ledge, peering down into the abyss, Jacob could not discern its bottom, which was lost in darkness far, far below. At last, the ledge broadened, leading into a forest. Never had Jacob seen such trees! They seemed to rise into the sky. Their canopy formed a solid roof leaving only a few patches for light to filter through. Moss dangled from dripping branches. There was little underbrush, only a carpet of ferns. Riding between the majestic trunks was easy. At eventide Jacob came to a clearing, a small open space in the gloom. There he and his animals rested. Suddenly, Jacob awoke. A pale moon was shining. He heard a deep rumbling in the clouds. Flashes of lightning lit up the sky, but there was no rain. And then Jacob saw them, ghostly huntsmen galloping in the clouds after a ghostly White Hart—a diabolic crew, a fear-inspiring sight.

"Gott steh mir bei!" Jacob exclaimed. "It is the wild hunt, die wilde Jagd!" He trembled and his teeth chattered. He watched the phantom host, the spectral horses, the Ratchet Hounds pursuing their ghostly prey amid thunder and the wind's howling. The appearance of the Wild Hunt meant bad luck. Everyone but Jacob would have given up, but he had gone too far to relinquish his quest.

For weeks Jacob searched the forest for his elusive prey. In vain. Everywhere he saw the tracks of a giant stag, but never a glimpse of the Great White Hart himself.

"I've seen his imprint, I know he is here, know that he is watching me!" Jacob was turning into a specter, his eyes glowing with fever, his hands trembling. And then one day he saw the stag in the distance, far away. Digging his heels into the Raven's flanks, he rode like the wind. But no matter how fast he rode, he could never come nearer. Like a will-o'-the-wisp, the stag seemed to float before him, always at the same distance. Jacob blew his horn, but no sound emerged from it. Wacker barked, but his barking was mute. Raven neighed soundlessly. Jacob loaded his rifle with one of his three silver bullets. He aimed, he fired. There was a flash in the pan but no report. Again and again Jacob sharpened the flint, measured out the exact amount of powder, and rammed down another silver bullet, but twice more the gun misfired with inaudible report.

All of a sudden, the stag turned around and came to Jacob. The Great Hart was so beautiful, such a perfect example of the Creator's art, that Jacob fell to his knees and burst into tears. When he dared to look up, Jacob perceived that the stag was even larger than he had ever dreamed. He towered over his pursuer, his mammoth antlers spread out like the branches of an oak tree. His body seemed to be covered with fine, glistening silk. His eyes shone like two large sparkling rubies; a golden cross was imbedded in his forehead. Jacob could only gaze in awe and wonder.

"It is true," he said at last, "you were never meant for me. You belong to God."

The hunter turned back, searching a long time for the ledge. It was already growing dark when he finally found it, but he was now in a desperate hurry to get away from that place, to get home. He rode out onto the ledge, trusting his horse and his own skill. Coal black night overtook them. A storm rose. Wind tugged at his rawhide shirt and at his hair. He was only halfway up the ledge. He could not see his hand before his eyes. He became aware of an unseen, evil presence. He could feel it, sense it. Jacob's hair stood on end, Raven shuddered, Wacker growled and howled woefully. The dog seemed to struggle against something trying to pull him off the ledge. Jacob heard a frightful, anguished howling growing fainter and fainter below him.

"The dog is gone," cried Jacob. "God have mercy on me!"

Jacob felt a violent tugging, a pulling at his clothes, his arm, his horse's body. It was not the wind. Raven screamed in terror. A furious jerk almost tore the reins from Jacob's hands. He realized that an evil spirit was trying to pull him and his horse off the ledge and down into the abyss to their doom. The pull became stronger, irresistible. Already the stallion was about to go over the edge. Already one of his hooves was frantically groping in thin air. Quick as a flash, Jacob drew his hirschfänger, desperately slashing with its heavy blade alongside his horse's neck and head. At once the pulling ceased. Raven regained his footing. Silently, numbed, Jacob rode on. He regained the land beyond the ledge. He slid down from his saddle in utter exhaustion. For hours he lay as if dead. When he awoke, it was daylight. Raven was grazing. Then Jacob saw it and trembled—a skeleton hand, a hand of bleached bones still clutching the reins.

Jacob had been away for a whole year. He had set out on his last hunt as a vigorous forty-year-old man. He returned as a babbling dotard. His long hair and beard had turned snow white. His eyes were rheumy, his limbs shaky. He was no longer able to care for himself. Some relatives in the settlement took Jacob in. They hardly knew him and had little chance of getting acquainted now. He never spoke again, just mumbled something nobody could understand. During the day he huddled near the fireplace. At night he slept on an old bearskin. Silently, he ate and drank what was set before him. His eyes kept wandering, gazing at something that was not there. Thus he lived a few years longer. One evening, as the candles were lit, Jacob suddenly cried out loud, "The stag is calling me," closed his eyes, and was dead.

The Wild Hunter of the Juniata

The skeleton of history wrapped in the flesh of legend.

At the time of the French and Indian Wars, when the land west of the Susquehanna was a forbidding wilderness, fought over by English soldiers, American settlers, French regulars, Canadian coureurs de bois, and a host of Indian tribes, there lived on the banks of the Juniata River, deep inside the disputed territory, a man whose name might have been Bell or Reilly, but who was known far and wide as Captain Jack, the Wild Hunter of the Juniata. Some called him the Half-Indian on account of his dress and manners. He was also known as the Black Rifle. The Indians had their own name for him—Stalking Death.

Captain Jack was a frontier pioneer of herculean stature, swarthy and keen-eyed. Land-hungry, he had taken his family where land could be had for the taking, provided one was either overbold or mad enough to make one's home in the country of the Crimson Tomahawk. Captain Jack was a dead shot, the finest marksman in the territory. He could hit the eye of a squirrel at a hundred paces and once, on a bet, had suspended a walnut by a string from a branch, shattering it at his first shot at 150 paces.

The chase was Captain Jack's delight, the country a huntsman's paradise, "aswarm with Turkee, Deere, Elke, Beare, Woolfe, Catamount," and, beyond the Monongahela, with an occasional "Buffaloe." That the hunter could become the hunted in the twinkling of an eye only added spice to the sport. Captain Jack was inured to the horrors of border warfare, as well as to heat and cold, hunger and thirst. He was also a patriot.

To help his people in their war against the French, he organized a company of hunter-rangers, skilled in woodcraft, expert in Indian fighting, clad like their leader in fringed buckskin. Armed with skinning knife and tomahawk, besides their long rifles, they were as ready to scalp a Mingo or Shawanoe as to be scalped themselves. They neither asked nor expected mercy. Neither did they expect pay. Whatever they could take from the French and Indians was all the reward they asked. They insisted, however, to be allowed to dress, march, and fight as they pleased without being subject to army discipline. General Braddock refused to have them take part in his expedition against Fort Duquesne, calling them the "damndest set of rogues and gallowsbirds, the most insolent, disobeying, curseing and swearing rascals in the world, worse than the most depraved savages."

They only grinned, calling him a damn fool to his face, and went home to their rude cabins to fight their own private war in defense of their homes and families. In his hour of need the general might have wished them back.

Ornery as a wolverine and unsociable to the extreme, Captain Jack was yet a caring husband and doting father, loving his family "as bread and meat loves salt."

One evening, Captain Jack came in from the forest and found his cabin burnt, his wife and children murdered. As he looked at the ruin, a tempest of fire swept through his being. In a moment the waving foliage of hopes, of sympathies and compassion were burnt out, leaving his nature like the charred trunks of trees through which has passed a roaring forest fire. A demon entered into and possessed him. As he walked to and fro before the heap of ashes which had borne the precious name of home, his clenched fist was shaken against the surrounding forest. His teeth were gnashed together. A storm came up. The rains of heaven beat down unnoticed upon his unprotected head. The crack of the thunderbolt, the flash of the forked lightning alike failed to attract his attention.

It was midnight. By the dull glow of the cabin embers the man could be seen, still walking backward and forward. The storm ceased, but not the walker. At last, morning dawned. A bird caroled its early song from the leafy branches of a mighty tree. The man paused. He looked around with a bewildered air. At a distance, in a puddle of water, lay his hat, where it had fallen the night before. He picked it up. As he did so his eye fell upon the corpse of his child. With heavy heart he dug a grave and reverently laid to rest the bodies of the dead. One mighty burst of tears and he was gone. Henceforth all aims, all hopes and affections were fused into one overmastering passion—*Revenge*. Caves and mountains became his dwelling-place.

Thus spake the oldtime chronicler.

The real man was turned into the ogre of legend. Pioneers and pathfinders came upon the corpses of Indians, left to the wolves and birds of prey. That they were invariably scalped was not remarkable but, horrible to relate, their hearts had been torn from their bodies to be devoured by Him, as some said, or to be carried dried in a satchel on his person as mementos or talismans. When a man chanced upon the mutilated body of an Indian, he said, "He has been here." They heard the crack of a rifle at midnight and said: "It is He." One night a settler heard a shot near his cabin and opened the door. A dead Mingoe lay before it and from the woods beyond a hollow voice sounded: "I have saved your lives!"

The German settlers called him the Rächer, the Dark Avenger, and feared him almost more than they feared the hostile Indians, even though they were thankful for his sometimes spooky protection. One settler swore that, when attacked by an Indian, a huge wolf had leaped at the warrior, tearing out his throat. The wolf then assumed the shape of Captain Jack, blood trickling down his chin. The specter grinned horribly, waved his farewell, turning back into a wolf once more. Another frontiersman related that he had seen Captain Jack face-to-face with a fierce catamount. "Come on, friend," the wild hunter had challenged the beast, "let's fight, bare fist against claw, tooth for tooth. I need the practice." The panther cowered and slunk away.

Once Captain Jack fought four Indians at one and the same time. He dispatched the first three, one after the other. One was a lithe, brawny warrior who grappled the Avenger, and a long, bloody fight with knives ensued. It ceased only when both were exhausted by loss of blood. The warrior got away, leaving Captain Jack the victor on the field of battle. Weak and faint as he was, Captain Jack proceeded to scalp the three dead Indians. He then worked his way back to the settlement to have his many stab wounds dressed. This was the one and only time a victim escaped him.

The Wild Hunter of the Juniata had killed more than a hundred Indians, but his thirst for revenge had not been assuaged. There lived in a native village deep in the wilderness a mighty chief, the terrible Cotties. In the space of one single day Cotties had taken the scalps of no less than sixteen settlers to prove himself worthy of his chieftainship. It was Cotties and his band who had burnt Captain Jack's cabin and murdered his family. For years the Indian Killer had searched for him in vain. Cotties was unaware of this. The burning of a single log cabin, the wiping out of a single family, was not worthy of remembrance. The event had simply slipped the chief's mind. But when Cotties was told of a man called Stalking Death, he was seized with a fierce desire to fight him, to match strength against strength, guile against guile. With both men determined to find each other, the fatal meeting would not be delayed for long.

They came face-to-face in a dark forest clearing. "Are you the one they call Stalking Death?" asked the Indian. "Are you Cotties the Terrible?" asked the white man. "Enough words," was Cotties' answer. They fought hand-to-hand for three days. Every morning they got up to renew their battle, stabbing, hacking, dodging, advancing, and retreating. Every evening they fell to the ground, bloody and exhausted. Came morning and, at daybreak, they were at each other's throat again. While the Kilkenny cats had fought until only their claws and tails were left, nothing at all remained of either Cotties or Captain Jack except a hatchet and a crimsoned knife. This an old pioneer woman told her grandchildren. The same woman would frighten the little ones whenever they were naughty: "Cotties the Terrible or Captain Jack will get you if you don't behave yourselves."

After his epic battle with Cotties, Captain Jack vanished, never to be seen again in the flesh. Grateful settlers named a towering eminence, "Jack's Mountain," after him. At its base, some said, the Wild Hunter of the Juniata was buried in 1772. "Not so," protested others, "he simply went West." On one point all agreed: every night, at the stroke of twelve, Captain Jack's ghost revisited a favorite spring to drink from its clear depths and then dissolved into nothingness. For many years, respectable, sober-minded farmers maintained that they had seen the spirits of Captain Jack and Cotties renewing their terrible fight in the clouds among thunder and lightning. Who is there that can say it was not so?

There stands a monument at Chambersburg, Pennsylvania, bearing the inscription COLONEL PATRICK JACK, AN OFFICER OF THE COLONIAL AND REVOLUTIONARY WARS—DIED JANUARY 25TH, 1821, AGED NINETY-ONE YRS. Could this be Captain Jack, the Wild Hunter of the Juniata? No one seems to know.

The Consequences of Not Letting
a Man Have His Drink

There once was a man called Hintze. He was a gunsmith and married to a mean wife. Hintze was not a very good gunsmith because he drank too much. You got to have a very steady hand to rifle a barrel or to fashion a fine flintlock. You have to be reasonably sober to do that. Hintze was, however, good enough to repair rifles or reset triggers, cobble together a new part, do some filing here and a little hammering there. A man can be in his cups and still do that kind of work.

Hintze figured that if he could get far enough from the other gunsmiths, way out into the wilderness where only the most daring would go, he could still earn a living while going on hitting the bottle to his heart's delight, because the backwoodsmen would come to him rather than travel nearly a hundred miles to York or Lancaster to have their long rifles fixed. So he settled down in the farthest settlement, called Dinwiddie Town to honor Virginia's governor, but named Deadmensburg by the locals for very good reasons, on account of the woods beyond the last dwelling being full of ferocious creatures, both two-legged and four-legged. This godforsaken place had some twenty log cabins, a forge, and a tavern called the Stag's Head. There was also a blockhouse. If things got rough, men, women, children, together with their livestock hastened to seek safety behind its stout walls, and the devil take the hindmost.

Hintze took up a few acres, put together a ramshackle abode, and set up shop. Thus he tippled and worked, worked and tippled, his wife taking proper care of the kitchen garden, three razor-backed pigs, and a few scrawny chickens. Now the old woman was always quick to get her hands on whatever money came in from gun repairing in order to prevent Hintze from drinking it up. In this matter man and wife were forever at war trying to outwit each other. As far as Hintze was concerned, it was a losing battle because the woman had an easy time emptying Hintze's pockets whenever he was drunk, which was most of the time.

One day Hintze told the woman: "Goodwife, you have picked

my purse again, leaving me nothing. Let me have two bits. I feel like going to the Stag's Head for a dram."

"You low dog," screamed the woman, "you sorry tosspot, you bumbling fuddler. You shall have nothing from me. Go to the devil for it!"

"Well then, goodwife, I have a mind to swap the suckling pig for a keg of tipple."

He went into the pigsty, grabbing a piglet by its forelegs. His wife got hold of the hind legs and they started pulling in opposite directions while the piglet squealed loud enough to make a man deaf. The woman was strong and won that tug-of-war.

"I shall take my gun and go out and shoot a deer," said Hintze. "I'll swap the meat for a barrel of rye."

There were deer enough in the nearby woods, but years of imbibing the good creature had made Hintze's hands tremble, his aim shaky, and his eyes rheumy. He fired off many bullets but hit nothing.

"Der Teufel soll es holen!" cried Hintze in frustration. "The devil take it. I'd sell my soul to the Teufel for a guinea."

On the way home from his fruitless hunt, crossing a bridge over the stream that flowed on the hamlet's outskirts, Hintze met a stranger, a wee manikin, very hairy, with a black pointed goatee and unkempt mane, tufts of hair protruding from ears and nostrils. The little man wore a small funny hat and wooden clogs much too large for his feet. His face was pockmarked and his skin as dark as that of a chimney sweep. The wee fellow's eyes were like buttons, moving all the time, darting here and there, missing nothing.

"A good day to you, sir," said the stranger, dropping a shiny guinea into the palm of the very surprised Hintze. "A very good day and a most pleasant evening," the words turning into loud cackling, not unlike the screeching of a bird. With that the odd fellow doffed his hat, bowed, and vanished in the twinkling of an eye.

It had happened so fast Hintze thought for a moment that it had all been a dream, but the coin in his palm was proof that the encounter had been real. So Hintze whistled up a merry tune, went to the Stag's Head, and was soon so besotted that he barely managed to find his way home.

For a short while Hintze remained sober, but soon the old story repeated itself. "Goodwife," Hintze said to his old woman, "you got again into my pockets. Let me have a shilling. Things have not been too good lately. I want to go to the Stag's Head and drown my sorrows."

"You good-for-nothing boozer, you rascally knave!" his wife screamed at him. "Not a farthing shall you get from me!"

"In that case I shall swap a chicken for a brimmer," said he. "Yes, a fowl for a fuddle, that's it!"

But already the woman stood in front of the henhouse threatening her husband with a pitchfork: "You sot, you rum-hound, you swill-all! The devil take you!"

"I shall shoot a rabbit," said Hintze, taking up his gun. "Yes, I shall load this with Pulver and Blei. A rabbit for a toddy!"

But again his aim was poor, and his hand unsteady, as he used up great amounts of powder and lead without hitting anything. "Donner und Blitz!" he cursed, "I'd give my soul for a guinea."

And once more, at the bridge, waited for him the hirsute mani-kin, saying "At your service, friend," dropping a freshly minted coin into Hintze's palm. And, as before, Hintze whistled a merry tune, went to the Stag's Head, and drank the tavern dry.

His little spree was followed by a month of sobriety until the urge came upon him again as he told his old woman: "Goodwife, you have filched my money. Let me have a shilling, not for liquor, just for a little 'baccer."

"I know you, you wine-bibbing low-down rogue, you guzzling, villainous toper. A clout on your red-glowing nose I'll give ye. Go to the devil!"

This time Hintze did not say anything in return but tiptoed to the stable, got the calf by the halter, and tried sneaking off to swap it for a barrel of brandy. Naturally, his wife was on to his tricks, knocked him flat with the blunt end of an ax, and led the calf back into the stable.

"There's not a penny's worth of pity in you, you miserly old hag," said Hintze when he came to. He then staggered off in the direction of the tavern, mumbling to himself: "They'll let me have a dram for old times' sake. Der Teufel soll mich holen for a mug of hot, buttered rum!"

"Over here, over here, by the bridge," a cackling voice called out to him. It was the pint-sized stranger who once more handed Hintze his coin. "This is the last time," said the hairy little fellow. "Repayment will be in order shortly."

Hintze was happy. He tossed off a large mug of hot buttered rum, followed by a tumbler of Barbados rum. He treated all his friends to round after round. He zigzagged home and collapsed on his bed with a happy smile.

A few months later, at the witching hour, with a pale moon shining and a storm brewing, with the dog howling pitifully and the wind rattling the windowpanes, Hintze and his wife were awakened by a loud thunderclap. A mighty gust of wind blew the door open, and amid swirling clouds of dust the wee stranger made his appearance. The unexpected visit instantly sobered the befuddled gunsmith. His teeth were chattering, his limbs trembling. Even his old woman, usually afraid of nothing, broke out in goose pimples.

"What do you want, good friend," stammered Hintze. "This is no time to come visiting."

"Come, come, sir, you know very well what I've come for," said the stranger, who, quick as lightning, thrust his thin hairy arm into Hintze's throat, deep, deep down, coming up in his fist with something resembling a fluttering moth emitting an insectlike wail—the drunkard's soul.

"Now you owe me nothing, sir, I am well paid," said the wee manikin as, with a triumphant screech, the fluttering soul in his pocket, he made his exit via the chimney.

"Consider, wife, what comes from not letting a man have his drink," said Hintze. Then he fell back on his pillow and was dead.

"Good riddance!" was his goodwife's only comment.

The Laughing Head

There was a young lad, lately come to the country of the benighted heathen, to the edge of the world wherein Christians worshiped in churches, slept in beds as was proper, tilled the soil, and lived as the Good Book commanded.

Young Tom, for that was his name, took up land, built himself a home, with much toil cleared a few acres, rooting up tree stumps and rolling away boulders. He then put in his first crop. Thus he prospered. Only one thing was missing—a wife. There was a great dearth of white, godly women because such desirable creatures would not come willingly to the wilderness.

But a wife young Tom must have. So he took his rifle and powder horn and also a sackful of baubles, such as were wont to bedazzle the heathen Indians, and betook himself to a Shawnee village where he espied a comely maid who smiled at him because he was young and good-looking. He went to her father's wigwam and spread out his gifts—sharp axes and knives, sparkling Bohemian beads, vermilion cloth, looking glasses, and many such-like trinkets. These he swapped for the girl whose father was a sorcerer and conjurer of the kind one finds in every heathen village. This witchman let Tom and his intended jointly hold up a sacred pipe, placed a large bear robe around their shoulders, and, with many magic incantations and strange rituals, indicated that the happy couple were now man and wife after the custom of his tribe.

Tom took his newly won bride, whose name was Mahotsee, back to his settlement, where he changed her name to Maud and wedded her for a second time in the proper Christian manner. And just as he had not comprehended any of his savage father-in-law's spells and invocations, so the dusky Maud did not understand a word of what the minister said, finding the doings in church exceedingly strange.

At first, Tom and Maud communicated with signs and gestures, but he soon taught her to speak English tolerably well, made her exchange buckskin for shift and petticoat, and instructed her in the use of soap and water instead of greasing her satin skin with bear fat. In this fashion they lived happily.

Now Tom had taken a fancy to his wife's folks and to their strange but fascinating ways. Now and then he would travel to their village to smoke the calumet with their sachems and watch his father-in-law do his conjurations. Always he brought gifts, and always he came home laden with venison and curiously fashioned objects. He even learned a little Shawnee, though he never used it when conversing with his wife, as he did not wish her to go back to her former heathen ways. The settlement's parson, Peter Peabody, took a dim view of young Tom's frequent visits to the Shawnee village: "Let me warn thee, Thomas, it is not meet for a Christian to have such truck with these godless folks, especially with your wife's father, a foul necromancer and practitioner of the black arts, as I am told. I tell thee, Thomas, your immortal soul is in peril. There are ghosts there, and demons, enchantments, and bewitchments. Danger lurks, Thomas. I fear for thee."

"I neither believe in ghosts, nor am I afraid of demons," said Tom, and went on visiting Maud's folks.

Once, sitting by his father-in-law's campfire, he said, offhandedly, "Our parson thinks that you are a magician who can do what is eerie, untoward, and unhuman. But I don't believe this. You are just a good fellow like myself who can do some sleight-of-hand tricks like our mountebanks at the fair."

Instantly, the old Shawnee twisted off his head, placing it at Tom's feet. Looking up at Tom, the head winked at him with a big grin, saying, "Tricks like this, my son?"

Tom was thunderstruck. He screamed with fear and ran, ran, ran away as fast as his legs would carry him. Wild-eyed, disheveled, and trembling like a leaf, he arrived home.

"Why, what is the matter with thee, Tom?" asked his wife. "Has something frightened thee?"

"Wife, I saw something terrible, fearful, diabolic, so utterly terrifying that I cannot tell thee."

Instantly, Maud twisted off her head, placing it in Tom's hands. And her head looked up at him, and her lips were smiling as she said, "Is it this that frightened thee, Tom?"

CHAPTER 2

The Long Hunters

There was no end to the land in the West and no end to the men who wanted it. During the second half of the eighteenth century, tales of a wonderful country called Kentucky set minds aflame in Pennsylvania, Virginia, and North Carolina. "Kaintuck," so it was said, was swarming with game, and a man with a rifle need never go hungry. A Dr. Walker who, in 1750, ventured beyond what was then the western edge of the British Colonies, reported that, within a comparatively short time, his party had bagged 13 buffaloes, 8 elks, 53 bears, 20 deer, 4 wild geese, and 150 turkeys.

In 1752 another early explorer described the land beyond in glowing terms: "This is a good country, ideal for settlement. It is fine, rich, level land, well timbered, with large walnut, ash, sugar maple, and cherry trees; well watered with a great number of little streams and rivulets; full of beautiful natural meadows with wild rye, blue grass, and clover."

The first white men to venture into this New Eden were the "Long Hunters," so called because they ranged over long distances over long periods of time, staying away from home in the wilderness for many months or even a full year. Some never returned. These were the Indians' hunting grounds and many a long hunter left his bones moldering there, a victim of tomahawk and scalping knife. For this reason some dubbed this New Eden that "Dark and Bloody Ground."

Long hunters went into the wilderness for furs and deerskins, which they cached in some place of concealment until it was time to go home. Often Indians found these hiding places and helped themselves to the hunters' peltry. One leader of a hunting party, finding their cached goods gone, disgustedly carved on a tree: "2300 DEERSKINS GONE. RUINATION BY GOD!"

Long hunters were just about the most self-sufficient men that ever lived. They penetrated the wilderness for long periods of time with nothing more than their long rifle, powder and lead, strike-a-light, hatchet, knife, some tobacco, and a little salt. If their hunting shirts or moccasins wore out, they made themselves new ones out of deerhides. If they were wounded, or fell sick, they doctored themselves. They adopted the lifestyle of the Indian and were away from home so long that their own children hardly recognized them when they came back. They were Anglo-Saxons, with a tiny sprinkling of Pennsylvania Dutchmen, and of the same bodily type— lean and bony, but lithe, with sharp, pinched noses, prominent cheekbones, pugnacious chins, eyes hard, keen and deep set, the mouth just a thin slash across the face, the hair long and unkempt. They were watchful, wary, and impatient of all restraint. They talked little and did much. They were the pathfinders who blazed trails for the earliest settlers. Sometimes they turned settlers themselves. Such a one was Pennsylvania-born Daniel Boone, the most famous long hunter, who started as a teamster and blacksmith in General Braddock's ill-fated army and then turned pathfinder, hunter, Indian fighter, scout, and, finally, wilderness farmer and founder of settlements.

Tarzan Boone

Daniel Boone was born a most unusual Quaker, who did not quake at the sight of blood and battle. He owned a rifle called Tick-licker and a dog called Cuff. In his old age he kept tame beaver and otter cubs. He never slept in a bed if he could help it, preferring to take his rest on a bearskin or wolfskin before the chimney fire. He was thin-lipped, which was why the Indians named him Sheltowee, meaning "Wide Mouth." He believed in dreams. His sense of humor, whatever he had of it, was exceedingly dry. He once came upon an Indian fishing in a stream and described the incident as follows: "As I was looking at the fellow, he tumbled into the river and I saw him no more," meaning that Boone had shot him from ambush.

Daniel wanted elbow room—lots of it. He wanted no neighbor within ten miles of his home and used to say that if you could see chimney smoke other than your own, it was time to move on. He was not one of those turn-the-other-cheek Quakers but an eye-for-an-eye Old Testamentarian. When, as a small boy, he had fallen asleep beneath a tree, two frolicsome young girls played a trick on him by emptying a pail of rotten fish guts over his head. He did not see any fun in this and gave each of them a black eye, a fat lip, and a bloody nose.

His mother was not a shining example of Quaker meekness either. When the little girls' mamas came to complain she told them, "If thee have not brought up your daughters to better behavior, it is high time they were taught good manners."

Boone was the very epitome of the far-roaming long hunter. Once, alone in the woods, he found himself pursued by four Indians. Trying, unsuccessfully, to get them off his tracks, he grabbed a loose grapevine, climbed up on it until he had gained sufficient height, and, trusting in his luck, swung himself—an early American Tarzan

—across a wide ravine. The Indians thus lost his trail, concluding that Sheltowee was a wizard who could fly through the air like a bird.

Boone always maintained that a man needed four things to succeed—a good rifle, a good horse, a good dog, and a good wife, in that order. The first three articles he already possessed. He wanted the fourth. One night he went out "fire hunting," that is, he fastened a lighted torch to the bow of his birchbark canoe, paddling it slowly and silently along a sluggish stream. Deer are nocturnal creatures seeking out water to drink during the dark hours. They are also curious and attracted by light. The trick was to fire at the light reflected in their eyes. Boone caught a gleam of eyes peering at him from the forest, raised his rifle, and fired—or rather tried to, because the powder had got wet and there was only the click of the hammer. Boone screamed in frustration "like a cougar," as he heard the deer escaping through the underbrush. The deer turned out to be a girl named Rebecca Bryan, who came flying home to her parents' log cabin, crying that she had been pursued by a "painter."

Soon after, panther and deer met and took a liking to each other. Daniel, clad in a blackened rawhide shirt, his long hair "clubbed," went sparking to win the pretty, strapping Rebecca, who was fifteen years old, just the right age to get married. She met him in a cherry orchard, showing off her white cambric apron, the very height of frontier elegance. Daniel, shy and awkward, more used to the company of bears than of a young lady, tried to hide his embarrassment by playing idly with his hunting knife, tearing a hole in her priceless cambric—"a good way to try her temper," as he said later. She forgave him.

It was the custom for a young swain to bring a deer to his true-love's cabin and dress the venison while she watched. Rebecca and her sisters and girlfriends made somewhat ironic comments on his sloppiness as he spattered a great deal of grease and blood all over his hunting shirt. Daniel pretended to have heard nothing, but as they sat down to eat in her father's long house, he picked up his bowl of milk, admonishing it, "You, like my hunting shirt, have missed many a good washing."

They married notwithstanding. The wedding was the occasion for a frontier feast of bear paws, squirrel pie, and corn pone. A gallon jug of potent Monongahela rye went round and round. There was the usual earthy, good-natured banter about the young couple's duty to forthwith increase and multiply. As the feast neared its end, Rebecca's girlfriends, one by one, climbed the ladder leading up to the loft and there, with many giggles and jests about lost maidenheads, put the bride to bed.

A little later Daniel's male friends went up and put him under the bearskin, next to Rebecca. An hour or so later, a "heartening cup" of hard cider and a platter of venison were sent up to the pair "to maintain their strength." There were rumors, true or false, that the panther had not been the first to share the deer's bed. If so, nobody minded very much. It turned out to be a very happy, long-lasting marriage, Daniel and Rebecca setting up housekeeping in a "half-face" lean-to, meaning a three-sided primitive shelter the front of which was entirely open. They had many children, and so many grandchildren that they themselves could no longer keep track of them, this in spite of Daniel having itchy feet that often kept him for many months away from home.

Boone had the habit of carving little notes about events, which to him seemed worth recording, into the trunks of beech trees, as for instance: D. BOONE KILLA BAR ON THIS TREE 1773. He killed a great many "bars." One time he heard a loud noise as from a thumping, traipsing giant and concluded, correctly, that it was caused by a bear, a "she-bear" in fact. He fired and, for once, merely wounded the huge beast, rather than killing it. The enraged animal charged—so fast that Boone had no time to reload. The formidable creature reared up on her hind legs as if wanting to engage in a wrestling match. Boone whipped out his large hunting knife, holding it with out-stretched arm in order to keep the growling beast as far away from him as he could. The obliging she-bear was so intent upon hugging Boone to her bosom in a loving embrace that she slowly impaled herself on the keen blade, pointed at her heart, until the whole knife was swallowed up in her body. She never caught on until she was dead. Possibly not even then. That night the Boone family supped on roast bear and rejoiced at having a new covering for Rebecca's tick bed.

Boone was the hero of innumerable fights with Indians. Once, traveling with his wife, he noticed a Shawnee lurking behind a tree. He quickly fired and scored a hit. "Dearest," Rebecca remarked, "methinks you killed an Injun."

"Pshaw," he answered, "what's *one* Injun?"

Sometimes he ended up second best. He was badly wounded on a number of occasions, lost brothers and children, and, more than once, fell into captivity. Like most frontiersmen, he always carried a few gunsmith's tools on a long hunting trip in case of emergencies.

Therefore, rather than burning him at the stake, his Shawnee captors employed him as their gun repairer. He used the opportunity to purloin some of their powder and bullets. Also, from discarded bits and pieces he secretly fashioned for himself a crude firearm. When he was ready, he appeared among his captors, saying, "Well, my friends, it is time for me to leave you," walking some forty paces away from their campfire. The chief called after him: "If Wide Mouth tries to escape, we will shoot him dead!"

"Go ahead and try," answered Boone, smiling.

During the night, while the Indians slept, he had drawn all the balls from their barrels, leaving only the powder. A dozen Shawnees fired their guns at him. Guffawing and capering, Boone made a great show of snatching their nonexistent bullets out of the air, pretending to gather them up in his hunting shirt. He then emptied out from it his small heap of stolen lead balls, letting them fall to the ground.

"Wide Mouth has heap big bullet medicine," the chief exclaimed.

"Goodbye, my friends," said Boone, and walked off without the Shawnees trying to stop him.

Daniel was superstitious and believed in dreams. Often his dead father appeared to him in visions. If the specter looked angry, then whatever Boone tried to do would turn out badly. If, on the other hand, his father's ghost smiled, all would turn out well. This he firmly believed.

Once he was confronted by a party of Indian braves. Their leader told him: "Sheltowee must not come here. This is our hunting ground. If you trespass upon it, we will be like wasps and sting you to death!" Shortly afterward, Boone dreamed that he was stung by a whole nest of yellow jackets. On his next hunting trip he was badly wounded by an arrow. He called the place where this happened Dreaming Creek.

Boone grew tobacco that he swapped with the Indians for pelts. He had built himself a two-story, grass-thatched drying shed, the tobacco leaves hanging from slender sticks in three tiers, one above the other. He was just about to take the completely dried stalks down, beginning with the topmost tier, when he was surprised by a Shawnee war party. He found himself precariously perched some eighteen feet off the ground, unarmed, at some distance from his cabin. The leader of the band approached him with a big grin on his face.

"How, Sheltowee. This time Shawnees got you. This time no escape. This time no tricks."

"Why would I try to escape from old friends like you," said Boone. "I shall be glad to go with friends to their village, but I must first finish my work here. Then my Shawnee friends will go home with plenty of kinnikinnick." He kept up his chatter, lulling them into a false sense of security, and then, with a mighty heave, brought all three tiers of dried tobacco down upon their heads, filling the air with a dense cloud of pungent tobacco dust. The Shawnees sneezed, coughed, and spat, frantically rubbing their eyes, trying to fight their way out of the swirling, suffocating, air-filling powder. When the dust finally settled, Boone had vanished.

When Daniel felt that his end might not be far off, he settled his debts, which gave him a great sense of accomplishment. He also paid his taxes—in deerskins.

Daniel and Rebecca lived to be eighty-six years old—a veritable miracle considering the dangers and hardships they had been exposed to. An even greater miracle was that the long hunter and Indian fighter died peacefully in his bed. This would not do for the legend makers who composed their own version of Boone's demise. They had him die as he had lived, sitting on a rock near a deer lick, hidden by shrubs and branches, his trusty Tick-licker resting on a log, primed and cocked, his finger on the trigger, his left eye closed, his right sighting along the barrel, waiting for the game to approach. Thus death overcame him as, in a last spasm, his finger pulled the trigger and the already dead hunter bagged yet one more deer.

His death went almost unnoticed. His old home, Kentucky, had never had much use for its greatest hero. Twenty-five years later they remembered him. His bones were exhumed for a fitting reburial. There was much pomp and circumstance, the rolling of muffled drums, the firing of salutes, many fine speeches. But before they put Old Daniel under for the second time, they made a cast of his skull. If you should by any chance know what became of it, please let the writer know.

Swallowing a Scalping Knife

Daniel Boone was once resting in the woods with a small number of his followers when a large party of Indians came suddenly upon them and halted—neither party having discovered the other until they came in contact. The whites were eating, and the savages, with the ready tact for which they are famous, sat down with perfect composure, and also commenced eating. It was obvious they wished to lull the suspicions of the white men and seize a favorable opportunity for rushing upon them. Boone affected a careless inattention, but, in an undertone, quietly admonished his men to keep their hands upon their rifles. He then strutted towards the reddies unarmed and leisurely picking the meat from a bone. The Indian leader, who was somewhat similarly employed, arose to meet him.

Boone saluted him, and then requested to look at the knife with which the Indian cut his meat. The chief handed it to him without hesitation, and our pioneer, who, with his other traits, possessed considerable expertness at sleight of hand, deliberately opened his mouth and affected to swallow the long knife, which, at the same instant, he slipped adroitly into his sleeve. The Indians were awed. Boone gasped, rubbed his throat, stroked his body, and then, with apparent satisfaction, pronounced the horrid mouthful *very good*.

Having enjoyed the surprise of the spectators for a few moments, he made another contortion, and drawing forth the knife, as they supposed, from his body, coolly handed it to the chief. The latter took the point cautiously between thumb and finger, as if fearful of being contaminated by touching the weapon, and threw it from him into the bushes, The pioneer sauntered back to his party, and the Indians, instantly dispatching their meal, marched off, desiring no further intercourse with a man who could swallow a scalping knife.

That's John's Gun!

At the disastrous battle of Blue Licks there were a few reported slain who had been captured, and, after running the gauntlet, had been allowed to live. Among them was a certain husband, who, with eleven other captives, had been painted black, the sign of death. The twelve of them were stripped and placed on a log, the husband being at one extremity. The cruel savages now slaughtered eleven, one by one, but when they came to this one, though they drew their knives and tomahawks over him ready to strike, they paused and had an animated powwow, ending in sparing his life—why, he never could find out.

For over a year his wife awaited his return, hopeful against all arguments to the contrary. She almost gave up at last, but, wooed by another, she postponed the day from time to time, declaring she could not shake off the belief that her husband would yet come back. Her friends reasoned on her folly; she reluctantly yielded, and the nuptial day was set, when just before dawn the crack of a familiar rifle was heard near the lonely cabin. At the welcome sound she leaped out like a liberated fawn, ejaculating as she sprang, "That's John's gun! That's John's gun!" It was John's gun, sure enough, and in an instant she was in her beloved husband's arms. Nine years later, however, that same husband did really fall at St. Clair's defeat, and the same persevering lover renewed his suit and at last won the widow.

A Clever Runner

A settler named Morgan was skinning a wolf that he had taken from his trap. He was out in the forest at a considerable distance from his home. He saw a rider coming toward him and recognized his neighbor's horse; however, the man on the horse was not his neighbor but a Shawnee Indian who was followed by three more braves who were on foot. Morgan took shelter behind a rock and fired at the rider, toppling him from his mount. Instantly grabbing his powder horn to reload, he found to his dismay that it was empty. While skinning the wolf the stopper had come loose and the powder had been spilled. Flight held out the only hope for survival. Morgan ran for dear life, the Indians at his heel. Morgan was a good runner and two of his pursuers quickly fell behind, but the third was fast gaining on him. Morgan's empty rifle had become an impediment and he discarded it, hoping that the Indian would pick it up and be thereby delayed, but the Shawnee ignored it. Morgan next threw away his three-cornered hat, but the Indian wasted no time on it either. Morgan flung away his blue coat with its shining brass buttons, sure that this, at least, would cause his tomahawk-waving pursuer to stop. It did not. Barely reaching the top of a little knoll ahead of his adversary, the desperate settler had recourse to another stratagem. He waved his arms and shouted, as if calling upon some friends for help: "Come on, boys, shoot the son of a bitch before he gets away!" This fooled the Shawnee warrior, who stopped in his tracks, convinced that he had fallen into a deadly ambush of armed pioneers. The Indian turned on his heels and fled back into the forest. Morgan hastened home, happy to have lost only his hat, coat, and gun, rather than his hair.

Some ten years passed. A treaty of eternal peace and friendship between the Shawnees and the palefaces was about to be signed. The Great White Father had sent some bigwigs in gold-laced uniforms to preside over the event. Shawnee chiefs arrived to "touch the pen." Morgan also came, together with his wife and half-grown offspring to witness the proceedings. The commissioners and the Indians sat in a circle. Gifts were spread. The smoking calumet went from hand to hand. Among the Shawnee elders putting their thumbprints on the treaty documents was a solemn fellow in a faded and frayed blue coat with brass buttons, cradling a Germantown rifle in the crook of his arm. Both coat and gun seemed familiar to Morgan. The Indian looked at him, nodded, and grinned. Morgan smiled back.

After the ceremony the chief walked over to Morgan to shake hands. They reminisced about the day when they had almost killed each other. "Me a warrior then," said the Shawnee, "now big chief. We never finish race."

"Well then," said Morgan, "why not finish it now?"

The news that there was going to be a running contest spread swiftly. A crowd gathered. One of the self-important bigwigs with a cocked hat arrived at the scene to take over the management of the affair. He pointed to a large distant tree: "You fellows run to that tree and touch it, then race back here to the mark."

The chief stripped to his breechcloth, Morgan to his drawers. The man with the cocked hat gave the signal and they were off. Both rivals touched the tree almost simultaneously, but when arriving back at the mark, Morgan was about twenty steps ahead. Panting, the loser sat down on a tree stump, rubbing one knee and ankle: "Stiff, stiff, too old to run."

"Well, you got the better of me last time," said Morgan, "and thereby got my gun. Now I got the better of you and should have it back." With that he smilingly took the rifle and walked off, leaving the Shawnee somewhat surprised.

A Damn Good Jump

This is the story of Sam Brady's famous leap, which gets longer and longer with every telling. Colonel Brady (every self-respecting frontiersman of his time laid claim to the title of colonel, or at least captain) was born in 1756 in western Pennsylvania, into a family of grim and enthusiastic fighters with a propensity for getting themselves killed. His father, John, was a surveyor by profession, a soldier by inclination, an officer of the Continental Army, and chief of rangers, who greatly distinguished himself at the Battle of Brandywine. John Brady once was so rash as to prevent an already booze-blind, scar-faced Indian from demolishing an additional keg of fine brandy. Temporarily disabled by too much firewater, the Indian vowed, "Sometime, for this, I heap kill you." Years later, as Captain John was riding home with a friend, a shot rang out and the old soldier dropped dead from his horse. His friend later reported that the assassin had been a scar-faced redskin.

The victim's son, "Leaping Sam" Brady, soon became famous as a daring long hunter and Indian fighter. Many were the tales, some of them true, of his many gallant exploits. Among the first was the story of his fight at the disastrous Battle of Paoli, during the Revolutionary War. Escaping from a crowd of lobsterbacks, Brady was jumping a fence when a British bayonet pierced his coat, pinning him to a fence post. Leaping Sam tore himself loose, shot dead a dragoon who was galloping after him, and clubbed a grenadier insensible with the butt of his rifle. He then made good his escape, hiding in a swamp.

Years later we find the doughty frontiersman in Ohio, engaged in fighting all sorts of Indians ornery enough not to take kindly to losing their ancient hunting grounds to land-hungry pioneers. On one occasion Brady fell into an ambush and was captured by his savage foes. There was jubilation among his captors at having landed so big a fish. There was to be no quick death for the killer of so many of their fellows. A slow barbecue was to be his fate. Brady was bound to the stake and a low fire kindled around him. Stoically, he endured his ordeal until he felt that flames, licking at his bonds, had weakened the rawhide rope with which he was bound. An Indian squaw, with a child in one arm and a huge war club in the other, dealt Brady a terrific blow just as he was ripping apart his bonds. Quick as lightning, he snatched the woman's infant and threw it into the fire, making his escape in the ensuing confusion. The fastest long-distance runner on the frontier, Brady managed, for a full twelve hours, to keep ahead of the human wolfpack snapping at his heels. As one after the other of his pursuers fell behind, panting and exhausted, Brady ran on and on to seek safety in the nearest settlement.

But it was his great jump, "Brady's Leap," which became his most famous exploit. In company with a party of rangers, the intrepid colonel was hot on the trail of a war party of Sandusky Indians. He overtook them, and his men had slaughtered most of the band when all of a sudden the pursuers became the pursued. It seemed as if the whole Sandusky tribe was upon them. Having become separated from his men, Brady was making a run for his life, a mob of tomahawk-swinging braves after him, eager for his scalp. Without warning he found himself face-to-face with a gaping abyss—the Cuyahoga River, flanked on both sides by towering cliffs. The air was already filled with the triumphant howls of the Indians, who were feeling sure of capturing their prey. Brady seemed lost. Behind him the merciless foe, before him the fatal gorge. Capture meant death by torture. In the words of a nineteenth-century writer:

> Yet how could one man bridge the chasm more than twenty-five feet wide? But there is no other way of escape from the yelling fiends, and summoning all his courage, with one mighty leap he bounds over the yawning gulf. Convulsively his hands clutch at the bushes growing on the bluff he had gained; but they give way; down, down, he slips almost his own height; but the iron nerves do not fail him, the sinewy hands grasp still other supports, and he continues his flight. The savages stand on the other bank, for a moment motionless with astonishment; quickly recovering themselves, three or four fire at him, hitting him in the leg.

Limping badly from his wound, Brady knew that it was only a matter of time until his pursuers would find a ford across the river and catch up with him. Outrunning them was now out of the question. He managed to reach a lake, known ever since as Brady's Lake,

well before them and without hesitation plunged into the water, swimming into a cluster of waterlilies, where he lay completely submerged, breathing through a hollow reed that protruded but a bare inch above the surface.

The Indians followed his bloody tracks to the water's edge where they ended. They carefully searched all around the lake, but could find no footprints emerging from it. They concluded that, weakened by loss of blood, their prey had drowned. They gave up the hunt and went back to their village. After dark, when they were long gone, Brady rose from his underwater refuge and joined the survivors of his party.

Later the Indians went back to the place of his great leap and concluded that no man of flesh and blood could have jumped over this frightful abyss. Only a sorcerer could have done so, one with the power of turning himself into a bird. "He no man," they said. "He no jump across the river; he wild turkey," the war party's leader exclaimed. "Brady made damn good jump! Indian not try."

To propitiate the spirit of the jumper, the Sanduskies carved upon the rock on the far side, upon which Brady had landed, the likeness of a wild turkey's foot. In 1856, as the rock was to be quarried, a Pittsburgh judge obtained permission to chisel the carving out of the cliff in order to preserve it. On this occasion the distance over which Brady had leapt was measured at twenty-seven and a half feet, and the height from the cliff's top down to the river at forty feet. Later, legends made Leaping Sam's jump thirty-five feet in length over a hundred-foot-deep chasm.

In 1786 Samuel Brady celebrated his wedding to Miss Drusilla Swearingen, the daughter of one of Washington's more prominent officers, who objected strenuously to the marriage, looking upon the suitor as an uncouth backwoodsman. But Drusilla, romantically enamored of the gallant Samuel, eloped with him, and the two of them lived happily ever after. Brady's jumping days, however, were over. For the rest of his life he limped and was slow afoot, the result of the

ball, still carried in his leg, a painful reminder of his big leap. Long hours spent underwater, hiding in the lake that bore his name, had impaired his hearing, leaving him almost deaf. Long years of living in the woods under the most trying circumstances had ruined his health. He died, comparatively young, in 1800, in West Liberty, West Virginia, survived by the legend of his great leap.

The Warrior Woman

The strange creature of whom we write was born in Liverpool, about 1750. Her maiden name was Hennis, her husband being Richard Trotter. Together with other adventurous spirits of the time, she and her husband emigrated to America, and, as if by instinct, sought the perils and excitement of border life. Trotter was an Indian fighter. He became a volunteer in Dunmore's War, and was killed in the bloody Battle of Point Pleasant. From that day his widow led that strange career which spread her name far and wide through the border settlements, and which will perpetuate it so long as the stories of the border struggle are read among men.

Thenceforth, she followed but one pursuit—that of fighting the Indians. She unsexed herself, wore men's clothes, and instead of household tasks, she took upon herself the toilsome life of a scout. She became a dead shot with a rifle. She learned to throw the tomahawk with all the accuracy and strength of an Indian warrior. As a hunter, she had no superior on the border. Wherever prizes were offered in contests of rifle shooting, tomahawk throwing, or other athletic sports, she always appeared at the last moment as a contestant, and carried off the prize. She rode a powerful black horse, called Liverpool, after her birthplace. It was the only living creature she loved. Her horse and rifle were her constant companions.

She spent her time as other scouts, roaming the forests in search of game, or stealthily watching in ambush for some wandering Indian. Among storms of rain and sleet, beset by the rigors of winter, followed by wild beasts, or pursued by Indians, her immense frame of iron strength knew no fatigue, her restless rancor no slumber. As she bestrode her horse, her male attire, her weather-beaten features, her black, wiry hair, cut short in men's fashion, her cold, gray eyes and grating voice, her rifle easily thrown over her shoulder, revealed the Amazon. No service on behalf of the settlers was too arduous, no mode of injury to the savages too cruel or bloody for her fierce zeal.

The story of one incident has come down to us. She was making her headquarters at Charleston Fort, in West Virginia, when the fort was besieged by an overwhelming force of Indians. Unable to subdue it by force, the besiegers undertook to reduce it by famine. The brave pioneers defended it resolutely until their hearts were chilled to find the supply of ammunition nearly exhausted. The nearest point from which supplies could be had was more than a hundred miles away. The way lay through dense forests, bottomless morasses, vast ranges of mountains, terrible precipices, and rushing rivers. Worse than all this, the whole country was overrun with war parties of savages. Great as was the peril of the fort, great as was the peril of the journey, this bold woman alone would undertake the task of procuring the supplies. Avoiding all trails, roads, and regular passes, she took her way directly across the mountains of West Virginia for more than a hundred miles.

Reaching her destination in safety, she procured lead and gunpowder, loaded it on a packhorse, and commenced the fearful return. Followed by raving packs of wolves, at every step beset by hissing serpents which still infested the mountains, discovered and pursued by Indians, hardly daring to sleep a moment, she crossed the mountains by a different route, swam her two beasts across foaming mountain torrents, and, after exposure to every conceivable peril, and escape from all, delivered her precious load to the beleaguered. This service became famous throughout the border. On her return she again took her place among the resolute defenders of the fort, doing guard duty, or sharing in the fray of every attack.

At some point in her career, this strange, unsexed creature, with her disordered intellect, was actually wooed and won by a man named Bailey, but this marriage made no changes in her life, except that, instead of being known as Mad Ann, she was thereafter Mad Ann Bailey. Her numerous services to the settlers caused her to be as much loved by the whites as she was feared and hated by the Indians. In the later part of her life, when times had become more settled, she used at times to visit the families she had known and served in her earlier years. From such visits she never failed to return laden down with presents.

The Corcondyle Head

The village had been at peace for nearly a dozen years now. The hostile tribes had retreated far back into the wilderness before the onslaught of white settlers. Speckled cattle grazed in the meadows. Corn and rye grew in the fields. The start of an orchard could be discerned. There was a meetinghouse, crude, to be sure, and Preacher Jones, who doubled as schoolmaster. Last but not least, there was the Pig and Whistle tavern, administered by the widow Anderson.

Goodman Anderson had died a few years since of apoplexy, leaving his wife with five children to care for. The widow had applied to the town council for a permit allowing her to continue in her deceased husband's footsteps. She pointed out that it was not unheard of for a woman to keep a tavern and that a refusal would force her and her children to become public charges upon their neighbors' purses. The elders got the point and quickly passed an ordinance that licensed her to carry on in her departed husband's position as tapster. She and her brood made their home in the tavern's back rooms, together with a young indentured serving wench. A grizzled odd-job man lived in a nearby barn. The widow provided simple but wholesome fare for weary travelers and served exhilarating, foaming cups of strong waters to the thirsty.

One day there appeared in the village a wandering quack and mountebank, traveling in a creaking wagon drawn by a spavined horse. Perched on the quack's shoulder was a small monkey beating a drum. The stranger took up his quarters in the tavern and, on the morning after his arrival, nailed a notice to the door reading:

> To be exhibited to the discerning PUBLICK, at the Pig-and-Whistle, by the universally acclaimed DOCTOR HIPPOCRATES SANITARIUS, a curious Creature called a UNICORN, with a Sheep's body, a bird's wings, a Lion's tail, and a head not unlike a STAG'S, adorned by a yard-long HORNE.
>
> Also a rare TWO-HEADED DOG and the head of a MONSTER never before seen in these parts, called a CORCONDYLE. Like-wise a LIVE monkey who beats the drum and performs diverse comick tricks.
>
> Also sold, by the aforesaid Doctor Sanitarius, a Sovereign JULEP esteemed in the Whole WORLD, an infallible perfect cure for CON-

SUMPTIONS, CATARRHS, AND ALL OTHER DISTEMPERS. Also a most excellent elixir and remedy that certainly cures the STONE and saves those that have been designed to be cut for it. It wonderfully dissolves GREAT stones and brings them away. Both remedies cheap at 1S 6D per bottle. The curiosities may be seen and examined by the PUBLIK for fifty sents, children under the age of seven GRATIS!

The unicorn was made up of the stuffed parts of different animals. However, implanted in its forehead was a real narwhal's horn. The two-headed dog was an outrageous fake. The corcondyle's head was actually the dried, hollowed-out head of an alligator. The sovereign remedies and juleps were concoctions made of riverwater, honey, pepper, and an inferior brand of Barbados rum. The monkey was indeed very much alive and performed as promised.

The exhibition was a success. The narwhal's horn was greatly admired. The two-headed dog was much commented upon. The corcondyle's head drew forth satisfyingly frightened screams from the children. The monkey, as his kind had never been seen before by the simple pioneers, was the life of the party. Numerous bottles of the sovereign julep and the royal remedy were sold, and a great many bumpers of hot buttered rum quaffed. Somebody said something about a renewed outbreak of Indian trouble, but far away, and therefore nothing to worry about. The happy widow got her cut. The crowd went home. The hired man retired to his barn. The widow, her children, and the serving wench went to bed. To his own chamber went Doctor Sanitarius in the certain hope that the young wench would join him there.

Sometime after they had fallen asleep, the lusty wench in the doctor's arms, they were wakened by horrifying war whoops. Rushing to the window, the widow Anderson saw her barn in flames and the village green swarming with howling Indians painted for war, saw her hired man staggering from the burning barn, saw him tomahawked and scalped. She just had time to bar the door, while the quack and the wench closed the window shutters. Some of the Indians had retrieved a large and thick wooden beam from the collapsing barn, losing no time in using it as a battering ram to break the door down. There seemed to be no hope for anybody inside the tavern. After mere minutes the door gave way and more than a dozen savages burst into the taproom, but an apparition, frightful to behold, stopped them in their tracks. Advancing toward them was an evil spirit, half human and half monster, the open maw of its hideous head studded with rows of wicked teeth, emitting blood-curdling growls. On the demon's shoulder, jumping up and down, perched a hairy little man beating a drum. There was a glimpse of a two-headed wolf terrifying to look at. This was bad medicine, sure death for anyone trying to fight these white man's monsters. Panic spread among the invaders. They fled in terror, vanishing as suddenly as they had come.

The settlers emerged in varying states of undress, frantically priming rifles and ramming down leaden balls into barrels, clutching axes and pitchforks, yelling louder than the Indians. They all gathered at the tavern, the first and only building attacked.

Preacher Jones, clad only in his nightshirt, came running too, fervently praising God for having delivered His children from the heathen fiends. "Glory to the great Jehovah!" he shouted, "who put the fear of God into the red devils! Glory, hallelujah!"

They crowded into the taproom, questioning the widow Anderson, asking what had caused the Indians to flee so abruptly. The good woman asked to be excused for a moment and then disappeared into her bedchamber. She reappeared shortly with the alligator's head hiding her own, on her shoulder the chattering monkey in a scarlet grenadier's jacket, wildly beating his drum, under her right arm the two-headed dog.

"I think it is this which frightened them," said the widow, her voice coming out in an unearthly fashion from the corcondyle's maw.

"Mistress, you are a beauty!" exclaimed Pastor Jones. "This calls for a brimmer of your best!"

Soon the red-hot, hissing poker was plunged into bumpers of potent rum. The cheering cups were passed around, and toasts were drunk to the resourceful hostess.

"Let us praise the Lord and get back to bed," said the scantily attired preacher, "before my freezing arse turns to ice!"

CHAPTER 3

Backwoodsmen

The backwoodsman was but slightly removed from the long hunter. Sometimes he was merely the hunter grown to full manhood, wanting not only to blaze a trail through the wilderness but to make his home there. The typical backwoodsman lived in a stump-dotted clearing of two or three acres, in a rude one-room cabin with an earthen floor, which had just replaced the open-faced lean-to that had been the family's first shelter. The new cabin usually had a chimney made of mud-daubed sticks that were forever catching fire. He usually had a string bed and a mattress of corncobs, with bearskins for blankets. He might also have a fireplace made of stone slabs and a chair or two carved from a tree stump. The number of his tools, utensils, and other belongings was limited by what he, his wife, and his horse could carry on their backs—that is, if he had a horse. A dog he had always. Poor beyond a modern American's imagination, he was a settler, a forerunner of "civilization," even if he could not sign his name. He might have put his crop in, but still supplemented his diet in large part by hunting.

Wherever the frontiersman went, the ringing sounds of axes could be heard clearing new ground in the deepest recesses of the primeval forest. Trees were notched and girdled as the frontier advanced by leaps and bounds. The red nomads of the woods more and more often found themselves surprised by surveyors with pole and chain, encounters which led to much bloodshed.

The pioneer had a voracious appetite for land: "The instant I enter on my own land, the bright idea of property, or exclusive right, of independence, exalts my heart. Precious soil, I say to myself, by what singular custom of law is it that thou wast made to constitute the riches of the freeholder?"

Oddly enough, once the backwoodsman had got hold of some land, he no longer cared for it. He was almost as footloose as the long hunter had been. He had hardly settled down in one place when his feet itched to move on. Usually, he moved two or three times during his lifetime—always westward. It was time to leave when you could see your nearest neighbor's chimney smoke. As Daniel Boone said when he left Kentucky for new horizons: "Too many people! Too crowded! Too crowded! I want more elbow room!"

The backwoodsman was a uniquely American type, rough-hewn, fiercely independent, fond of a rough-and-tumble fight, of politicking, of women, dogs, and hard liquor. He was also a storyteller par excellence, developing in the process a pungent, explosive, and picturesque frontier jargon.

The Irrepressible Backwoodsman
and Original Humorist

Davy Crockett, the irrepressible backwoodsman, who adopted the coonskin cap for his symbol, was a walking bundle of contradictions—a fairy-tale character and a real live historical personality, an innocent child of nature and a wily politician, a semiliterate butcher of the King's English who penned a quite readable (probably ghostwritten) autobiography, a friend of wild critters who killed forty-seven bears inside of one month, an Indian lover whose rafters were decorated with numerous redskins' scalps, a buffoon and frontier comedian who died a hero's death, a one-time Tennesseean who ended his life as a Texican.

He could play the fiddle, dance the Irish jig, and shoot out a squirrel's eye at a hundred paces. "The Yaller Blossom of the Forest" was born in Tennessee on August 17, 1786, in a crude cabin near the Nolichucky. His Irish father, John, had fought at King's Mountain during the War of Independence. He later erected a water mill that was swept away by a flood. His mother, née Rebecca Hawkins, was a right sprightly woman who, so the legend has it, could still in her old age jump a seven-foot fence backward, dance a hole in the puncheon floor, and make love three times a day without flinching. She was one of those frontier women who danced so hard on Sunday nights that Davy had to rake up their toenails on Monday mornings.

Young Davy had little schooling because he ran away from a birching. He "jest loved the wimmin," and got a number of girls in the family way. At one time he was paying court to a Quaker girl. In his own words: "For though I have heard people talk about hard loving, yet I reckon no poor devil in this world was ever cursed with such hard love as mine has always been, when it came on me."

She would have none of him as her heart was set upon a sober-minded, nonswearing, mild-mannered Quaker cousin.

"This news was worse to me than war, pestilence or famine; but still I knowed I could not help myself. I saw quick enough my cake was dough, and I tried to cool it off as fast as possible; but I had hardly safety pipes enough, as my love was so hot as mighty nigh to burst my boilers."

She married the Quaker and Davy got hitched to a Scottish girl, Polly Findlay, reputedly a direct descendant of King Macbeth, with a disposition to match. To escape her Davy joined Old Hickory Jackson in the War against the Crees. When he returned, Polly was gone. "Without a tender and loving wife," Davy looked for, and found, a substitute in an ample-bossomed "widder-woman" named Lizzy Potter. In time, Davy became known as the King of the Wild Frontier, who could outshoot, outdrink, outtalk, outhunt, outjump, and outfight any other two-legged creature in creation. Always he had with him Teazer, his dog, Kill-Devil, his rifle, and Big Butcher, his bowie knife, the longest and heaviest in the whole country.

He was a genius at bragging: "I'm a screamer and have got the roughest racking horse, the prettiest sister, the surest rifle and the ugliest dog in the district. I'm a leetle the savagest crittur you ever did see. For bitters I swallow a whole keg of aquafortis, sweetened with brimstone, stirred with a lightnin' rod, and skimmed with a tornado. I can swim like a catfish, run like a fox, and fight like the devil. I make love like a mad bull and kin swallow an Injin whole if you butter his head and pin his ears back."

In 1827 Crockett was elected a member of Congress. In 1835, he lost his seat. He castigated his constituents who had failed to reelect him: "I told them, moreover, of my services, pretty straight up and down, for a man might be allowed to speak on such subjects when others are about to forget them; and I also told them of the manner in which I had been knocked down and dragged out, and that I didn't consider it a fair fight anyhow they could fix it. I put the ingredients in the cup pretty strong I tell you, and I concluded my speech by telling them that I was done with politics for the present, and that they might all go to hell, and I would go to Texas."

He went to Texas to keep his tryst with destiny. The legends show us Davy Crockett at the Alamo, his last bullets expended, gripping his Old Betsy by the barrel, wielding it like a club amid heaps of his fallen enemies. A postscript to his autobiography describes the hero's end:

> The battle was desperate until daylight, when only six men of the Texian garrison were found alive. They were instantly surrounded, and ordered by General Castrillon to surrender, which they did, under a promise of his protection, finding that resistance any longer would be madness. Colonel Crockett was one of the number. He stood alone, the barrel of his shattered rifle in his right hand, in his left hand his large Bowie knife dripping blood. There was a frightful gash across his forehead, while around him there was a complete barrier of about twenty Mexicans, lying pell mell, dead or dying. . . .
>
> General Castrillon was brave and not cruel, and disposed to save the prisoners. He marched them up to that part of the fort where stood Santa Anna and his murderous crew. The steady fearless step and undaunted tread of Colonel Crockett had a powerful effect on all present. Nothing daunted he marched up boldly in front of Santa Anna, and looked him sternly in the face, while Castrillon addressed "his excellency," "Sir, here are six prisoners I have taken alive; how shall I dispose of them?" Santa Anna flew into a violent rage, and replied, "Have I not told you how to dispose of them? Why do you bring them to me?" At the same time his brave officers plunged their swords into the bosoms of their defenceless prisoners. Colonel Crockett, seeing the act of treachery, instantly sprang like a tiger at the ruffian chief, but before he could reach him a dozen swords were sheathed in his indomitable heart; and he fell and died without a groan, a frown upon his brow, and a smile of scorn and defiance on his lips.

Grinning the Bark off a Tree

That Colonel Crockett could avail himself, in electioneering, of the advantages which well applied satire ensures, the following anecdote will sufficiently prove:

In the canvass of the Congressional election of 18——, Mr. ***** was the Colonel's opponent—a gentleman of the most pleasing and conciliating manners—who seldom addressed a person or a company without wearing upon his countenance a peculiarly good humoured smile. The Colonel, to counteract the influence of this winning attribute, thus alluded to it in a stump speech:

"Yes, gentlemen, he may get some votes by grinning, for he can outgrin me—and you know I ain't slow—and to prove to you that I am not, I will tell you an anecdote. I was concerned myself—and I was fooled a little of the wickedest. You all know I love hunting. Well, I discovered a long time ago that a 'coon couldn't stand my grin. I would bring one tumbling down from the highest tree. I never wasted powder and lead, when I wanted one of the creatures. Well, as I was walking out one night, a few hundred yards from my house, looking carelessly about me, I saw a 'coon planted upon one of the highest limbs of an old tree. The night was very moony and clear, and old Ratler was with me; but Ratler won't bark at a 'coon—he's a queer dog in that way. So, I thought I'd bring the lark down in the usual way, by a grin. I set myself—and, after grinning at the 'coon a reasonable time, found that he didn't want to come down. I wondered what was the reason—and I took another steady grin at him. Still he was THERE. It made me a little mad; so I felt round and got an old limb about five feet long, and, planting one end upon the ground, I placed my chin upon the other, and took a rest. I then grinned my best for about five minutes; but the cursed 'coon hung on. So, finding I could not bring him down by grinning, I was determined to have him—for I thought he must be a droll chap. I went over to the house, got my axe, returned to the tree, saw the 'coon still there, and began to cut away. Down it come, and I ran forward; but d——n the 'coon was there to be seen. I found that what I had taken for one, was a large knot upon the branch of the tree and, upon looking at it closely, I saw that I had grinned all the bark off, and left the knot perfectly smooth.

"Now, fellow citizens," continued the Colonel, "you must be convinced that, in the grinning line, I myself am not slow—yet, when I look upon my opponent's countenance, I must admit that he is my superior. Therefore, be wide awake—look sharp—and do not let him grin you out of your votes."

▲▼

Davy Crockett on the Stump

▲▼

"Friends, fellow-citizens, brothers and sisters: On the first Tuesday previous to next Saturday you will be called on to perform one of the most important duties that belong to free white folks— that are a fact. On that day you will be called upon to elect your members to the Senate and House of Representatives in the Congress of the United States, and feeling that in times of great political commotion like these, it becomes you to be well represented, I feel no hesitation in offering myself as a candidate to represent such a high-minded and magnanimous white set.

"Friends, fellow-citizens, brothers and sisters: They accuse me of adultery; it's a lie—I never ran away with any man's wife, that was not willing, in my life. They accuse me of gambling, it's a lie—for I always plank down the cash.

"Friends, fellow-citizens, brothers and sisters: They accuse me of being a drunkard, it's a d——n eternal lie,—for whiskey can't make me drunk."

▲▼

The Drinks Are on Me, Gentlemen

▲▼

While being on the stump during a local election, Davy Crockett found himself among a group of constituents, all of them dry as powder horns and, consequently, exceedingly thirsty. He had to treat them, but was helliferociously short of the wherewithal. Leading the crowd of voters to the nearest watering hole, he was eyed with great suspicion by the tightwad boniface. Not in the least fazed, he slapped his famous headgear on the counter, calling for a cooncap's worth of whiskey, telling his eager constituents: "Gentlemen, the drinks are on me."

The bardog measured out the cap's worth in likker while the crowd broke into enthusiastic "Huzzahs for Crockett!" The publican picked up the coonskin cap and threw it up into the loft behind him. As soon as the glasses were empty, Davy called for another round. While the tapster's back was turned, Davy, observing that there was a lot of space between the logs which formed the loft, took his ramrod and fished out his skin cap from out between them. "I brung a passel of these to sell. Might as well swap 'em for some of the good creature." With that he put the same cap on the bar while the voters drank toasts to the Cunnel an' the Dimmicratic Party. This game the Yaller Blossom of the Forest played again and again, until the whole company had been well watered into insensibility, the boniface included. Assured of the necessary votes from his appreciative constituents, the Original Frontier Humorist retrieved his coonskin cap for the last time and departed whistling a merry tune.

▲▼

Gouging the Critter

▲▼

In 1797 a Kaintuck long hunter took his ax and went into the woods to cut a broom handle for his wife. He was but a short way from his cabin when he was set upon by a large, ferocious bear. He was about to tackle the "varmint" with his ax, but his four-legged opponent snatched this weapon from him. So the two of them, bear and man, went at each other tooth and nail. Unfortunately, from the bear's point of view, the human contestant was of the half-horse–half-alligator type, an experienced rib staver who had bitten off many an ear during a lively election-day fight. He now went about "gouging the critter," using the same methods he had employed when fighting river rats and card cheats—namely, by fastening his teeth upon the beast's nose, while doing some eye gouging and groin thumping. In no time at all the poor bear was reduced to "crying uncle" by crying so loud and pitifully that neighbors from a mile off came running to the rescue—of the man, they thought.

Soon Bruin's skin was lying in front of the bold "gouger's" fireplace after a great feast of roasted bear for the whole settlement. "How didje an' the bar make it?" one of the neighbors inquired of the happy ring-tailed squealer.

The victor flapped his wings and crowed like a rooster: "T'war nuthin'. Bars can't stand Kentucky play. Gougin' and twistin' of the privities is too hard on 'em."

Jim Bowie and His Big Knife

Colonel Jim Bowie, now there was a man! A southern blueblood, he was fair-haired, and blue-eyed, jovial, soft-spoken, and ever polite to the ladies. He could rip apart a fellow with his knife, from the groin to the throat with a single swipe. He was born, in 1796, in Old Kaintuck, though there are some who say that he hailed from Georgia. It doesn't matter. The main thing is that he was born. Jim had four brothers of whom only one, Rezin, is worth mentioning. In 1802 Jim's Pappy took the whole gang of them to Catahoula Parish, Louisiana, where young Jim amused himself riding alligators, lassoing them and killing them with his butcher knife, making good money by selling the hides. Such doings gave people the idea that Jim was big and burly, but in truth he was a not overly tall, delicate fellow.

Jim and Rezin were tolerably good shots, but when it came to fighting, they preferred knives. As Jim used to say: "A knife is always loaded." How did Jim come by his famous knife? Well, according to some, he once found himself in a scrape with two mean-eyed sons of bitches with only a sword for a weapon. He tried to chop the head off of one of these fellows, but the blade broke in half and he had to finish his fight with the stump. He did so well with it (he ripped up both these gents' bellies) that Jim said to himself: "A knife's the thing for me!"

But whoa! Hold on! The truth is that Jim didn't invent the bowie knife. His brother Rezin is the one who did it. Rezin was about to go on a hunting trip but had somehow lost his knife. He made himself a new one from a blacksmith's rasp, on account of the admirable quality of its steel, and so came up with the most formidable close-quarter weapon ever. Rezin later made a present of it to his brother Jim, saying: "You may some time find it useful. Should the occasion ever come, you may depend upon its temper and its strength."

Whoa, hold it right there. This sounds too highfalutin. As a matter of fact, some folks tell a different story. Rezin did not make his mancarver himself but went to a knifesmith by the name of Jim Black. This fellow, then a blacksmith's apprentice, had run away from Philadelphia to set up shop for himself in the West. He had his own secret way of hardening steel, and his knives were famous for keeping their blades keen and razor-sharp forever. It was said that a man could cut hickory wood with one of Black's knives for a month and still have a blade keen enough to shave himself with. Rezin went to this fellow and asked him to make a knife to his specifications—not for picking his teeth, but for "killing stuff." Black came up with a man-slicer whose blade was fourteen inches long—the first bowie knife.

Whoa! Hold on again, because some friends of the Colonel vowed that the genuine original article had a blade exactly nine and a quarter inches long and one and a half inches wide. It broadened along the spine, tapering to a point, single-edged, but double-edged at the tip. This was a mighty handy tool. Besides being ideal for picking your teeth, it was good for shaving, whittling, trimming your nails, and cutting your beard. You could use it for slicing, and stabbing, and even throwing, because it was weighted at the tip. It was the ideal widow-maker. You could stab a fellow with it in the heart so nice and easy that he hardly felt a thing. As for cutting a throat, it was the dreamiest thing ever.

There are some folks saying that the colonel was so noble and dainty that he used his knife only once for its intended purpose. They are dead wrong. In 1827, on the most famous occasion, Jim Bowie used it during a free-for-all duel which came about by the colonel being dead broke. He went to a banker, Norris Wright, and applied for a loan. Wright told him that he was a bad risk. That made the colonel kind of wrothy. The anger simmered and came to a boil. To settle matters both men, together with several friends and supporters, met on a sandspit in the middle of the Mississippi River that the locals used for such affairs of honor. The parties lost no time palavering but went at it with a will. Wright shot Bowie down, "ventilating" him through hip and shoulder. Thinking that he had settled the colonel's hash for good, Wright stabbed him in the chest and, for good measure, gave him a terrific clout on the head, but there was still enough wildcat left in Jim to fight back. With a deft upward slash of his knife he neatly opened up Wright from pubis, via pelvis, to the shirt collar. He then proceeded to make coleslaw out of two other fellows to teach them not to stick their noses into other folks' business. A handful of gents bit the dust on this occasion, and word of the wonderful bowie knife spread through the whole country.

But whoa! Hold on! There are some so-called historians who say that the bowie knife had not been invented yet and that Colonel Jim had done his slicing with an ordinary butcher knife. It doesn't matter. Wright was dead and Bowie came out of it alive to do more deeds of derring-do.

During another battle royal, Bowie was set upon by three knife fighters, gents with their bark on who had been hired by a bardog whom Bowie had once carved up like a turkey. The colonel neatly decapitated the first would-be killer with a slash of his two-pound blade. The second assassin managed to inflict a leg wound on bold Jim who, in a tit for tat, disemboweled the fellow with a one-two-three swipe. The third hombre ran away, but Jim, though limping, caught up with him, cleaving his skull in two, "from crown to shoulder."

Not all of Jim's encounters had such bloody endings. In 1832 a lady traveling on a stage coach requested a fellow passenger to put his pipe away because it emitted clouds of vile, suffocating smoke. The ruffian ignored her and went on puffing and blowing, but another passenger quickly persuaded him to behave by holding a monstrous knife to his throat. The gallant passenger's name was Jim Bowie.

In 1813 Jim and Rezin moved to Texas where they opened the first steam-operated sugar mill in the state, but whoa! Hold It! The Bowies' real business was slaving. They got friendly with the pirate Jean Lafitte, who had built himself a fort on an island in the Gulf of

Mexico. Lafitte and the kindhearted gentlemanly brothers, blessed with the gift of winning every man's heart (and every woman's love), began a brisk trade in "black ivory." The pirate brought in the slaves fresh from Africa. Jim and Rezin bought them at one dollar a pound, smuggled them into the States, and sold them there at three dollars per pound for a neat profit. The importation of slaves from Africa had by then been outlawed even though the "peculiar institution" was to endure for some fifty years more—until Lincoln's Emancipation Proclamation.

Jim and Rezin settled down at San Antonio de Béxar, the colonel becoming, for a while, a citizen of Mexico. When the colonel's money ran out, he found a solution, both romantic and financially beneficial —he married beautiful Ursula de Veramendi, daughter of the Texas vice-governor, a rich caballero who settled a dowry of fifteen thousand dollars upon the teenage bride. The happy husband took to living high on the hog and to drinking more tequila and mescal than was good for him. When he found himself broke again, he and Rezin went prospecting for gold and silver, starting a legend within a legend —the Saga of the Lost Bowie Mine.

It began with Jim bribing Xolic, chief of the Lipan Apaches, with the gift of a silver-plated rifle, to adopt him into the tribe and show him their secret mines containing a million dollars' worth of silver. Rather than let the Bowies have their treasure, the chief told Jim where to find a still richer mine, on the San Saba River, near an ancient, deserted Spanish fort. On November 2, 1831, Jim and Rezin set out to recover this treasure. They took along with them eight others for mutual protection, six white men and two black slaves. Soon they found themselves waylaid by no less than 164 Caddo and Tehuacana Indians, determined to keep the treasure for themselves. The odds were fifteen to one. Jim had his men entrench themselves in a great hurry and put up some sort of a breastwork. Behind it the treasure seekers made their stand.

Before the shooting started, Jim tried to negotiate his party out of their predicament, sending Rezin and a man called Buchanan to parley with the Indians, who responded by crying: "How d'ye do? How d'y do? and firing a salvo that shattered Buchanan's leg. The ensuing do-or-die fight lasted all day. Bowie lost one man dead and three wounded. Of the Indians no less than fifty were killed and thirty-five wounded. They decided to leave Colonel Jim alone. There was no surgical kit in Bowie's party, "not even a dose of salts" to treat the leg. Jim "boiled some live oak bark, very strong, and thickened it with pounded charcoal and Indian meal, made a poultice of it, and tied it around Buchanan's leg. They then sewed a piece of wet buffalo hide around the leg to hold the whole mess together. Miraculously, Buchanan recovered completely. Eventually, Bowie found the mine, which was even richer than he had hoped for. He began shipping wagonloads of silver to San Antonio. But whoa! Hold it! Some low-down skunks insisted that there never was a Bowie Mine, and that Jim got his silver by robbing mule trains carrying precious ore from established mines to a number of refineries.

The search for the Lost Bowie Mine has never stopped since. Mexicanos and gringos, settlers, ranchers, prospectors, city slickers, clergymen, ruffians, and gentlemen, even grimly determined women, have torn up the earth, tunneled into hillsides, drained ponds, diverted lakes, and dug up huge boulders to get at Bowie's treasure—all in vain, though a stone gatepost of the old Spanish fort was found, bearing the inscription BOWIE MINE, 1832.

In 1833 tragedy engulfed Jim Bowie. A cholera epidemic struck San Antonio. Jim sent his wife and two small children to her parents' home in Monclova. There all five died of the dread disease, while Jim, in San Antonio, remained immune and unscathed, drowning his grief in oceans of whiskey.

In 1835 the outbreak of the Texas War of Independence made impossible any further treasure hunts or silver mining (or the robbing of bullion-transporting mule trains). Leading a ragtag company of volunteers, Jim Bowie was commissioned its colonel. With thirty men he joined the Americans and Texicans defending the Alamo, vowing to die rather than retreat. Davy Crockett also arrived at the head of a dozen marksmen calling themselves the "Tennessee Mounted Volunteers." Such reinforcements heartened the defenders, but their enthusiasm cooled when Colonel Bowie and his men went on a colossal drunk, parading, reeling, through the streets of San Antonio, frightening sober-minded citizens out of their wits. In the course of events Colonel Bowie and Colonel Travis jointly assumed command of the Alamo. Well enough when he had arrived, Jim was at death's door toward the end, succumbing to the last stages of consumption. (But whoa! Hold it! Some said he was mainly suffering from a broken leg, the result of a fall from one of the Alamo's walls.)

General and Jefe Supremo Antonio López de Santa Anna, arrived to besiege and take the Alamo with 5,400 men and twenty-one cannon. Of defenders there were barely 180. The outcome was never in doubt. The Texicans withstood assaults and bombardments for eleven days. On the twelfth day the Mexican bands played the degüello, a trumpet call signifying "no quarter," as Santa Anna launched his final assault. The defenders were overwhelmed and every male survivor put to the sword.

> When the oncoming hordes of the Mexicans swept into and through the battered breaches, they found Bowie stretched upon his cot, his life fast ebbing away from attacks of his dread disease, consumption. With an unquailing eye he looked upon approaching death and seizing his pistols he determined to sell his life as dearly as possible. Two of the cowards who dashed toward him, fell beneath his steady aim and then he grasped the trusty knife that had served him so well upon that sandy battle-ground on the far-off Mississippi. The blood of the hero for a moment gave him strength and the noble steel was plunged into the bodies of three of his murderers, before his gallant spirit took its flight from that frail tenement now pierced by almost a hundred wounds.

The Mexicans tossed his body on their bayonets until his blood covered their uniforms and dyed them red. Thus ended the life of a knife fighter.

◆　◆　◆

The mythmakers were as busy with Bowie as they were with the likes of Davy Crockett or Calamity Jane. There are therefore almost as many versions of Bowie's death as there were mythmakers. One sample:

> Two Mexican officers were detailed to pile up the bodies of the defenders and burn them. In the search they found a man still alive, lying sick on a stretcher.
> "Do you know him?" asked one.
> "I think," replied the other, "it is the infamous Col. Bowie." They berated him for fighting against the Mexican government; he replied by denouncing them for fighting under such a tyrant as Santa Anna; they commanded silence, he answered:
> "Not when ordered by such as you."
> "Then we will relieve you of your tongue," rejoined one of the officers.
> The brutal order was given to the soldiers nearby, and speedily obeyed. The bleeding and mutilated body of the gallant Texan was thrown upon the heap of the slain, the funeral pile of the patriots saturated with camphene, and the tall pillar of flame that shot upward bore the soul of Bowie up to God.

▲▼

Won't You Light, Stranger?

▲▼

A gentleman was once traveling where water was not the most abundant article, when he discovered a specimen of a one-mule cart—such as some good citizens use for purposes of emigration, when they are necessitated to seek a new location, in consequence of the supply for the manufacture of tobacco failing in the old homestead. Every appearance indicated a camp for the night, though the only person moving was a "right smart chunk of a boy," who was evidently in trouble. The inside of the cart gave a constant strain of baby music, and a succession of groans, indicating deep distress. This, and the grief of the boy, aroused the kind sympathy of the traveler, and he rode up and inquired if anything was the matter.

"Is anything the matter?" replied the boy—"I should think there was. Do you see that old feller lying there, drunk as thunder?—that's Dad. Do you hear them groanings?—that's the old woman; got the ague like blazes! Brother John he's gone off in the woods to play poker for the mule, with an *entire* stranger. Sister Sal has gone scooting through the bushes with a half-bred Ingen, and durn if I know what *they* are up to; and do you hear that baby? don't he go at it with a looseness!—well he does that—and he is in a bad fix at that, and it is a mile to water, and there isn't the first drop of licker in the jug; and ain't that matter enough? Won't you light, stranger?—Dad'll get sober, and Sal will be back arter a bit. Darn'd if this ain't moving, though. *Is anything the matter?*—shouldn't think there was much, no how. Give us a chaw of terbacker, will ye, stranger?"

▲▼

Ohio Poem

▲▼

Come all ye fine young fellows
who've got a mind to range
Into some far-off countree
Your fortunes for to change.
We'll lay us down upon the banks
of the blessed O-Hi-o,
Through the wild woods we'll wander,
And we'll chase the buffalo.
Take your powder, boys,
And keep your rifles handy,
Take your whiskey and your rum,
And don't forget the brandy!

CHAPTER 4

Ring-Tailed Roarers of the Western Waters

When George Washington visited Pittsburgh in the 1770s, it was a desolate caricature of a town, consisting of some twenty hovels inhabited by about a hundred bedraggled settlers. But there was already talk of Pittsburgh being destined to become the great metropolis and commercial center of the West, the springboard to the Far West. By 1786 the population had grown to five hundred but, in the words of an early traveler, "The town is inhabited almost entirely by Scots and Irish, who live in paltry log houses, and are as dirty as in the north of Ireland, or even Scotland." The town had one great asset, though; it was strategically situated at the confluence of the Ohio and the Allegheny rivers, the Ohio being looked upon as the great liquid highroad to the Far West.

The country west of Pittsburgh was still a near wilderness. The only way for land-hungry settlers and their goods to move westward was by river. This gave rise to a particular mode of transportation by means of rafts, barges, bateaux, arks, pirogues, flatboats and keelboats. Arks have been described as floating homes conveying whole families and their chattels, sometimes as movable saloons or general stores. Pirogues were oversized canoes, smaller than arks, serving the same purpose. Often encumbered with odd-looking additions, like warts on a toad, they were referred to as monstrous craft, defying classification. Slow and lumbering, they could be used on the largest rivers. Such craft were not the stuff out of which legends are made—neither were the humble barges and rafts—but the flatboats and keelboats were the darlings of the wild rivermen.

The typical flatboat resembled a large box on top of a huge rectangular plank. It had no draft at all and could float, so it was said, on an inch of water. It was equipped with two large, slanted steering oars on either side, which gave it its other name—broadhorn. It could be rowed, but was most often poled. If not too big or heavy, and with a sufficiently large crew, it could be lifted up and carried around an impassable stretch of the river. It could only go downstream.

The keelboat, as the name indicates, had a keel and, in rare cases, provided with a sail, managed to attempt a poor imitation of tacking against the wind. Usually, it was moved along with the help of poles. The typical keelboat, called a "bateau" by the French, was pointed at bow and stern, of light draw, between twenty and forty feet long. It had a crew of fifteen to twenty-five men. They were equally divided between each side and took turns on the walking boards that extended the whole length of the craft. The men planted their poles firmly in the river bottom and then, facing toward the stern, "walked" their boat against the current. Arriving at the stern, each man picked up his pole and went back to the bow, repeating the whole performance again and again. It was hard, backbreaking work that demanded strength and hardihood. Flatboats and keelboats went out of fashion on the Ohio sometime between 1815 and 1820 with the appearance of the first steamboats. On the far side of the Missouri they lasted some fifteen years longer until replaced by steam-driven craft there also.

The rivermen were an amphibious breed, extravagant boasters who could outrun, outjump, outfight, knock down and drag out more men than any other cuss form the Roarin' Salt to the Massassip. They loved to brawl for the sheer fun of it, "Kentucky style," that is with no holds barred. Favored battle tactics included groin kneeing and eye gouging. Some brawlers let the nails of their little fingers grow to monstrous length, so that they resembled bobcat claws, to rip out their opponents' eyes. Biting off an ear or a nose was part of the fun. Cruel practical jokes were looked upon as welcome entertainment, sometimes ending in death. The rivermen had a gift for inventive swearing and created a language all their own, yeasty and flavorful. When old age had tamed them, out-of-work boaters became easy prey for eastern writers of almanacs and weeklies who plied them with tanglefoot, being in return regaled with tall tales that the writers further expanded and exaggerated with wonderful skill. Thus a new species of legend was born.

The most written-about ring-tailed roarer was Mike Fink, the "king of the Keelboat men," also known as the "Ohio Snapping Turtle," the "Salt River Roarer," the "Snag on the Massassip," the "Prince of Moosecatchers," or the "Last of the Flatboat Men." Mike kept generations of nineteenth-century writers busy inventing endless new feats accomplished by their favorite subject. However, Mike did exist in the flesh as well as in some author's head. He was born at Pittsburgh, in 1770, some say of Scotch-Irish parents, while others insist that he came from Pennsylvania Dutch stock. The country was still swarming with not overly friendly natives as Mike began his career as hunter and scout, wise in "Ingin ways." When a wave of pioneers took to the water in order to go west, Mike found his true vocation as a riverboatman. He was not an endearing character—a liar, braggart, brawler, even murderer. Yet he was also a hero of sorts—a superb marksman, fearless, of herculean build, with immense physical strength and endurance. He could be at the same time gallant and insanely cruel toward women, kindly or brutal toward his fellows. In his time and peculiar environment such "horse-alligators" had admiring followers.

Mike Fink was described as being swarthy, muscular, and dark-haired, walking around in a red flannel shirt, moccasins, and a coonskin cap, a huge hunting knife stuck in his belt, never without his rifle, lovingly called Betsy or Bang-all.

Early writers who claimed to have known him, or to have known somebody who had known him, made their readers believe that they had jotted down some of Mike's typical brags, such as: "I walk tall into varmints and Ingins, it's a way I got, and it comes as natural as grinning to a hyena. I'm a regular tornado, tough as hickory, longwinded as a nor'wester. I can strike a blow like a falling tree, and every lick makes a gap in the crowd that lets in an acre of sunshine. I'm a Salt River Roarer, and I love the wimmin, and am chockfull of fight. Whew, boys!"

One of these writers was honest enough to admit that he and his rivals had invented so many yarns about Mike that their readers began having doubts that there ever was a man called Mike Fink.

Mike got around. Starting out on the Ohio, he went on to pole his crafts on the Salt, the Mississippi, and the Big Muddy. In 1822 he joined General William Ashley on his epic fur-trapping expedition to the Rockies, eventually having his brains blown out on the Yellowstones, dying a true westerner.

Seymour Dunbar, in his *History of Travel in America,* gives a wonderful description of flatboat men and their crafts.

They resembled—those unwieldy vessels of such a short time ago—a mixture of log cabin, fort, floating barnyard and country grocery. At night, as they drifted on the dark waters, their loopholes often spurted jets of rifle fire, while women loaded the hot rifles of the men in the flickering light of pine knots held by silent children, and watched for the answering shots of red enemies through the fog which hid them. By day, on a more kindly voyage, some backwoods genius on the cabin roof would touch the resin to his fiddle-bow and send the wild strains of a hoe-down to the wooded shores and back again, while the family mule gave vent to his emotions in a loud heehaw, the pigs squealed, the children shouted and danced to the melody of the combined orchestra, and the women rolled up the bedding, milked the cow, hung up the wash and killed a few chickens for dinner. . . .

Dunbar described the typical broadhorn:

He was of the restless type that in every period of American development has done the unusual and dangerous thing just for the love of doing it. . . . He was an epicure of excitement. Work no other men would do was his one luxury. . . . In his normal state he was silently waiting for something to happen, knowing quite well that it certainly would. When the bomb of circumstance exploded the human creature was on the dot of time transformed into a combination of rubber ball, wildcat and shrieking maniac, all controlled by instantaneous perception and exact calculation. After the tumult he subsided again into his listless lethargy of waiting, the monotony being endured by chewing tobacco and illustrating the marvelous accuracy with which he could propel a stream of its juice for any distance up to fifteen feet.

Still another distinguishing feature of the professional flatboatman was his iridescent vocabulary. He spoke in a ceaseless series of metaphors, similes and comparisons. Everything was described, whether the thing discussed was an inanimate thing or human action, by likening it to something else. . . . When a boatman wanted to say that some act had been performed with celerity he declared it had happened "quicker nor a alligator can chaw a puppy."

A Shooting Match

"I expect, stranger," said Davy, "you think old Davy Crockett war never beat at the long rifle; but he war, though. I expect that there's no man so strong but he will find someone stronger.

"If you haven't heerd tell of one Mike Fink, I'll tell you something about him, for he was a helliferocious fellow, and made an almighty fine shot. Mike was a boatman on the Mississip', but he had a little cabin at the head of the Cumberland, and a horrid handsome wife, that loved him the wickedest that ever you see.

"Mike only worked enough to keep his wife in rags, and himself in powder and lead and whiskey, and the rest of the time he spent in knocking over b'ar and turkeys, and bouncing deer, and sometimes drawing a bead on an injun. So one night I fell in with him in the woods, where him and his wife shook down a blanket for me in his wigwam.

"In the morning says Mike to me, 'I've got the handsomest wife, and the fastest horse, and the sharpest shooting iron in all Kentuck, and if any man doubt it, I'll be in his hair quicker than hell could scorch a feather.'

"This put my dander up, and sez I, 'I've got nothing to say agin your wife, Mike, for it can't be denied she's a shocking handsome woman, and Mrs. Crockett's in Tennessee, and I've got no horses, Mike, I don't exactly like to tell you you lie about your rifle, but I'm damned if you speak the truth, and I'll prove it. Do you see that are cat sitting on the top rail of your potato patch, about a hundred fifty yards off? If she hears again, I'll be shot if it shan't be without ears!'

"So I blazed away, and I bet you a horse, the ball cut off both the old tom cat's ears close to his head, and shaved the hair clean off the skull, as slick as if'd done it with a razor, and the creatur never stirred, nor knew he'd lost his ears till he tried to scratch 'em.

" 'Talk about your rifle after that, Mike!' sez I.

" 'Do you see that are sow off furder than the end of the world,' sez Mike, 'with a litter of pigs around her?' And he lets fly.

"The old sow gave a grunt, but never stirred in her tracks, and Mike falls to loading and firing for dear life, til he hadn't left one of them are pigs enough tail to make a toothpick on.

" 'Now,' sez he, 'Colonel Crockett, I'll be pretticularly obleeged to you if you'll put them are pigs' tails on again,' sez he.

" 'That's impossible, Mike,' sez I, 'but you've left one of 'em about an inch to steer by, and if that had a-been my work, I wouldn't have done it so wasteful. I'll mend your shot.' And I let fly, and cuts off the apology he's left the poor creatur for decency. I wish I may drink the whole Mississip', without a drop of the rale stuff in it, if you wouldn't have thort the tail been drove in with a hammer.

"That made Mike sorter wrothy, and he sends a ball after his wife as she was going to the spring after a gourd full of water, and knocked half her comb out without stirring a hair, and calls out to her to stop for me to take a blizzard at what was left of on it. The

angeliferous creatur stood still as a scarecrow in a cornfield, for she'd got used to Mike's tricks by long practice.

" 'No, no, Mike,' sez I. 'Davy Crockett's hand would be sure to shake, if his iron was pointed within a hundred miles of a shemale, and I give up beat, Mike.' "

Did Such a Helliferocious Man Ever Live?

One early writer asked: "Did such a man like Mike Fink ever live, and did such a man ever die? And if so, how and where did he go to the happy hunting grounds?" Well, here is one tale.

In 1822 Mike Fink and two friends—if there were human beings who could call themselves the Ohio Snapping Turtle's friends—Carpenter and Talbot, hired on in St. Louis with Andrew Henry and William Ashley to go up the Missouri in search of beaver. Mike as the "admiral," running one of the seventy-foot keelboats, "cordelling" his clumsy craft yard by yard upstream, Talbot and Carpenter as trapper and hunter. Mike, being the "William Tell of the Prairie," also doubled as huntsman, supplying plenty of meat to the expedition with the help of Betsy, his never-failing rifle.

Together with some sixty other adventurous mountain men, the party reached the mouth of the Yellowstone and there built a fort and stockade as protection against the "Terrible Blackfeet." From there Major Henry, Ashley's second-in-command, sent out small parties of about a dozen men each to trap beaver along the many streams and ponds of the region. Fink and his two companions, together with nine others, were sent to the Musselshell River and there trapped all summer and fall until winter set in. When it got too cold and the snow was too deep, they returned to the fort. In its vicinity they built themselves a dugout, preferring their primitive abode to the crowded, evil-smelling quarters inside the stockade. Then they holed up like hibernating bears during the bleak winter months. There was nothing to do but gamble and get drunk. Idleness breeds mischief and in the background, always, lurks the devil, ever ready to cause trouble. The place attracted many 'Hang-around-the-fort Indians," spoiled by contact with the white traders and their kegs of "Injin whiskey," a devastating mixture of raw alcohol, rattlesnake heads, and gunpowder, the latter ingredients added to give the hellish brew "a kick." Among this crowd were many squaws who, either at the order of their men or on their own account, sold themselves to the trappers for rotgut or foofaraw—trifles such as vermilion paint, red trade cloth, tobacco, or glass beads. One of these girls, called either Moon Woman or Red Leaf, was comely and willing to share Mike's blanket, but she got tired of her "Mississippi Roarer" and soon was found in the bed of Carpenter, who was said to be gentle and very handsome. Mike took it exceedingly ill.

"Give her back, you cussed, landlubbery, yellow-livered varmint! Give her back, you double-soaked whiskey pipe, or you can hang me up for bar meat if I don't cut you down to size like a Massassip alligator chaws up a puppy!"

With that, Mike seized one arm of his erstwhile girlfriend while Carpenter got hold of the other, and they proceeded to have a good old-fashioned tug-o'-war, the squaw hollering and howling like a wolf cub caught in a trap. "Come along, you infernal, two-timin' possum," shouted Mike, while Carpenter yelled back that he would cut out Mike's liver and lights and eat them raw for breakfast. Both then let go of the girl and had a go at each other, Carpenter, being younger and faster, getting the better of Fink.

After having been knocked down several times Mike began to holler for mercy: "Avast, you kankariferous ripscallion, I never bar a grudge agin a feller who whupped me in a fair fight. Thar's no use fur old friends killin' each over a louiserous she-catamount!"

With that he gave the girl a clout on the head, saying, "There, that'll larn you to be makin' eyes at that feller when you could 'ave been stayin' with your Mike, still the top man when it comes to makin' love to the wimmin. Now, let's have a drink!"

This seemed to settle the matter in an amiable way, but Mike was not a man to forget a slight. With the coming of spring, as both Mike and Carpenter were drawing their rations of hardtack and whiskey, getting in a new store of powder and lead before going on another trapping expedition, Carpenter remarked to Fink, "Old hoss, I sure hope you don't bear me a grudge on account of that injin hussy. She left me long ago for another feller."

Mike patted her erstwhile companion on the back, shouting to the bystanders: "I'll tell you boys, the fort's a skunk-hole, and I'd rather live with the bars than stay in it. Some of ye's been trying to part me and my friend, that I love like my own cub, and tried to pizen me against him, but we remain the best o'friends as afore and no mere she-injin can come between us! There, to show you how I trust this 'ere boy, we'll sky a copper, play the game as we used to." With these words Mike walked off some sixty paces, placed a glass of whiskey on his head, and challenged Carpenter to shoot at it. "There, that's how I trust this here boy. Come on, old hoss, shoot it off like you used to do!" Carpenter raised his rifle, let fly, and missed. "Carpenter, my boy," exclaimed Mike, "I taught you to shoot differently from that last shot. Your hand trimbled, but never mind. Waal, it's my turn now."

"Hold it, Mike," cried Carpenter. "There's somethin' I jest got to do first."

He went aside and asked someone who could write to put it on paper that he bequeathed his rifle, pistol, powder horn and shot pouch to Talbot in case he should be killed. Carpenter had seen a certain glint in Mike's eyes that made him do this. In the meantime, Mike loaded his Betsy, primed it, and picked his flint. Without further ado, Carpenter took his position at sixty yards opposite Fink and, with a brave smile, put the cup of whiskey, filled to the brim, on his head as a target for Mike to shoot at. Mike leveled his rifle and drew a bead, but at once lowered his Betsy and, laughing loudly, shouted at Carpenter, "Hold yer noddle steady, old hoss, and don't spill the whiskey, as I shall want some presently!"

With that, Mike cocked his rifle, aimed, and fired. Without a sound Carpenter slumped down to the ground, the ball having smashed into the center of his forehead, killing him instantly.

"Carpenter, you cussed critter," yelled Mike. "you've spilt the good whiskey. Get up!"

"He'll never get up agin, Mike." shouted a bystander. "You've gone and killed him!"

"The devil I have," said Mike, coolly putting down his piece, blowing the smoke from Betsy's muzzle. "T'war an accident, for I took as fair a bead on the cup as I ever took on a squirrel's eye. Maybe I've lost the tech, or maybe he moved. Waal, no use to cry over spilt whiskey!"

There was many a boatman and trapper who thought it was cold-blooded murder, that Mike had used the shooting contest to pay off his old grudge over the Indian woman who had left him for the sake of Carpenter, but nothing could be proved.

But talk would not stop, because Mike had never been known to miss his aim. It was Talbot who most vehemently denounced Fink as the murderer of their mutual friend, and Mike, in turn, called Talbot a cussed, lying varmint. Some months later Mike went to the fort and made a bee-line for the gunsmith's shop where Talbot had a job repairing the trappers' rifles. Talbot saw Mike approaching, his Betsy, as always, cradled in his arms.

"I'm a-warnin' you, Mike," cried Talbot, "don't come any closer!" Mike came on.

Talbot went for his double-barreled pistol, the same that Carpenter had bequeathed to him. "Fink, ef you come any nearer, I'll fire, by God!" Mike came on. "One more step," warned Talbot, "and you're a dead man!"

Mike came on. He stepped through the door and Talbot let him have both barrels. Mike's last words were "I didn't mean to kill the boy!" Thus died "the last of the keelboatmen."

Talbot died a year later, drowned when trying to cross the Missouri in a bullboat.

Like Father, Like Daughter

Mike Fink's daughter Sal became a legend in her own right. She was known as "Sal, the Mississippi Screamer."

I dar say you've all of you, if not more, frequently heerd this great she human crittur boasted of, an pointed out as "one o' the gals,"—but I tell you what, stranger, you have never really set your eyes on one o' the gals, till you have seen Sal Fink, the Mississippi Screamer, whose miniature pictur I here give, about as nat'ral as life, but not half as handsome—an' if that ever was a gal that desarved to be christened "one o' the gals," then this gal was that gal —and no mistake.

She fought a duel once with a thunderbolt, an' came off without a scratch, while at the fust fire she split the thunderbolt all to flinders, an' gave the pieces to Uncle Sam's artillery men, to touch off their cannon with. When a gal about six years old, she used to play see-saw on the Mississippi snags, and arter she was done she would snap 'em off, an' so cleared a large district of the river. She used to ride down the river on an alligator's back, standen upright, an' dancin' the Yankee Doodle, an' could leave all the steamers behind. But the greatest feat she ever did, positively outdid anything that was ever did.

One day she war out in the forest, making a collection o' wildcat skins for her family's winter beddin', she war captured in the most all-sneaken manner by about fifty Injuns, and carried by 'em to Roast Flesh Hollow, whar the blood-drinkin' wild varmints detarmined to skin her alive, sprinkle a little salt over her, an' devour her before her own eyes; so they took an' tied her to a tree, to keep till mornin' should bring the rest o' that ring-nosed sarpints to enjoy the fun. Arter that, they lit a large fire in the Holler, turned the bottom o' thar feet towards the blaze, Injun fashion, and went to sleep to dream o' thar mornin's feast; well, arter the critturs got into a somniferous snore, Sal got into an all-lightnin' of a temper, and burst all the ropes about her like an apron-string! She then found a pile o' ropes, too, and tied all the Injuns' heels together all round the fire—then, fixin' a cord to the shins of every two couple, she, with a suddenachous jerk, that made the intire woods tremble, pulled the intire lot o' sleepin' red-skins into that ar great fire, fast together, an' then sloped like a panther out of her pen, in the midst o' the tallest yellin', howlin', scramblin', and singin', that war ever seen or heerd on, since the burnin' o' the Buffalo Prairie!

She Fought Her Weight in She-B'ars

Sal Fink once got into a helliferocious scrimmage with the biggest of all she-b'ars that ever was, and her two outlandishly large cubs. Sal was out in the woods gatherin' acorns for her pet pig when she heerd a loud buzzin' an' hummin'. She followed the sound and came to a large hollow tree with about a bushel full of obstreperous bees. "Sal," she sez to herself, "whar thar are bees, thar must be honey," an' with that she stuck her arm into this thar hollow tree to get some of that sweet stuff. But there waren't only bees inside. There was a mighty loud growl that made the whole tree trimble, an' out o' that durned tree shot the she-b'ar with her maw wide open and them huge teeth a-glitterin' in the sunshine, already mighty displeased on account of them buzzin', stingin' insects havin' a go at Sal. Behind her came the cubs like so many wildcats, growlin' an' grumblin'. All three critters were detarmined to have themselves a bite out of Sal's delishious shoulders and appetizin' hinder cheeks, but Sal greeted the varmints with a kick worthy of the Great Stallion of the West, an' arter that she kicked 'em into turnin' somersaults, rollin' all over each other. But the cussed she-b'ar reared herself up on her hind legs a-goin' to embrace Sal in one of them speshial hugs for which Bruin is famous. Not at all intimidated, Sal got into a stance like a champeen boxer, givin' the huge pestiferocious critter a hail of blows between wind an' weather, which knocked the breath out of the she-b'ar so that she had to sit down. But the beast got her wind back fast enuff, getting her paws with those big claws, an' her teeth, into Sal's hair, holding on tenashiously, like burrs stickin' to a horse's tail, but our brave girl, unfazed, got ahold of the varmint's jaws and

turned the hull critter clean inside out, an' when the cubs saw their poor ma treated that way, they took to their heels mighty fast so that they wouldn't get a sim'lar treatment. Sal dragged the she-b'ar home whar her family made a big delishiferous meal o' that b'ar meat, Sal gettin' the paws which, as everybody knows, are the best parts.

He Crowed and Flapped His Wings

Mike Fink was not the only keelboatman who loved a knock-down-and-drag-out fight. A goodly number of his fellows likewise were always willing and eager to engage in an old-fashioned free for all. Roaring Ralph Stackpole was also known as Tom Dowdle, the Rag-man.

"Cunnel," said he, "you're a man in authority, and my superior officer; warfo' thar' can be no scalping between us. But my name's Tom Dowdle, the rag-man!" he screamed, suddenly skipping into the thickest of the throng, and sounding a note of "My name's Tom Dowdle, the rag-man, and I'm for any man that insults me! log-leg or leather-breeches, green-shirt or blanket-coat, land-trotter or river-roller—I'm the man for a massacre!" Then giving himself a twirl upon his foot that would have done credit to a dancing master, he proceeded to other antic demonstrations of hostility, which when performed in after years on the banks of the Lower Mississippi, by himself and his worthy imitators, were, we suspect, the cause of their receiving the name of the mighty alligator. It is said, by naturalists, of this monstrous reptile, that he delights, when the returning warmth of spring has brought his fellows from their holes, and placed them basking along the banks of the swampy lagoon, to dart into the center of the expanse, and challenge the whole field to combat. He roars, he blows the water from his nostrils, he lashes out with his tail, he whirls round and round, churning the water into foam; until, having worked himself into a proper fury, he darts back again to the shore to seek an antagonist. Had the gallant captain of horse-thieves boasted the blood, as afterwards he did the name, of an "alligator half-breed," he could scarce have conducted himself in a way more worthy of his parentage. He leaped into the center of the throng, where, having found elbow-room for his purpose, he performed the gyration mentioned before, following it up by other feats expressive of his hostile humor. He flapped his wings and crowed, until every chanticleer in the settlement replied to the note of battle; he snorted and neighed like a horse; he bellowed like a bull; he barked like a dog; he yelled like an Indian; he whined like a panther; he howled like a wolf; until one would have thought he was a living menagerie, comprising within his single body the spirit of every animal noted for its love of conflict. Then, not content with such a display of readiness to fight the field, he darted from the center of the area allowed him for his exercise, and invited the lookers-on individually to battle. "Whar's your buffalo-bull," he cried, "to cross horns with the roarer of the Salt River? Whar's your full-blood colt that can shake a saddle off? H'yar's an old nag can kick off the top of a buck-eye! Whar's your cat of the Knobs, your wolf of the Rolling Prairies? H'yar's the old brown b'ar can claw the bark off a gum tree! H'yar's a man for you, Tom Bruce! Same to you, Sim Roberts! to you, Jimmy Big-nose! to you, and to you, and to you! Ar'n't I a ring-tailed squealer? Can go down the Salt on my back, and swim up the Ohio! Whar's the man to fight Roaring Ralph Stackpole?"

A Fight Between Keelboatmen Averted

Well, boys, there I wuz, at the bar of my favorite waterin' hole, when a gennelman next to me made a remark I didn't like. So I made a remark he didn't like. He spat in my face. I spat in his face. He knocked me down. I got up and knocked him down. He knocked out three of my teeth. I knocked out four of his teeth. He kneed me in the groin. I kneed him in the groin. He bit off my right earlobe. I bit off half of his left ear. He invited me to step outside and we war jest a-goin' to have a nice fight when some cussed pussy-footin' Yankees pulled us apart. Friends, that would've been a grand old scrimmage ef only they would've let us!

Stranger, Is This a Free Fight?

The story is familiar of the man who took passage in a flatboat from Pittsburgh bound for New Orleans. He passed many dreary, listless days down the Ohio and Mississippi, and seemed to be desponding for want of excitement. In course of time the raft upon which he was a passenger put into Napoleon, in the State of Arkansas, "for groceries." At the moment there was a general fight extending all along the "front of the town," which at that time consisted of a single house. The unhappy passenger, after fidgeting about, and jerking his feet up and down, as if he were walking on hot bricks, turned to a used-up spectator and observed:

"Stranger, is this a free fight?"

The reply was prompt and to the point:

"It ar'; and if you wish to go in, don't stand on ceremony."

The wayfarer did go in, and in less time than we can relate the circumstance was literally "chawed up." Groping his way down to the flat, his hair gone, his eye closed, his lips swollen, and his face generally "mapped out," he sat himself down on a chicken coop and soliloquized thus:

"So, this is Na-po-le-on, is it?—upon my word it's a lively place, and the only one at which I've had any fun since I left home!"

The Screaming Head

Emigrants who traveled by boat faced many dangers other than snags in the river, water moccasins, drowning, or swamp fever. The greatest danger came from murderous river pirates, and the spot most feared by rivermen and passengers alike was the ill-famed Cave in the Rock near the confluence of the Ohio and Mississippi rivers. This was the dreaded "Cavern of Death," which for some generations served as the lair for several gangs of robbers and murderers.

Many were the ways by which these human fiends lured the unwary wayfarers to their death. One of these cutthroats took up his station at a short distance upstream from the cave, calling out for help to passing rivercrafts, pretending to be shipwrecked and marooned on the rocky shore. When the would-be Good Samaritans came ashore to rescue the "poor castaway," the members of the gang emerged from their hiding places and fell upon their victims, plundering the boat and murdering the passengers, showing mercy neither to man, woman, or child.

Another bandit put up a crude tavern on the riverbank whose lights were a welcome sight to many a tired and hungry crew seeking food, drink and a real bed to sleep in. Once the "guests" slumbered, the murderer and his gang set upon them with club, ax, and bowie knife amid scenes of horror.

Then there was Billy Potts, the demon ferryman who, once in midstream, pounced upon those who had entrusted their lives and goods to him, beating them to death with an iron cudgel.

The worst of all these fiends were the Harpe Brothers, enemies to humankind, surpassing all other river pirates in cruelty and the lust for blood. They had remade the Cave in the Rock into a satanic castle, decorated with wine-red velvet curtains, French gilt-framed mirrors, chandeliers, and other booty from their robberies. Murder alone did not satisfy these human hyenas unless it was accompanied by torture—mental and corporeal. Even the worst of the other bandits gave the Harpes a wide berth, afraid to fall into the clutches of the murdering siblings. It was whispered that if the Harpes found themselves short of meat they were not above devouring human flesh, cutting out lights and livers, even boasting of their "own, special kidney pie, and guess from what kind of critter this side meat came from."

If a comely woman fell into their hands, they sometimes spared her life—for a time only. Keeping her as their slave, they treated their captive cruelly until, having become tired of her, they tossed the unfortunate into the river to drown. Legend had it that they fashioned the skulls of some victims into drinking cups, toasting each other with infernal laughter. Outlaws such as they could not come to a good end. It was fated that their reign of terror should come to its fitting climax.

A reward of a thousand dollars in gold for the capture of either of the Harpes, dead or alive, had been posted up and down the river, but none, not even the boastful ring-tailed roarers who ran the keel-

boats, were tempted to claim the reward. The two outlaws had a gang of four other cutthroats to abet them in their bloody work. One night, by the flickering light of their crystal chandelier, the six bandits sat around the fire, swearing and drinking raw whiskey. All of a sudden, the younger of the Harpe brothers grinned wolfishly, exclaiming, "If none of those lily-livered sons of bitches has the guts to try to collect those thousand dollars, why, I'll claim it myself!" Having uttered these words, he fixed his eyes upon one of the four gang members, sprang upon him and knocked him to the ground with a tremendous blow from the butt of one of his pistols. Laughing, as if this had been merely a boyish prank, the younger Harpe severed his erstwhile companion's head from its shoulders and wrapped the ghastly, dripping trophy in some rags, shouting, "Here are my thousand dollars! Will his noggin not do for a Harpe's head? Now for the reward!" With these words he took up his bloody bundle and sauntered off, leaving the four others behind in the cave. As soon as the older Harpe was asleep, the three remaining companions in crime crept silently away, no longer having the stomach to stay.

As soon as the younger Harpe reached the next town, he sought out the sheriff and the local judge, exhibiting his trophy, telling everybody present: "This here is the head of one of the Harpe Brothers. I cut it off myself. I've come to get the reward!"

Some months before, a man had fallen into the clutches of the murdering brothers, had been struck down and left for dead. Having only been beaten into unconsciousness, he had come to and, once the Harpes were gone, had effected his escape. He had come to see what the commotion was all about and realized that his moment of revenge had come. He spoke up loudly, telling the crowd: "That fellow here is one of the Harpes. I could pick him out from among thousands. It's a Harpe, all right, with a face hard to forget. As to the head, I'm sure it belongs to someone they have murdered."

Another bystander then spoke: "Yes, it's one of them, one of the Harpes. I've seen them only from afar, but it's true enough, their faces you don't forget. They were after me, but I got away."

The younger Harpe began to stutter and tried to lose himself in the crowd that had quickly gathered around him, but they got hold of him and he could not escape. He was tried on the spot, found guilty, and strung up on the nearest tree. The cutoff head was buried in a potter's field.

The older Harpe now lived alone in his gloomy hideout, but justice was now on his trail. One sole survivor of a large family the Harpes had murdered sought and found the monster's lair and near it lay in wait until Harpe emerged to prey on some unlucky traveler who might chance his way. As the outlaw stood in front of his cave, scanning the horizon, his form silhouetted against the sunlight, the avenger shot him dead. As Harpe had done to many of his victims, so it was done to him. His killer severed his head and wedged it into the fork of a huge, dead nearby tree. He hurled the rest of the body into the river. But that is not the end of the story.

For some years after, emigrants who passed the Cave in the Rock in their boats could hear a loud, piercing, bansheelike wailing that seemed to come out of nowhere. Shuddering, they hurried on, not caring to stop and find out what, or who, caused this frightful eerie screeching. But one traveler, more daring than the others, determined to discover the source of all that wailing. He rowed ashore, saw the tree and, in its fork, the dreadful, shriveled, eyeless head. Its pale flaxen hair was stirring in the wind, its lips were moving. Shocked beyond words, the traveler could, in between the unnerving screams, hear words escaping from the gaping mouth:

Listen well,
In hell I must dwell.
Do not do as I have done,
Or to the devil you'll be gone!

The curious traveler was curious no longer. He plied his oars as fast as he could to get away from that accursed spot. He told his tale, and others traveling by boat shunned the Cave in the Rock, making a wide detour around it. Those who were driven by wind and waves to the shore averted their eyes and stopped up their ears to avoid hearing the ghostly wailings. The screaming head kept other would-be river pirates from occupying the Cavern of Death. Not even outlaws could stand to be within the sound of the lamenting head. As the years went by, flesh and hair fell from the head, which became a naked skull gleaming in the moonlight. It ceased its wailing and at last grew silent. Maybe it is still there.

Stopping Drinking for Good

Boys, I'll tell you a tale. It happened a long time ago. I was floatin' down the Big Muddy in my broadhorn, the Cougar Kate. I was quite a hell-raiser in those days and had taken aboard a big load of blue ruin. I was as drunk as a skunk, but not too drunk to steer. The mist was all over the river and it was like driftin' through buttermilk. Now and agin' I was floatin' by some old dead cottonwoods and, as I passed them by, they all looked like ghosts wavin' their arms at me. The fog threw a blanket over everything. It was so quiet you could hear a mosquito hiccup. The wind and the river were barely whisperin'. The silence made me skittish, though I couldn't say why.

All of a sudden, out of that buttermilk, I spied a flatboat comin' ward me. Up on the box I could make out some men, wimmin, and children, all huddlin' together as if they war freezin'. Among them was a catgut scraper. He had his fiddle tucked 'neath his chin and his bow on the strings, but there was no sound and his hands didn't move. He was like bein' petrified. And when that boat came so close

I could almost tech it, I noticed that I could see through these folks as if they had been made of glass.

In the stern was sittin' a man havin' ahold of the big steerin' oar. He was dressed all in black, gaunt and skinny, and I didn't specially like the looks of him. He looked infernally unhuman and witchlike. His cloak, his broad-brimmed slouch hat, and his boots were all black. Even blacker were his hair and beard coming all the way down to his waist, and one of his eyes, lookin' straight at me, glowed like a hot coal. But where his other eye ought to have been there war jest a hole with a baby cottonmouth peekin' out o' it. It gave me the trembles jist to see him like that. And in the feller's lap sat a big black tomcat, and by his side crouched an oversize black hounddog. I don't mind tellin' you that I was skeered. My hands were tremblin', my legs shakin', and my teeth chatterin' and clickin' like them castanets the Mex wimmin use when they're dancin'. And I could look through that stranger and his pets too because they were jist like made out of gossamer, and when I teched the boat I teched nothin' but air.

All of a sudden the scary silence was shattered as the dog reared up on his hind legs and started barkin' and howlin', and the cat started caterwaulin' and meowin', and the man in the stern stood up. He was wavin' his arms at me, and I saw that his fingers were jist bones, bleached bones picked clean. He was wavin' his arms so viggerously that it made his head fall clean off, but he caught it and put it on his shoulders. I'm tellin' you, boys, my hairs were standin' up like cornstalks and my lights and liver turned to jelly. Then this critter started to talk while the little snake kept slitherin' in and out o' his empty eye socket, which was mighty discombobulatin'. The feller's voice was hollow and helliferous, turnin' my veins to ice. Here's what he said to me:

"Hulloe, stranger, look at me, full of worm holes and half-eaten by crawfish. I used to be a real land screamer and rib staver, all porcupine quills and aquafortis. One time I got wolfish and went on a tear. I got as drunk as a skunk, as drunk as you are today," and here he took to cacklin' and guffawin' horrible-like. "I was so drunk I opened my shirt collar to piss, and I didn't take keer of this boat, and run her on a snag, and she sank. And all these innocent folks here, who had put their trust in me, drownded. And I drownded too. Stranger, I'm a-warning you, if you don't stop drinkin', you'll wind up like me afore the year is over!"

Boys, I was so ramsquaddled that I stopped drinkin' for good right then and there, teetotaciously—leastwise for a whole week.

CHAPTER 5

Mountain Men

The mountain man, who chose to spend his days in the western wilds trapping beaver, has been called "the free-est human who ever was," free from the straightjacket of civilization, free from the constraints of law, convention, domesticity, religion, or authority. For his freedom he paid a price that to the "normal" citizen seemed exorbitant—the ever-present danger of being killed by an enraged grizzly, or gored by a wounded buffalo, of having his hair lifted by an Indian brave, of being "rubbed out" by a fellow trapper during a drunken free-for-all, of dying of hunger, or of freezing to death amid the snows of savage winters. If the mountain man, "being exceedingly tenacious of life," survived all of these perils, he was apt to end his days crippled by rheumatism, a result of constantly wading in icy streams to set his traps. But no matter what hardships he had to endure, the trapper looked upon them as a cheap price to pay for what mattered to him most—his absolute freedom. In a way, "mountain man" is a misnomer. One could with equal justification call him a plainsman, or a riverman, as he plied his trade wherever the pickings were rich. He made his living, if it can be called that, by trapping beaver, swapping the skins for the few things he needed to exist. His possessions were few—whatever he could carry on his person and his packhorse: seven traps, a Plains rifle, preferably a Hawken, whose heavy ball would drop a charging buffalo in its tracks, two pounds of gunpowder, four pounds of lead, a bullet mold, a spare pair of moccasins, a strike-a-light with tinderbox, an awl, and a good supply of "chawin' 'baccer," most of which he carried in his "possible sack." He also had a blanket or buffalo robe, a hatchet, a camp kettle, and his indispensable Green River knife. Sometimes he also toted a bag of foofaraw—trinkets such as beads, bells, small mirrors, and vermilion paint, to induce a good-looking squaw to share his blanket.

The trapper's way of life was made possible by a rage for beaver hats among fashionable city dwellers, both in America and Europe. The beaver plew was the standard medium of exchange where ordinary money was scarce. In the halcyon days of the fur trade, a prime skin fetched from four to six dollars a pound in the mountains. Once every year, the trappers gathered at the "rendezvous," a sort of wilderness fair and carnival, held at a previously agreed-upon place, such as Pierre's Hole, the Popo Agie, or the Green River–Siskeedee. At the rendezvous as many as a thousand mountain men, traders, and Indians with their squaws came together to swap pelts for coffee, whiskey, powder, blankets, and tobacco a man needed to last through the next trapping season. As the mountaineer skinned the beaver, so he was fleeced by the trader who sold him his basic necessities at an exorbitant 2,000 percent profit.

An equally powerful inducement to attend the rendezvous was the opportunity to "cut one's wolf loose" during one glorious, long-lasting orgy to

make up for many months of loneliness and danger, a time for "uncouth frolics of semi-savages," riotous, picturesque, alcoholic, and splendiferously barbaric. According to George Ruxton, who witnessed it.

The rendezvous is one continued scene of drunkenness, gambling, and brawling and fighting, as long as the money and credit of the trappers last. Seated, Indian fashion, round the fires, with a blanket spread before them, groups are seen with their "decks" of cards, playing at euker, poker, and seven-up, the regular mountain games. The stakes are "beaver," which here is current coin; and when the fur is gone, their horses, mules, rifles, and shirts, hunting packs, and breeches, are staked. Daring gamblers make the rounds of the camp, challenging each other to play for the trapper's highest stake—his horse, his squaw (if he has one), and, as once happened, his scalp. "There goes hos and beaver!" is the mountain expression when a great loss is sustained; and, sooner or later, "hos and beaver" invariably find their way into the insatiable pockets of the traders. A trapper often squanders the produce of his hunt, amounting to hundreds of dollars, in a couple of hours; and, supplied on credit with another equipment, leaves the rendezvous for another expedition, which has the same result time after time, although one tolerably successful hunt would enable him to return to the settlements and civilised life, with an ample sum to purchase and stock a farm, and enjoy himself in ease and comfort the remainder of his days. . . .

But of course, to become a farmer was not something a mountain man took a shine to.

The first rendezvous was held in 1825, the last in 1842. The glorious age of the free trapper lasted barely thirty years. By 1846 beaver hats were out of fashion, displaced by tall headgear made of silk and felt. As for the beaver, it had been trapped into virtual extinction. But the legends of the mountain men endure.

> The fur trader, trapper, beaver-hunter, or mountain man was a peculiar product of the American frontier. He belonged to a calling that had no counterpart. He started from frontiers at which more cautious pioneers were glad to stop. He was an adventurer for whom danger became a daily commonplace, an explorer who took tribute of the wilderness and wandered through the reaches of the outer West with all the freedom of the lonely wind. He was the predecessor of the missionary, the gold-seeker, the cattleman, the settler, and all kindred pioneers. The feet of a nation walked his half-obliterated trails, the course of empire followed his solitary pathways to the western sea.

Little Big Man

In 1826 an advertisement appeared in the *Missouri Intelligencer:*

NOTICE: To whom it may concern: That Christopher Carson, a boy about sixteen years old, small of his age, but thickset, light hair, ran away from the subscriber, living in Franklin, Howard County, Mo., to whom he had been bound to learn the saddler's trade, on or about the first day of September last. He is supposed to have made his way to the upper part of the State. All persons are notified not to harbor, support, or subsist said boy under penalty of the law. One cent reward will be given to any person who will bring back the said boy.

(Signed) *David Workman*

The measly reward leads one to suspect that Christopher's master did not greatly value his services and had not seen any signs of future greatness in him.

Kit Carson was born in 1809. When he was still a child, his family moved from Kentucky to Missouri. In appearance Kit was unprepossessing, only about five feet four inches tall, but "endowed with extraordinary elasticity." He had light-colored eyes and sandy, shoulder-length hair. Some said that he was bowlegged. His voice was as gentle as a girl's. Kit was something of a dandy. His hunting shirt was fringed and richly embroidered with designs of beadwork and porcupine quills. His horses were always richly accoutered. Unlike his fellow trappers, Kit was clean-shaven.

The little chap was versatile—a sometime saddler's apprentice, teamster, hunter, pathfinder, scout, guide, trader, Indian fighter, amateur surgeon, farmer, rancher, and soldier, rising to the rank of brigadier general. Above all else he was a beaverman, the very embodiment of a Rocky Mountain trapper.

When Kit was fifteen, his father apprenticed him to the worthy saddlemaker. He stood it for about two years, "but mourning over the awl, the hide of new leather, the buckle and strap" did not "shine" for him. The wee lad yearned, as his biographer said, "for the glorious shade of mighty forests; the wild battle with buffalo and bear; the crack of the unerring rifle, pointed at the trembling deer." At age seventeen he abruptly fell off his saddler's stool and lit out in search of adventure. He started inauspiciously as a teamster on the Santa Fe Trail, but soon became the eminent supertrapper, known as the "Monarch of the Prairie," and the "King of Pathfinders." Fanciers of other peoples' horses called him the "Thief-taker." At the height of his fame a prominent Londoner remarked that, as a result of books written about him while he was alive, Kit was better known in England than the Duke of Wellington, possibly a slight exaggeration. His fellow trappers simply called him Kit, which suited him fine.

He unceasingly roamed the whole length and breadth of the American West, covering immense distances without benefit of railroad or stagecoach. For years he never saw the face of a white woman or slept under a roof. Like many other western heroes, Carson was the subject of many "adorned" tales. An early writer described one of Kit's scrapes with Indians:

> Discharging his rifle and pistols at the first he came to, Carson raised himself in his stirrups, and swinging the former weapon over his head, with as much apparent ease as if it were a mere whisp, he brought it down upon the dusky horde around him with fatal effect. Not less than a dozen in the space of twice as many seconds bit the dust beneath its weight, while his horse, madly rearing and plunging, trod down some four or five more.

Swinging his heavy Hawken like a "whisp" must have been quite an effort for the diminutive Monarch of the Prairie, weighing all of 125 pounds.

On another occasion Kit's small party was attacked by a band of over a hundred Comanches. As the distant drumming of their ponies' hooves reached his ears and his eyes caught the glint of their lance points, Kit, quick as lightning, whipped out his bowie knife and slit the throat of his own horse, pulling the thrashing animal to the ground, using its still-twitching, blood-spurting body as a rampart behind which he crouched, resting his Hawken on the still-warm corpse. Instantly grasping his intent, Kit's companions, just as quickly, cut the throats of their horses and mules, doing their ghastly work in such a way that the bodies formed a circle inside which they took cover. As the mass of Comanche horsemen charged upon their, as they thought, easy prey, they themselves fell prey to the trappers' terrific volley, which toppled them by the score from their rearing, terrified ponies, maddened by the scent of reeking blood from the trappers' slaughtered mules and horses. A second salvo convinced them that they had picked the wrong men to furnish trophies for their scalp poles, and they galloped off even faster than they had come.

There was romance mingled with danger in Kit's life. "His heart had spoken," as the Indians were wont to say, meaning that he had his eye on a dusky bundle of loveliness, an Arapahoe lass named Singing Grass. It happened during one of the annual rip-roaring, murderously exuberant rendezvous of the mountaineers, an occasion for drunken orgies, extravagant gambling, wild horse races, epic fisticuffs, and a frantic search for woman flesh.

There was a fly in Kit's ointment in the shape of a gigantic, red-bearded Canadian voyageur, with a jaw like a bear trap, named Shunar. This unwholesome specimen, six and a half feet in his moccasins, was a much feared ruffian and fire-eater, always on the prowl for likely victims of his brutality, always boasting of the many men he had personally sent to the happy hunting grounds. He announced that he was wolfish, intent to crush some bones and bite some fellow's head off. He was searching for a worthy subject. Frenchmen were too soft. He had already disposed of too many Injuns. Americans were no fun either. He'd get himself a pliant branch and switch them. Thus he went around swearing, cussing and bellowing, making a great nuisance of himself.

This blustering behemoth, likewise, had taken a shine to Singing Grass, trying to seduce her with baubles and foofaraw, such as glass beads and vermilion ribbons. When this did not have the desired effect, he tried to rape the girl. In this he also failed, despite his enormous size and strength, because of the hair rope the girl wore between her thighs as a sort of native chastity belt. He went at it like a mad bull, but he could not hold Singing Grass down while at the same time trying to untie the rope. His wolfish mood was not improved when he discovered that the Arapahoe girl had permitted Kit to get rid of the impediment.

Shunar swaggered around the camp, swearing to have Kit for breakfast, calling him a bougre and a berdache, a fellow playing the woman to degenerate trappers. Kit's early biographer, Doctor De Witt Peters, discreetly omits all references to the Arapahoe beauty and describes what happened in his own Victorian way:

> Among the men congregated at the rendezvous, there was a Captain Shunar, a powerful Frenchman. The Captain was exceedingly overbearing in his intercourse with all around him. Upon the slightest pretext, he was sure to endeavor to involve some of the trappers in a fight. The result was that he was heartily despised by all, although, for the sake of peace, he was allowed to go unmolested. One day his conduct was particularly offensive to the entire command; for, after having had two fist fights with a couple of weak and inoffensive men, he commenced boasting that he could easily flog all the Frenchmen present; and, as to the Americans, he said that "he could cut a stick and switch them." Such actions and manners, at last, attracted Kit Carson's notice and caused him to be greatly annoyed. He thought the matter over and concluded that if Captain Shunar was allowed to gather many more such detestable laurels, he would soon become even more bold and troublesome. As no other member of the company seemed disposed to put a check upon such unmanly behavior, he quietly determined to make the affair his own.
>
> An opportunity soon presented itself. A number of the company had congregated together and were engaged in conversation, when Captain Shunar began anew his bullying language; this a little more boisterous than usual. Kit Carson, advancing into the centre of the company and placing himself in front of the Captain thus addressed him:
>
> "Shunar, before you stands the humblest specimen of an American in this band of trappers, among whom there are, to my certain knowledge, men who could easily chastise you; but, being peaceably disposed, they keep aloof from you. At any rate, I assume the responsibility of ordering you to cease your threats, or I will be under the necessity of killing you."

To this Captain Shunar did not reply; but immediately after Kit Carson had closed his remarks, he turned upon his heel and walked directly for his lodge.

Kit Carson was too well versed in trapper rules not to read the meaning of this action. He, therefore, walked off also, but, in the direction of his own lodge. In a brief space of time, both men appeared before the camp, each mounted on their respective horses. The affair had drawn together the whole band, and they were now, quietly, so many witnesses of the facts here recorded.

Captain Shunar was armed with his pistol and rifle. Kit Carson had taken merely a single-barrel dragoon pistol which happened to be the first weapon that had fallen in his way, because of his hurry to be on the ground. The two men now rapidly rode towards one another, until their horses' heads almost touched, when both horsemen reined up, and Kit Carson addressed Captain Shunar as follows:

"Am I the person you are looking for?"

Captain Shunar replied, "No!"

It was apparent that this reply of Captain Shunar was a falsehood; for, while giving it utterance, he raised his rifle in the act of shooting, bringing it to his shoulder and covering his antagonist. Before, however, Captain Shunar could discharge his gun, the ball from Kit Carson's pistol shattered his forearm, causing the rifle to tilt upwards, which changed the direction of its contents in such a way that Kit Carson received a wound in his scalp while the powder severely burned his face.

It was the universal opinion of the spectators of this event that both parties of this unhappy scene fired nearly at the same instant. The facts of the case show very plainly, first, that Captain Shunar intended to kill his antagonist. Why did he aim at Carson's breast? Second, that Kit Carson's shot was delivered perhaps a second or two in advance of Captain Shunar's; third, that Kit Carson did not desire to kill his antagonist, but merely to save his own life by disabling his adversary.

Things were not quite as neat and elegant as in this account. Shunar's language was a good deal more colorful. Kit Carson, by his own account, did not say, "I will be under the necessity of killing you," but instead offered to rip his opponent's guts out. In addition, as some witnesses maintained, he reloaded his pistol and finished off the Frenchman for good.

A less bloody embroidered story tells of Kit's pet beaver: "It war a whopper. That beaver slept ev'ry nite with Kit in his tent, an' when Kit left for the day to do his trappin', that doggone beaver fell to work and make a dam acrost the floor usin' chists and possible bags and whatever foofaraw he could find. That thar beaver was as nigh human bein' as any trapper."

Eventually, Kit married his little Arapahoe squaw, who bore him a daughter whom he later had properly brought up in St. Louis. Singing Grass died of mountain fever when the child was still a baby. Carson then married a lively señorita from Santa Fe and settled down as a rancher in Taos. He died in 1869 at Fort Lyon, Colorado, of heart failure. Calmly awaiting the end, his last words were "I am gone, Doctor! Compadre, adiós!"

Kit Carson and the Grizzlies

One quiver ran through the frame of the beautiful elk when he breathed his last. The echoing sound of the rifle shot had hardly died away, to which the true hunter ever listens with un-feigned pleasure as the sweetest of music to his ear, when the last faint melody was broken in upon and completely lost in a terrific roar from the woods directly behind him. Instantly turning his head to note the source of this sound, the meaning and cause of which he well knew by his experienced woodman's ear, educated until its nicety was truly wonderful, he saw two huge and terribly angry grizzly bears. As his eye first rested upon these unwelcome guests, they were bounding towards him, their eyes flashing fiery passion, their pearly teeth glittering with eagerness to mangle his flesh, and their mon-strous forearms, hung with sharp, bony claws, ready and anxious to hug his body in a close and most loving embrace. There was not much time for Kit to scratch his head and cogitate. In fact, one instant spent in thought then would have proved his death warrant without hope of a reprieve. Messrs. Bruin evidently considered their domain most unjustly intruded upon. The gentle elk and deer mayhap were their dancing boys and girls; and, like many a petty king in a savage land, they may have dined late and were now enjoying a scenic treat of their ballet troupe. At all events Kit required no second thought to perceive that the monarchs of the American forest were unappeasably angry and were fast nearing him with mighty stride. Dropping his rifle, the little leaden bullet of which would now have been worth to him its weight in gold could it by some magic wand have been transferred from the heart of the elk back into its breech, he bounded from his position in close imitation of the elk, but with better success. The trees! he hoped and prayed, as he fairly flew over the ground with the bears hot in chase, for one quick grasp at a sturdy sapling. By good fortune, or special Providence, his hope, or prayer, was answered. Grasping a lower limb, he swung his body up into the first tier of branches just as passing Bruin brushed against one of his legs. Bears climb trees and Kit Carson was not ignorant of the fact. Instantly drawing his keen-edged hunting knife, he cut away for dear life at a thick short branch. The knife and his energy conquered the cutting just as Messrs. Bruin had gathered themselves up for an ascent, a proceeding on their part to which Mr. Carson would not give assent. Mr. Carson was well acquainted with Messrs. Bruin's pride in, and extreme consideration for, their noses. A few sharp raps made with the severed branch upon the noses of the ascending bears, while they fairly made them howl with pain and rage, caused them hastily to beat a retreat. This scene of ascending, getting their noses tickled and again descending, howling with pain and rage now kept Messrs. Carson and Bruin actively busy for some time. The huge monsters and monarchs of the mountains were determined not to give it up so quickly. Such a full and fair chase and to be beaten by a simple white man on their own domain! This evidently galled their sensitive natures. It is true the roaring of the bears in his rear had stimulated Mr. Carson in the race, so much, that he undoubtedly ran at the top of his speed; and, being naturally, as well as by long practice, very fleet of foot, he had managed to outstrip his pursuers in the race. It is true he had made short work of climbing the tree and here again had very innocently beaten the bears at their own game and one in which they took great pride. It is more than probable that the bears were in too good a condition to run well. Had it been early springtime they would doubtless been much lower in flesh. That was their own fault too; they should have known that racing time cannot be made on high condition. After leaving their hibernating quarters they should have been less given to a sumptuous habit at the table.

Affairs were, however, by no manner of means settled. They had the daring trespasser on their domain treed, and almost within their reach; and, indeed, to keep out of the way of their uncomely claws,

Kit was obliged to gather himself up in the smallest possible space and cling to the topmost boughs. The bears now allowed themselves a short respite for breathing, during which they gave vent to their wrath by many shrill screeches. Then they renewed their endeavors to force the hunter from his resting place. Mounted on their hind paws, they would reach for him; but, the blows with the stick, applied freely to their noses, would make them desist. In vain did they exhaust every means to force the man to descend; he was not to be driven or coaxed. The hard knocks they had sustained on their noses had now aroused them almost to madness. Together they made one desperate effort to tear Kit from the tree. As in all previous attempts, they were foiled, and their ardor dampened and cooled by the drumming operations upon their noses, which this time was so freely and strongly applied upon one of them as to make him lachrymate and cry out with pain. One at a time they had been out of sight and hearing for some time so that Kit considered it safe to venture down from the tree; when, he hastened to regain and immediately reload his rifle.

Thus ended an adventure in which Kit Carson considers that he failed to lose his life and limb by the narrowest miss that ever occurred to him.

Run for Your Life, White Man!

The saga of John Colter is one of great courage, superhuman endurance, and a great deal of luck. Born in 1775, in Virginia, Colter moved to Kentucky and, in 1804, set out for the unknown, unmapped West as a member of Lewis and Clark's famous scouting expedition, one of nine "Kaintuck fellers, blessed with an open and pleasing countenance." He took to the prairies like a duck to water, possibly the first white man to get a glimpse of the Tetons and to cross a forbidding region of spouting geysers and bubbling, boiling sulphur springs known ever since as Colter's Hell.

By 1807 John Colter had become a hardy, accomplished trapper, determined to make his fortune in beaver plews. At first, he did his hunting along the upper Missouri, but when this area became trapped out, he began looking for richer beaver grounds.

Beaver was plentiful in the country of the "Terrible Blackfeet," so named because they would not suffer a white man to invade their hunting grounds and live. In 1808, in company with a fellow trapper named Lemuel Potts, Colter entered the forbidden land. He took more chances than others to have his hair lifted because, as one of Lewis and Clark's men, he had shot and killed a Blackfoot brave whom he had caught in the act of horse stealing. The danger was great, but the lure of prime beaver pelts at five dollars a piece was greater. Colter and Potts exercised extreme caution, always setting their traps after nightfall and gathering in their catch before sunrise.

During the day they remained hidden among the cottonwoods and underbrush lining the banks of all western streams. One morning at daybreak the two men were paddling their birchbark canoe along the Jefferson fork of the Missouri, examining their traps. On both sides rose riverbanks so high that they were not able to see the plains above.

"Thar's a heap of Injin sign hyar," Colter remarked. "This hoss don't take a shine to this." Potts said nothing.

Suddenly, they heard the sound of a mighty trampling of numberless feet.

"Injins," whispered Colter. "We must git away afore they seed us."

"Don't be sech a yellow-livered cuss," said Potts, "it's jest a herd of bufflers."

Colter only shrugged as they paddled on, but he had been right because they soon saw the tops of the bluffs aswarm with Blackfeet. The Indians motioned for them to come ashore. Flight was impossible. Over Potts's objections, Colter steered for the riverbank. As soon as their craft touched ground, an Indian snatched Potts's rifle from his grip. Quick as lightning Colter jumped ashore, wrested the weapon from the Indian's grasp, and handed it back to his companion. Frantically, Potts paddled away into midstream.

"Come back, you darn fool!" shouted Colter. "Come back or they'll kill you!"

But Potts had made up his mind. Taking a chance of being killed instantly by bow or bullet was preferable to a slow death by torture in case of capture. He raised his rifle and fired. One Blackfoot brave fell dead. Hideous yells and a volley of arrows was the answer. So many shafts found their target that poor Potts, to Colter, seemed transformed into a human porcupine.

"They made a riddle of him," he was to say later, recounting the scene. Soon Potts's reeking scalp was waving on a stick above the milling crowd.

The Indians stripped Colter of everything but the hair on his chest. Naked as he was born, they dragged him to their village. They brought him to their chief. In his years of trapping Colter had learned enough of the Blackfoot language to understand what his captors were talking about. They were discussing various methods of putting him to death, methods highly amusing to them, less so to him. Fortunately, the chief was something of a sportsman.

"Is the white man a good runner?" he inquired.

Colter understood at once. He was to furnish entertainment by running for his life. Here was a glimmer of hope. He strengthened the chief's whimsical fancy by assuring him: "This white man is a very poor runner, slower than a turtle."

His captors grinned, enjoying the game. The chief motioned them to stay back. He then led Colter to a spot some four hundred yards distant to give him a sporting chance. Then he slapped Colter on the back and said, "Run for your life, white man! Save yourself if you can!"

The chief signaled to his braves that the race was on. The Indians howled like demons, waving their lances and tomahawks. The odds seemed hopeless. Colter was outnumbered five hundred to one. His pursuers were armed. He was naked and defenseless. Nowhere could he see a place to hide. The river, lined with timber in which he might seek concealment, was six miles away. Still, he did not despair. One chance in five hundred was better than none. He flew rather than ran. On and on he raced, the war whoops of the Blackfeet ringing in his ears. He did not dare look around for fear of losing one inch of ground. Moccasins protected his pursuers' feet; his were bare. Prickly pear, thorns, and sharp stones reduced his soles to a reddish mass, yet, bent on survival, he did not even feel the pain.

Constant yelling and howling after their human prey was knocking the wind out of many Indians, who kept dropping out of the race, one after the other. Those who continued after him were strung out over a great distance. The yells and the sounds of pounding moccasins behind him grew fainter. He was gaining on his hunters. He dared to look. Only about a dozen Blackfeet had been able to keep up with him, but the foremost, a gigantic, spear-wielding warrior, was only about a hundred yards behind him. On and on went the race. Colter strained every muscle and spent his last ounce of energy. His lungs were about to burst. Blood gushed from his nostrils, spattering his chest. His gigantic pursuer was in no better shape. He could not get nearer his two-legged game, but Colter could not get farther from him. Thus both raced on. The trapper now held a slight advantage. He was running for his life, the warrior only to earn an eagle feather, but the latter had finally driven himself to within twenty yards of his intended victim. It left him incapable of a further effort. Despairing of closing this last gap, he hurled, or rather tried to hurl, his spear at Colter, but he stumbled and fell, breaking his weapon in the process. Colter had turned around, arms outspread, to face his pursuer. In a flash he saw and seized his only chance. Grabbing the spear's pointed part, he impaled his foe with such tremendous force as to pin him to the ground. Then he ran on.

One after another the braves arrived, stopping for a few moments to mourn their fallen comrade, breaking into frightful howls of anguish, giving Colter a further chance of getting ahead of them. He reached the timber alongside the river and disappeared in the undergrowth. Seconds later he plunged into the sluggish river. In its midstream he discerned a huge, brush-covered beaver hut. The trapper knew beavers better than he knew men. He was aware that a beaver house always was partly under and partly above water, the entrance lying below the surface. Above was the comparatively dry upper chamber—the beaver family's home. Without the slightest hesitation Colter swam to the dome-shaped structure and dived, fumbling for the entrance opening in the murky water. He was alert to the great risk involved. A man is bigger than a beaver. He might get stuck in the narrow channel leading to the upper part. Then it would be all over. He would drown. But he would try his luck. He found the entrance and, as he had feared, got stuck. With a mighty effort he managed to squeeze himself through and into the beavers' den. The outraged occupants hurriedly left their home in the opposite direction, leaving Colter sole master of the place. He crouched there alone, in darkness, panting and retching.

The Blackfeet warriors followed Colter's tracks to the river's edge and began searching for him. They combed the shore on both banks without finding his footprints, proof that he had nowhere gone ashore. Some even swam to the beaver hut and stood on its top to get a better view of their surroundings, unaware that only a foot of earth and tangled branches separated them from their prey. Colter could feel his roof trembling above him and feared that one or the other of them might break through. He could hear them talking, could even make out a word or two. The Indians looked for him everywhere, even in the most unlikely places. Colter heard them shouting to each other across the river for a long time, but after several hours everything was quiet at last. The Blackfeet had given up, thinking that the trapper in his weakened state, possibly wounded in his fight with their slain comrade, must have drowned.

The fugitive stayed in his strange hideout the rest of the day and the following night. He was weary unto death. His lacerated feet gave him great pain. He was cold and hungry. Through chinks in his domed roof he could discern a little light—the dawn of another day. Once more he squeezed himself through the entrance channel. Cautiously, his head hidden in tangled driftwood, he scanned the river in every direction, making sure that his enemies were gone. He felt something against him—his unwilling hosts reclaiming their home. He swam to the far shore and stood for a moment, caught up in revery. He was alive. He had escaped.

He had escaped his human foes but not the forces of nature. He was naked and defenseless, without any means of killing game. His feet were lumps of suffering flesh. A chance encounter with a grizzly or a pack of wolves would be his end. He was over a hundred miles from the nearest place of refuge, Manuel Lisa's fort and trading post on a branch of the Yellowstone River, but with renewed hope and grim determination he set out upon his awesome trek. He stilled his hunger by eating toads, snakes, insects, and roots. A jackrabbit's partly decomposed body made a welcome feast. What was left of its skin, and a fragment of fur he found in his path, he wrapped around his bleeding feet. Out of reeds and grass he fashioned himself the poor imitation of a garment. Years in the wilderness had given him an eye for the land and a sure sense of direction. He reached the fort in the incredibly short time of seven days. To the men watching from the stockade Colter appeared as a stumbling ghostlike shape, a two-legged bundle of reeds barely dragging itself along. He was at last

recognized amid thundering cheers, clad, and fed. A bumper of brandy did him no end of good. After ten days he was fit again, his mind fixed on beaver.

A choice lay before him—to go back to trap, or to St. Louis and his bride, Sally, whom he had married two years before. Incredible as it may seem, he chose the mountains and returned to the land of the Terrible Blackfeet where beavers were a-plenty. At five dollars a plew the lure was too great. In the month of May 1810 a small canoe arrived at St. Louis from the headwaters of the Missouri, sagging under a huge load of beaver pelts, paddled by none other than John Colter. He had paddled his frail craft over 2,500 miles of winding streams and rivers, covering the distance in a mere thirty days. Whether walking, running, or paddling, Colter was the fastest man on the prairies. He sold his pelts at a good profit and returned to his Sally.

The rest of his life was anticlimactic. He bought land and livestock. He built himself a house and set up as a farmer. Together with his wife he raised chickens, milked cows, and stuck pigs. What the wilderness and the Blackfeet failed to accomplish, civilization did. It killed him. John Colter died in 1813, at the age of thirty-eight. The legend of his epic race lives on.

The story is almost too good to be true—almost. It is much more factual than the tales of most western heroes. Events happened as described—except for one bit of later embroidery, namely the beavers. As Colter himself told it, it was not inside a beaver hut he was hiding, but under a natural raft of tangled tree trunks, branches, driftwood, and other debris, lying almost motionless in mid-river. With nose and lips above water, his head concealed between tree trunks, he stayed there, waterlogged, until his skin shriveled, while his pursuers actually cavorted on top of his floating island, "yelling like the devils." But true or not, the beavers, added by later story tellers, give the Colter saga that "extra touch."

Old Solitaire

Old Bill Williams was a semilegendary character, famous among the free trappers, often called the "ultimate mountain man." He himself sometimes signed his papers proudly "Bill Williams, Master Trapper." A Ute chief commented that Old Bill was "a great trapper, good hunter, took heaps of beaver, great warrior, many scalps hanging from his belt, but no friends, always by himself." One observer described him as six foot one inch, tall, gaunt, red-headed, with a hard, weather-beaten face, marked deeply with smallpox. He was said to be all muscle and sinew, the most indefatigable hunter in all the West, "a shrewd, cute, original man." His hardihood was incredible. He could outrun a deer, outfight a bear, and run all day with six traps on his back. He wolfed down his meat raw and was in like measure impervious to the searing desert storms of summer and the icy blizzards of winter. He was very profligate of life, killing Indian men, women, and children with the same lack of feeling as when bringing down a deer or jackrabbit.

No one ever accused Old Bill of being fastidious. He outdid his fellow trappers in dirtiness and never washed if he could help it, a gent carrying a few pounds of topsoil around on his body. He went about in a filthy, reeking buckskin shirt, so stiff he could stand it upright on the ground. His pants, shrunken and clinging to his bony shanks, were full of holes, leaving parts of his buttocks exposed. His lousy hair hung down to his shoulders, his unkempt beard to his waist, yet he loved to deck himself out in barbaric finery, fringed, beaded, and quilled, his cap of otter fur decorated with hawk and eagle feathers. The best description of Williams was left us by an early British traveler, George Frederick Ruxton, who knew him well:

> Williams always rode ahead, his body bent over his saddle-horn, across which rested a long heavy rifle, his keen eyes peering from under the slouched brim of a flexible felt hat, black and shining with grease. His buckskin hunting shirt, bedaubed until it had the appearance of polished leather, hung in folds over his bony carcass; his nether extremities being clothed in pantaloons of the same material (with scattered fringes down the outside of the leg, which ornaments, however, had been pretty well thinned to supply "whangs" for mending or pack saddles), which, shrunk with wet, clung tightly to his long, spare, sinewy legs. His feet were thrust

into a pair of Mexican stirrups made of wood, and as big as coal-scuttles; and iron spurs of incredible proportions, with tinkling drops attached to the rowels, were fastened to his heel—a bead-worked strap, four inches broad, securing them over the instep. In the shoulder belt which sustained his powder-horn and bullet-pouch, were fastened the various instruments essential to one pursuing his mode of life. An awl, with deerhorn handle, and a point defended by a case of cherry-wood carved by his own hand, hung at the back of his belt, side by side with a worm for cleaning his rifle; and under this was a squat and quaint-looking bullet-mold, the handles guarded by strips of buckskin to save his fingers from burning when running balls, having for its companion a little bottle made from the point of an antelope's horn, scraped transparent, which contained the "medicine" used in baiting traps.

The old coon's face was sharp and thin, a long nose and chin hob-nobbing with each other; and his head was always bent forward giving him the appearance of being hump-backed. He appeared to look neither to the right nor the left, but, in fact, his twinkling eye was everywhere. He looked at no one he was addressing, always seeming to be thinking of something else than the subject of his discourse, speaking in a whining, thin, cracked voice, and in a tone that left the hearer in doubt whether he was laughing or crying.

The legend of Old Bill is controversial. He is described as kindly and true, a faithful friend and honest fellow, but is also accused of being a murderous fiend, a horse thief, a scalp-hunter, and a booze-blind drunkard. Some said that he had gone to school and could read and write in a legible hand; others said that "he had no glory except in the woods." The truth probably lies somewhere in between. On one thing all who knew him agreed: of all the free trappers Old Bill was "the most tattered, toughest, and notoriously the least trammeled." It is also certain that he was a loner who had no use for the company of man or beast except, of course, during the mating season. Among his fellows he was known as Old Solitaire.

There is an old joke that our hero was known as Old Bill Williams before he was weaned. At any rate, the epithet "Old" was a moniker of affection, bestowed regardless of age.

William Sherley Williams was born in 1787, on Horse Creek, North Carolina, of pious Baptist parents. His father had been a soldier in the army of the Revolution who had taken up farming after the war was over. In 1794 the family settled in the vicinity of St. Louis, then a village of roughly a thousand inhabitants ruled by Spain. Old Bill therefore grew up in the shadow of the fur trade. As a boy, he worked on the farm from "can see to no can see." In 1806 he went West on a stolen horse with his pappy's Hawken rifle. He was nineteen then, a ginger-haired, walking, six-foot human skeleton. God grabbed him by the scruff and shook his soul mightily so that he looked heavenward. He fell under the influence of a wandering hellfire-and-brimstone Baptist preacher, the Reverend John Clark, a Scotchman and one-time sailor, privateer, pirate, British foretop man, deserter, and schoolteacher. Clark so worked for Bill's salvation that he was "saved" and himself set up as an itinerate sermonizer, swapping the Word of God for a meal and a place to sleep. His orations were mighty powerful. He put the fear of God into his trembling listeners, threatening them with hellfire everlasting for a variety of transgressions. Once, seized by the spirit, he preached with such tremendous effect that his listeners were rendered "as slick as peeled onions," their sins peeled off after having been washed thoroughly in the Blood of the Lamb. One day, as he worked himself up into a frenzy, with foam-flecked mouth holding forth on the always-interesting subject of fornication, his eye fell upon a comely, high-bosomed lass who smiled back at him, which put an aching into his loins. Then and there he decided that, like the fellow who crept into a harem disguised as a eunuch, "he was not cut out for his job." He gave up preaching and went farther West to live among Osage Indians. On rare occasions he was still seized by an urge to preach the gospel to the heathen children of nature. He had no great luck with this endeavor. Once he regaled them with the story of Jonah and the Whale. The Indians commented: "We have heard the white people tell lies, we know they always lie, but this is the biggest lie we ever heard." He did not missionize the Osages, but they missionized him. He began worshiping the Sun as Giver of Life, the Moon as Goddess of Propagation, and Grandmother Earth as the Great Nourisher of Men and Beasts. His Indian brothers called him Pah-Hah-Soo-Gee-Ah, the Redheaded Shooter. He then took to wife the daughter of the chief of the Big Hill Band and with her begat ginger-haired offspring. He then became an interpreter at trading posts, for the government, and for a company of dragoons. In 1820, Bill's father died after having predicted, correctly, the exact minute, hour, and year of his demise.

In 1825, at the age of thirty-eight, Bill began his somewhat belated career as a mountain man. He took to it with the enthusiasm of a hungry cat pouncing upon a succulent mouse. He soon had a squaw in every tribe, for political as well as physical reasons, and also in order to learn as many native languages as possible. He became fluent in seven, a great asset for a man after beaver plews. He likewise cemented relations with the Hispanic people of the Southwest, attracting a beautiful señorita who, on her part, presented him with a strapping carrot-haired son. As a trapper, Old Bill ranged far and wide, from the Texas Panhandle to the Pacific and from the Rio Grande all the way up into the Yellowstone country. Shunning human company, he talked to his Hawken rifle, named Knockumstiff, and conversed with his old nag Calico, reportedly the ugliest horse on the Plains. Above all others he hated the Terrible Blackfeet, the mountain men's perennial enemies. It was said that Old Bill could smell a Blackfoot from ten miles off. In the words of Ruxton:

> When with a large party of trappers anything occurred which gave him a hint that trouble was coming, or more Indians were about than he considered good for his animals, Bill was wont to exclaim —"Do 'ee hyar, boys, thar's sign about? this hoss feels like caching"; and, without more words, and stoically deaf to all remonstrances, he would forthwith proceed to pack his animals, talking the while to an old, crop-eared, raw-boned Nez-percé pony, his own particular saddle-horse, who, in dogged temper and iron hardiness, was a worthy companion of his self-willed master. This beast, as Bill seized his apishamore to lay upon its galled back, would express displeasure by humping its back and shaking its withers with a wincing motion, that always excited the ire of the old trapper; and no sooner had he laid the apishamore smoothly on the chafed skin, than a wriggle of the animal shook it off.
>   "Do 'ee hyar now, you darned crittur!" he would whine out, "can't 'ee keep quiet your old fleece now? Isn't this old coon putting out to save 'ee from the darned Injuns now, do 'ee hyar?" And then, continuing his work, and taking no notice of his comrades, who stood by bantering the eccentric trapper, he would soliloquise —"Do 'ee hyar now? This niggur sees sign ahead—he does; he'll be afoot afore long, if he don't keep his eye skinned—he will. Injuns is all about, they ar'; Blackfoot at that. Can't come round this child—they can't, wagh!" And at last, his pack animals securely tied to the tail of his horse, he would mount, and throwing the rifle across the horn of his saddle, and without noticing his companions, would drive the jingling spurs into his horse's gaunt sides, and muttering, "Can't come round this child—they can't!" would ride away; and nothing more would be seen or heard of him perhaps for months, when they would not unfrequently, themselves bereft of animals in the scrape he had foreseen, find him located in some solitary valley, in his lonely camp, with his animals securely picketed around, and his peltries safe.

Kindly Old Bill would often lecture the greenhorn, introducing him into the mysteries of trapper life: "Do 'ee hyar now, you darned greenhorn, grizzlies air bad, but Blackfeet is worse. Them's the ornariest Injins fer sure. When yee git into their diggin's yer hair's already half offen yer skull, do 'ee hyar? Blackfoot diggin's won't shine in this crowd. No, stranger, Blackfeet air worse than a painter defendin' her cubs. Oncet I war trappin' beaver at the head of the Yellerstone with nary an Injin sign around. W-a-a-l, this child lit his fire an' wuz a-smokin' his pipe. I knowed I hadn't orter, but I did. I war b'ilin' beaver tails when, all of a sudden, thar they be, the cussed varmints, Blackfeet, four o' them, and me with but me old toothpicker. I gutted one o' the red divils with me knife, brained the second with me tommihawk, kneed the third in the groin, and got ahold o' the fourth by the nose with me teeth, taken keer of all four varmints at the same time. Hang me up fer b'ar meat, if I didn't. Yessir, Blackfeet are bad, but this hoss is badder. Them Injins air pizen, son, steer clear o' them, do 'ee hyar?"

Old Bill might have admonished a newcomer in the same vein as a fellow trapper named Long Hatcher: "This child hates an American what hasn't seen Injuns skulped or doesn't know a Yute from a Shian mok'sin. Sometimes he thinks of makin' tracks for white settlement but when he gits to Bent's big lodge on the Arkansa and sees the bugheways, an' the fellers from the States, how they roll thar eyes at an Injun and yell worse nor if a village of Camanches was on 'em, an' pick up a beaver trap an' ask what it is—jest shows whar the niggurs had thar brungin' up—this child says, "a little bacca ef it's a plew a plug, an' Dupont an' G'lena, a Green River or so,' an' he leaves for the Bayou Salade. Darn the white diggins while thar's buffler in the mountains!"

Old Bill ate whatever walked, ran, hopped, crawled, crept, slithered, swam, or flew. All others scorned painter meat. Even the hardiest trappers found it too strong for their taste. Old Bill relished it. Rattlesnake stew did shine. Locust, roasted to a crisp, would do when nothing else was to be had. When starving, he had recourse to eating the parfleche soles of his moccasins. As Ruxton remembered: "Old Bill, however, never grumbled! He chewed away at his shoes with relish even, and as long as he had a pipeful of tobacco in his pouch, he was a happy man. On his one visit back to civilization, at his brother's farm in Missouri, he grabbed the intestines of a freshly slaughtered calf and squeezed out their contents into his gaping mouth, swallowing it all down with grunts of delight and an expression of sheer ecstasy. He flavored his food with buffalo gall and put more than just a pinch of pepper and gunpowder in his whiskey "to give 'er a kick." He was accused of having eaten a fellow trapper during John Charles Frémont's disastrous winter expedition, and was rumored to have boasted that "it war mighty good eatin', speshly the liver lights." Surprisingly, in view of his barbaric fare, he could, at times, be finicky. To quote Ruxton again:

On one occasion, they had come upon a band of fine buffalo cows, and shortly after camping, two of the party rode in with a good supply of fat fleece. One of the party was a "greenhorn" on his first hunt, and, fresh from a fort on the Platte, was as yet uninitiated in the mysteries of mountain cooking. Bill, lazily smoking his pipe, called to him, as he happened to be nearest, to butcher off a piece of meat and put it in his pot. Markhead seized the fleece, and commenced innocently carving off a huge ration, when a gasping roar from the old trapper caused him to drop his knife.

"Ti-yah," growled Bill, "do 'ee hyar, now, you darned green-horn, do 'ee spile fat cow like that whar you was raised? Them doin's won't shine in this crowd, boy, do 'ee hyar, darn you? What! butcher meat across the grain! why, whar'll the blood be goin' to, you precious Spaniard? Down the grain I say," he continued in a severe tone of rebuke, "an' let yer flaps be long, or out the juice'll run slick—do 'ee hyar, now?" But this heretical error nearly cost the old trapper his appetite, and all night long he grumbled his horror at seeing "fat cow spiled in that fashion."

At that time, Old Bill and his party were deep in Blackfeet country. Beaver were plentiful, but so were signs of Indians. Some of the men suggested finding a more congenial place to trap. Old Bill wouldn't hear of it. Usually shunning the Blackfeet like devils incarnate, he now declared:

"Do 'ee hyar now, boys, thar's Injuns knocking round, and Blackfoot at that; but thar's plenty of beaver, too, and this child means trapping anyhow." He went on to say that no matter where they went they were bound to run into tarnal red fiends, and they might as well stay where prime plews could be gotten. While old Bill stayed behind to guard the camp, three parties of two men each went off to look for beaver sign. One pair was made up of Markhead and another newcomer named Batiste. These two were waylaid by a passel of Blackfeet. Markhead was wounded and Batiste killed. Markhead galloped off, a volley of balls and arrows whistling after him. He drew no bit until he reined up at the camp-fire, where he found Bill quietly dressing a deer-skin. That worthy looked up from his work; and seeing Markhead's face streaming with blood, and the very unequivocal evidence of an Indian recontre in the shape of an arrow sticking in his back, he asked—"Do 'ee feel bad now, boy? Whar away you see them darned Blackfoot?"

"Well, pull this arrow out of my back, and maybe I'll feel like telling," answered Markhead.

"Do 'ee hyar now! hold on till I've grained this cussed skin, will 'ee! Did 'ee ever see sich a darned pelt, now? It won't take the smoke anyhow I fix it." And Markhead was fain to wait the leisure of the imperturbable old trapper, before he was eased of his annoying companion.

Old Bill had no word of regret for the death of the unfortunate Batiste, declaring it was "jest like greenhorns, runnin' into them cussed Blackfoot," and commented that pauvre Batiste was only a no-account vide-poche frog-eater. He had, however, lost his appetite for trapping in that particular location, packed his possibles, got on his horse—this time another ungainly beast named Santeefé, and "put out."

Old Bill had the reputation of being a fine marksman. During shooting competitions he bet as much as a hundred dollars' worth of pelts on himself. Ruxton wrote that Williams was "a dead shot with his rifle, though he always shot with a double wobble, for he never could hold his gun still, yet his ball went always to the spot."

He was the hero of innumerable Indian fights, One of these he might have described thus: "I tellee, stranger, Blackfeet air pizen. I calkilate this hoss'd rather shoot an' skulp an Injun than eat, even if it war fat buffler cow. W-a-a-l, thar I wuz trappin' along the Columbia, plumb in the middle o' Injun diggins, when I seed b'ar sign. Grizzly, by ned! I war wolfish fer b'ar meat, fur sartain. W-a-a-l, instead b'ar I run into a passle of them cussed Blackfeet. I tellee, friend, I thought I war a gone beaver, mity nigh to losin' his hair. When them varmints seed me, they started yellin' like the divils, owgh-owgh! makin' an orful racket. I knowed I wuz in fur a scrimmage. Quicker 'an a greased fart I raise me trusted Knockumstiff, all primed and loaded fur b'ar, and let fly! Wagh, I keeled one o' them, a precious big bastard. I tellee, this child didn't stop to reload but made fur the timber with three o' the darned niggurs arter me, froze for hair. I wuz swift as a roadrunner then an' gained 'nuff head-start on 'em to reload an' as them tarnal critturs came out o' the piñon, I let fly again an' drop the foremost, by Jihosaphat! Whoopee!

"Stranger, I tellee, agin I get a start on them miscreants an', hidin' behind a rock, ram down 'nuther wad an' G'lena, an' let fly. Hang me up fur b'ar meat if I didn't hit that consarned savage plumb between the eyes. Sez this old coon to hisself, 'Hurraw, ye're rid of them divils when, I'll be doggone, 'nuther three Blackfeet are comin' out of a side canyon. Wagh! This child's plew warnt whuz a cussed plug o' baccer. 'Ye're goin' under fer sure,' I sez to myself. That war hard doin' then, by Ned! I wuz plumb tired out but put on one more spurt, gittin' away from 'em for a mite, hidin' in the timber, an' then doublin' back like a grizzly fer some two or three hunnerd yards come up behind them precious bastids an' shoot one dead, gut the next with my Green-River, an' brain the last with me tommihawk. Thar wuz some more but they didn't wait for similar treatment, but lit out fer home like deer with a painter arter them. W-a-a-l, this old coon retraced his steps an' took thar skulps, all six o' them, an' hung 'em on his belt to dry, an left the rest o' them sonsabitches fur wolf meat. Wagh! I reckoned that thar mought be more Injuns knockin' about, an' this hoss didn't want to leave any tracks fur 'em to follow, so this child jumped astride a log floatin' down the river an' used his fore-paws to paddle all the way home to camp. Wagh! I swar, that's what happened, an' ye better believe me, do 'ee hyar!"

The era of the free trappers and mountain men lasted, at the most, some thirty years and came to an abrupt end around 1840. The reasons were twofold—the beaver had been virtually trapped out and, in Europe, beaver hats were no longer the rage, especially as the newly manufactured felt was so much cheaper than pelt. The trappers did not want to believe that their way of life was coming to an end. One of Ruxton's friends, a mountain man named Killbuck, soliloquized: "Howsever, beaver's bound to rise; human natur can't go on selling beaver a dollar a pound; no, no, that ain't agoing to shine much longer, I know. There was the times when this child first went to the mountains: six dollars the plew—old 'un or kitten. Wagh! But it's bound to rise, I says agin." But it never rose again and, reluctantly, one by one, the free souls of the wilderness had to look for another way to earn their plugs of 'baccer and gallons of "red uprising."

For a while Old Bill tried his luck as a storekeeper in Taos, but selling foofaraw, calico, and ribbons to señoritas and old crones just was not his meat—it "did not shine." One day, exasperated at one female haggling over mere centavos, he flung his bolts of cloth and calico into the dusty street, threw the bolts out as far as they would unroll, shouting in his squeaky voice:

"Hyar, damn ye! If I cain' sell ye my goods, I'll give 'em to you fer free. Thar, ye cussed hyenas, fight fer them!"

While the ladies pulled hair, bit, scratched, and kicked in a frenzied free-for-all, Old Bill saddled his ancient crop-eared nag, took his old Hawken and possible sack, and trotted off to his beloved mountains. He tried some more trapping for a while, without much luck, and then bethought himself of another profession. Legend has depicted Old Bill Williams as an ornery, eccentric, picturesque, but kindly and lovable character. There was, however, another, different side to the old coon.

It has been said that the mountain men looked upon horsestealing as a perfectly legitimate undertaking, provided that it was "properly directed." By this was meant that, if one could avoid it, one should not steal horses from fellow trappers or friendly Indians upon whose good will one depended. Stealing horses from Mexican "greasers" and Californios, on the other hand, including killing the owners if they resisted, was not only profitable, but also a glorious, thrilling sport. Old Bill went into horse stealing in a big way. He teamed up with the likes of Pegleg Smith and other rough, not to say murderous, characters to organize veritable horse-stealing expeditions in the grandest manner. On his first venture he came back to Bent's Fort, the horse thief's heaven, with about three hundred stolen horses and mules. The fort's "bourge-way," Charles Bent, did not ask any awkward questions as to the caballada's origin, nor did he want to see bills of sale, but shelled out enough dineros for a colossal binge that lasted until the liquor gave out.

On one monster horse-stealing raid, kindly Old Bill joined Captain Bonneville, Sylvestre Cerré, Walker, Joe Meeker, and some other trappers, because beaver was scarce while there were horses aplenty in California. On the way, they killed twenty-five Indians just for the fun of it. In the Pueblos of the peaceful Moquis (Hopis) they plundered the people of their blankets and corn, killing a few who were bold enough to protest. Having arrived in California, they settled down in Monterey and "reveled in a perfect fools' paradise," spending their days in a wild orgy of fiestas, bullfighting, bullbaiting, cockfighting, gambling, wenching, fisticuffs, knife fights and, above all, drinking, "pursuing a career toward California which emulated the Forty Thieves of the stirring story of Ali Baba." They then rounded up an immense herd of stolen horses and mules and, in a cloud of dust visible for thirty miles, retraced their steps homeward. The fact that the injured hacendados had sworn to tie any of the marauders they could catch to a horse and drag him through the cactus until only little bits were left for the coyotes gave the whole enterprise its special zest.

Old Bill's and his companions' endeavors were not always crowned with success. On one veritable Jornada del Muerte, Old Bill tried to drive a herd of 1,500 stolen animals through the Mojave Desert. Closely pursued by the enraged owners, two-thirds of the horses and most of the mules died of thirst and exhaustion, the rest were stampeded by a Ute war party.

Suffering badly from Indian raids, Mexican officials hired a band of former trappers to wipe out the marauders, promising fifty dollars for every scalp brought in. Old Bill took part in this atrocity. They came back with 1,000 horses, 300 sheep and goats, 183 scalps, and 18 women. As the Mexicans wanted to pay only ten dollars per live woman, a ferocious trapper called Spiebuck offered to kill the female captives to sell their scalps at the higher price. Be it said that Old Bill balked at this and sold the women as slaves.

Old Bill once went to visit his folks back in Missouri. His brother John did not recognize the strange, outlandish creature before him.

"Wagh," exclaimed the offended visitor, "don't ye know yer own brother, ye old hoss?"

"I would if I seed him, but ye're no kin of mine, that I know of," answered John.

"Thyar, ye old mule, I'll prove it to ye," said Bill, exhibiting a half-moon-shaped scar on his forearm. Satisfied as to Bill's identity, John invited him in. At night Bill couldn't stand the agony of sleeping in a bed and settled down on the floor.

Old Bill's last escapade occurred when Frémont, the "Great Path-finder," hired him as a guide to map out a way for a railroad to the Pacific. The expedition started out in November 1848 and ended in disaster. Frémont insisted upon crossing the mountains in midwinter —a desperate undertaking. To make matters worse, he chose the wrong route. Old Bill and other experienced mountain men pointed out the dangers involved, but Frémont was vain, self-centered, and convinced that he knew better. The expedition was ravaged by bliz-zards and marooned in hip-deep snows. Food gave out. Men ate their moccasins, horses nibbled on each other's tails and manes—and died. Frémont was stuck in the icy wastes of the La Garita Mountains. Not being able to go forward, he yet could not bring himself to go back. Some men froze to death. Old Bill nearly shared their fate. In the words of Micajah McGehee, one of the survivors, "Bill dropped down upon his mule in a stupor and was nearly senseless when we got into camp." Frémont sent Williams and three others on a 160-mile trip to the rear to get supplies. There were no horses left and they had to make the terrible journey on foot. Each was given a blanket, a small bag of frozen mule meat, a handful of sugar, a Hawken rifle, and a dozen bullets. Plagued by howling snowstorms, they crept back at a snail's pace. On some days they made only one mile. Their food ran out. For days they had only a small hawk and the carcass of an otter to divide among themselves. One of them, a man called King, col-lapsed and had to be left behind. One of the remaining three, Breck-inridge, managed to bring down a deer and drag it back to Old Bill and McGehee. "Old Bill took the meat in his bony hands and began tearing off great mouthfuls like a savage animal." It took the three men ten days to crawl and limp the remaining forty miles to the nearest settlement. The last survivor of Frémont's party staggered into Taos on February 9, 1849.

Frémont placed all the blame for the catastrophe on Old Bill, accusing him not only of incompetence as a guide, but of having misled the expedition so that he could later plunder its cache of abandoned stores. He also spread the rumor that Old Bill was a can-nibal who had eaten the unfortunate King. It did Bill no good point-ing out that "King wuz as dead as a buzzard when we left him." The cannibal label stuck to him until his death.

Bill's father had been something of a mystic and, as mentioned, had correctly predicted the day and hour of his death. Old Bill had inherited this penchant for the supernatural. He believed in the transmigration of souls. He was sure of turning into a buck elk after his demise. He implored his friends, "Don't ever shoot buck elk at the Bayou Salade arter I've gone under, do 'ee hyar?" He said he would die "when a b'ar'll put his cussed paw on me shoulder." Having somewhat regained his strength, Old Bill and a certain Dr. Kern set out in March 1849 to recover some of the cached possessions they had been forced to leave behind in the mountains. Old Bill was uneasy. Twice in a row he had dreamed that a bear had put a paw on his shoulder. The two men were never seen alive again. They had been surprised at their campfire by a band of Ute warriors. Old Bill had greeted them without suspicion. The Utes were his blood brothers. He had married into their tribe, but a search party found him and Kern "porcupined by Ute arrows."

In 1913 Charles Johnson wrote this epitaph:

> A party of trappers were crossing the stream near the place where the old fellow had laid down, and saw a pony nibbling the bark from a cotton-wood tree. He was gaunt, famished, and his ribs were fairly sticking through his flesh. They rode up to him and were much distressed to see the form of a man lying beneath the white mantle of newly fallen show. They brushed this away and found "Old Bill"; his grizzled head bent forward upon his breast, and his clothing stained with the wounds which had sapped his very life-blood. He had gone to the Great Beyond.
>
> With tears in their eyes the trappers hollowed out a grave for the lone refugee. Here they buried him, and finding his faithful steed unwilling to leave the place where he had carried his master, shot the emaciated animal. They placed both in the same grave, and over their forms erected a huge pile of stones, not only to mark the last resting-place of "Old Bill," but also to keep the wolves and coyotes from digging up the remains.
>
> Thus, in a wild canyon perished the aged solitary, and in the peace and quiet of that wilderness in which he loved to wander, hovers the spirit of the lonely man of the plains. His last resting-place well suited the career of "Old Bill": trapper, scout, and fearless adventurer among the savage men, wild beasts, and inhospitable wastes of the then unpeopled West."

Mountain men did not make water through their eyes, nor was Old Bill a character to shed tears over. The Victorian Age demanded even more pathos for the end of the Old Bill Williams saga:

> Old and gray, marked with the scars of a hundred hand-to-hand combats, and skirmishes innumerable, "Old Bill" at last met his fate at the hands of his most hated foes. Flying single handed and alone from the swarming Blackfeet, who had driven him from the headwaters of the Missouri, he fought like the retreating lion, ever and anon making a stand and dealing death to his foes. For six days

and nights they trailed him, often by the blood that poured from his many wounds, and at last, almost within reach of a trapper's camp, on the Yellowstone, the cowardly jackals dealt the brave, old lion his death blow.

Still he would not give up, and swearing that his scalp should never dry in the smoke of a Blackfoot lodge, he once more fought them off and turned in flight. The savages, despairing of ever capturing this man, who defied fatigue and wounds, turned back, and Williams rode on into the night of oblivion. . . .

Very touching, indeed, except that this was, of course, pure fiction. The question of whether Old Bill was the scurrilous, kindly curmudgeon of legend or the murderous horse thief and scalp hunter of history will not be answered in these pages.

Pegleg Smith and Headless Harry

Tom Smith entered this world on October 10, 1801, at a place called Crab Orchard and consequently grew up to be a very crabby fellow. Like so many other trappers, he was born a Kentuckian. He ran away from home at age sixteen because of the severe beatings administered to him daily by his father, mother, schoolteacher, and divers others. Why he received these floggings is not known. One can only guess. He used to say later: "I don't keer about the old woman wallopin' me, but the old man had no right to treat me so blame bad."

As a grownup, he was a swiller of whiskey, the ruination of all women who had the misfortune to cross his path, a superman when it came to horse stealing, the owner of a fictitious gold mine, and a scoundrel in general. If his Pa and Ma intended to beat the badness out of him, they were spectacularly unsuccessful. He was, however, a true specimen of that "reckless breed of men"—the wild, untamed fur trappers—surpassing most of his fellows in hardihood and durability. He was, at times, the companion of such great beaver men as Milton Sublette, Old Gabe Bridger, Kit Carson, and Cerain St. Vrain, who accepted him as one of their own. Those who complained so bitterly about his rascalities belonged chiefly to only three special groups—virgins he deflowered, rancheros whose horses he stole, and Indians who fell victims to the hellish rotgut he sold them.

After running away from his birch-wielding father, Pegleg hired on as a cook on a Mississippi flatboat. He got into numerous fights and was slashed across the face by an irate customer suffering from the aftereffects of one of Pegleg's meals. For a while he lived with Choctaw Indians and later worked as riverfront stevedore, barkeep, and bouncer in St. Louis. For a few years he was employed by Antoine Roubidoux, a fur trader and outfitter. In 1824 he joined a party of mountain men on the Santa Fe Trail and soon was trapping beaver along the southwestern streams. He cemented relations with various Indian tribes and, for political as well as biological reasons, "married" a number of squaws, acquiring a small harem in the process. He boasted that he never shared his lodge with less than three "wives" and that he never failed to take the scalp of any man he had killed.

Pegleg got his nickname while trapping along the North Platte in company with Sublette, St. Vrain, and other mountain men. He was ambushed and shot, the ball shattering his leg below the knee. He contemplated the damage and concluded that the leg had to come off. He asked his companions to do the job. They refused, pleading lack of experience. The main reason was that amputations usually ended in death within a few days due to gangrene and blood poisoning, and his friends were averse to being blamed for such an unsatisfactory outcome.

"Yer chicken-livered bastards," Pegleg growled. "I'll do it myself, but fust get me plenty of Old Towse!"

They had an ample supply of Taos Lightning at hand, an infernal mixture of Mexican aguardiente and raw corn whiskey guaranteed to maim and kill. He downed a few tin cups full of the fierce stuff, tied a tourniquet tightly around his splintered leg above the wound, took his time honing his bowie knife to a keen edge, had some more Old Towse, and then circumcised his leg, cutting to the bone, having enough savvy to leave a flap of skin and flesh for further use.

"This child needs a tommyhawk," he informed his friends watching the proceedings with great interest. The desired item was produced. Pegleg took another swill:

"Take ahold of the flap, Cerain," he demanded.

"Enfant de Garce," said St. Vrain, pulling the skin to one side, "but you're a cool niggur for sure." Pegleg swung the tomahawk, bringing it down with tremendous force, cutting halfway through the bone. He took a deep breath, had another swig from the proffered tin cup, chopping down with his tomahawk a second time, and—presto—the leg was off. "Wagh, ain't she some!" was Pegleg's sole comment.

Sublette got out his awl case, needles and sinew thread, and under Pegleg's direction sewed the flap like a patch over the bleeding stump. Then Sublette wrapped up the remainder in a dirty shirt: "Thar she is, pretty as a pitcher."

Using a horse travois, Pegleg's companions managed to get him to winter quarters on the Green River. There his three Shoshone squaws took over, treating the stump with Indian herbs to whose miraculous powers, Pegleg said, he owed his survival. For some time large bone splinters worked their way out of the stump, which Sublette gingerly pulled out with a pair of bullet molds. The following spring Pegleg chopped a large chunk of wood out of an old oak tree. From it he whittled himself the peg leg which became his trademark. He also carved himself a wooden socket that he tied to the side of his horse. It fit his wooden leg so that he could ride as well as before. From then on he was called Pegleg by the whites, 'Wee-He-To-Cha (Wooden Leg) by the Indians, and El Cojo (The Lame One) by the Mexicans.

The painful incident left Pegleg with a great fondness for Old Towse. He not only consumed great quantities of it, but set up a still and manufactured his own potent brand, a great deal of which he sold or traded to other trappers, Utes, Shoshones, and Comanches. Thus he became a whiskey peddler. He then branched out into another commercial venture—the kidnapping of Indian children and selling them, mostly to Mexicans, as future slaves. This did not lower his reputation among fellow trappers, who had little use for their red competitors. A mere kidnapper, they said, was a damn sight better than a bounty hunter, who made his living killing and scalping Indian men, women, and children, bringing in the scalps, at five or ten dollars apiece, as proof of ridding the country of unwanted folks standing in the way of civilization. Bounty hunters were detested, not on account of killing Indians, but because they were apt, whenever they ran out of Indian scalps, to replenish their supplies by lifting the topknots of dark-haired white Americans.

Nor did it bother his friends that Pegleg became the greatest horse thief in the West, and not just stealing a horse here and there. He set himself up as the chief of an ungodly crew, who strayed into

California on tremendous horse-stealing raids, driving caballadas of up to three thousand head back to New Mexico, selling them at a huge profit to traders and trappers, usually at Bent's Fort. Once, heading east with a stolen herd of horses, Pegleg and his band of rustlers were chased by a posse of aggrieved rancheros. During a dark moonless night, Pegleg and his rascally crew crept into the camp of their pursuers and stole their horses too, forcing the most unhappy caballeros to walk two hundred miles back to their homes. This, likewise, failed to lower him in the eyes of most beaver men because the victims were "greasers."

What did, however, turn the whole trapping community against Pegleg was his "absquatulating" with a huge load of pelts, entrusted to him for delivery in Santa Fe by Ewing Young, leader of a company of mountain men. Instead of doing what he was supposed to do, Pegleg, in cahoots with another bandido, named Maurice Le Duc, lit out for California to sell them there, keeping whatever money they got for themselves.

At this point Pegleg becomes a fairy-tale character, the discoverer of a mysterious mountain made of black gold. In order to reach California, Pegleg and Le Duc had to cross the forbidding "American Sahara"—waterless, treeless, and trailless, a country of scorpions, tarantulas, Gila monsters, and sidewinders, where every plant bristled with thorns or spikes and where a furnacelike heat turned men into parched, shriveled-up ghosts. Surprised by one of the fierce sandstorms so frequent in the area, Pegleg and Le Duc lost their way and became completely disoriented. Some of their pack mules broke down or got lost, one together with their water supply. As the wind abated and visibility increased, Pegleg could make out, a few miles ahead, three hills which to him looked like "maiden breasts"—the famous "Golden Hills of Pegleg Smith." He climbed the highest of them to get his bearings. He saw in the distance a range of forested mountains where he and his companion were sure to find water. As he sat down to take a short rest, he felt a stab of pain as his hindquarters came into contact with a sharp, pointed stone. It turned out to be a blackish nugget, heavy for its size, sprinkled with yellow spots. Looking about him, he saw that the whole hill was strewn with these nuggets as with hailstones after a storm. Out of curiosity he gathered up a bagful of these strange rocks. Together with Le Duc he then cached some of their pelts since, due to the death of some of their pack animals, they were no longer capable of carrying everything.

The two bedraggled scalawags finally reached El Pueblo de Nuestra Señora de Los Angeles and there sold their furs to a sea captain in the China trade. Pegleg later claimed that his strange black nuggets were made of pure gold and that he sold them for fifteen hundred dollars. Pegleg went on a monumental tear, drinking the little town dry and getting into numerous saloon brawls. On several occasions he took his wooden leg off, using it like a club to beat his opponents senseless. While his ability to hop around nimbly on one leg while cracking skulls was greatly admired, he was encouraged to leave Los Angeles before becoming the central figure at a necktie party. He took the advice and returned to New Mexico, where he organized a few more horse-stealing raids and opened a trading post. He traveled to San Francisco to cash in on the Gold Rush of '49.

From about 1850 on, however, the decayed, prematurely aged rapscallion went downhill fast. He squandered whatever money he had left on oceans of tanglefoot. He haunted the saloons of San Francisco, a fumbling soak, cadging drinks. He found, however, one last source of income by becoming the originator of the innumerable "Lost Mine" yarns which have kept thousands of gold hunters and amateur prospectors busy to this day. He always carried one lump of gold-bearing quartz in his frayed pockets, using it to lure greenhorns into investing in his phantom mine. He even sold maps, showing the location of his fabled treasure, for five dollars apiece, to the credulous pilgrims. True believers helped him to organize an expedition to recover the golden milk of the three maidens' breasts, but the adventure was stillborn when, on the second day, their horses were run off by a band of bandidos hired, but of course, by Pegleg himself. Eventually, the pilgrims lost faith in his phantom gold and the old horse thief finally died of delirium tremens and a rotting liver in a San Francisco hospital. The dying former mountain man bequeathed his last treasure map and wooden leg to his doctor, who kept these objects for a while as conversation pieces. This, however, was not the end of the tale.

Soon after Pegleg's demise a new Pegleg appeared, not as a ghost, but in the flesh. This miraculously resurrected Pegleg Redivivus also had a wooden limb and his pockets full of black nuggets sprinkled with yellow. He held court in the watering spots of Yuma, regaling the shorthorns with tales of the three lost golden hills. This kept him in pocket money and enough free liquor to float a battleship. Pegleg Redivivus disappeared without a trace as miraculously as he had come.

In 1871 an army deserter tottered into the town of San Bernardino clutching a rawhide bag full of black nuggets sprinkled with yellow. Dehydrated and emaciated, he landed in the hospital, where he told all who would listen that he had stumbled upon a dead man, lying faceup in the desert, by his side the selfsame bag of yellow-sprinkled nuggets. The corpse, whose eyes had been picked out by birds, had a wooden leg. Therefore, it had to be Pegleg Smith! The soldier promised his doctor to lead him to the corpse as soon as he was well. He added that the dead man's tracks seemed to come from three distant hills—surely the fabled, gold-rich "Maidens' Breasts." Unfortunately, the soldier did not get well, but died. His tale and bag of nuggets, however, set off a new stampede to find Pegleg's treasure.

Some seventy years later an individual appeared, two-legged, but claiming to be Pegleg's grandson and only heir. He carried in his pockets a quantity of blackish lumps sprinkled with yellow. He also had a map showing where his grandfather's treasure could be found. Likewise, he cadged drinks and made money promoting search parties to recover the Pegleg gold. Then Pegleg Number Three also vanished into nothingness, but some hardy souls are still looking for the three golden hills.

The Saga of Pegleg Smith gave rise to the Saga of Headless Harry, the hardy mountain man who outdid his peg-legged predecessor by a considerable margin. Headless Harry had been Pegleg's friend and companion. Setting his traps in an out-of-the-way stream, he was surprised by a war party of Comanches. He fought them off with rifle, pistol, knife, tooth, and nail, until he was surrounded by dozens of their lifeless bodies, but was finally overcome by numbers. The cussed redskins scalped him so thoroughly that his whole face,

deprived of the crown that had held it in place, slipped down around his neck, leaving him with a naked skull, but with his eyes still in their sockets. He staggered back to his lodge, hoping that his Crow squaws could sew his face back into its proper place, but they took one look at him and fled, shrieking with terror. Harry then critically examined his reflection in the nearby stream, coming to the conclusion that he could not "shine" in his present condition and that what he needed was a brand-new head. He first carved himself a new noggin out of wood and then proceeded to cut his own head off with his butcher knife. Cutting your own head off is very hard to accomplish and it takes a real rugged and determined fellow to do it. But Harry was up to it. And so he chopped and cut, and sawed and twisted until the job was done. After burying his old head he put on his new one and was mighty pleased with it. He then teamed up again with his old friends trapping beaver. His companions insisted that Headless Harry with his wooden noodle was much smarter than when he had a brain, which had been second-rate. To amuse his numerous half-breed children, Harry sometimes took his wooden head off, using it as a ball to play with. Headless Harry died when, caught in a prairie fire, his wooden pate went up in flames until nothing but a little heap of charcoal remained.

Mind the Time We Took Pawnee Topknots?

"Mind the time we 'took' Pawnee 'topknots' away to the Platte, Hatch?"

"Wagh! ef we didn't, and give an owgh-owgh longside of thar darned screechin', I'm a niggur. This child doesn't let an Injun count a coup on his cavyard always. They come mighty nigh rubbin' me out tother side of Spanish Peaks—woke up in the mornin' jist afore day, the devils yellin' like mad. I grabs my knife, keels one, an' made for timber, with four of thar cussed arrows in my meatbag. The 'Paches took my beaver—five pack of the prettiest in the mountains—an' two mules, but my traps was hid in the creek. Sez I, hyar's a gone coon if they keep my gun. So I follers that trail an' at night crawls into camp, an' socks my big knife up to the Green River, first dig. I takes tother Injun by the har and makes meat of him too. Maybe thar wasn't coups counted an' a bug dance on hand ef I was alone. I got old bull-thrower, my rifle, made medicine over him, an' no darned niggur kin draw bead with him since."

Lover Boy of the Prairies

Including

THE SAGA OF PINE LEAF, THE INDIAN AMAZON

By his own account Jim Beckwourth was the greatest lover ever to arouse yearning in the hearts of dusky Indian maidens (and not a few white married ladies). He also claimed to be the mightiest of all Indian fighters—greater than Daniel Boone, Kit Carson, and Old Gabe Bridger rolled into one. Those who knew him called Beckwourth "the biggest liar west of the Mississippi" and pronounced his fanciful stories "unbelievable and unverifiable." Jim dictated his "autobiography" to Thomas Bonner, a journalist from San Francisco. When the book was published, in 1856, a group of denizens in a Colorado mining camp appointed from among them one illiterate old codger to procure a copy. He returned, not with Beckwourth's autobiography, but with a Bible. One of the miners eagerly opened the book and began to read at random: "Now the Lord had prepared a great fish to swallow up Jonah. And Jonah was in the belly of the fish three days and three nights. . . . And the Lord spake unto the fish, and it vomited out Jonah upon the dry land." At this point one irate listener could stand it no longer, and shouted, "Hold it right thar, I'd knowed that for one of Jim Beckwourth's damn lies anywhar!"

Jim was, if one is to believe him, the son of a Virginia gentleman who had been an officer in General Washington's army and one of his slaves, a beautiful "high-yaller" girl. He was born in 1798, at Fredericksburg, one of thirteen children. The family moved, en masse, to Missouri. Young Jim was apprenticed to a blacksmith. "Among other indiscretions," Jim acknowledged later, "I became enamored of a young damsel, which, leading me into habits that my boss disapproved of, resulted finally in a difficulty between us." The difficulty was twofold: (1) the damsel was the blacksmith's daughter, and (2) she was soon "wearing her apron high." The blacksmith got into the habit of throwing hammers at the adolescent Casanova, who promptly fired them back at his master's head. Jim decided to quit before somebody got killed, particularly since his amatory adventures got him into trouble with the law and also because the prospect of fatherhood did not appeal to him.

Jim found in Papa Beckwourth an understanding father who in his own youth had been caught in a similar predicament. The old man gave Jim a horse, a rifle, and a handful of dollars, telling him to make tracks. Jim did.

In 1823 the young reprobate hired himself out to General Ashley, as body servant, groom, and blacksmith, setting out for the Rockies to trap beaver in company with such famous Plains characters as Jedediah Smith and Thomas Fitzpatrick, thus beginning his career as a mountain man. He soon bragged of being a great killer of Indians as well as also being a peerless athlete. He told of having set out with a certain "Black Harris," a free trapper of "great leg" who was said to be able to outwalk, outrun, and outlast every other two-legged creature. He also had the evil reputation of abandoning any companion who could not keep up with him. Jim and Harris ran out of food and were starving. It was Harris who weakened and could not go on. "Oh, Jim," he pleaded, "don't leave me here to die! For God's sake, don't let the red divils get my skulp!" Summoning up his last ounce of strength, iron-willed Jim managed to crawl to the nearest fort to organize a rescue party.

In 1825 Jim took part in his first mountain man rendezvous on the Green River, a meeting of a thousand untamed savages, white and red, wallowing in an orgy of wenching, begetting, fighting, gambling, cheating, swapping squaws and lies, wolfing down mountains of buffalo meat and, above all, downing oceans of Uncle Sam's "Oh, be joyful." It was not long before Jim, following in his father's footsteps, had sired a number of little black, white, and red papooses. Jim credited himself with rescuing Ashley, who could not swim, out of a raging whirlpool; of saving a fellow trapper from an equally raging grizzly; and of single-handedly saving the whole expedition from destruction. Upon Ashley's return to St. Louis, all engaged in a three-day spree with many lasses, among them one Eliza who, probably

with good reason, believed herself engaged to Jim, who promised to marry her but went back to the mountains and never thought of her again.

After another trapping season Jim, amorous as well as practical, took on as a "servant" the widow of a companion who had been "rubbed out" by a party of Blackfeet. "She was of light complexion, smart, trim, and active, and never tired in her efforts to please me. She seemed to think that she belonged to me for the rest of her life," a mistake made by many. Thus began Jim's career as the "West's Greatest Squaw Man."

Some women are drawn to macho males who treat them rough. This might help to explain Jim's luck with masochistic ladies. When a trading post was established in Blackfoot country, the tribesmen were highly pleased. As Jim put it, "I soon rose to be a great man among them, and the chief offered me his daughter for a wife." Jim accepted avidly and "without any superfluous ceremony" became the son of the head chief. Profit was the aim, "more than hymeneal enjoyments." His trade prospered greatly as he obtained prime beaver plews in exchange for worthless baubles. After a few days of married bliss, "he had a slight difficulty in his family affairs." A party of braves rode into camp with a number of white men's topknots. This was the occasion for a scalp dance. Jim's wife told him that she wished to take part in the festivity. Jim objected: "No; these scalps belonged to my people; my heart is crying for their death; you must not rejoice when my heart cries; you must not dance when I grieve." The wife went anyhow and outdanced them all.

Jim decided to teach her a lesson. He jumped into the dance circle and gave his disobedient wife a tremendous clout on the head with his battle-ax. She slumped to the ground as if hit by lightning. He dragged her to his tepee and left her there for dead. Her friends and relatives were aroused. They surrounded Jim's lodge, shouting, "Kill him! Kill him!" It was his father-in-law who came to his rescue, crying out loudly: "Stop! Hold! Warriors! Listen to your chief!" He turned to Jim: "My son, you have done right. That woman I gave you had no sense; her ears were stopped up. You had a right to kill her. But I have another. She is more beautiful. She has good sense and good ears. You may have her in place of the bad one."

"Well," thought Jim, "this is getting married again before I have even had time to mourn."

While Jim was busy consummating his new marriage, he heard loud sobbing at the door. It was the first wife, who had only been stunned and had regained consciousness after a few hours. Promising henceforth to be a good and obedient wife, she crept under the blanket with the other two, thus starting a ménage à trois.

Over the years, Beckwourth "married" eighteen "official" wives, beside amusing himself with numberless "unofficial" one-night stands. He once kept seven wives at the same time. Being a man of some delicacy, he kept them, together with their respective off-spring, in seven separate tepees.

During one trapping excursion Jim Beckwourth visited a village of Crow Indians. One of his fellow trappers, almost as big a liar as Jim himself, told the Indians that Beckwourth was a member of their tribe, a long-lost brother, abducted as a child by Cheyenne warriors. White trappers, the man explained, had bought Jim to raise him as a mountain man. The gullible Crows believed the fanciful tale. An ancient couple among them at once recognized in Jim their own son, long mourned as dead. Admiring the many scalps dangling from his belt, they promptly named him the "Great Brave." Thus he became a member of the Crow tribe. As such he had to have a good-looking wife. He was asked to pick one from among the three daughters of a mighty chief. Their names were Still Water, Black Fish, and Three Roads. Jim chose Still Water because she was the prettiest. The two scorned ones wailed with disappointment. Being a compassionate fellow who could not stand seeing women weep, Jim married them also. The triple wedding was celebrated with song, dancing, feasting, and the drinking up of the trappers' store of firewater.

Jim became not only a mighty man of war among the Crows, but was soon elevated to the rank of chief. After a battle against the Sioux, a fourteen-year-old girl became part of his war booty. What could the poor man do but marry her? His harem grew.

"A little girl, who had often asked me to marry her, came to me one day, and with every importunity insisted upon my accepting her as my wife. I said: 'You are a very pretty girl, but you are only a child, when you are older I will talk to you about it.' But she was not to be put off. . . . The little innocent used such powerful appeals that, notwithstanding I had already seven wives and a lodge for each, I told her she might be my wife." Jim just could not say no.

The ever-victorious Jim won so many fights against Sioux, Black-feet, Cheyennes, and Assiniboines that he was made the head chief of all Absarokas, as the Crows called themselves. His many triumphs were ascribed not only to his prowess but also to an all-powerful protective medicine—a perforated magic bullet and two large, ob-long, rainbow-colored beads that he wore in a bundle around his neck. As chief, he was invested with the magic name of Medicine Calf. He had finally arrived, as he put it, "at the pinnacle of his fame." His seven (or eight) wives outdid each other in cooking, tanning, quilling, beading, and sewing for him. They fed him suc-culent boudins, tender meat of plump puppies, buffalo tongues, and well-aged smoked bear paws. They fought each other for a place under his blanket. But there can be too much of a good thing. Jim got bored. He bemoaned having wasted twelve years of his life among heathen savages. He was about to return to civilization when a woman named Pine Leaf came into his life—an enchantress who drove him to madness because she would not be his.

Pine Leaf was the queen of Indian amazons, a woman with the strength of a buffalo, the ferocity of a wildcat, the fleetness of a deer, and the courage of a mountain lion. Her beauty and sensuous feline way of moving drove the great lover into a frenzy of desire. When Pine Leaf was twelve years old, her twin brother had been killed by the Blackfeet and she swore never to marry until she had killed one hundred enemies to avenge him.

Jim was obsessed with the desire to add the doughty amazon to his harem. He implored her to be his wife: "She flashed her dark eyes upon mine: 'You have too many already!' " As he laid siege to her, day after day, she told him she would be his "when pine needles turn yellow." It occurred to him that pine needles remain forever green. She said, "I shall be yours when I come across a redheaded

Indian." This too was little comfort. She assured him: "I shall take no other man but you for my husband *if* I should ever wish to marry." This also was not very encouraging. During a raid upon a Sioux village Pine Leaf took two pretty Lakota girls prisoner and offered them to Jim as a substitute for herself. He added them to his seraglio, but still yearned for her. During a scrimmage with an enemy war party, Jim was about to be "rubbed out" by a gigantic Cheyenne warrior when Pine Leaf came up at a dead run, pinning Jim's opponent to the ground with her lance, calling out cheerfully, "Ride on, friend, I have him safe now!"

For a short period only, Jim was temporarily distracted by a surpassingly beautiful girl called Red Cherry. Unfortunately, she was already married to Big Rain, a dour warrior chief jealous of his possessions, whether horses or women. As Jim recalled: "Big Rain possessed the most beautiful squaw in the whole village; she was the admiration of every young brave, and all were plotting (myself among the rest) to win her away from her proud lord."

Jim crept into her lodge one night when her husband was away, but she resisted him, saying, "I am the wife of a big chief. He will kill you." But Jim was a most persistent fellow and kept at it until the comely Red Cherry succumbed. Big Rain found out and exacted the customary penalty. As Jim related it: "I was seized by Big Rain, supported by a dozen of his relatives, all armed with whips, and they administered a most unmerciful beating." They took from Jim his entire horse herd—eighty fine animals—and stripped him of all he owned, except his weapons. He thought it "a pretty stiff price for a pretty woman."

In spite of a sore back, Jim went on seeing Red Cherry and had to run the gauntlet—again and again. It was Big Rain who finally tired of the game and sold his wife to Jim for the consideration of one war-horse, ten guns, ten chiefs' coats, scarlet cloth, ten pairs of new leggings, and the same number of moccasins. He now had the exclusive rights to Red Cherry without fear of further whippings, but forbidden fruits taste better than those grown in one's own garden and he soon tired of her as he resumed wooing the untouchable Pine Leaf. Years went by. The heroic amazon was now minus two fingers. One had been shot off during a battle, the other she had cut off herself in mourning for a fallen comrade. Fighting a party of Blackfeet, she was severely wounded, a bullet passing through her left breast, touching the heart, and coming out through the shoulder blade. Her face had been scarred by knife and tomahawk. She bore the scars of a hundred fights. Suddenly, she made up her mind to call it quits and marry while she still retained some of her good looks.

She addressed her friends: "Warriors, for many winters I have been on the warpath with you; I shall tread that path no more. I shall take up the needles and my beads. I said I would kill one hundred foes before I married any living man. I have more than kept my word. I have fought my last battle, and hurled my last lance. I am a warrior no more." She went to Jim and told him: "And now, my friend, I am yours after you have so long been seeking me. Take me to your lodge."

It was Jim's last marriage among the Crows. The connubial bliss lasted exactly five weeks. Then James Beckwourth left to go back to the "white man's diggings." He never saw Pine Leaf again. He wreaked havoc among pale-faced lasses after learning how to deal with the impediment of crinolines. He impressed naive listeners with tales of being the only man to survive the storming of the Alamo. He claimed to have done great deeds in the Seminole War. Then, one last time, he gave in to a great yearning for the fleshpots of the Crow Nation. His old friends welcomed their great chief, Medicine Calf, with cries of jubilation. Many of his former wives, with numerous offspring, overwhelmed him with kindness and caresses. They mollycoddled him until he could stand it no longer and was ready to leave for good.

Jim Beckwourth had led a torrid life of romance. It was fitting that he should die a romantic death. When Jim told his Crow friends that he had to leave them forever, there was much weeping and lamenting. The chiefs and elders got together to smoke the pipe and take council. "He won't come back," they said. "He will take with him his great medicine, the rainbow-colored beads and the magic bullet. Then it will protect us no longer. This must not happen." His wives and many pretty young squaws also came together to talk matters over. "He is fickle," they said. "He will abandon us and our children. We love him so much, we'd rather see him dead than in the tipis of strange white or black women." They all invited Jim to a great farewell feast. There was splendid fare—liver pudding, kidney pemmican, dog soup, buffalo ribs, antelope meat—but for the mighty Chief Medicine Calf they had prepared a special dish of the most tender and succulent buffalo calves' tongues, garnished with fragrant, wonderfully tasting mushrooms. "This," Jim's wives told Jim, "is for you alone." He filled his bowl, and filled it again, and filled it for the third time. "This is the best food I ever ate," he pronounced, smiling, licking his fingers. Then he fell asleep. The Crow men and women watched him slumber, knowing that he would wake up no more. The mushrooms were of the most poisonous kind. Thus died the Great Lover of the Western Plains. The Crows gave him a most splendid funeral, painting his face vermilion, dressing him in the finest ornamented chief's coat, putting on his feet death moccasins with beaded soles, killing his great war-horse to serve him in the spirit land. They put him up on the lofty death scaffold, giving him to the wind and to the eagles. His wives cut off their hair and their little fingers in mourning, saying, "Now he is ours forever."

Putrefactions

There are many American yarns about petrified humans, animals, and forests. This is the oldest one.

The darndest liar was Black Harris—for lies tumbled out of his mouth like boudins out of a buffler's stomach. He was the child as saw the putrefied forest in the Black Hills. Black Harris came in from Laramie; he'd been trappin' three year an' more on Platte and on the other side; and, when he got into Liberty, he fixed himself right off like a Saint Louiy dandy. Well, he sat to dinner one day in the tavern, and a lady says to him—

"Well, Mister Harris, I hear you're a great trav'ler."

"Trav'ler, marm," says Black Harris. "This nigger's no trav'ler; I ar' a trapper, marm, a mountain-man, wagh!"

"Well, Mister Harris, trappers are great trav'lers, and you goes over a sight of ground in your perishinations, I'll be bound to say."

"A sight, marm, this coon's gone over, if that's the way your stick floats. I've trapped beaver on Platte and Arkansa, and away up on Missoura and Yaller Stone; I've trapped on Columbia, on Lewis Fork, and Green River and the Hely. I've fought the Blackfoot, and damned bad Injuns they are; I've raised the hair of more than one

Apach, and made a Rapaho 'come' afore now; I've trapped in heav'n, in airth, and hell; and scalp my old head, marm, but I've seen a putrified forest."

"La, Mister Harris, a what?"

"A putrified forest, marm, as sure as my rifle's got hind-sights, and she shoots center. I was out on the Black Hills, Bill Sublette knows the time—the year it rained fire—and everyone knows when that was. If thar wasn't cold doin's about that time, this child wouldn't say so. The snow was about fifty foot deep, and the buffler lay dead on the ground like bees after a beein'. Thar was no buffler, and no meat, and me and my band had been livin' on our moccasins, leastwise the parflesch, for six weeks; and poor doin's that feedin' is, marm, as you'll never know. One day we crossed a cañon and over a divide, and got into a peraira, whar was green grass, and green trees, and green leaves on the trees, and birds singing in the green leaves, and this in Febrary, wagh! Our animals was like to die when they see the green grass, and we all sung out, "Hurraw for summer doins."

"Hyar goes for meat," says I, and I jest ups old Ginger at one of them singing-birds, and down come the crittur elegant; its darned head spinning away from the body, but never stops singing; and when I takes up the meat, I find it's stone, wagh! "Hyar's damp powder and no fire to dry it," I says, quite skeared.

"Fire be dogged," says old Rube. "Hyar's a hoss, as'll make fire come," and with that he takes his axe and lets drive at a cottonwood. Schr-u-k—goes the axe against the tree, and out comes a bit of the blade as big as my hand. We looks at the animals, and thar they stood shaking over the grass, which I'm dog-gone if it wasn't stone, too. Young Sublette comes up, and he'd been clerking down to the fort at Platte, so he know'd something. He looks and looks, and scrapes the trees with his butcher knife, and snaps the grass like pipe-stems, and breaks the leaves a-snapping like Californy wolves.

"What's all this, boy," I asks.

"Putrefactions," says he, looking smart; "putrefactions, or I'm a nigger."

"La, Mister Harris," says the lady, "putrefactions! why did the leaves and the trees smell badly?"

"Smell badly, marm!" says Black Harris; "would a skunk stink if he was froze to stone? No, marm, this child didn't know what putrefaction was, and young Sublette's varsion wouldn't shine nohow, so I chips a piece out of a tree and puts it into my trap-sack, and carries it in safe to Laramie. Well, old Captain Stewart, a clever man was that, though he was an Englishman, he comes along next spring, and a Dutch doctor chap was along too. I shows him the piece I chipped out of the tree, and he called it a putrefaction too; and so, marm, if that wasn't a putrefied peraira, what was it? For this hoss doesn't know, and he knows fat cow from poor bull, anyhow."

Well, old Black Harris is gone under too, I believe. He went to the Parks trapping with a Vide Poche Frenchman, who shot him for his bacca and traps. Darn them Frenchmen, they're no account any way you lays your sight. ("Any bacca in your bag, Bill? this beaver feels like chawing.")

●●●
The Injin Killed Me Dead
●●●

Oncet I wus settin' traps in the Yellerstone country when I wus treed by a pack of tarnally hungry timber wolves. To save myself I shinnied up a tall tree, the varmints below me makin' a divilish racket, howlin', growlin', yawpin', lookin' up at me, waitin' for this child to come down to be made a meat of. Waal, I warn't in no mood to be wolf meat an' just set thar on the top-most branch, waitin' for the cussed critters to go away. Waal, arter 'bout two hours, they gave up an' vamoosed. I warn't wroth to see 'em go an wus jest 'bout to climb down when the whole damn pack of 'em came back— snarlin', an' yawpin', an' barkin' as before. Waal, sez I to myself, I'll jest set up hyar a spell longer till the varmints get tired of the game, but I hadn't larned yet how savvy them Yellerstone wolves can be, cause the dratted critters had brung with 'em just 'bout the most humongous beaver ever to chaw my tree down. When I seed that beaver, I don't mind tellin' you, I got skeered. An' with good reason for the consarned thing started right away to chomp an' chew an' gnaw away at the trunk. An' he warn't slothful either. That dad-burn beaver war gnawin' with a rare fury as if he knowed that I had his dead pappy's plew in my possible bag. Hang me up for bear meat if he didn't chomp plumb through the trunk in less'n three minnites. Down the tree comes this child, traps, possibles, branches—the whole shebang. The whole pack of wolves war 'pon me in a second. It's a sad story, gennelmen, for the varmints ripped me apart into bite-sized chunks an', if yer pardon the pun, wolfed me down, leavin' nary a bone.

As to the weather, gents, in winter it's so cold down in Ute country, that the hump meat freezes in yer stummick an' the boudins inside your bowels turn to ice. Thar's some folks had to wait until spring to go to the privy an' ease their 'ntestines, if thar was a privy, which, natcherally thar wus not. Waal, in Febbr'y of 1830 it snowed down thar for seventy days w'thout stoppin', an' the snow piled up seventy feet high, an' all the bufflers in the valleys froze to death an war buried unner the snow. When spring came, all I had to do war to tumble 'em into the Great Salt Lake, an' I had pickled buffler 'nuff for myself an' the whole fur brigade for years.

You arx me 'bout the tightest spot this child found himse'f in as far as the red divils are concerned. I'll give it to you straight. I war in Blackfoot country. Them Blackfeet don't shine for me, an' the feelin'

is recipercated. 'Bout 1838, arter the last big rendyvous at Pierre's Hole, I was jumped by six of them red fiends. They war on horseback, an' so was I. This hoss had only one of them newfangled Colts to fight with, a six-shot gewgaw. Waal, I start blazin' away at 'em an' with every shot I killed one of them varmints, five 'n all, but thar wus still one of 'em left.

We wus nearin' the edge of a deep an' wide gorge, an' a fall to the bottom meant sartin death. I turned my hoss suddint an' the Injin was upon me. We both fired to once, an' both horses war killed. We now engaged in a han'-to-han' fight with Bowie knives. He wus a powerful Injin—tallest I ever seed. It was a long, desp'rate scrape. One moment I had the best of him, an' the next the infernal cuss had the upperhan'. It went on an' on, knife, tooth, an' claw. You arx me, stranger, how it came out—badly, very badly. The Injin killed me!

Heaven According to Old Gabe

Is thar a hell? Is thar a heaven? This hoss don't know. Howsomever, if this paw's child had his wish, I'd make ye a proper heaven, wagh! Not one of 'em state fixin's heavens whar folks sit on clouds in thar nightshirts a-playin' harps. That kind of heaven ain't the holler tree fur this beaver nohow. It don't shine. This child's heaven is like Brown's Hole, the Popo Agie, an' the Bayou Salade, all rolled into one at rendeevoo time, wagh!

This child's heaven is akin to a valley, with grass ass-high, green as em'rals, with a river plumb across, an' its water pure awardente fur the fellers to dip thar tincups into it, agin an' agin, an' be joyful. An' no matter how much they swaller, that Ole Touse never quits aflowin'. An' close by thar's a mountain, nigh upon a mile high, an' sculp me, if it ain't made up totally of twists of 'baccer, an' it never gits smaller an' the pilgrims can have as many chaws as they want, in all eternity. Wagh!

An' buffler's thar by the thousands, an', doggone, no matter how many of 'em you shoots down, the herd's never gittin' less. As soon as one is down, thar's 'nuther comin' up, weedlike, by ned! An' ev'ry one of them fellers has his Jack Hawken fusee, an' they all shoot plumb center, whoopee! Thar's fun everlastin' runnin' meat, an' no one's ever hungry, but ev'ry pilgim has his meatbag full—nothin' but fat cow, an' tender buffler tongues, an' sweet roasted boudins to tickle a man's ribs. Wagh!

Thar's never any hard doin's, an' beaver hats never go out of style, an thar's beaver a-plenty, fightin' each other fur a chance to git themselves trapped, an' it's ten dollars a plew, old-un or kitten, prime plews all. An' no matter how many of the critters ye trap, thar's allus more a-waitin' thar turn. An' longside that Tangleleg River thar's tepees 'sfar as the eye kin see, full o' squaws awaitin' the mountain men's pleasure—wanton like minks, Shyan, an' Sioux, an' 'Pache, an' Yute—all plump an' pretty, with shiny, greased faces, a-cookin', an' a-beadin', an a-tannin', with that lovin' look in thar eyes, whoopee! They're virgins, all of 'em, an', hang me up fur b'ar meat, ef they're not turnin' back into virgins, agin an' agin', arter ev'ry set-to, hurraw! An' ef a feller gits plumb tired of all them squaws, thar's the Mexican señoritas—"Ay, bonita, mi corazón, let's you an' me fandango." I tellee, old pard, that's heaven fur sure. Wagh!

An' ev'ry day thar's a rendevoo, makin' all other rendevoos prior tharto look like Sunday school doin's. Whoopee! Nigh upon a thousand beaver men, mountain men, pilgrims, bushways, traders, mangeurs de lard, Injuns, squaws an' squawmen, hosses, mules, dawgs —all a-yellin', singin', barkin', neighin', hollerin', screechin' like the devils! The fellers all in thar finest beaded an' quilled outfits, the squaws in all thar foofaraw—I tellee, no better sight fur sore eyes, "enfant de garce!" as the Frogs say. Thar's nothin' too rich fur my blood, wagh!

An' ev'rywhar boys swappin' stories, takin' horns of red up-risin', chawin on thar 'baccer, sweet-talkin' Injun gals, tradin' plews fur gold an' silver. Thar are no vide poches. All are rich. They gamble—all honest games, not a kyardsharp among 'em!

"Ho, boys, hyar's the deck an' hyar's the beaver. Who war' set his hoss? Wagh!

Some mountaineers gratify their dry; papoose-makers with squaw fever are a-gropin' an' a-squeezin, makin' thar sloe-eyed partners squirm an' giggle. Others take a shine to hagglin' over foofaraw, or indoolge in a game of Injun poker. But most, like this hoss, have a hankerin' fur sports. I tellee, this coon loves to cut his wolf loose, by ned! An' what's the greatest sport? I tellee. It's fightin'. Us trappers love it. The Injuns love it. The coureurs de bois love it. So we grabs our weapons, an' the bucks put on thar war paint, an' at it we go! This hoss is a man-killer, never curried below his knees, a two-legged airthquake an' prime specimen of chain-lightnin'. I tellee, stranger, this beaver's the champeen eye-gouger an' hair-lifter of the Rockies, whoopee! So we lift topknots an' whip out our butcher knives an' wade into liver up to the Green River. So we cuts throats, an' shoot, an' stab, an' hack with tommyhawks, an' arrers, an' pistols, but it's all friendly-like, an' no hard feelin's. Jest good fun, doee hyar? Come evenin', those who have gone under, git up agin, eyeballs pop back into thar sockets, teeth sprout again, skulps grow back on bleedin' skulls. Trappers an' Injuns set around the fire, smoke the pipe, take a swig of snakehead whiskey, an' brag about thar great deeds. Come mornin', all start fightin' agin, wallowin' in blood up to thar armpits, amoosin' themselves with manly sports. It shines, wagh!

I tellee, stranger, arter this hoss has chewed his last plug of 'baccer, that's the kind o' heaven he'd take a shine to, not to a psalm-singin', hippercrit preacherman's paradise, but a real man's heaven, wagh!

••

Damn Good Shootin'

••

Four grizzled mountain men sat hunkered down around their campfire—Jim Bridger, Bill Jackson, Captain Ben Bonneville, and Bill Williams, the Old Tanglebeard—drinking whiskey straight from tin cups, chomping on a mess of boudins, reminiscing while spitting ambeer all over their hunting shirts. Everything was as right as right can be. The whiskey, for once, had not been adulterated, the boudins were lightly roasted, almost raw, just as they liked them, and the 'baccer was strong and muscular. Numberless buffalo were there for the taking, and the young Absaroka squaws were obliging.

Yet the four trappers were a sad-looking bunch, sitting there with an expression as if they had been sucking lemons.

"Beaver don't shine anymore," grumbled Old Jim. "Some dratted cuss in London invented that disgustin' stuff they call felt to make hats of 'stead of from beaver. Beaver don't shine no more. Wagh!"

"Cain't git a dollar fer a plew what usta go fer five, enfant de garce!" added the captain.

"Beaver's trapped out, anyhow," said Bill Williams, "an' trappers like us is trapped out too. Whar are they now? Gone under, by Ned, an' the grass a-wavin' over 'em."

"An their topknots wavin' from tepee poles," lamented Jackson. "This hoss has had enough. I'm goin' to sell my traps to some greenhorn who hasn't caught on yet that beaver's gone."

"Gone under an' rubbed out, Brother Beaver an' the Montagne Man, wagh! Beaver don't shine now, that's sartin fur sure," said the captain.

"Waal," said Old Jim, "no use whinin' like a coyote a-howlin' at the moon. Thar's still sumphin fer a man to do. Thar's still some fun to be had. This child's headin' fer the white man's diggin's to scout fer them settlers' wagon trains."

"Beaver's gone, sartinly," Jackson added, "but Injuns ain't. Thar's plenty of them red fiends left, an' they are half-froze for hair. Them pilgrims and their prairie schooners need our protection an' got to shell out fer it."

"Merde! This coon ain't goin' to wet-nurse a bunch o' cussed tenderfoots. I druther be gut-shot, by gar!" grumbled the Captain.

"Durn it all!" said Jackson, "stop yer belly-achin'. Jim's right. Thar's a wagon trail yonder in the cottonwoods. This hoss is goin' to scout for 'em."

"Don't go, Bill," said Old Tanglebeard, "thar's nuthin' there fer you but squalling kids, baby shit, an' mollycoddlin' the pilgrims. An' in front of you nuthin' but a thousand miles of rattlers an' horny toads. You kin allus overtake 'em if you got a mind to, but stay, leastwise while thar's whiskey in the keg."

"That's a reas'nable proposition, friend. Like you said, while thar's whiskey in the keg."

The four of them drank in silence, taking on quite a load.

"We wus friends, waren't we, Bill, an' you, Cap, an' you, Tanglebeard, good friends all, tried and true. Wagh!" Jim was getting just a wee bit maudlin. "Reckon it's this child's last rendyvous," he went on, "jest the four of us. Pierre's Hole, the Bayou Salade, them war the days!"

"Pierre's Hole, Brown's Hole, the Popo Agie!" the captain fell into a reverie. "Le Grand Rendezvous, the stacks of pelts, the available loveliness of the Nez Percé mademoiselles, the gamblin', the merveilleux fisticuffs, the glorious drinkin' bouts, the horse races, the shootin' matches! How good it was!"

"The matches, wagh!" mused Jim, "thar wus good shootin' then. No more, no more."

"Thar's some good shots left, Jim," said Jackson, offhandedly.

"Tell me who. Whar's the fellows could still do the trick we usta indulge in, shootin' tin cups full of whiskey from each other's heads, an' narry a drop spilt."

"You an' me, Bill, you an' me, that's who. We can still do it, I bet."

"Mayhap we could. I did it more'n oncet. This child's hand is still stiddy like a rock. Let's do it once more, fer old time's sake."

"One more tam, enfant de garce!" exclaimed the captain. "Mille tonnères!"

"Let's have a few more drinks fust," insisted Old Tanglebeard.

"Do-ee trust me, Bill?" Bridger asked. "Ain't you skeered?"

"This old hoss skeered? Never! I trust you, Jim, I know ye can shoot. Harraw! I git my old Hawken, an' you git your Kaintuck long gun, an' we have a go at it, wagh!"

"An' I'll get two new tin cups from the booshway," volunteered Old Tanglebeard, ambling off on somewhat unsteady feet to the nearby fort.

"You both are a leetle ivre, a wee bit drunk, Mes amis," said the captain. "The shootin' match, it could be peut-être dangereux."

"I can drink up an ocean of whiskey," vowed Bridger, "an' still hit a fly on the wing."

"Likker cain't get me drunk," boasted Jackson.

Old Tanglebeard came back with two new shiny tin cups. Bonneville picked out a piece of charcoal from the fire, using it to mark each cup with a black spot for a bull's-eye. Bridger lost no time filling them with whiskey.

"Let's git on with it, old hoss," said Jackson, "let's shoot 'em off each other's head like we usta do at the rendyvous!"

"Have ye wiped yer barrel, Bill?" Bridger asked.

"We'll wipe her now." They both withdrew their ramrods and carefully wormed their muzzle-loaders. Old Tanglebeard measured out the usual eighty paces and marked the spot for the two contestants to stand on. "Toss fer the fust shot," he told them.

Bridger won the toss. "If I win, I'll git yer mule. If you win, you can have my pony."

"Neither's worth a pitcher of warm spit, but it's a deal."

Bridger primed and loaded his iron. "Go, take yer stand whar I marked the scratch," Tanglebeard told Jackson, who took his position without the slightest hesitation, while the captain placed the full tin cup on his head without spilling a drop.

"Are ye ready?" Bridger shouted.

"Ready as a bridegroom on his wedding night," answered Jackson, standing motionless like a gravestone.

"Stiddy now, old hoss, stiddy," Tanglebeard warned Bridger.

"Ne bougez pas, mon vieux," the captain needlessly reminded Jackson. "Don't move, by gar!"

Ever so slowly, Jim Bridger raised his Hawken, sighted carefully along its octagonal barrel, and let fly.

"Hurraw! Bull's-eye, bull's-eye!" Old Tanglebeard shouted triumphantly as the tin cup flew high in the air, spattering him with whiskey.

Jackson picked up the cup and stared at the hole the ball had made, plumb center through the bull's eye. "Purty, purty," he remarked, "but nary good enough, old chap."

"What didje say, not good 'nuff, by Ned!" Bridger shouted, getting wrothy. "What the divil didje mean with yer consarned *nary* good 'nuf?!"

"Yer spilled the likker, Jim, an' nary a drop left in the keg. That's very wasteful."

"How in hell kin I shoot the bulls-eye outer yer cup w'thout spillin' some of that whiskey?"

"I'll show yer, Jim." Jackson took the other cup, scraped up some mud from the ground, rolled it up into a little ball and filled the cup's handle with it. "Thar," he said, "this here mud in the handle is our bull'e-eye. This child'll shoot it out w'thout spilling any of that whiskey."

"I never seed it done that way," said Bridger, "but it's all the same to me. Whang away an' see if I flinch."

Gingerly, with great care, Captain Bonneville placed the full-to-the-brim cup upon Bridger's head. Bridger stood at his mark as calm and unruffled as a cool spring morning. "Put her more sidewise, Ben, to give me a fair shot," Jackson called out, and the captain adjusted the cup to Bill's liking. Jackson raised his Kaintuck iron and aimed. Bridger's eye never blinked. Bill pulled the trigger. There was a flash, a puff of smoke, the crack of the old rifle. Bridger remained standing as if carved from stone. The cup had not moved. The ball had gone clear through the handle without touching it.

"Careful with the likker!" Jackson shouted.

Gently, Jim took the cup down. It was still full to the brim. The four men examined it. "Damn good shootin'!" said Old Tanglebeard, and all agreed. Jim Bridger raised the cup and took a sip: "Here's to the old days when beaver war plenty and plews war five dollers apiece." He half-emptied the cup and passed it to Bill Jackson. "Thar, have a sip, yer old wood-tick."

"An' here's to the free trappers who've gone under," said Bill, draining the proffered tin cup with one gulp. Tanglebeard and the captain did likewise. "The whiskey's gone," said Bill at last, "an' I've got to ride herd on them pilgrims. You, Jim, kin keep yer pony."

"Waal, old hoss, it won't be long now an' me too will have to go back to the white man's diggin's. I don't like thinkin' 'bout it an' I hate to see yer go."

"I hate it too, durn it. Take keer of yerself."

They shook hands. And then Bill Jackson got on top of his old lame mule and the two of them ambled off into the sunset. Bill looked back but once, lifting his hand in a last farewell. The other three, at the end of their own trail, waved back.

Uncle Joe the Humorist

"Uncle Joe" Meek was a famous mountain man, muscular, handsome, with a luxuriant beard, a jungle of hair, and dark, flashing eyes. He was absolutely fearless, a man who could stare down a grizzly and take on three enemy braves at the same time. Like "Old Gabe" Bridger, Meek was a mighty storyteller, with a great sense of humor. When beaver gave out, Meek became a guide nursing pilgrims along the newly opened Oregon Trail. He eventually settled down as a farmer, dying in Oregon at the age of sixty-five. Like Kit Carson and Jim Beckwourth, Uncle Joe dictated his life's story to a writer, Frances Fuller Victor, who was a better writer than many others, because she managed to preserve the flavor of Meek's way of expressing himself.

◆ ◆ ◆

On the Yellowstone, Hawkins and myself were coming up the river in search of camp, when we discovered a very large bar on the opposite bank. We shot across, and thought we had killed him, fur he laid quite still. As we wanted to take some trophy of our victory to camp, we tied our mules and left our guns, clothes and everything except our knives and belts, and swum over to whar the bar war. But instead of being dead, he sprung up as we come near him, and took after us. Then you ought to have seen two naked men run! It war a race for life, and a close one, too. But we made the river first. The bank war about fifteen feet high above the water, and the river ten or twelve feet deep; but we didn't halt. Overboard we went, the bar after us, and in the stream about as quick as we war. The current war very strong, and the bar war about halfway between Hawkins and me. Hawkins war trying to swim downstream faster than the current war carrying the bar, and I was a trying to hold back. You can reckon that I swam! Every moment I felt myself being washed into the yawning jaws of the mighty beast, whose head war up the stream, and his eyes on me. But the current war too strong for him, and swept him along as fast as it did me. All this time we war looking for some place to land where the bar could not overtake us. Hawkins war the first to make shore, unknown to the bar, whose head was still upstream; and he set up such a whooping and yelling that the bar landed too, but on the opposite side. I made haste to follow Hawkins, who landed on the side of the river we started from, either by design or good luck; and then we traveled back a mile to whar our mules war left—a bar on one side of the river, and *two bares* on the other.

Ba'tiste's Nightmare

"Bien, excusez, Monsieur, you must know first place, de 'Medicine Bag' is mere humbug, he is no medicine in him—no pills; he is someting mysterieux. Some witchcraft, suppose. You must know that tous les sauvages have such thing about him, pour for good luck. Ce n'est que hocus pocus, to keep off witch, suppose. You must know, ces articles can nevare be sold, you see dey cannot be buy. So my friend here, Monsieur Cataline, who have collect all de curiosités des pay sauvages, avait made strong applique to me for to get one of dese medicine bags for his Collection curieux et I had, pour moimême, le curiosité extreme for to see des quelques choses ces étranges tings was composé.

"I had learn much of dese strange custom, and I know when de Ingin die, his medicine-bags is buried wis him.

"Monsieur, so it never can be got by any boday. I hap to tink wen we was live in de mous of Yellowstone, now is time, and I avait said Monsieur Cataline, que pensez vous! One of de chiefs of des Knisteneux has die. Il avait une medicine-bag magnifique, et extremement curieux; il est of de wite wolf skin, ornament et stuff wid tousand tings wich we shall see, ha? Alors, suppose Monsieur Cataline, I have seen him just now. I av see de medicine-bag laid on his breast avec his hands crossed ovare it. Que pensez-vous? I can get him to-night, ha? 'Tis no harm—'tis no steal—he is dead, ha? 'But, would you not be afraid, Ba'tiste, (said Monsieur Cataline), to take from dis poor chap his medicines on which he has rest all his hopes in dis world, and de world to come?' Pardon, je n'ai peur, non, Monsieur, ne rien de peur. I nevare saw ghost I have not fear, mais, suppose, it is not right, exact; but I have grand disposition pour for to obligé my friend, et le curiosité moimême pour to see wat it is made of; suppose to-night I shall go, ha? 'Well, Ba'tiste, I have no objection (says Monsieur Cataline) if your heart does not fail you, for I will be very glad to get him, and make you a handsome present for it, but I think it will be a cold and gloomy kind of business.' Nevare mind, Monsieur Cataline, (I said) provide he is well dead! I had see les Knisteneux when dey ave bury de chap—I ave watch close, and I ave see how de medicine-bags was put. It was fix pretty tight by some cord around his bellay, and den some skins was wrap many times

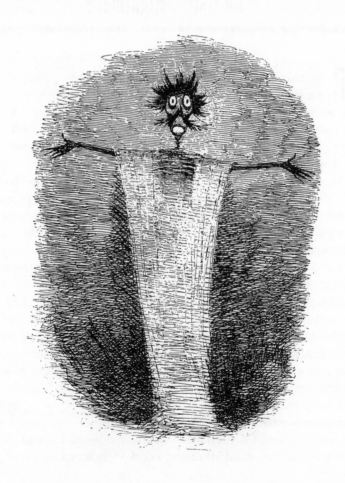

around him—he was put down in de hole dug for him, and den de hole was to be fill up; now was de only time possible for de medicine-bag, ha? I ave very pretty little wife dat times, Assineboine squaw, and we sleep in one of de stores inside of de fort, you know, ha?

"So you may imagine, I was all de day perplex to know how I should go, somebody may watch—suppose he may not be dead? not quite dead, ha? nevare mind—le jour was bien long, et le nuit dismal! Oh, by gar it was dismal! plein of apprehension, mais je n'avais pas peur! So some time after midnights, when it was bout right time pour go, I made start, very light, so my wife must not hear. Oh diable l'imagination! quel solitude! well, I have go very well yet, I am pass de door, and I am pass de gate, and I am at lengts arrive at de grave! B'atiste, courage, courage! Now is de times come. Well, suppose I am not afraid of DEAD man, mais, perhaps, dese medicine-bag is give by de Grand Esprit to de Ingin for something? Possibe! I will let him keep it. I shall go back! No, Monsieur Cataline will laughs at me. I must have him, ma foi, mon courage! so I climb down very careful into de grave, mais, as I descend, my heart rise up into my mouse! Oh mon Dieu! Courage, B'atiste, courage! ce n'est pas l'homme dat I fear, mais le medicine, le medicine. So den I ave lift out de large stones, I ave put out my head in de dark, and I ave look all de contré round; ne personne, ne personne—no bodé in sight! Well, I ave got softly down on my knees ovare him and when I ave unwrap de robe, I ave all de time say, 'pardon, courage!' until I ad got de skins all off de bodé; I ave den take hold de cord to untie, mais!! two cold hands seize me by de wrists and I was just dead—I was petrifact in one instant! Oh, St. Esprit! I could just see in de dark two eyes glaring like fire sur upon me! and den, it spoke to me, 'Who are you?' (Sacré vengeange! it will not do to deceive him, no,) 'I am Ba'tiste, poor Ba'tiste!' 'Then you are surely mine, (as he clenched both arms tight around my boday) lie still! Ba'tiste.' Oh, holy Vierge! St. Esprit! O mon Dieu! I could not breathe! miserable! Je suis perdu! oh pourquoi have I been such a fool to get into dese cold, cold arms! 'Ba'tiste? (drawing me some tighter and tighter) do you not belong to me?' Yes, suppose! oh diable! Oui, oui, je suis certainement perdu, lost, lost, for evare! Oh! can you not possibe let me go? 'No, Ba'tiste, we must nevare part.' Grand Dieu, c'est fini, finis, finis avec moi! 'Then you do not love me anymore, Ba'tiste?' Quel! quoi! what!! est-ce vous, Wee-ne-on-ka? 'Yes, Ba'tiste, it is the Bending Willow who holds you, she that loves you and will not let you go. Are you dreaming, Ba'tiste?' Oui, diable, ——!' "

"Well, Ba'tiste, that's a very good story, and very well told; I presume you never tried again to get a medicine-bag?"

"Non, Monsieur, je vous assure, I was satisfy wis de mistakes dat night, pour for je crois qu'il fut l'Esprit, le Grand Esprit."

Song of the Voyageur

Ax' heem de nort' win' w'at he see
   Of de Voyageur long ago,
An' he'll say to you w'at he say to me,
   So lissen hees story well—
I see de track of hees botte sau-vage
   On many a hill an' long portage
Far far away from hees own vill-age
   An' sound of the parish bell.

I nevair can play on de Hudson Bay
   Or mountain dat lie between
But I meet heem singin' hees lonely way
   The happies' man I know—
I cool hees face as he's sleepin' dere
   Under de star of de Red Rivière,
An' off de home of de great white bear,
   I'm seein' his dog traineau.

De women an' chil'ren runnin' out
   Of de wigwam of de Cree—
De leetle papoose dey laugh an' shout
   When de soun' of hees voice dey hear—
De oldes' warrior of de Sioux
   Kill hese'f dancin' de w'ole night t'roo,
An' de Blackfoot girl remember too
   De ole tam voyageur.

C H A P T E R   6

Timber!

The western logger has always been a tantalizing subject for legends. All the stories about the bold, shaggy-bearded lumberjacks finally became concentrated in one supernatural figure—Paul Bunyan, the loggers' demigod. Some say that the real Paul Bunyan was Paul Pierre Bonhomme, a giant Canuck axman and fearless leader among Papineau's rebels against the British Crown in Canada's year of trouble—1837. But like Bunyan, Bonhomme is merely a figment of the imagination. Paul Bunyan lives on in the minds of Canadians and Americans, young and old. The fact that he never existed, except in mythology, matters not at all.

Paul Bunyan and His Little Blue Ox

Paul Bunyan is an oddity among the legendary frontier characters because, like Deadwood Dick, he never existed. No matter how outright fabulous and fairy tale–like some of the stories told
about David Crockett, Mike Fink, or Doc Holliday, they all were at
some time alive and walked the earth, while the King of Lumberjacks
was entirely the product of a writer's imagination. He also was different from the other, once living, western heroes in being something
of a newcomer, first mentioned in a Detroit publication of 1910. Tales
of giant axmen of the Bunyan type seem to have originated in Canada. There are even claims that anecdotes about a herculean Canuck
logger named Bonjon had inspired the first Paul Bunyan stories. But
there is no proof of this. Though Bunyan's home grounds were the
logger camps of northern Canada, he jumps the Mississippi, drives
his oxen across the Bering Strait, and gives birth to Puget Sound by
uprooting a giant redwood tree. Paul Bunyan is a true westerner.

Paul Bunyan was big like hell, fought like hell, and lied like hell.
He was as tall as a redwood tree. He was so strong that he could pick
up an ox between his thumb and forefinger. He made himself an ax
handle out of a whole pine tree trunk. He chopped a ten-foot branch
off an oak tree and used it for a toothpick. He once uprooted the
biggest tree that ever was with his bare hands. The hole where the
roots had been filled up again with water, and that became Puget
Sound. Paul was a great jumper. He could jump over the Mississippi
River and back again without ever touching ground. Paul loved to
dance. He danced so hard he caused a number of major earthquakes.
He once slipped and fell into Lake Superior, which made it spill
over. This created the great flood that covered the states of Wisconsin
and Minnesota, as well as the province of Ontario.

One day, absentmindedly, Paul Bunyan put one of his loggers in his pocket and then forgot about him. The pour soul nearly starved to death before Paul rummaged around in his pocket for a chaw of 'baccer.

Paul cut his hair and beard only once every three years. After he had his barbering, there was usually a mountain of hair left, as big as a haystack. Paul always combed it out and, on the average, got about fifty pounds of salt pork, a hundred pounds of beans, and ten gallons of molasses out of it.

Paul had an appetite to match his size. Once, leading a tote team to his campsite, he came to a large lake. It was growing dark. The sky was covered with clouds and there was no moon. They decided not to go on but to camp right there by the lake. Paul and his lumberjacks had worked up an elephant-sized hunger. Luckily, they were also carrying a year's supply of food with them and Paul dumped all those beans and the salt pork into the lake. He built fires all around the lake until the water was boiling, turning the whole huge pool into bean soup. Paul and his loggers drank up the lake and it took years until it was full again.

The camp's cooking oven covered an acre of ground and the frying pan was just as big. When pancakes were called for, the cook lit a whole forest fire underneath the pan and then had some of the boys tie the side of a hog to the bottom of their snowshoes, having them skate all over the pan to grease it up.

Everything having to do with Paul Bunyan was larger than life. He had a daughter called Peg who could chop down the biggest tree with one cut and break it to pieces over her knee for kindling. His horse was so big that an ordinary fellow needed a six-story fireman's ladder to mount it, provided Paul let him.

Even the bugs in Paul Bunyan's camp were considerably bigger than other bugs. Once, one of the loggers was working high up in a tree when a bunch of mosquitoes got right under the seat of his pants, lifted him clear off the branch he was sitting on, and flew away with him over the treetops. It might have gone badly with that fellow if that cloud of mosquitoes had not come down on a fat steer. That gave him the chance to get off without falling to his death. He hit one of those cussed insects a solid whack with his ax and the darn critter bit a good-sized chunk out of the blade. When that bunch of mosquitoes finally got off the steer, there was nothing left of the poor beast but a heap of bones. The mosquitoes then settled down on some tree stumps, picking their teeth with meat skewers. Paul had heard that in Africa they had man-sized bumblebees whose favorite food was mosquitoes. Paul at once ordered a boatload of these bumblers, but it turned out that the bees and the mosquitoes took a shine to each other, producing offspring of mosquito-bees with stingers at both ends. Paul promptly sent for a passel of special sixteen-legged, thirty-two eyed spiders whose favorite food consisted of bumblebee-mosquitoes, but these finicky critters preferred to gobble whole oxen. Paul sold the stingers of those rambuctious insects to the army as bayonets.

One day Paul Bunyan was lying down in the sun to get a little rest. A lumberjack passing by thought he saw a large bullfrog jumping and dancing on Paul's bare chest. "What's that bullfrog adoin' dancin' and jumpin' up and down on you?" the fellow inquired. "That ain't no bullfrog," answered Paul, "it's only one of those goddam cussed fleas!"

Paul had a pet catfish that followed him wherever he went. But that fish came to a sad end. It accidentally fell into the Big Onion River and drowned.

Paul had an ox, a rather large beast that grew two feet every time Paul looked at it. It was called Babe, though some remember it as Benny. These folks are wrong. The name was definitely Babe. One morning, when Babe was still only a bull calf, the loggers saw a big barn wandering into camp. It was the calf, having outgrown the barn and walking away with it, carrying it on its back.

Babe was known as Paul's Little Blue Ox of the Woods. He measured twelve ax handles betweeen his eyes and weighed more than all the fish that ever got away. Babe saved Paul a lot of time and labor. Paul used to hitch him to hundred-acre plots of forest, one plot at a time. As he dragged these chunks of timberland along, Babe was driven right to the riverbank. There Paul cut the timber off, just as if he were shearing sheep, and then floated the logs down the Little Gimlet River.

In winter Paul hitched Babe to a huge sled instead of a wagon. Beside his regular load of logs, Babe also had to haul the water tank Bunyan used to ice over the road for the sled's runners. One time the tank burst and that's what started the mighty Mississippi River and keeps it flowing. Whenever the Little Blue Ox had to be shoed, it took a whole iron mine to make the shoes.

One year there was a big logjam, the biggest anybody could remember. The logs were piled up three hundred feet high and were backing up the river for thirty miles. Paul led old Babe right into the river at the point where the logs backed up the farthest. The Little Blue Ox stood in the water up to his belly. That was about fifty feet high. Paul put him in there with his hind end against the logjam. Then he took his big buffalo gun and shot Babe a dozen times in the rump. Babe thought the bullets were flies. His tail was just about thirty feet long. Babe switched it back and forth to drive the pesky flies away. The tail switching caused such a wind storm that it broke up the logjam.

Paul Bunyan tried to find a cow big enough to keep old Babe company. It took him a long time, but he finally found one. Her name was Betsy, but some say it was Bossy. That cow was so big that when it was wintertime around her head it was summertime at her tail end. When Betsy got mad and pawed the ground, she brought up an acre of dirt every time. Paul took good care of Betsy, feeding her corn, rye, and sour mash. Paul did the milking himself because no one else was big and strong enough to do it. Betsy gave a hundred gallons of milk every day. But there was a problem. The milk was too strong to use at the table. It had turned into pure 100-proof rye whiskey.

In winter the camp was so cold, more than a hundred degrees below freezing, that it turned the flames of the loggers' fires into icicles. They couldn't do anything with them. So they bundled them up and piled them somewhere near the camp. Came spring and the icicles turned into flames again, threatening to set the whole camp on fire. Paul and his lumberjacks managed to chuck them into the river. They set the waters boiling and that evening the loggers feasted on a great mess of well-cooked crawfish.

Paul Bunyan had a cook who was so ugly that, when he peeked into the pot of bean soup to see how it was doing, at the sight of him the soup began to sizzle, curdle, and ferment, and after it was strained, it was found to have turned into strong moonshine, the kind that, when a drop gets onto a boot, will at once burn a hole through the leather. Paul took the man off his cooking job and put him in charge of the camp's distillery.

And what became of Babe, the Little Blue Ox of the Woods? That ox lived entirely on flapjacks. Twelve cooks were busy night and day making flapjacks for him. One day the cooks were all sick with the flu and old Babe got so hungry waiting for them to recover that he gulped down the red-hot stove, and that was the end of him.

Paul Bunyan Helps to Build a Railroad

Paul Bunyan was weaned on corn whiskey. He grew three feet every morning. He was so tall you could see his head only on clear days. When he laughed, it caused an earthquake, so people asked him never to listen to a joke. Thereafter, he took to grinning silently. Paul Bunyan could cross the whole Indian Territory in three steps. Everything about him was big. Even the crumbs falling from his table were so large that the mice who gobbled them grew as big as timber wolves and chased all the grizzlies plumb out of the country. Paul's ax was so heavy it took seven of the brawniest loggers to lift it, and it took twelve men all day to sharpen the blade. His great blue ox, Babe, ate up ten acres of prime corn every morning for breakfast. Paul could log off a whole county every day.

When General Dodge ran into problems building the Union Pacific Railroad, he called upon Paul for help. That was after Paul dug out Puget Sound to sluice the water of the Pacific Ocean into a huge ditch he had scooped out in a day to float his logs. He later named this ditch the Columbia River.

As far as the railroad was concerned, Paul got together ten thousand live and frisky beavers to build the fence along the track. The obliging critters gnawed off the trees along the right of way, chewing them into six-foot-long fence poles. Then he got himself fifty thousand prairie dogs to dig out the post holes. For railroad ties he took only the tallest trees with trunks so thick that it took a whole crew of shanty boys three days merely to chop through the bark. Aided by his best lumberjacks—Sourdough Sam, Caleb Kanuck, and Sven the Swede, he sawed them down to the right size. Falling, the big trees raised such colossal clouds of snow that daylight could penetrate them only on Sundays, when Paul and his men stopped working. Babe, the blue ox, dragged the iron rails into place—three miles of them at a time. As for railroad engines, Paul fetched them from the shop and, with a locomotive under each arm, hauled them from Chicago to Omaha with seven mighty steps. Once, when Paul and his shanty-boys got thirsty doing all this work, they swallowed up Lake Huron in three gulps.

When General Dodge could not find a place to get through the Rockies, which barred his way like a solid wall, Paul just kicked the biggest peaks to the side with his iron-soled boots and thus made a pass for the Union Pacific. When Dodge ran out of wood in the Great American Desert, Paul just roped himself ten square miles of forest somewhere in Canada and had Babe drag it all the way to Utah. He and his loggers finished their job in record time, ahead of schedule, and got a big bonus.

Paul Bunyan celebrated the event by putting together a barrel as high as Pike's Peak and as wide as all of Texas. He filled it to the brim with all the whiskey in the United States, paying for it with the bonus money. Then he and his shantyboys went on a big drunk, though it took them an uncommonly long time, three days in fact, to lap up all that liquor. As a result, for a full three months all America was on the wagon. In gratitude, Carry Nation proposed to Paul Bunyan, but he wouldn't have her.

◆　◆　◆

Almost a hundred years later the government remembered how Paul Bunyan had helped to build the transcontinental railroad. Now the United States was at war with Nazi Germany, Fascist Italy, and the Japanese Empire. A very smart man by the name of Einstein proposed to make an atom bomb, just in case Hitler's scientists had the same idea. Nobody knew whether it could be done and, if so, how long it might take. Then somebody remembered Paul Bunyan.

At the time Paul was only some 150 years old—just reaching middle age, because longevity was his middle name—and as peppy as ever. The government started looking for Paul. They had quite a hassle finding him, but finally they did. When somebody discovered twelve-foot-long human boot prints in the snows of the Canadian north woods, they figured, correctly, that they had to belong to Paul. They followed the tracks to a round log cabin, the biggest ever seen, covering about a square mile, and sure enough, inside they found Paul soaking up his twists of chewing tobacco in potent corn whiskey to give them a kick.

"Can we talk to you about a matter of some importance, Mr. Bunyan?" the government men said to Paul.

"Sure, soon as I done my shavin'," Paul told them. He took his ax and hammered down his stubbles through his cheeks into the inside of his mouth, where he bit them off. That's how he shaved himself. He proceeded to comb his curly beard with a pine tree, then he put on his mackinaw and said, "What kin I do fur you, strangers?"

"Well," they explained, "as you know, there's a war on—"

"A war, by thunder! Let me git my licks in agin the cussed redcoats!"

"No, not with the British, Mr. Bunyan, but with—"

"With them danged Rebs, then, by Ned! Jest let me git my hands on 'em!"

"No, no, Mr. Bunyan, we are at war with the Germans and the Japs. Very dangerous chaps. They have us against the ropes. They might be building an atom bomb and will beat us to it. If they do, that's the end for us. They'd rule the world."

"You don't say. What's this atom bomb like?"

"It has the power of the sun, Mr. Bunyan. It can make a hole ten miles wide and ten miles deep in a second. It is the most powerful thing in the world. With it we could win this war."

"I kalkilate I kin make one fer you," Paul told them. "Loggin's kinda slow anyway this time of the year."

He jumped a wee bit up into the air, only just about a hundred feet, clicking his heels seven times before coming down. He did this three times. "That's for warmin' up," he explained.

Then he gathered himself up into a ball and then uncoiled for his real big jump, taking off like a cannon shot, leaping right out of the atmosphere and disappearing into space. The government men stood open-mouthed. They didn't know what to do. After a while they heard a great roaring and thundering as from a thousand express trains or jet planes. It was Paul Bunyan coming back. He carried something

glittering in his hands, a lump about the size of Mount Shasta. It glowed red-hot, emitting a light so bright that the government men would have gone blind had they not worn dark glasses.

Paul landed with such force that he sank into the earth up to his armpits. He flung the white-hot shining thing about a mile away from him. The strange object hit the ground with a force greater than a volcanic eruption, causing an earthquake measuring eight on the Richter scale, gouging out of the earth a hole twenty miles wide.

"W-a-a-l, thar she is," said Paul Bunyan, digging himself out, blowing on his scorched and blistering fingers. "Hot she war, so hot she burned plumb through my gloves!"

"What in heavens is it, the thing you brought?" inquired the stunned and trembling government men.

"I jumped purty high, I reckon," said Paul, "high 'nuff to break off this here piece outa the sun. Seems to be what you fellers want. I better cool her off."

Ole Paul went over to the river and swallowed up about ten miles of it, holding most of the water in his puffed-out cheeks. He went to the crater that had the chunk of sun in it and squirted the water all over it, enough to turn the crater into a huge lake. The heat of the piece of the sun was so great it made the lake boil.

"Isn't she sumpthin'?" said Paul. "Didje ever see a thing like that? I reckon I'll name this pond here Lake Winnipeg."

In three big jumps Paul moseyed over to the storage shack next to his cabin, and from it fetched a sack of coffee weighing ten tons. He dumped it into the hissing, bubbling lake. He then put two of his fingers in his mouth and whistled, so loud that it shook the leaves from the branches of all the trees within three miles. That brought all his shantyboys running. They were rolling before them what looked like big rubber wheels but turned out to be oversized dough-nuts. Each of them also brought along a large metal bucket that he filled by dipping into the lake, which had turned into strong coffee. Then Paul and his lumberjacks sat down to breakfast, filling up on hot java and doughnuts.

The boss logger asked, "What now?"

"Mr. Bunyan, what you brought us is an enormous lump of split atoms," said the government men. "We have to get it down to White Sands, our testing range in the Southwest. We got to anlayze it."

"Reckon me and Babe'll get her down thar," said Paul. He hitched the chunk of the sun to the blue ox with a ten-mile-long steel chain. As it melted from the chunk's heat, the chain had to be replaced two or three times on the way. Paul put a saddle on Babe's back, vaulted onto it, cracked his whip, and off they went, quick as lightning. The government men took a plane, but old Babe was so fast that he and Paul arrived at White Sands long before them. The piece of the sun was still so hot it turned the dessert sand into molten glass. A nearby mountain also was changed into glass and was made transparent. You couldn't see it because you could see right through it. The pilot of the government plane was about to crash into this invisible mountain, but Paul snatched it out of the air and put it safely on the ground. When the government men descended from their plane, they naturally stepped on a surface of sheer glass and slid and slithered around as if they had been on ice skates, and all fell on their behinds.

"What now?" asked Paul.

"Now we study the thing you have brought."

All the world's greatest scientists put on their lead suits and their darkest glasses and examined the sun chunk. "It is indeed a gigantic atom bomb," they told Paul.

"What do we do with it?" the boss logger wanted to know.

"Well, Mr. Bunyan," they said, "we will give you this exploder and then you fasten it to your sun rock, like so, and then you and your blue ox amble over to Japan."

"And then what?"

"Then you push this button here, and turn this dial on that timer, and plunge down this plunger, and then you and your ox run like hell."

"What happens next?"

"The bomb explodes."

"And then?"

"Then there is a blinding flash and all of Japan goes up in flames, turns into ashes, crumbles into little pieces, and disappears into the sea."

"With all the people?"

"With every living thing."

Paul Bunyan got to thinking. When Paul thinks, he runs round and round in circles. So he started. He ran round in circles for seven long hours. He ran so fast and with such tremendous force that he gouged out a hip-deep circular ditch. Hip-deep, for Paul, means about fifty feet or so. When he was done thinking, he told the government men, "Sorry, folks, but I ain't a-goin' to do it."

"Why not?" they asked.

"I brung this thing down to earth to do some good, to heat up the homes of folks too poor to pay for coal, not to kill."

"But Bunyan, those Japs are our enemies. And the Krauts too. Their turn comes later."

"Sorry ag'in, but you got the wrong man for this job. You fellers are 'bout three hundred years short of bein' smart 'nuff to handle this thing. I better bring her back to whar she belongs."

With that ol' Paul clicked his heels and jumped into space once again, where he glued the sun rock back to where he had taken it from. Then he jumped back to earth, figuring his path so exactly that he landed right at his doorstep where Babe and the shantyboys were waiting for him.

The government men looked very glum. "I guess," one of them said, "we'll have to make an atom bomb by ourselves."

They did.

Kidnapped by a Flea

An old Indian tale tells of the Great Spirit looking down from the sky upon the strange doings of the white men. One day his eyes chanced to fix upon Paul Bunyan's lumber camp. It was raining, and with nothing to do the axemen were bored stiff. There were, as usual, no women in the camp, and the nearest place where a fellow could make the acquaintance of a lady—that is, a pair of faded, horse-faced painted cats—was more than a hundred miles away. Those sorry bachelor-loggers had grown as ornery as badgers. There was just nothing going on in camp, nothing to occupy one's mind. It got to the point that, when the only fiddler in camp struck up a tune, the fellows had to waltz around with each other, and that game had grown mighty stale.

Well, the Great Spirit felt more than a mite sorry for that sad bunch of hermits. He tried to think up something to amuse them and to keep them occupied. He talked it over with the double-faced Moon Lady and the Great White-haired Wizard of the North, and they agreed that something ought to be done. Those loggers were white folks, mostly, but not the kind to bother their red brothers— not soldiers, or prospectors, or land speculators. Besides, Paul had more than just a smidgin of Cherokee in him. So the Great Spirit got out his big possible bag and rummaged around in all the foofaraw in it, and took out a bushel of wallpaper flounders, and a bushel of seam squirrels, and mixed it all together with a half-dozen handfuls of fleas, and sprinkled a mess of these active citizens over the loggers' camp-site. The little mattress lizards and bosom chums got busy right away and soon the old timber wolves were bored no longer, occupied with scratching and cussing, having a high old time, hunting the wee crimson ramblers.

From that day on, logging camps were never without their gen-erous quota of cooties and chinch bugs. The little fellows became regular pets, following the loggers like hound dogs, learning all kinds of tricks. There was laughter and merriment as the loggers raced their favorite graybacks and bedbugs against each other, having jumping contests among their favorite fleas, even setting up a flea circus with the little beasties jumping through rings or doing tightrope acts on threads of yarn. The six-legged inhabitants were real smart too. Whenever the lumberjacks were moving to a new camp, sending their gear and bedrolls ahead with the tote teams, the little bedcats made sure not to be left behind, and when the loggers arrived at the new place they found their pets waiting for them, waving their innumera-ble legs in greeting, jumping and hollering, making a dad-blasted racket.

Things went on like this harmoniously until one day some old bull whipper blew into camp, straight from Virginia City, making a great to-do about the great gold and silver strikes, telling of fist-sized nuggets lying on the ground like so many pebbles waiting to be picked up, of prospectors turning into millionaires overnight, of for-mer beggars building themselves palaces with crystal chandeliers, Turkey carpets, and ample stocks of blue ruin and aged-in-the-barrel Kentucky bourbon. Hearing this, all the loggers skedaddled, leaving in a body to make their millions in the goldfields. They were in such a hurry that they left their belongings, including bedrolls, behind, together with their little six-legged friends. Why bother with raggedy, moth-eaten blankets when everybody was already dreaming of sleep-ing in four-poster beds with silken sheets and eiderdown pillows. At first the little cooties and hoppers were not at all worried. They thought the loggers had gone to work as usual and would be home in the evening, as always, but the men never returned. When the wee varmints realized that they had been abandoned, left to fend for themselves, there was such a weeping and wailing as would have broken a wolverine's heart. Paul Bunyan did not go. He told Old Babe that the loggers were plumb locoed and that he, for his part, would take a long vacation until the fellows had come to their senses. So he and Babe leit out for their old home in the Canadian north-woods. There, in Paul's old cabin, they made themselves comfortable, sitting by the fireplace, sipping whiskey and playing pinochle.

Many years went by because, being the most stubborn folks on earth, it took the loggers that long to admit that their get-rich schemes had not panned out. None of them had hit paydirt. All of them were in rags and starving. They came to the conclusion that going back to chopping down trees for a living was not such a bad idea.

One fine morning the whole bunch of them was rapping at Paul's door, clamoring for work. They had aged a bit. Paul too was older now, with a good crop of white hairs in his beard, while Old Babe was showing a lot of gray between the horns, but they were all as strong as ever, eager to go back to doing what they did best.

They started up again at their last campsite. They found things as they had left them, except that the ground around the bunkhouse was littered with bones—rabbit, woodchuck, and gopher bones, to judge by their size. They also found a lot of tracks of a kind nobody had ever seen before. Otherwise there was no sign of life anywhere. "Mighty queer," said Sowbosom Sam, the belly robber. Then all had their pork and beans and went to sleep.

In the middle of the night Paul was wakened by a helliferocious racket. The loggers were hollering and screaming. One yelled, "Kangaroos! I'm being hassled by kangaroos!" Another cried, "Wildcats, I'm being savaged by wildcats!" Still another was yelling, "Badgers, badgers, one of 'em got a bite-hold on my nose!" They were all hollering like the devil and, somewhere, Old Babe was bellowing so loudly that it shook the leaves from their branches. Then Paul felt something stirring in his beard. At first, he paid it no mind, being accustomed to a bunch of birds always nesting in there, but all of a sudden he noticed sharp teeth nibbling at his ear. He made a grab at whatever was the cause of it, and came up with a beaver-sized critter that was scratching, biting, and squealing something fierce. Paul had to whack it at least a dozen times with his mighty fists, and stomp it with his half-acre boots, before he got the better of it. The loggers, in their long johns, were in a hellish uproar, kicking and hitting out at some unseen varmints. A few of the fellows lit their lanterns and by the light of them were dumbfounded to see passels of the weirdest outlandish critters scurrying about, snapping at their heels, jumping at their throats, snarling and growling, their gimlet eyes glowing like coals. The loggers were defending themselves as best they could with axes and sledge hammers, having their hands more than full. "Kangaroos!" screamed one man, beset by three strange beasts that could jump fifty feet into the air. One man was crying that he had a wolverine by the ears and was afraid of letting go. All night long, amidst an incredible turmoil, the loggers fought off the monstrous creatures, but as soon as the sun came up, they were all gone as if by magic, except one which Old Babe had trampled with his enormous hooves until it was dead.

The fellows crowded around to examine it. They shuddered at the sight. It was the queerest, awfullest thing that ever was seen. The devilish critter was about as big as a wolf, covered with brownish fuzz, and strangely flat, as if it had been squashed by a steam press. It had huge mandibles with rows of sharp, cone-shaped teeth, but the weirdest thing about it was that it had six stumpy, hairy legs. The fellows looked at it in stupefied wonderment. It had them puzzled.

Paul sat down on a boulder and started thinking, all the time contemplating the evil being. Suddenly, he jumped high in the air, clicked his heels, and shouted, "By the Great Swamp Gaboon and the Fire-breathing Windigo! Boys, I've got it! I'll break my pick if this here ain't an oversized bedbug!"

"How, in blazes, did it get so big?" the loggers wanted to know.

Paul gave it to them: "Boys, it's what they call nowadays the survival of the fittest. When we quit here, ten years ago, we left our little cuties with nothing to feed on. The fleas and mattress lizards plumb starved to death, except the biggest and most ferocious, who started feeding on grasshoppers, maybe, and those pests had litters, and the litters had litters, and always the smallest and weakest died off, leaving only the biggest sons of bitches to reproduce their kind. So our little pets became bigger and bigger, going on from eating rats and gophers to dining on cats and rabbits and sheep. Those rambunctious hoppers you called kangaroos are fleas. The rest are all graybacks and chinch bugs. They're all gone now, because they sleep during the day and feed at night."

"What do we do, Paul?" asked Sourdough Dave. "Come dark, they'll be back. I don't mind tellin' you, I'm skeered."

"Leave it to me, boys," said Paul. He saddled up Babe and galloped over to the nearby fort, talking the colonel into lending him two of those newfangled Gatling guns, and a platoon of cannoneers with a battery of quick-firing Napoleons. To top it all, he hitched Old Babe to a big twelve-pounder Parrott cannon. Before nightfall Paul was back in camp with all his artillery. He made the loggers and soldiers hide in and around the bunkhouse and set up woodpiles generously sprinkled with lamp oil. Beside each woodpile he had a lumberjack standing by with a box of lucifers, ready to set it ablaze as soon as Paul gave the word.

"Wait till you see the whites of their eyes, boys, and then let 'em have it!" Paul told his men.

As soon as it got dark, the lumberjacks could hear, coming from afar, a scruffling and scurrying, caterwauling and snarling, teeth-clicking and mewling to make the hair of even the hardiest woodsman stand on end. Soon they could make out hundreds of wicked eyes glowing in the dark amid a great noise of slavering, salivating, and chop-licking that set their teeth chattering.

Instantly, Paul gave the order: "Light your fires, boys, and give 'em a whiff of grapeshot!"

As soon as the fires illuminated the scene, the men saw a great mass of fearful varmints hopping, slithering, crawling, and scurrying toward them. At once the soldiers and loggers opened up with their Gatlings and Napoleons as the boom of cannon mingled with the sound of shotgun blasts and the whistling of rifle bullets. It was a massacre. Monstrous as they were, the giant insects could not stand up to the weapons of intelligent human beings. The men made short work of the ungodly pests whose carcasses soon were littering the ground. Old Babe had the time of his life, bellowing and stomping to death every critter that was still moving. When it was all over, the fellows gave a mighty cheer that made the mountains tremble.

Paul ordered a roll call and found that one man was missing—Sowbosom Sam, the cook. One of the loggers spoke up, saying that he had seen one of the kangaroo-fleas carrying off what seemed to be a human.

"Holy mackerel! That's Sowbosom Sam for sure!" cried the King of Lumberjacks as he jumped on Old Babe's back, "After him! Paul Bunyan to the rescue!"

Off like the wind they went. Luckily, a full moon was rising, giving Paul glimpses of the monstrous flea carrying off the poor cook in his claws. The critter was mighty fast, covering a hundred yards with each jump. Old Babe had to crank up his speed, slowly gaining on the misbegotten insect. When it came to the crunch, nobody and nothing could outrun the Little Blue Ox of the Woods. At dawn they caught up with the kangaroo-flea and his victim. The monster, sitting on a rock, had a stranglehold on Sowbosom Sam and was about to gobble him like corn on the cob. Paul had his trusted Hawken rifle ready and let fly at the flea. The heavy slug hit it right between the eyes, but it was so hardheaded that it merely shook the bullet off, looked annoyed, and turned back to nibble at Sam's rump. Then Old Babe charged. He caught the kangaroo-flea on one horn, flipped it upward a mile in the air, caught it on his other horn, and then kept tossing the cussed critter from one horn to the other until nothing remained of it but a few tufts of fuzz. That left Sowbosom Sam up in the air. Old Babe had flung him so high that it took the cook quite a while to come down. Paul caught him with both arms and set him gently down. Sam felt himself all over to make sure that all of him was still there and found that, except for a tiny nibble, he was still intact.

"That was mighty close," was Sowbosom Sam's comment.

Thunder Bay

A violent norther was blowing when Shot Gunderson, the iron man of the Saginaw, came across the ice to challenge Paul Bunyan.

The iron man had his back to the wind. Paul Bunyan's battle plan called for an exactly opposite position, but he was forced to make the best of this one. At any rate, the shantyboys were safe. The logger still hoped to make the iron man face the wind. Just how to maneuver him into that position was the question.

To spar for time Paul engaged in a preliminary to actual battle. Shot Gunderson sneeringly participated. The iron man did not care. He had no fear or doubt about the outcome. He was invulnerable. He was likewise irresistible. Water was his only weakness, and he stood on seventeen feet of ice. So he scornfully followed the logger's lead.

"Go ahead and sashay," rasped the iron man. "But it ain't goin' to do yer a particle of good."

Paul Bunyan said nothing. Leaning hard into the wind, he grimly eyed Shot Gunderson, at the same time hefting a bay-shore boulder in his left hand.

Suddenly he tossed it in the wind and instantly pulzerized the stone with a blow of his right fist. Clouds of grit blew down the necks of the wind-heaved shantyboys on the shore. Grinning harshly, Shot Gunderson hauled fistfuls of black stuff from a mackinaw pocket and shoved them into his mouth. Then he struck sparks from his flint. A violent explosion rocked down the wind. The iron man of the Saginaw had fired a charge of blasting powder between his jaws without loosening a tooth. Paul Bunyan did not change expression.

His next move was to draw a sixteen-foot log from his hip-pocket and set it on his shoulder.

"Dast you to knock the log off my shoulder here," Paul Bunyan growled.

Shot Gunderson responded by gouging a furrow five feet deep in the ice with the toe of his boot.

"Dast you to cross that line there," he rasped.

"I'm going to make you look human," growled Paul Bunyan then. "For that you got to be peeled. So here and now I start to peel off your iron hide."

"I'm making a patchwork cushion outer you there," rasped the iron man. "To make that I got to take you to pieces first. So I'm startin' in to make pieces of you now."

That ended the ceremonies, which were to serve as a model forevermore when men in the woods engaged in battle. They failed to swerve Paul Bunyan. The iron man had not budged from his position. He leaned back solidly into the norther, his anvil fists slowly but surely coming up for a fighting swing. The boss logger did not quail or retreat, though fully convinced by now that Shot Gunderson was actually invulnerable and irresistible. The rumors had not told the half of it about the iron man. . . .

Now the norther began to prove that the biggest storms indeed have the longest lulls. After the lull before dawn the wind had steadily increased, first with its barrage of gusts, then with its first massed forces, and at last with a terrific wedge of wind aimed and hurled with solid violence at Thunder Bay. Now the weather unloosed its last and mightiest effort against the boss logger. The wind was backing up Shot Gunderson.

That was the iron man's main trouble when he tried to set himself for one straight finishing punch. . . .

Just an instant too late Shot Gunderson unloosed his irresistible fist. Paul Bunyan was already lunging inside the blow. The iron man's arm shot harmlessly by Paul Bunyan's dodging head like a log plunging over a waterfall. Nobody was there.

It was the boss logger's great chance. The force of his missed blow and the drive of the wind hurled the iron man off balance. He whirled dizzily. Paul Bunyan felt his own feet fly off the ice, but he sturdily kept his grip on the iron man's corrugated throat. Shot Gunderson drove his spikes into the ice and hauled up, still on his feet. Paul Bunyan made his cleanest landing since the time he tumbled from the high jump of bucking Big Auger River. His vaulting feet curved down in a royal arc and struck true. Now Paul Bunyan had his back to the wind. Shot Gunderson, white-hot with frustrated wrath, leaned into the wind to seize his adversary in a death grapple.

The boss logger was at last set to carry out the battle plan his sagacity had formed. The iron man was hooking him close. At his rear the norther was battering with increasingly furious blasts. Paul Bunyan leaned back carefully into the wind. He dropped his left hand from Gunderson's neck, leaving his own jaw exposed.

Then he roared tauntingly into the iron man's funneled ear: "Scared to try another punch? Scared to fight and bound to wrassle? Where's your killer's punch, iron man?"

The taunt was shrewd. Certainly it was Paul Bunyan alone who had done all the wrestling so far, and it was Shot Gunderson who had tried to fire a punch. The iron man raged. He heard nothing but the taunt, and he saw nothing but the exposed left jaw of the boss logger.

"Show yer who's skeered," he rasped. "Show yer who's a-wrastlin'! Right now I shatter that jaw of your'n into shavin's!"

Even as he rasped out the boast, the iron man dropped his anvil of a fist down to his boot top, to start an inside uppercut which would smash into the logger's unguarded jaw. At that, Paul Bunyan took a yet heavier lean back into the norther. He tensed every muscle. The iron man's irresistible fist started up like a huge rock heaved by a power enormous. In the very same instant of an instant Paul Bunyan yanked the iron man toward him with his right hand and pivoted himself out to the right like sheet lightning. The battering norther hammered by him, driving with full force into Shot Gunderson.

The iron man's fist was shooting up like seventeen cannonballs in one. The norther hit the irresistible fist when it was only inches from its mark and deflected its course. Shot Gunderson himself took the blow. The inside uppercut ended under his own chin with a shattering impact, lifted him explosively, hurled him backward in an enormous arc—and then the bay earned its loud name as the iron man of the Saginaw drove head first through the ice with a crash that resounded in echoes for five hours.

Huge foaming waves and ponderous floes broke upon the boots of horseshoe iron that turned their calks toward the sky. The boots quivered once and were still. That quick Shot Gunderson gave up the ghost.

CHAPTER 7

Gold! Gold! Gold!

It all started on January 24, 1848, at Sutter's Mill in California's Sacramento Valley, when Jim Marshall picked up a nugget and cried, "Boys, I think I found a gold mine!"

The gold rush was on. Prospectors came from the East Coast in sailing ships around the Horn, or traveled across the whole width of the continent, some with nothing more than a handcart. The Great Melting Pot was born here—California swarmed with Yankees, southerners, ex-farmers and city dwellers, Mexicans, Chileans, Australians, Kanakas, Chinamen, Indians, blacks, and Europeans in general. Among these comers were titled English men, a longtime mistress of the king of Bavaria, men who claimed descent from Napoleon, famous writers, actors, and actresses, adventurers, card-sharps, duelists, and whores. All of them arrived sick with gold fever, con-sumed by greed and hope, lured by the shiny yellow metal, which made a very few of them rich, and made a very many of the "Fools of Forty-nine" wish they had never heard the word "gold."

Yearning for gold peopled the West, drove the Indians onto reserva-tions, gave an impetus to the building of the transcontinental railroad, and spelled the end of the buffalo.

The California Gold Rush was followed by gold strikes in Colorado, Montana, South Dakota, Arizona, and Alaska. Denver, Tombstone, Sacramento, Helena, and Deadwood owed their birth to gold. When the gold gave out, men could still make a fortune in silver, copper, or lead. Every strike brought on a new avalanche of immigrants. Gold inspired adventure stories, songs, and poems. In particular, it inspired legends—legends of jubilation and despair, of love and lust, murder and self-sacrifice, of devils and ghosts, and, most often, of lost treasures and mines—the Lost Dutchman's, the Lost Frenchman's, the Lost Jim Bowie, the Lost Bonanza, the Lost Breyfogle, the Lost Crazy Woman's, the Lost Phantom, the Lost . . . There just is no end of them and, occasionally, one can still encounter a wild-eyed Oldtimer, with a map, wielding pick and shovel in search of buried treasure. The mines and treasures may be lost forever, but their legends endure to this day.

Tommy-Knockers

The mines of Park City, Utah, are haunted by "tommy-knock-ers," dwarfish ghosts, both disembodied and corporeal, some of them good and some evil. The mine shafts and galleries are also the abodes of a beautiful, nude, pale-skinned female spirit, with flowing, gossamer tresses, sometimes, but not always, astride a white headless horse.

Perkin Basset, a "Cousin Jack"—that is, one of thousands of Cornishmen who came to America to work in the gold and silver mines—had a special cross to bear when it came to tommy-knockers, who, for reasons beyond this ken, singled him out for their unwanted attentions. It might have been that Perkin imbibed too much "conversation fluid," which induced him to tell strange stories of being kept awake at night by the "click and ping" of single-jacking coming from the nearby mine, the eerie sounds of jack against drill caused by invisible imps. It got so bad that poor Perkin was robbed of his sleep by this infernal, persisting hammering, reverberating in his ears right inside his humble shack until it seemed to him that the ghost was driving the steel right into his throbbing head. The desperate miner had recourse to a bottle of the good creature that he kept right by the straw sack which served him as a bed, but the more of the stuff he knocked down, the worse it got. Finally, it dawned on him who it was that kept him awake.

It was a tommy-knocker who, in his earthly existence, had been one Joe Trelawney, an old Cousin Jack and hard-rock man who had gone up the flume during a gas explosion in the Chinaman's Pit. From this fellow Perkin had borrowed five dollars and the man had gone over the range before Perkin had a chance to pay him back. "That's why he's makin' a noosance o' himself," Perkin told his friends while bending his elbow at the Free Soil saloon. "He"'s worried about his goddam five bucks."

Perkin went down into the pit and there, sure enough, he heard Joe's voice coming right out of the rock, whining, "I want my sawbuck."

Perkin even got a glimpse of Joe, or rather his ghost, looking exactly as in life, except that he had shrunk to the size of a little two-foot gnome—transparent to boot.

Worse than Joe's specter was another devilish imp, the ghost of one Pat O'Brien, a shovel stiff with whom Perkin had locked horns, "pattin' him on the lip," as the saying went, over a shanty queen named Lou. Pat had gone under when the timbering had caved in on him. Pat too had become a shriveled midget manikin, tripping over his beard and, like Joe Trelawney, was a "see-through" ghoul, though, sometimes, he appeared in a more solid form. He was Perkin's special curse, leering at him from crevices, hissing, "I'll teach ye to mess around with my Lou, begorra!"

It did no good at all that Perkin tried to quiet this uncouth apparition, saying, "Lou ain't any concern of yours or mine anymore. She's messin' with every Tom, Dick, an' Harry nowadays. Why don't ye stop yer cussed pranks?"

But the mischief-making troll kept knocking ladders from under Perkin's feet, tripped him up, plagued the poor miner with rock falls, and almost managed to have him crushed under the wheels of a heavy ore cart.

On the other hand, there was the phantom woman, on foot or on her headless steed, floating before Perkin, her pale flesh glistening in the flickering beam of her "miner's friend," luring him on through endless galleries, enshrouded in her long, silver-blond hair. Perkin could make out her shapely form and sinuous limbs, but her face was veiled as by fog and mist. Perkin was consumed with longing, but whenever he stretched out his hands to touch her, the enticing ghost instantly dissolved into nothing, slipping through his fingers like a gust of cold air.

One day Perkin was drilling into a vein of auriferous ore when, to his horror, water gushing from a seam turned to blood. He put this down to a case of jitters and wild imagination, caused by excessive tippling. He dismissed the frightful vision from his mind, convincing himself that what he thought had been blood was merely water discolored by an outcrop of iron ore.

A few days later the phantom woman appeared again, motioning him to "come on." Perkin followed her through gallery after gallery into parts of the mine he had never entered before—a labyrinth of natural caves where stalactites, gleaming like giant icicles, encircled him like prison bars. The phantom suddenly turned around and faced him. The veil of fog lifted from her face, and in the light of his miner's lamp he recognized her as Sukey, a girl he had, a few years before, befriended and callously discarded. The hairs on his head stood up in terror and his legs turned to water as cold, ghostly hands caressed his cheeks and icy lips pressed themselves against his mouth. And then, in a flash, the specter vanished. In its stead appeared the dwarfish tommy-knocker that once had been the living Pat O'Brien, leering, mocking, and screeching, causing a hail of rocks and stalactites to hail down from the cave's roof upon the hapless Cornishman. Perkin fled in mortal fear, and suddenly his lamp gave out, maliciously extinguished by the evil imp. Pursued by its hellish laughter, Perkin groped in utter darkness, blindly, trying to feel his way back along dripping rock walls. He came to a dead end. He was utterly lost. He cowered in a coyote hole, a little side gallery, not knowing where to turn. Then he noticed, with mounting dread, that the air around him was "dead," that he was being enveloped by a gaseous "choke-damp." As the venomous vapors rose from the ground, his breath gave out. He panted for air; he felt himself suffocating with the tommy-knockers' mocking laughter ringing in his ears. "So this is the end," he was thinking when someone took him by the hand, leading him away. Choking and on the point of death, he let himself be carried off with prodigious speed. The air began to clear and so did his head. A tiny, distant spot of daylight showed itself at the end of a long gallery, beckoning, opening a path to deliverance. Soon Perkin found himself at the mine's entrance. He turned to thank his rescuer, a fellow miner, he thought, but it turned out to be Joe Trelawney's ghost, saying gruffly, "Better make it a tenner."

Perkin stumbled into the open, deeply inhaling the air imbued with the exhilarating scent of pine needles and wild flowers. He holed up for many weeks in his lone cabin, not going down to his diggings, deep in thought, drinking soda water instead of his usual forty-rod. He emerged, as if from hibernating, went to the mine, and stuffed ten silver dollars into the crack where Joe's spirit had first appeared to him. Next he went into town, looking for the girl named Lou, finding her at her favorite man-catching watering hole. He persuaded Lou to let him have a tintype of her still-pretty mug in return for a small bag of gold dust. He made tracks to the boneyard and placed the tintype on Pat O'Brien's grave with a heartfelt: "Ther, you old bastard, thet's the best I can do for ye. Our lovely Lou is now a bride of the multitude, n' you wouldn't want to hev anythin' to do with her, 'specially as she'd be makin' you a present in the form of a powerful dose of the pox. Well, pal, enjoy yerself wherever ye are."

After that he wrote a letter to Washoe, to a friend of Sukey's, whose name and address he remembered:

Miss Molly Ludlow,
at the Long horn Saloon,
Washoe, Nevada

Dear Miss Ludlow:

Ye mite recall me. I'm Perkin Basset, the feller usta go with Sukey. I'd deeply appreshiate it ef ye would let me know what happent to her. Pleese rite to me, care of the Silver Doler, Park City, Utah.

Yer obeedent sarvant,
Perkin Basset

After six weeks he received an answer to the effect that Sukey had died in childbirth while bringing into the world a child—namely his daughter—now five years old and called Jenny. The girl lived in Washoe's poor imitation of an orphanage.

Perkin cleaned out his cabin, put up curtains at his single window, got a second bed, bought a new pair of pants, and took the stage to Washoe. He returned to Park City with an overjoyed Jenny, adopted her legally, and found a lady, neither young nor beautiful, to move in with him, taking care of the little girl while he tried to hit pay dirt in his diggings.

Single-jacking, clicking, and hammering no longer disturbed Perkin's slumber. Tommy-knockers henceforth shunned his company. The unclad lady on her headless horse was never seen again.

It Had a Light Where Its Heart
Ought to Have Been

Somewhere in the Superstition Mountains the Lost Phantom Mine is still waiting for its discoverer. The exact location is known, and detailed maps exist, but the darn thing is—you just can't find it. Plenty of fellows have tried, drawn by stories of millions of dollars' worth of gold in that mine, but they all had to go home empty-handed. And there's another thing: the mine comes with a ghost. Actually, the ghost does not really come with the mine, but seems to be looking for it, just like everybody else.

The first one to come across it was Arizona Charlie, an old hand at prospecting. He was out camping when his mule got frightened by something and started to scream and kick and shiver. Charlie thought that maybe a bear or cougar was spooking his old mule, but there was no sign of any such critters. Charlie spent the day looking for some evidence of ore or mining, but found nothing. When it got dark, the mule started carrying on again, but this time Charlie found out what was spooking it—it was a flickering light circling around the campsite. Charlie remembered that he couldn't figure out what kind of light it was, except that it was a mighty queer one. When the light came nearer, Charlie saw that it belonged to an eight-foot-tall skeleton. The light was inside the rib cage where the heart ought to have been. The skeleton sat down for a while by the campfire, opposite Charlie, which made him feel very peculiar. It just sat there in a sort of palsy-walsy way, and then got up, waved one bony hand jauntily, and left. Charlie was hanging around for a few days more, looking for the Lost Phantom. He met the skeleton again, always at night, always with the strange light inside its rib cage. It too seemed to be looking for something, like a she-bear looking for her wayward cubs. Some nights the spook kept Charlie awake by rattling its bones, but Charlie got used to that, as the skeleton was very peaceful, meaning no harm. Whenever the rattling grew too loud, Charlie would yell at the skeleton to stop it, saying, "Hombre, you're making too much of a racket for a man to get a good night's sleep. Go and do your rattling someplace else." Then the skeleton would scamper off meekly to where Charlie could not hear it. After a while Charlie gave up on the Lost

Phantom Mine and never went back to the Superstition Mountains. So that was the end of what one could call a sort of friendship with the skeleton.

Some years later two other old-timers were prospecting for the lost mine. They were sitting by the fire, washing down their frijoles with some hot, black java, when one of them saw an eerie light flitting about like a butterfly. "What the hell is that?" he said to his partner, who told him, "It's just our fire reflected on that rock wall." But then they both saw that it was a monstrously tall skeleton with something like a miner's lamp shining through its ribs.

"Holy Moses!" said one prospector. "Let's vamoose. That thing scares the shit out of me!"

"It doesn't seem to be mad at us," said the other. "Maybe it owns the mine. Let's stick around. It may lead us to it."

"Seems to me just the opposite. I think he wants us to find it for him," said the first.

"How do you know it's a 'he'?"

"Stands to reason. What would a female skeleton be doing wandering around in this godforsaken place?" He turned to the skeleton: "Hey, you old bag of bones, let's agree, whether we find the Lost Phantom, or you do, we split half and half, though I don't know what you'd spend your share on. What do you say? Is it a deal?" The skeleton nodded, but they didn't find a trace of the mine.

Some years later a fellow from Dallas came riding along on a horse. He had a map and was sure he'd find the Lost Phantom. The moon was shining and he had just stretched out in his bedroll when his animal started neighing and trampling as if a whole wolf pack had been after it. Then the Dallas fellow heard a loud rattling, too loud for a snake. He thought it was a log of dry wood crackling in the fire, but saw that it was a huge skeleton rattling its bones with light shining out of its empty eye sockets. The Texan screamed, jumped on his horse, and lit out at a dead run, leaving all his stuff behind. Later he went to all the bars in the nearest towns, drowning his horrors in whiskey, telling everybody who would listen about the dreadful ghost skeleton.

Among these listeners were three bold men who were out for treasure, and hearing about the tall skeleton, they concluded that it had something to do with the Lost Phantom Mine. Maybe, they said, part of the mine had caved in on the ghost and it tried to get its body back to have it properly buried. For the sake of gold the three were ready to tackle any old skeleton.

"We only have to stick around that old dry-bones and he will lead us to the treasure," they told each other. So they went up into the Superstitions, and the skeleton was there all right.

"How do you do, sir?" one of them addressed the ghost. "Fine weather we've had lately."

The skeleton nodded.

"Seen anything of an ancient mine around here lately?" The skeleton shook its skull. "Well, sit down by the fire, old fellow, and warm your bones."

The skeleton did. It stuck to them, and they stuck to it. They became right friendly. The skeleton used to come and sit by the fire, listening to them swapping stories. When the men told jokes, the skeleton slapped its thighbones while its skull grinned horribly.

Sometimes it let its light shine upon a dated copy of *Playboy* magazine, leafing with rattling fingers through the dog-eared pages.

"We brought it specially for you," the men told the ghost. The skeleton started to collect firewood for the men to show his appreciation. One of the fellows, just for the heck of it, handed the specter a tin cup full of hot coffee, and he took it and dropped it as if it had burned his finger bones. The men named their strange compadre "Boney." "Hey, Boney, what do you say?" one of them shouted, "why don't you show us where your gold is buried, seeing as you don't have any use for it. Why, not even a broken-down old whore would do it with you, no matter how much money you'd give her. But we could use some of that yellow stuff all right, couldn't we?"

But Boney only shrugged his shoulders, putting up his skeleton hands as if to say, "No can do."

So they finally gave up on each other. The skeleton's still there, and so is the Lost Phantom, some place. But what good is that? I ask you.

He Ate All the Democrats of Hinsdale County

Some years ago a new cafeteria was opened at the Department of Interior in Washington. A wag gave it the name of "Packer Hall." Some people wondered who the exalted personage might be after whom the cafeteria was named. It turned out that it was Packer the Cannibal, a treasure-seeker who in 1873 had gone into the mountains with five fellow prospectors in search of gold and who had killed and eaten his companions when their food gave out. The higher-ups in the department were not amused and the cafeteria's name was quietly changed.

◆　◆　◆

It was November, and late in the season to go into the San Juans looking for the shiny yellow metal men dream of, but the six men at Chief Ouray's camp on the Uncompahgre River were consumed with gold fever. They partook of the chief's food and smoked the pipe with him. Ouray consulted his wise old men who had the gift of foretelling the future. The chief told his visitors: "Your medicine is bad. If you go into the mountains, winter and hunger will claim you. You will not come back. Instead of gold you will find death waiting for you. This medicine man here has had a vision—in it he saw five skeletons and one live fat man. It is a very bad vision. Wait until spring before you go."

Among the prospectors was Alfred Packer, a tall man, with long, dark curling hair, a dark mustache and goatee, and deep-set, shifty eyes. "We ain't a bunch of goddam red savages," said Packer. "We don't believe in sech drivel. I know these mountains. I say we can do it. The woods 're full of game an' the weather is mild. We ain't goin' to sit here on our butts, waitin' like a passel of durn fools for spring. We're a-goin' now. We aim to git rich!"

They took a vote among themselves and decided in favor of going on. They picked Packer for their guide. The names of his companions were Swan, Miller, Humphreys, Noon, and Bell. With the exception of Packer, not one of them was ever seen alive again.

It snowed and snowed. The winter was the worst in men's remembrance. Elk and deer came down from the mountains into the valleys where it was warmer and where they could find things to feed on. In January, Mrs. Charles Adams, the wife of the Indian agent, was plagued by nightmares and premonitions. Clouds of icy white fog enveloped the agency, filling the valley from end to end. For days the clouds would not lift, so people could not see the hand before their eyes. Mrs. Adams was obsessed with the thought that some place out there in the snow and mist a poor soul was lost. She imagined hearing piteous cries for help. She put up a light high up on a pole to serve as a beacon that might guide a freezing, famished wanderer to safety.

One day a wild-eyed, almost incoherent man with matted hair and beard staggered into Chief Ouray's camp. It was Packer. When asked what had become of his five companions, he cursed. He said that he had sprained an ankle and gone lame, and that his partners had gone on without him, leaving him helpless and alone in the snowbound wilderness to starve. During the following weeks it was noticed that Packer was drinking heavily, throwing a great deal of money around, and betting recklessly on games of chance. People wondered where all that money came from and how Packer had acquired a watch that one miner recognized as having belonged to

Swan. Of his five companions nothing was heard. They seemed to have simply vanished. People whispered of terrible things that had happened in the mountains and began feeling uncomfortable in Packer's presence.

In 1874 the thaw came late to the high country of Colorado, but when it finally arrived, three prospectors ventured up into the mountains in their perennial search for the elusive glittering gold. They made camp near Slumgullion Pass. Their dog chased a rabbit, but instead of returning with a bunny, it came back with a human arm between its teeth. The three men investigated and, at the spot where the dog had dug up the arm, came upon the grisly remains of four men, killed and butchered, most of the flesh stripped from their bones. Nearby they found a fifth, headless corpse. They quickly determined that these were the bodies, or what was left of them, of Packer's missing companions.

Faced with the evidence, Packer confessed, though he tried to make it appear that the killing was either done by others or in self-defense. A week after leaving Ouray, Packer said, the party had run out of food. No game could be found. They dug up roots but, as Packer explained, they were not very nutritious. After one more week the members of the party became restless, looking upon each other with a certain longing, "like castaways on a drifting boat offering up a shipmate as a sacrifice to the others." Packer, so he said, went from their camp to gather firewood and when he came back found that his partners had poleaxed Swan, because he was the eldest of the group and could not put up much resistance. The remaining four were busy cutting up the body, slicing off strips of flesh from the chest, thighs, and calves. Roasted, these were quite palatable. Packer admitted that he soon developed a fondness for chest meat, which he thought was better than breast of chicken. The killers divided among themselves Swan's belongings, including several thousand dollars.

Humphreys, Noon, Bell, and Packer next agreed among themselves that Miller should furnish the next meal, because he was young, tender, and fat. He was killed with a hatchet while stooping to collect firewood. The survivors now eyed each other with a great deal of apprehension, but men have to sleep sometime. Humphreys and Noon did not manage to stay awake and wound up in the cooking pot, but Packer pronounced them not nearly as succulent as Miller.

Packer and Bell were now alone. Calling God to witness, they made a solemn pact not to kill each other, even if they starved to death. Each had a rifle and they were hoping to find game. Their hopes were disappointed. Again they were living on a thin diet of roots. Bell, with that certain hungry glint in his eye, began to shout: "I can stand it no longer. One of us must make meat for the other, right here and now!"

Raging like a maniac, and baring his teeth like a wolf, he took a swing with his rifle butt at Packer, who parried the blow and, in return, buried his hatchet in Bell's skull. Packer gorged himself on his companion's flesh, packed up what was left of it, and stumbled on. Wading hip-deep in snow, and utterly exhausted, he spied a distant light. It came from the Ouray Agency. He had come full circle.

Packer was held for trial, but escaped. For nine and a half years "he got lost." There were rumors that he had gone to Australia, where a gold rush attracted thousands of prospectors. But nothing was really known of his whereabouts. In March of 1883 an old gold miner named Frenchy was tossing restlessly on his bed in a Fort Fetterman boardinghouse, being kept awake by particularly voracious bedbugs. Through the thin partition between his and the adjoining room, he heard the voice of a man slinging woo at a "lady of the night." Frenchy recognized the voice as belonging to none other than the long-sought "Packer the Cannibal." He at once rousted out the local sheriff, who arrested the man in question who said that his name was John Schwartze. But it was Packer all right, and he was speedily brought to trial. The Saga of Packer the Cannibal ended on a dramatic note. Sentencing Packer to death, Judge Gerry concluded with this historic and memorable pronouncement of doom:

PACKER, YAH REPUBLICAN, MAN-EATING SON OF A BITCH, THERE WERE FIVE DIMMICRATS IN HINSDALE COUNTY, AN YAH VORACIOUS BASTARD HEV EATEN 'EM ALL! I SENTENCE YAH TO BE HUNG BY THE NECK UNTIL YOU'RE DAID, DAID, DAID, AS A SOLEMN WARNIN' AGIN' REDOOCIN' THE DIMMI-CRATIC POPULATION OF THIS COUNTY. AN' MAY THE LORD HAVE MERCY, FOR I DON'T, ON YER DAD-BLAMED CANNIBAL SOUL!

◆ ◆ ◆

Packer's sentence was eventually commuted to forty years in the Canon City penitentiary. He vowed never to speak again and silently spent the next eighteen years braiding ropes and making hair bridles. Then Polly Pry, a pretty lady journalist working for the *Denver Post*, "rediscovered" the man-eater and got a good story out of him. "PACKER THE CANNIBAL REDIVIVUS!" read the headline. The *Post* started a campaign for the cannibal's release, and on January 1, 1901, Packer was pardoned to become the doorman and elevator operator for the *Denver Post,* giving those passengers, riding alone with him to the top floor, a wonderful case of the jitters. The man-eater finally went up the flume, as the miners put it, on April 24, 1907. Democrats are now in the majority in Hinsdale County.

A Golden-Haired Fellow

A miner named Nugget Nick had struck pay dirt—about five thousand dollars' worth of gold dust and nuggets. On the spur of the moment, he decided to go to town for a little spree—get soused, buck the tiger, visit the scarlet ladies. He set off as he was, mud in his ears, mud between his toes, mud in his hair. When he got to town, the first thing he saw was a barbershop with a big sign: SHAVE & HAIRCUT 25 CTS.

It occurred to him that his beard had not been trimmed in almost a year, that his face was hidden behind a veritable jungle of hair, and that his appearance could conceivably frighten the Daughters of Babylon. He entered the tonsorial parlor and told the barber: "Here's your chance to make some money. Will you cut my hair for what you can get out of my beard?

"You're crazy," said the barber, "it's two bits or vamoose."

"Suit yourself," said the miner, "but I'll pay you double if you catch all the hair you cut off my head and beard in one of them shavin' basins of yourn. Be sure to catch it all."

"It's a deal," said the barber.

When the job was done, the miner said; "Now fill this here basin with water and then watch me."

The barber did as told. Nugget Nick started sloshing the water round and round, washing every last speck of dirt out of his hair. Then he removed the hair and started panning for the yellow. Nugget Nick got thirty-one buckaroos' worth of gold out of the basin. The barber was the saddest tonsorialist in all the West.

Treasures of Various Kinds

There was a poor man named Juan living halfway between Santa Fe and Chimayo. Pobrecito! This Juan was indeed very poor —poorer than poor. His wife was a nag, telling him every day about the rich and handsome men she *could* have married, men who would have kept her in style, giving her fine things to wear, and jewels, and servants to do all the housework. Juan's son, Jesús Eulalio, was a pícaro, a no-good hombre, doing time in the calabozo for horse theft. Juan could thank his patron saint, San Juan Nepomuceno, that his Jesus was merely jailed and not hanged. And there was Pablita, Juan's daughter, who had so far forgotten herself as to have borne a child out of wedlock to that poltrón Pedro, an idler given to drink. The good padre, Fray Domínguez, had persuaded this Pedro to marry Pablita, threatening him with everlasting damnation, but what satisfaction could there be in a marriage with the fruit of their sin squalling all through the ceremony, reminding all present of this scandal. And what good was a son-in-law like Pedro, not a respectable hardworking muchacho who contributed something to the family, but a holgazán, a lie-a-bed, eating up more than his share of food and wasting time in idle chatter while hitting the bottle.

Pobre Juan! To add to his misery, his fields were small, full of rocks, insufficiently irrigated, and yielding little. His sheep suffered from blackleg; his lambs were devoured by coyotes and bobcats. His single horse had glanders and the blind staggers. His mule was vicious, waiting for an opportunity to kick Juan in the hip or groin. His sow had the lamentable habit of eating her piglets. His chickens were succumbing to parasites and refused to lay. Cutworm had gotten into Juan's beans, cornworm into his maize. There were more wiggling, voracious grubs in his orchard than apples. "Madre de Dios!" Juan cried out in despair. "What am I going to do?"

Juan's father had also been poor. He had left his son nothing but an old map, drawn on deerskin, indicating a spot where an ancient treasure might be found. Now there had always been talk about lost bonanzas and hidden eldorados. Almost every one of the older families had such a map of forgotten mines and hidden treasures, maps drawn on the skins of animals, on cowhide, on parchment, on faded paper, written in Latin, Spanish, or English, maps of the conquistadores who had ridden with Coronado, Oñate, and de Vargas, maps accidentally lost by gringo prospectors or palmed off by larcenous hucksters. Juan had not paid much attention to the map because his father, and grandfather, and great-grandfather had already gone treasure hunting with it and found nothing. But now, with hunger knocking at the door, he remembered it. Quién sabe? His father might have searched in the wrong place, or could have overlooked something, or misread the map. Might Juan not succeed where his father had failed? He had forgotten where the deerskin map had been stored and had to search long and hard for it. He found it at last at the very bottom of an old trastero filled with heaps of worthless things. He carefully unfolded the map and studied it. The treasure, according to his ancient mapa, seemed to be located somewhere in the Jemez Mountains, in or around an old mission church, destroyed by idol-worshiping indios during the great Pueblo Revolt of 1680. But of its history Juan knew nothing.

Before he set out on his quest, he invoked the help of his patron saint. He had not one but two images of his santo, two ancient bultos of faded colors and full of worm holes. One image was big and the other small. Juan concluded, not unnaturally, that the little one represented the saint's son, his niño. Juan lit a candle before his two santos, knelt down, and prayed: "Señor Santo, you see how it is. We are so poor, muy pobre. We need your help. It costs you nothing. So why not do it. I have only enough centavos to light this one small candle for you, but if you help me find the treasure, I'll light a dozen candles for you all the time. And I'll cover you and your little niño with gold leaf and build an altar for you. Do this for me, por favor, Señor San Juan Nepomuceno. It is your job to do it."

Juan said this because his special saint was martyred for refusing to break the secrecy of the confessional, which indicated to Juan that the saint was in charge of secrets, particularly secret tesoros. He took the smaller image and put it away in the trastero in which he had found his mapa.

"Señor Santo," he informed the larger bulto, "I have taken your little son away from you and you won't get him back until you let me have that treasure. So get busy, por Dios!"

After having settled matters with the santo, Juan saddled his limping horse, took the mapa, pick and shovel, a skin of wine, and an ancient muzzle-loading pistola as protection against bandidos who might rob him of his treasure if he should be lucky enough to find it. Thus, equipped, he set out for the Jemez Mountains. He had no trouble finding the ruin, but the ground around it was all torn up, telling him that there had been many treasure hunters there before him. He was not discouraged. He had prayed to San Juan Nepomuceno. They probably had prayed to some other saint. He dug, he shoveled, he gouged, he scooped out for many days—all in vain. His food was giving out, his wine was gone, his sorry nag had plucked up all the grass growing around the ruin. Juan was finally ready to give up when he noticed that one of the stone slabs that formed the ruin's floor was raised a little above the others. With great effort he was able to pry the slab loose and dig underneath it. What he found was no treasure but a grave containing a moldering skeleton turned brown with age. Juan looked at the skull and the skull looked back at Juan. Juan was thinking.

"Señor Espectro, Señor Ghost," he said at last, "I am sorry to see you lying there like this, but it happens to all of us. But, hermano, you have been lying there for a long, long time, for hundreds of years, maybe. You must know everything that happened here. I think you are guarding that treasure. I don't have to tell you that it is of no use to you in the condition you are in. It can't buy you a tortilla, a bottle of wine, or the love of a woman. I, on the other hand, have great need of this treasure. I have a nagging wife, a no-good son, a daughter who makes babies before she is married, and her child, as well as a lazy good-for-nothing son-in-law to support. My fields are poor, my beans and corn are worm-eaten. Look at my old nag here, ready to drop dead at any moment, and if she does, I have no dineros to buy another horse. Look at the rags I'm wearing. Look at the holes in my pants! I can use the treasure, you cannot. If you give it to me I will do many good things for you. I will gather up your bones and put them in a fine velvet-lined coffin with silver handles, and I will have you buried in consecrated ground right in the cemetery of the big church at Albuquerque. I will have many masses said for the saving of your soul, and I will light candles for you, not a few, but many, and not small ones either, but the biggest, tallest ones I can find. But you understand that I cannot do all this until you show me the treasure without which I can neither buy the coffin, nor the candles, nor pay for the masses so necessary to shorten your time in purgatory. You must see, compadre, that it is in your own interest to give me that treasure. For the love of God, Señor Ghost, do it!"

All at once, the grave was filled with a wondrous light, and amid sweet odors there rose from the jumble of bones a smiling, transparent spirit, dressed like a caballero of the times of El Rey Felipe, in a gold-brocaded doublet and a cartwheel of fine lace around his neck. In his hands the smiling ghost carried a chest held together with metal bands. The ghost was made up of light and air and gauzelike mist. Juan could see right through him, and when he tried to touch him he could feel nothing but air. But the chest was real and solid. It was a true miracle that a ghost made of nothing could carry such a heavy arca. The friendly ghost made a courteous bow, put the chest down in front of Juan, and smiled. Juan asked: "I do not know how to thank you, Señor Ghost, but, being on such good terms, tell me, are there women ghosts, and if there are, can you make love to them?"

The ghost looked annoyed at such impertinence and vanished in a shimmering cloud.

Juan felt around the chest. There was nothing ghostly about it. It had a lock, and stuck in it was a key. With trembling hands Juan turned it and lifted the cover. He could hardly believe his good luck as he stared at the fabulous treasure the arca contained—gold escudos, maravedis, florins, duros, caroluses, cruzeiros, doubloons, tostons, and coronas, making altogether an enormous fortune in coins. Juan sank to his knees to give thanks: "Gracias, gracias, Señor Espectro, gracias, San Juan Nepomuceno, thank you, thank you, Madre Santíssima, Lady of Light!"

Juan loaded the heavy chest on his old horse, which staggered under the burden. He gathered up the skeleton in his ragged coat, and hurried home, a most happy fellow—a muy feliz hombre. He arranged for his bag of bones a magnificent funeral, gave alms with both hands to the poor, covered his santos, both the big and the small, with gold leaf, and invited everybody he knew, and some he did not know, to a big fiesta.

Juan had a neighbor, a certain Don Fernando. He was a well-to-do rancher, but mean-spirited, miserly, and covetous. He always made fun of Juan, laughed at his ragged clothes, at his sorry-looking horse, and made insulting remarks about Pablita, who, he said, had given birth too early and married too late. Juan's good fortune kept Don Fernando awake at night with envy. A no-account pauper like Juan, in Don Fernando's opinion, did not deserve to have found so rich a treasure. What did such a low fellow know about money? He would only squander it. But a caballero like himself would know so much better what to do with such a tesoro. Where there was one chest of gold there might be another. Juan had made no secret of how and where he had found his. And so Don Fernando too saddled his horse, a sleek and blooded animal, took pick and shovel, a flask of the finest amontillado, and his pair of silver-handled pistols, and rode off to the Jemez Mountains.

He had no trouble finding the ruin, and he too discerned on its stone floor a slab that was slightly out of position. He pried it loose and underneath also found a grave containing a skeleton. Playfully, he picked up the skull, tossing it from hand to hand.

"You little son of the devil," he addressed the brittle cranium. "For certain you have been a bandito sitting on your ill-gotten gains. You do not deserve them. They belong to the finder, namely to me! Don't make any fuss! Hand them over and be quick about it! I don't want to waste much time on you."

He sat there, expectantly, on what had once been a column. After a little while a mist arose from the grave and from it rose the shape of a spectral caballero in old-fashioned attire, similar to, but not, the one Juan had buried. This ghost too was made of nothing but air, and also carried a heavy chest.

"It's about time," said Don Fernando to the apparition. "Don't stand there like a fool. Give me the chest!"

The ghost obeyed, grinning horribly. "Now go," said Don Fernando, "you are no longer wanted. Get lost. Vamoose!"

The ghost laughed in a most unnatural hair-raising manner and vanished without a trace.

"Good riddance," said Don Fernando. "Now let's see what we've got." Impatiently, he pried open the lid and groped in it for the expected gold coins. Then he began to curse in the vilest, most shameful way. The chest contained no treasure but . . . but what? Ah, it would be indelicate to tell you.

The Missing Chest

About one hundred miles southwest of Santa Fe lies the sleepy village of Manzano, at the time of the events to be described a jumble of low adobe buildings baking in the sun, exclusively inhabited by Spanish-speaking folks. Time meant little in Manzano then, at least time as conceived by gringo historians. The year in which it all happened is therefore undetermined. It happened "some time ago," or "long, long ago," or "when grandmother was a young girl." An educated guess can be made from the tradition that it happened before the railroad came to New Mexico and before the first Anglo settled in the vicinity of Manzano. Something can also be deduced from the appearance of the mysterious stranger who, like an alien from another world, one day showed up in the village plaza. He wore, all agreed, an elegant knee-length frock coat resembling the one President Lincoln wore. It was remembered by the earliest tellers of this story only because it was held together in front by a long row of buttons—not ordinary ones, but buttons made of twenty-peso gold pieces, something that stuck in the mind of the Manzano folks. The stranger also wore a stovepipe hat, never before seen in this part of the country. In view of this attire one may say with some confidence that the mysterious event took place some time between 1845 and 1870.

The stranger arrived in a handsome light carriage drawn by a team of mules, the finest, sleekest mules ever seen. He was a most imposing personage, portly and over six feet tall, and endowed with a stentorian voice that could be heard at a great distance. Of his face it was only remembered that it was dominated by a mouth engagingly smiling from ear to ear and displaying an extraordinary set of brilliantly gleaming teeth. He was an exceedingly cheerful, polite, back-slapping individual who called everybody "amigo" and "compadre" in spite of being, obviously, a very important caballero, a rico hombre. Of his name there are many versions. Suffice it to say that he was Don So-and-so from the town of Chihuahua in Mexico, come on a mission of utmost importance.

The gold-buttoned stranger addressed the folks who, being curious, had crowded around him.

"I have come, amigos," he explained, "because your wonderful town of Manzano is a pearl among cities, full of history, a town of holy martyrs. Yes, my good people, I have come to admire and venerate your sacred church with its cloister and mission, where so many poor indios were instructed in the faith and brought to Christ, and so many holy padres were slain by savage idolators, martyrs to the only true religion."

They showed him the tiny humble morada put up by the Brothers of Light, also known as Penitentes. "No, no, compadres," the stranger protested. "I mean the big church, built of stone, erected by the padres in the days of King Philip."

"There is no such church here, señor," the people informed him. "Maybe you mean the missions of Quarai and Abó, not far from here, but they are in ruins."

"I assure you, caballeros, that there was such a church here, in Manzano," and with that he drew from his ample pockets an ancient parchment brittle and yellowed with age, displaying a map of Manzano, showing the location of a large mission church with cloisters, a cemetery, outbuildings, and orchards.

"Maybe the godless savages destroyed this church when they murdered the poor friars. Maybe its ruins lie buried somewhere around here. For the glory of God, compadres, we must find it! Follow me!"

With map in hand, the man from Chihuahua paced off a hundred steps toward the east, starting at the stump of a centuries-old tree. He stopped at the weed-covered remains of an ancient well and measured some seventy steps to the south, arriving at the remnants of a round stone tower which long ago had served the early settlers as a refuge from Apache raiders. From there, consulting his map again, he took some two dozen steps to the east, coming to a mound of ancient potsherds, among them a piece of glass from a Spanish drinking vessel that bore the date of its manufacture—1703.

"Dig here, amigos," he cried, "dig here, por la gloria de la Virgen! You will find the church underneath all this dirt and rubble. It will become a center of worship. Pilgrims will come from everywhere to worship here. It will make all of you rich, compadres of mine. When we find it, I will give the biggest fiesta ever held in Nueva México, I promise. I will bear all expenses, for the glory of God and of the Holy Church. Get your picks and shovels, my friends, and dig!"

The good people of Manzano went at it with a vengeance, spurred on by the gold-button man, fired with visions of fame, riches, and the prospect of a great fiesta. The map turned out to be truly excellent, for, after digging for only one hour, the men discovered the corner of a large building, surely a church, and a short while later laid bare much of its flagstone floor. In the late afternoon they uncovered a finely carved altar and, amid the surrounding rubble, the only slightly damaged statue of San Francisco.

The stranger was weeping for joy. "We found it, amigos, just as I told you!" he cried. "On your knees, my friends! Let us pray!"

After they all had done so, the mysterious visitor made a solemn speech: "Compadres, look here, at the dark red spots on these stones —blood of your own ancestors who helped the padres building this mission. Think of it. Here is the very ground upon which they died for their faith at the hands of idol-worshiping brujos, of pitiless sorcerers. Now, at last, we can honor them by rebuilding this church! Glory to God and all the saints! Glory to Christ and the Virgin. Glory to you, amigos, as the descendants of holy martyrs! I shall bear all the costs. And, as I promised, tomorrow we celebrate by having a great fiesta with music and dance. I will purchase from some of you the four fattest sheep and two fattest pigs, and a whole ox, if someone among you should have such a one for sale. And there will be enough aguardiente to drink for everybody. Now go and rest from your labors!"

The fiesta was a truly great event. The ox was turning on a gigantic spit. Everywhere bubbling kettles of chili stew, full of succulent chunks of mutton, and equally large bowls of carne adobada, overflowing with delicious morsels of tender pork, were waiting for customers. After the feast came the baile, the dance. The overgenerous stranger had hired musicians from the surrounding countryside—fiddlers, harpists, guitarists, even a trumpeter, all making a glorious noise that made the feet of even the oldest folks dance. And there was, as promised, liquid refreshment enough to float a battleship. The stranger's carriage contained, a wonderful, sheer inexhaustible supply of kegs and bottles of aguardiente, tequila, and original mescal de Oaxaca con su propio gusano, and the caballero from Chihuahua ladled it out by the gourdful.

"Drink, my friends, and be happy," he encouraged the revelers, "don't be shy. Señoras y señoritas, this mescal is so smooth, so mild, so innocent that even you can imbibe it without fear or hesitation."

All night long the charming stranger saw to it that everybody's glass, cup, or gourd remained always filled to the brim. And so the good people of Manzano got muy borracho, muy ebrio, until they all

passed out. It was high noon when they finally came to. They rubbed their eyes, cleared their throats, got up on unsteady legs, yawned, stretched, and looked around. Someone noticed that the open-handed stranger was nowhere to be seen.

"His team of mules and his wagon are gone too," one of the campesinos observed.

An old lady added, "Surely, he went to the ruin of the church to pray at the altar."

The whole village went to see whether she was right, but the rico hombre and his wagon were not there either. What they found was a big hole, or rather a rectangular opening, very much like a freshly dug grave, that had not been there when they finished excavating the day before. Whoever had made the big hole had left a shovel lying next to it, also the stub of a cigarillo, the kind they had seen the kindly stranger smoke incessantly. They peered into the hole. It was empty, except for some decaying fragments of wood, the largest of them showing signs of having been carved.

The good people of Manzano scratched their heads and looked at each other. They cried out in unison: "Un tesoro! It was a treasure chest. That is what he came for. By right it belonged to us. It was *our* treasure! He has robbed us!"

Some men mounted their horses to go after him. They rode to the great Socorro Road leading down to El Paso and Chihuahua. Some rode south and others rode north, toward Albuquerque. The tracks of his team and wagon were lost among many other tracks and, in any case, he had too much of a head start on them. The whole affair had, however, whetted their appetites for treasure. Many Manzano folks hurried to all the church ruins in the area, to Quarai, to Abó, to Gran Quivira, to every spot showing the merest traces of ancient habitation, tearing up the earth in a frenzied, futile search for treasures. They never found anything worth a single centavo.

The mystery of the stranger with the gold buttons was never solved. Had there really been a chest? And, if so, what had it contained? No one will ever know. That is the Great Lost Treasure of Manzano Mystery, the mystery of the chest that was not there.

CHAPTER 8

Git Along, Little Dogies

Only in America could a cowherd be made into a romantic hero, celebrated in film and literature, subject of innumerable novels, songs, and poems, finding his apotheosis as a gaudily dressed, guitar-picking yodeler. Translate "cowboy" into any other language—garçon de vache or Kuhjunge—and you go immediately from the sublime to the ridiculous. Actually, even in America "cowboy" was originally a term of derision. During the War of Independence, a band of Tory marauders were known as cowboys, not because they were cattle herders, but because they stole cows. Some historians say that this was the first time the word "cowboy" appeared in our language.

The real-life cowboy, a vanishing species, was a bowlegged, hardworking saddlestiff, sometimes up to his ankles in manure, branding and castrating the little dogies—not a very romantic occupation. A Casanova our cowboy was decidedly not. It has been said that the only two things the typical cowhand feared was being afoot or finding himself in the presence of a decent woman. Cowboys were not the stuff of which husbands are made. A fellow who, on the average, made thirty dollars a month and spent 90 percent of his time out on the range was not what most girls were looking for. The formula for a good "oater" has always been "plenty of action, plenty of close-ups of a pet pony, and only one minute of kissing at the very end." And indeed, cowboys were most often depicted as being in love with their favorite cayuse rather than with their lady friend. This is supported by headstones such as these, which can be found in the cow country:

HERE LIES
"I'M HERE"

The Very Best of Cow Ponies,
A Gallant Little Gentleman.

HERE LIES
"WHAT NEXT"

He had the Body of a Horse,
The Spirit of a Knight, and
The Devotion of the Man
Who Erected this stone.

Few monuments exist extolling in such lyrical terms the virtues of cowhands' wives or sweethearts who had "gone over the range." One nasty fellow said that the cowboy realized himself with a pistol rather than with his pecker, but the pistol bit has also been overdone. Many cowboys did not pack guns, many who did never fired a shot in anger, and those few who used them on another human often missed. In the words of William Savage: "For the matter of a week, or per chance two—it depends on how fast his money melts—in these fashions will our gentleman of cows engage his hours and expand himself: He will make a deal of noise, drink a deal of whiskey, acquire a deal of what he calls 'action'; but he harms nobody, and, in a town toughened to his racket and which needs and gets his money, disturbs nobody."

The way in which romance has transformed the hardworking buckaroo into the Sir Galahad of the Open Range can be best seen in the typical John Wayne–style Western in which our hero is busy drilling holes into Injuns and bad hombres, smashing up saloons, and rescuing damsels in distress, but never, never, never doing what he is supposed to—working the cattle.

And yet the gallant, carefree cowboy makes a dashing figure as, tall in the saddle and silhouetted against the western sunset, he rides forth to endless new adventures.

The Saga of Pecos Bill

Pecos Bill wasn't a man of flesh and blood. He was an idea, a vision, a cowboy demigod. His voice broke while still in his mammy's womb and his first words upon emergin' were "Gimme a drink." He was born with a full set of teeth, a full head of red hair, and seven bristly hairs on his chest. Three days after he was born, he started chawin' 'baccer. He was weaned on panther piss, made in his pappy's portable still from a gallon of Pecos River water (hence his nickname), a gallon of pure, double-twisted and distilled white lightnin', a cupful of gunpowder for seasonin', and three rattlesnake heads for taste. At the age of three he was already a hell of a poker player.

It was precisely on his third birthday that Bill's pappy went to stake out a claim in the Texas Panhandle. He'd hitched up a team of oxen to their prairie schooner, tied a milch cow and a horse to the rear end, and stowed a cage with a dozen chickens and a barrel of his own brand of popskull someplace in the wagon. He put his children, all nineteen of 'em, among them a set of quintuplets, in the rear where they couldn't interfere with the drivin'. Bill was the youngest and he sat farthest back. Now, after crossin' the Pecos River, jest havin' reached the far bank, the left front wheel hit a big rock and the jolt chucked li'l Bill clear out of the wagon and into the river. (That's still another reason for Pecos Bill's moniker.) Well, with so many younguns an' all the squallin' and noise they made, Bill wasn't missed. In the evenin', when the whole gang of them made camp, their pappy rounded them up to count heads. He found out that they were one head short.

"Bill's jest a wee nipper," said his mammy, "nary six feet tall. We shorely had him around yestiddy. Mebbe we oughta go back and look for him?"

"Naw, he's all of three years old," said Bill's daddy, "old 'nuff to fend for hisself. He'll play his hand as it's been dealt to him. I ain't worryin' none."

"Waal, iff'n you say so," answered his wife.

Now, what happened to Bill was this: He crawled out of the river, spat out a dozen or so fingerlin's, and crawled off into the chaparral, where he found himself face-to-face with an ancient gray-haired grandpappy coyote by the name of Methuselah, on account of his age and wisdom.

"Here, little doggie, nice little doggie," said Bill.

"Doggie, hell!" said Methuselah. "I ain't no goddam dog. I'm a coyote, boy! Waal, you're like a lost calf a-lookin' for his mammy's teats. I reckon I've been dealt the hand to take care of you. Come along."

So that granddaddy coyote took Bill to where the whole pack of 'em was scratchin' themselves and chawin' on bones and introduced him all around. Methuselah took Bill to a lady coyote sucklin' two pups. "Thar's your chuckwagon," he told Bill. "Thar's nipples enough for one more."

"Heck," said Bill, "I never tech the stuff. I'd rather have whiskey."

Well, Bill settled in with the coyotes and in two shakes of a lamb's tail plumb forgot that he was human, being convinced that he was a coyote too.

In this new family of his Bill was known as "No Tail" for obvious reasons. Old Methuselah taught him everything a self-respecting coyote ought to know—how to catch a rabbit, how to lift his right leg to pee, how to howl at the moon. In no time at all Bill became the best moon howler in the pack. Methuselah also showed him how to run down a deer and told him to avoid skunks for the sake of his nose. The only varmint givin' Bill any trouble at all was the Wowser, a fearful critter sired by the Great Oligocene Saber-toothed Tiger of the West upon the Giant Fur-covered Catfish of the Big Muddy. This oversized monster had a tail like a fish, the body of a lion, and teeth like a chain saw. Its voice was thunder, its breath fire. Its glance could strike an ordinary feller dumb. Waal, li'l Bill fought the Wowser for a full day. In the end Bill whupped the varmint and knocked him down for the count. As the Wowser was lyin' senseless on the ground, Bill disdainfully lifted his leg over him and let him have it while the delighted coyotes whooped it up. Bill was now the champeen and top dog among the pack. A winsome young blondish coyote lass was makin' eyes at Bill, shakin' her rump at him, sayin', "It so happens that I'm in heat and willin'. How about it?"

Nobody knows what would've happened if fate hadn't interfered. It would've been a prime case of this here miscegenation, and god knows how the pups would've turned out, if a cowboy named Slim hadn't come gallopin' in at a dead run, a-shoutin' and a-shootin' his six-gun scatterin' the coyotes before him like chaff in the wind. Young Bill didn't run away like the others. He was busy with his freshly killed grizzly, tearin' off its legs and gnawin' on the paws.

"What in hell are you doin' mother-nakkid among those varmints and eatin' yer meat raw?" Slim wanted to know.

Bill had never seen human bein's since he fell off his pappy's wagon. He had plumb forgot what they looked like. He stood his ground, growlin' and barin' his teeth.

"Stop that tomfoolery," said Slim. "It ain't human."

"I ain't human," answered Bill. "I'm a coyote. My name's No Tail."

"You're ramsquaddled with loco weed. You ain't a coyote. You're human like me."

"You're a damn liar! Am I not the champeen moon howler? Don't I lift my right leg to pee? Hain't I got fleas?"

"Ev'rybody's got fleas. I got fleas. If you're a coyote, whar's your tail? Coyotes got tails."

"It was bitten off by a painter when I was a baby, Granddaddy Methuselah told me."

"You're a feather-headed fool. Come along. I'll show you somepin."

Slim took Bill to the nearest creek: "Look in the water. Whad-daya see?"

Bill looked at their reflections in the water. He was stupefied. "I'll be danged!" he exclaimed. "Leapin' lizards! I'm a friggin' human. I reckon I've got no choice but to jine up with your kind."

Bill mounted up behind Slim and they rode off in the gen'ral direction of civilization. Thus Bill rejoined the human race.

Pecos Bill got along well among the two-leggeds. Folks took to him, though they sometimes wondered about him when he took off all his clothes and hunkered down on his haunches, howling at the moon like a coyote. He turned out to be a born cowboy, better than the best. Fust thing he did was get himself a hoss. As he warn't an ordinary fellow, so his hoss warn't an ordinary pony. He raised him from a colt on a diet of strychnine juice, baked tarantulas, and bob

wire. That made him grow fast, but it also made him ornery. He grew
into a boomerang stallion, a can't-be-rode hoss, a one-man bronco.
Bill was the only one who could ride him. His name was Widow-
Maker 'cause nobody who ever tried to ride him survived the experience, except Bill's friend Slim. Slim was a one-A bronc buster and
Bill let him try. Slim got on and Widow-Maker boiled over, his ears
back, sidewindin', jackknifin', sunfishin', and chinnin' the moon. It
was a real whing-ding. Widow-Maker bucked Slim off, cat-backed
him all the way from the Panhandle to the top of Pike's Peak. He
would've froze and starved to death up there if Bill hadn't fetched
him back with his five-hundred-mile-long lasso. "Your hoss has a
bellyful of bedsprings," was all Slim had to say.

Bill was always mounted, never afoot 'xcept when he was haulin'
supplies in his buckboard. On those occasions he hitched a grizzly
bear and a saber-toothed tiger to his wagon, usin' a live twelve-foot
diamondback rattler for a whip. Talkin' of snakes, one day Pecos was
ridin' through Raton Pass when he came up against the Nueva Mexico Cascabela Grande, an outsized rattler, half a mile long, with yard-
long fangs, which amused itself by scarin' travelers out of tryin' to
use the pass.

"Git out of my way," Pecos told the sarpent. He had learned to
talk rattlesnake language from the coyotes.

"Make me!" said the Cascabela Grande.

To have a fair fight, Bill let the snake have three first bites. Then he let his wolf loose. First he yanked all the rattler's fangs out and then he whirled it round and round, the whole half mile of it, forming loops and straight lines, curlin' it around hills and tall trees, and that gave Bill the idea of calf ropin'. He invented it. Nobody had ever done it afore him. He was always amusin' himself with his reata. When a mountain got in his way, he jest threw a loop over it and drug it to one side. He roped himself a tornado and spurred it along from Denver all the way to Austin. When the tornado couldn't buck Bill off, it turned itself into rain and dripped away from under him. Bill shinnied down some thirty thousand feet on a streak of lightnin' and came down so hard on his ass that it had calluses like sheet iron from then on till to the end of his days. Thus he became the all-time champeen roper of the West.

One day Bill ran into his pappy. He didn't recognize him, but his daddy recognized Bill. "Son," he said, "by yore brand I know you for my young-one. I'm yore pa!" Bill was still a mite frothy over his parents not havin' gone lookin' for him arter he fell out of their prairie schooner, but he was happy, all the same, to be reunited with his family after all that time.

When they arrived at his folks' ranch, they surprised his mammy sweepin' a bunch of some forty howlin', tommyhawk-swingin' 'Paches out of her backyard with a broom. She was a hardy old lady whom Bill could admire. His pappy owned a spread of about a million acres on which he ran some fifty thousand cattle.

"You call that a ranch?" commented Bill. He staked out all Texas for a bigger ranch and fenced in New Mexico for a calf pasture. He built for himself, his pappy and mammy, and all his many brothers and sisters a house so big that he needed a relay of horses to get from the front door to the back door. He had to fence in his considerable spread. He did it all alone. He rounded up a million badgers, and a million gophers, and a million prairie dogs to dig the holes for his fence posts, somethin' those critters like to do anyhow. Once during a long dry spell he dug a deep trench and diverted into it most of the Gulf of Mexico. His ditch became known as the Rio Grande. From then on he never lacked water.

Bill's pappy had a large crew of buckaroos ramrodded by a feller called Hellfire Jake. Hellfire was ten feet tall, had hands the size of children's coffins, and had seven Colts .44 and a dozen large bowie knives stuck in his belt. Bill caught himself the biggest mountain lion he could find, put a saddle on the critter, and rode over to where his pappy's vaqueros were sittin' around the chuck wagon. Some feller offered him a king-sized plate of pork and beans but he waved it aside as no fit chow for a grown man. He fixed himself a meal of live horny toads, gila monsters, and scorpions, with a barbed wire salad on the side, washing it all down with a gallon of boilin' coffee fortified with three pounds of wolf pizen. After he was done, he wiped his mouth with prickly-pear cactus and inquired, "Who's the boss around here?"

Hellfire got up and said: "I was, but you be."

Like any good cowpuncher, Pecos Bill was afraid of only two things—a decent woman and to be seen afoot. He spent a good deal of dineros, though, on the soiled doves of the prairie and was a frequent, and welcome, guest in a hundred cathouses, from the Pecos to the Powder. But when he finally fell for a "good" woman, he fell hard. Her name was Slue-Foot Sue and she was every bit as red-headed as Bill. She was a first-class horsewoman and Bill was smitten when he saw her bareback astride the Great Fur-bearin' Rio Grande Catfish, which was twice as big as a whale. Sue was beautiful. She had green eyes and plenty of wood by the woodpile, front and back. You could span her waist with one hand, but couldn't set her down in a tub. Bill was crazy about her wondrous hourglass figure. He moseyed up to her and planted a big juicy kiss on her ruby red lips, sayin': "I'm Pecos Bill and you're the heifer for me. I'll put my brand on you."

They got hitched, but their love had a sad end. The morning after their wedding night Sue asked Bill for a favor: "Let me ride your Widow-Maker. I can handle him."

Here's whar Bill made his big mistake. He couldn't say no to Sue. Widow-Maker tossed her so high that she bumped into the moon and broke her neck.

After that, Bill took to drinking. As an infant, he had been reared on bumblebee whiskey—the drink with a sting. That was too tame for him now. He needed stronger stuff. No liquid refreshment was powerful enough to fill his need. One evenin' he came howlin' into the Bucket of Blood, in Virginia City. He told the bardog: "I want a man's drink, not a tenderfoot's tipple!" The bardog knew jest what Bill wanted. He had served him before. So he mixed Ole Pecos a cocktail of strychnine, wormwood, mashed blackwidow spider, gunpowder, fine-chopped chili peppers, snake venom, shredded locoweed, and tarantula juice. Bill spit it out, all over the bardog's counter.

"You call this swill a drink!" he roared. This is fit only for a
Yankee schoolmarm! I want a *real* drink!"

A miner sittin' next to him tried to be helpful. He filled a huge
beaker with bang-juice—that is, nitroglycerine—sayin', "Hyar, Bill,
try this for a kick."

Bill emptied the beaker with one mighty swallow. His eyes spar-
kled. He smacked his lips: "Now this is a hoss of a diff'rent color!
This here is what I call a *real* drink! Fill'er up!" The miner did. Bill
took another swig. There was a terrific explosion. When the dust
settled, there were Bill's pants still standin' upright, tucked into his
boots, but of Bill himself not a trace could be found. He had plumb
vanished, taken the Big Jump in a blaze of glory, gone to the Big
Roundup in the Sky. But some folks could never accept this.

"Bill didn't blow up into smithereens, into tiny pieces so small
you couldn't see them with a magnifyin' glass," they said. "He ran
into an eastern dude with gold-painted boots, a ten-foot-high velvet
Stetson, and chaps as big as the sails from a boat. The dude tried
playin' cowboy by chawin' 'baccer and was dribbling the ambeer all
over his fancy embroidered vest. Ole Pecos Bill watched it and jest
laughed hisself to death."

The Taming of Pecos Bill's Gal Sue

Pecos Bill was born in the middle of a big storm, amid thunder
and lightning. He was different from his brothers and sisters,
emerging from the womb with hair on his chest and a big boner. He
was weaned on red likker and panther piss. He was raised on bear
meat and mountain oysters sprinkled with strychnine. The day after
Bill's birth was clear and the sun was shining. Ole Man and his whole
gang were camping out, feasting on bobcat-liver pudding and scor-
pion salad when all of a sudden the sky darkened, turning day into
night. At the same time, the air was filled with a tremendous hum,
as from a hundred railroad engines. The din made the earth tremble
and the cows stampede.

"By Ned!" Ole Man shouted. "It's a swarm of them cussed monsterquitoes. Doggone, Ole Woman, get me the big kettle!"

Ole Woman went over to the wagon to fetch the outsized kettle they used for rendering lard. She covered little Bill, who was playing in the sand, with this huge iron pot to protect the newborn from the ferocious, bloodsucking giant monsterquitoes. She also put in a chopping ax for Billy to use in case of need. She didn't notice the big coon-tailed rattler also crawling under the kettle to get away from the ferocious insects. It was so dark she had to light up her lamp to do all this. The rest of them crawled into their prairie schooner, covering themselves as best they could.

Well, the monsterquitoes smelled that tender flesh and blood of the newborn baby and started diving on the big kettle. So powerful were these pesky critters that their stingers went right through the kettle's iron walls, but little Bill knew just what to do. As soon as one of the nippers penetrated through the kettle wall, he chopped it off with his ax. The monster insects then lifted off the kettle but found that they still could not get at his rich sweet blood, because their stingers were gone. They set up a big wailing and howling and flew off. Ole Man and Ole Woman found Billy sitting on the ground, playing with the coon-tailed snake. Billy was giggling. The rattler struck again and again, but the snake venom was too weak to cause even a slight rash on Billy. Ole Man killed and skinned the twelve-foot varmint and Ole Woman fried up a big dish of snake meat. With the skin Ole Man made himself a handsome hatband. Ole Man and Ole Woman claimed a hundred acres, built themselves a sod house, cleared some land, and began farming. One day when Bill was one year old and the whole gang of them was outdoors doing one thing or another, Bill was left alone in the sodhouse where he cut his teeth on a bowie knife. Suddenly, a loud roaring, growling, and screaming came from the cabin.

"What's that?" said Ole Woman.

"Nuthin'," said Ole Man, "Billy is jest worryin' a grizzly who got in thar. I can't help that varmint none. That b'ar has to fend fur hisself."

Bill strangled the bear with his bare hands and had nary a scratch. When the folks got to him, he had already cut up the grizzly into steaks with his bowie knife. For a few weeks they dined on bear stew, bear soup, bear pudding, bear lights and liver, and bear sausage. They were glad when it was gone and they could eat something else than just bear.

When Bill was three years old, he played by the Pecos River, fell in, and was carried away by a flood. He was swept downriver for some ten miles. He was sailing along, close to the shore, when a big coyote leaned over the embankment, grabbed him by the scruff and so saved his life. Her name was Granny, because she was female and a grand-mother many times over. She was the boss lady of the pack and took a liking to Bill, adopting him into the tribe. It didn't take long for Bill to become the pack's chief. He quickly forgot that he was human. He thought that he was a coyote. He took on coyote ways. He tore around on all fours hunting rabbits, prairie dogs, gophers, and mice. He howled at the moon with the best of them. He had a coyote gal to cuddle with.

When Bill had been swept away by the flood, Ole Man and Ole Woman had been busy with the other twelve younguns—too busy to miss him. A day later Ole Man was counting noses. "Whar in tarna-tion is Billy?" he said. "That boy's always lost."

"My darlin' Billy is gone an' lost," said Ole Woman "Oh, what's become of my Billy Boy?"

"Don't git yerself all riled up," Ole Man told her. "He's all of three years, old enough to fend fur hisself."

"Iffen you say so," said Ole Woman. When they thought of him, which wasn't often, Ole Man and Ole Woman called their lost son Pecos Bill, because it was the Pecos River that had carried him off. That's how Bill got his nickname.

Bill lived with the coyotes for seven long years. One fine morning he went down to the river to quench his thirst. There was somebody there before him, the strangest living thing he had ever seen. The weird creature was walking on two legs. One of its cheeks was swollen and brown juice kept dripping from its mouth. Something monstrous was attached to the top of its head and around its neck hung a bright red flap of what had to be part of its skin. Its fur was exceedingly strange too—blue over its legs and blue-and-white-checkered all over its upper body, even the forelegs. Its feet were horrible to behold, hairless and leathery, with spurs like a wild turkey's at the heels, shiny and glittering, making a tinkling sound whenever the creature moved.

"What in hell are you a-doin', boy?" the creature said to Bill, "mother-nakkid an' runnin' around on all fours?"

"I'm a coyote," answered Bill. "Coyotes walk on all fours. I'm naked because I have no fur. It's a birth defect. I can't help it. You shouldn't rub it in."

"Stop pulling my leg, boy," said the creature. "You ain't a coyote. You are a man like myself."

"No!" said Bill. "I ain't."

"Look at your reflection in the water, you darn fool," said the creature.

Bill looked and got the shock of his life. He looked like the creature, not like a coyote. In this way Bill found out that he was no coyote but a man.

"What's your name, boy?" asked the man.

"Bill, I think. I remember somebody at some time calling me that. What's yourn?"

"Snaggletooth Charlie is my moniker."

"Well, Charlie, since I turn out to be a man, I'll jine up with you to live among humans." With that, Bill got on his pet grizzly, using his pet rattlesnake like a whip. "That's a funny pony you're ridin'," commented Snaggletooth.

Bill followed Snaggletooth to his cattle camp to meet Bowlegs Jim and Big Ears Dick and the other cattle herders. He was also introduced to Cowchip Kate, Snaggletooth's girl.

His new friends were called herders, not cowboys. Cowboys hadn't been invented yet. It was Pecos Bill who invented them. It happened this way: Bill asked the fellows, "How do you catch them steers and cows?"

"Well," they said, "we take a rope, and make it into a loop, and lay it on the ground, and put a lump of salt in the middle. Cattle are crazy about salt. Then, when they step into the noose to lick up the salt, we pull the rope and catch them in the loop, one at a time."

"That seems to be a poor way of doin' it," said Bill, "and what then?"

"Then we drag 'em into the barn, into the stable."

"Why do you do things in sech a dumb way? Why don't yer let 'em run free, feed on all that prairie grass?"

"They'll scatter over the whole countryside. They can outrun us. We could never catch 'em again."

"There must be a better way than that," said Bill. "Let me be by myself for a while and think of somethin'."

Bill went out into the prairie. He caught himself a mustang for riding. Then he made himself a long rawhide rope and put a loop into it. Then he practiced catching cows with his rawhide rope. When he had got the hang of it, he returned to camp. He showed his new friends how to rope cattle on horseback.

"Now this here," he told them, "I call a 'lasso,' an' what we're a-doin' is 'roping.' "

Pecos Bill taught them everything. He taught them how to get the whole herd together into one bunch. "Let's call this a roundup," he said. He then invented a gadget with which he could mark the cattle to identify which outfit the animals belonged to. He made a big fire and in it heated up his new gadget. "That's a brandin' iron," he explained, "an' now we're a-goin' to do some brandin'." After they had done this, Bill told them, "Let's see who's the best bronco rider in this bunch." So they competed against each other in bronc busting and fancy riding. Naturally, Bill won. "This was a rodeo," he said, "and now you are no longer herders. From now on, you're *cowboys!*" In this way Pecos Bill, on the spur of the moment, invented the American cowboy.

Bill, as you can imagine, was very popular with the girls. He had used them up at a prodigious rate, but not until he met sweet Slue-foot Sue did he fall for one. Sue was very pretty, and spunky and great fun, but she was very bossy. In any kind of relationship she wanted to wear the chaps. If Bill told her not to do a thing, she was sure to do it. If he told her to do something, she would not do it even for a million. So there was a problem. On the morning after their wedding he told her not to go near the river at a spot where it rushed through a narrow canyon, ending at a waterfall with a hundred-foot drop. Naturally, that's exactly where she went for a swim. Bill saw her being carried away by the swift current. Quick as a flash, he got out his lasso and jumped on the back of the Great Pecos Catfish, which was twelve feet long and a lot faster than the current. "Yippie-tie-hie-oooh!" yelled Bill, "Come on, Cat! Let's get her afore she gits to the falls!" After an exciting chase downriver Bill managed to get his rope over Sue just as she was about to go over the edge. He sat her before him on the Great Pecos Catfish, which swam upriver as fast as if it was swimming with the stream. Safely ashore again, Bill told Sue, "Never do this again!" "Maybe I won't," answered Sue.

Now the day after, Sue got it into her mind to go out riding while Bill was busy herding cows. "That's fine by me, my pretty li'l coy-ote," said Bill, "only never go over thar to them blue mountains younder, 'cause that's Apache country." (Bill loved his Sue so much that he called her his pretty little coyote, and whenever there was a full moon, he sat down before her window and howled. It was a throwback to his days as a coyote.)

Naturally, that's exactly where Sue went riding—in the Blue

Mountains. It was not long before she had plenty of company—fully a hundred Mescaleros painted for war. Again it was a case of Pecos Bill to the rescue. He came riding up like a storm, twirling his lariat, and he roped all those hundred Apaches into one loop, dragging the whole bunch of them, at a dead run, through about ten miles of prickly pear and chaparral until they cried "Uncle."

"You all better behave yerselves from now on!" Bill told those Mescaleros, and they swore a solemn oath never to bother Sue or anyone else from Bill's ranch again.

Bill had a horse called Widow-Maker. It was sure death for anyone but Bill trying to ride him. Bill told Sue: "Sluefoot, my purty li'l coyote, never, never git on Widder-Maker. He'd break yore neck fer sure!" And what did Sue do on the third day after their wedding? You guessed it. She jumped on Widow-Maker's back, digging her spurs into his flanks. Widow-Maker didn't take it kindly. He catbacked, skydived, blowed the plug, sunfished, warped his backbone, jackknifed and, finally, chinned the moon, bucking Sue right out of the atmosphere into space.

Now Sue always wore her fanciest outfit when she went out riding, trying to make an impression on the menfolks. So she had put on her very chic dress with an enormous bustle made of whalebone and horsehair. When she came down to earth out of space, she landed

hard on her fanny and bounced right back again, and again, and again. She tried to hold on to one of the moon's horns, but couldn't do it. She kept coming down and bouncing back, higher and higher and higher, while Bill sat on a fence, chomping on a chaw of 'baccer, grinning from ear to ear. "Help, Help! Billy, save me!" Sue screamed. But Bill just sat there, twirling his thumbs, doing nothing.

Finally, Sue bounced back so high she landed on the moon, plumb in the middle. She kept rocking back and forth up there, yelling for all she was worth: "Please, Billy, please, get me down from here. Please, Billy, and I'll never disobey you again!"

So Bill took his lariat and threw a loop over one of the moon's horns and pulled the whole shebang down to earth—moon, Sue, and all. He threw the moon, which was like a huge crescent, back into space and it acted like a boomerang, going clear around Mars and coming back again. So Bill had to throw it back a few times more until it stayed put where it belonged. Then he said to Sue, "My purty li'l coyote, will you keep your promise and do what I tell you?"

"Maybe I will," said Slue-Foot Sue.

Coyote Makes a Texas Cowboy

Coyote, the Creator, the Earth-Maker, the Trickster, had already made the world and all the animals living in it. He was very self-satisfied: "I have done a good job," he said.

"Friend Coyote," the buffalo reminded him, "you were supposed to make a creature called 'Man.' You didn't do it."

"*Now* you tell me" complained Coyote. "I'm supposed to have everything finished before sundown. I have a deadline. Well, amigos, gather around me and help me to figure out how this creature should look."

So all the animals gathered around Coyote according to rank—first the buffalo, then the whale, the eagle, the bear, the mountain lion, and so on.

"It's easy," said the buffalo. "Give him horns and a big hump. Then he'll be beautiful—like me."

"Nonsense," said the whale. "Humps are ugly. No horns! Let him have skin. Hair only gets in the way of swimming. And flippers, of course. Then he'll be at home in the water."

"Water, swimming—bah, humbug," exclaimed the eagle. "Give him wings to soar up to the sky, the sun, the stars. Cover him with feathers."

"You are mad, brother eagle," roared the mountain lion. "What this new human creature needs are claws and big teeth to catch his prey."

"Claws, fangs, my word," said the elk, "how gross! Antlers, my friends, majestic anglers and fast legs."

Then all the animals started shouting together: "Give him horns, no, wings, a big tail, please, shoveling paws are a must, hooves, no, claws, give him scales and flippers, no, no, no, give him a thick pelt!" And so on and on. Coyote lost patience: "Be quiet, all of you. We haven't got much time. I'll start with the basics, just four legs, a body, and a head. Then we can try out different things, see what looks best—lots of hair or no hair, horns or antlers, flippers or wings."

So Coyote formed up a body with a little mud and attached a head and four legs, holding the whole thing upright, contemplating his work. "I think I'll cover him with reddish fur," said Coyote. "That will look nice." Just at that moment the sun went down.

"You messed up, friend," the buffalo chided Coyote. "Everything had to be finished by nightfall. Now you have to leave him like he is. Now you can't add anything more."

"You've put too much brain in his head," complained the bear. "He'll be too smart. He'll rule over us. Make the brain smaller."

"Too late, friend," said Coyote. "The sun is down. We must leave things as they are."

"Look what you've done, Coyote," said the mountain lion. "You've got the critter propped up standing upright when the sun went down. So now he has to walk on his hindlegs only. He'll be very slow."

"Can't be helped, can't be helped now," answered Coyote.

"He looks just awful standing there," remarked the moose, "all naked and without any hair except on top where you started to cover him up. He's so ugly."

"Can't be helped, can't be helped."

"He looks like a big white worm with four legs," said the badger. "I can't stand the sight of him, and he's shivering, all naked like that."

And indeed, the creature seemed to be cold, as if he were about to freeze to death.

"I can't take away or add anything in the way of living matter," said Coyote, "but I can fashion some artificial things, not made of flesh, to cover him up." Having said this, Coyote made a Stetson hat to put upon the human being's head. "We must start at the top," explained Coyote. Then he made a shirt with mother-of-pearl buttons, a Levi jacket, and a silk handkerchief and put that on the strange creature. After that he clothed him below the waist in red long-johns and blue Levi pants and, as a last touch, put high-heeled boots on his feet.

"The creature is thirsty," remarked the fox. "It wants to drink." As the animals watched, the upright walking creature waddled over to the stream, cupped his hands, filling them with water, but as soon as he began to drink, he spat out what he had swallowed.

"He doesn't like water, imagine," said the wolf.

"I'll make a special liquid for him to drink," said Coyote.

"What will you call it?" inquired the mule deer.

"Wooble," answered Coyote.

"That doesn't sound right," commented the pronghorn.

"All right, all right," said Coyote, "we'll call it whiskey."

"He was sagging at the moment of sundown," said the prairie dog, "and that left him bowlegged."

"That's all right," said Coyote. "I'll put it into his mind never to walk on foot but always to ride on the horse's back. For that kind of life bowlegs are ideal."

"What shall we call this special kind of being?" asked the buzzard.

"Bomble-Womble," suggested the weasel.

"Shmeedle-wheedle," proposed the squirrel.

"Wagagaga," said the owl.

"Be quiet, all of you," shouted Coyote. "I made him and it is up to me to give him a name. Let me think." Coyote was silent for a while, thinking hard. Finally his face lit up. "I've got it," he said. "I'll name him the *Texas cowboy!*" And that was that.

The Heart-Shaped Mark

R ance Wilson was a rancher—not an ordinary, run-of-the-mill rancher—but the richest cowman in the county, with the biggest spread, the biggest herd, and the biggest house. He was a proud man, proud as Lucifer. Few men were allowed to call him by his first name. His wife had died during childbirth, much too young. He had never been able to get over it, though he gave no outward sign of this, as he wanted no pity. He had never remarried. His wife had left him with a daughter whom he named Regina—the Queen—because in his mind a daughter of his was a queen. He doted on her, spoiled her, indulged her in every whim, but also watched over her like a hawk. The girl was eighteen, hot-blooded, headstrong, and very beautiful, with a deer's alluring eyes, contrasting with a moist, inviting, and generous mouth, and a cat's sinuous way of moving. Her father thought that there was not a single man within a hundred miles worthy of her. Therefore, he watched over her, or tried to, because it is easier to watch a bagful of fleas than a high-hearted girl.

One early dawn Wilson's cowhands brought in a young fellow whom they had caught red-handed with a heifer, burning his own brand over Wilson's Lazy-W. The rustler was shifty-eyed, unkempt, and very scared. He was not at all bad-looking and had a way of endearing himself that was lost on Rance Wilson. On his right cheek was a small, cherry-colored, heart-shaped birthmark. Confronted by the grim-faced rancher, he managed a sickly grin, trying to joke his way out of his predicament, kidding about "slow elk," pleading that folks should go easy on a young fellow down on his luck, and really not meaning to carry through the theft. "I was only foolin' around with the iron," he repeated a few times, giving Rance a pitiful, trembling smile.

But at that time and place cattle rustling was not a joking matter, nor something to fool with, nor did one go easy on the thief.

"You know what to do, boys," said Wilson.

One of his men made a loop in his lariat—he had done this before —and threw the looped end over the sturdy branch of a right handy tree. Others tied the rustler's hands behind his back and lifted him onto his horse. They led the horse to the tree and placed the noose around the young man's neck.

"I wanna say a prayer," he requested.

"Say it," replied Wilson.

The condemned man got halfway through "Our Father" and faltered. "I have plumb forgotten the rest," he mumbled stupidly.

"The part you remembered will do," said Wilson, nodding to his cowpunchers. Somebody slapped the horse's rump and it ambled off from under its rider, leaving him hanging in midair. He dangled for a short while, his legs kicking in a mad dance, and then kicked no more. They let the body down, self-consciously, grinning with embarrassment, waiting for Wilson to tell them what to do next. The rancher was a hard but God-fearing man. "We'll bury him proper," he told his men, "somebody get a shovel." Somebody did. They dug the grave.

"What do we do for a coffin?" asked a young buckaroo, new to the game. There was raucous laughter.

"There's an old blanket hanging on the fence," said Rance Wilson. "Use that."

They wrapped the body, leaving the face exposed, and lowered it into the waiting hole. Rance Wilson motioned to an elderly bystander: "Tom, you once studied to be a preacher. Say a few words."

Tom took off his misshapen and stained hat, holding it before him like an oversized fig leaf, and cleared his throat: "Lord, you know this feller here was a no-good rustler an' hoss thief but, mebbe, he was a Christian deserving of Your mercy. So go easy on him, Lord. Amen."

They were about to shovel the sod over the body, but at that moment Wilson's daughter came riding up in a hurry, carrying a crude wooden cross, its two pieces hastily tied together with a bit of string: "Cook told me you boys hanged a rustler. I thought there should be a cross." She dismounted and walked to the open grave, glanced at the body, saw the heart-shaped birthmark, let out a small cry, and fainted away.

"Must be something she ate," remarked Rance Wilson, lifting her up on his horse, slowly trotting off with her toward his big house.

His men buried the rustler under a mound of earth, not forgetting to stick the cross into it.

Sad to relate, it was not something Regina ate. As the weeks went by, Rance Wilson turned into a hermit. He had often invited fellow ranchers to lavish dinners in his house, to barbecues and a little fiddling. Now he invited no one. Those who arrived uninvited were not encouraged to enter his home. He seldom was seen outside his house, and Regina was not seen at all. He dismissed all members of his household, save Doña Concepción, who had been his daughter's wet nurse and now did the cooking.

Regina was big with child and every day grew a little bigger. Rance Wilson thought that he could not bear it and was willing to die of shame. He was unable to figure out how this misfortune could have happened. He had watched over her, knowing how impulsive she was, and how defiant she could be, but after all, an eighteen-year-old girl cannot be chaperoned twenty-four hours a day, not Regina, anyhow. So it had happened.

He wanted to know the name of the son of a bitch who had done this to him. She would not tell. Halfheartedly, he tried to beat it out of her, with no success. Both of them were having a hard time. At last, some eight months after the rustler's hanging, Regina gave birth to a squalling boy, with no one to help but the aged Mexican cook. Rance Wilson went into his daughter's room, had one look at his newborn grandson, and walked out again without uttering a word.

In the morning two of his cowhands found Rance Wilson, the richest and most important man in the county, in the barn, hanging from a crossbeam, as dead as dead can be. While one of them cut Wilson down, the other hurried to the house, knocked on the door, and told the cook. Shortly afterward a dissheveled Regina came running out the door, loudly wailing, in her fancy, frilled nightshirt, cradling at her breast the baby boy. Visible on his right cheek was a tiny, cherry red, heart-shaped birthmark.

The Skeleton Bride

In the year of our Lord 1861 there lived down Texas way a loose-jointed swashbuckling young fellow by the name of Travis Smith. Not far from his family's place, close by the river in a little 'dobe house, lived a languid, sloe-eyed girl by the name of Estrellita. Travis was sweet on Estrellita or, rather, she was sweet on him, permitting him to take liberties with her in the shade of a large cottonwood tree, liberties that put her in the family way.

"Marry me, mi corazón," pleaded Estrellita.

"I sure will, sweetheart," said Travis, "but jest now I got to jine Gin'ral Braxton Bragg's army to lick them Yankee bastards. I'll reckon we'll have 'em beat inside a month. Then I'll come back to marry my li'l Estrellita. That's a solemn promise."

He took his old muzzle-loader from the wall, filled his canteen with home-brewed white lightning, saddled his pinto, and trotted off to war whistling a merry tune.

The Rebs didn't lick the Yankees inside a month and Travis did not come back to his lonesome Estrellita. He did not write to her because he didn't know how and because it would have been a waste of time, as she couldn't read. Besides, he was much too busy to think of her. The war went on and on and years went by. At the Battle of Glorieta, Travis got hit in the thigh by a Minié ball, which did considerable damage and laid him up for months. He was taken to Las Cruces, where a comely widow who liked his looks and free and easy ways took him in and cared for his wound. One thing led to another. He took certain liberties with her, this time in the shade of a mighty oak, which somewhat changed her body's profile. The War Between the States ended. Still, Travis tarried at the generous widow's place. He had taken a liking to her cooking.

One day a shaggy-bearded, one-armed man in faded butternut came up limping to the widow's house. She gave a little cry and fell around his neck. Then she laid her head on his chest and sobbed. It turned out that she was not a widow after all. Presumably killed at Shiloh, her husband had merely lost a limb.

"Here's your little boy you haven't seen yet," said the almost widow, pointing to the little toddler playing in the yard. Her husband was truly amazed at having become a father during his two-year absence. Travis did not stay to witness the widow explaining things to her rumored-to-be-dead mate, but jumped upon his horse, not the same he had started out with, and took off in a great hurry.

The Reconstruction years were a sorry time for the Secesh veteran. Travis drove longhorns along the Goodnight Trail. The work was hard and the pay poor. Inside a Dodge City saloon he had his jaw and cheekbone broken during an argument over cards. It ruined his good looks. He drifted from ranch to ranch, punching cows and getting nowhere. Whenever the weather changed, his leg hurt where the Minié ball had hit it. Another couple of years went by. Travis yearned for the comforts he had known, yearned to be mollycoddled by a loving woman.

Drifting from one place to another, he found himself one day in the neighborhood of his folks' old homestead. He went there to have a look. The soddy was gone, and so were his parents. He had no idea where they had gone to, or whether they were still alive. It did not bother him much. He and his kin had never been close. Suddenly, he besought himself of Estrellita. He got on his horse and rode down to the river. The little 'dobe house was still there, looking mighty inviting, sunflowers growing by the porch. He went in without knocking. By the hearth, inside the neatly kept and swept room, sat Estrellita, as pretty as ever, just as he had left her.

"Howdy," he said, "remember me?"

She flew into his arms, covering his face with kisses. He started making a long excuse for not having come back to marry her. She stopped him, putting her hand over his lips, saying; "Don't talk. Come, my one and only love."

She took him by the hand, leading him to the table heaped with good things—carne adobada, still hot, chicken mole, posole, and a pitcher of red wine to wash it all down. While eating hungrily, Travis kept staring at Estrellita. He had never noticed before how truly beautiful she was, dressed in all her finery, her scarlet waist, the blue, flower-patterned skirt, the lace shawl over her head.

"What a fool I've been," he thought. "I should have come back sooner."

After he had finished eating, she led him to her bed and made love to him, tenderly and passionately. At last, they fell asleep in each other's arms.

Travis awoke with a start, drops of water falling on his face. He looked up and saw, in the dawn's early light, that the hut had no roof. It was raining and he was sopping wet. He could make out in the dusk, that the 'dobe house, which had been so alluring, was, in reality, a crumbling ruin with a collapsed fireplace. Instead of Estrellita's warm body he felt something hard and sharp digging into his side. He dared to look and his teeth began to chatter. Nestled in his arms was a skeleton, its bones covered with shrunken yellow skin, strands of hair still adhering to the skull covered by bits of frayed lace. Shreds of blue and red cloth lay mingled with the human remains. In the horrid thing beside him Travis still managed to recognize Estrellita.

In one corner of the ruin he could make out what seemed to be a crib containing a tiny skeleton in remnants of a baby's chemise. With a terrible cry he jumped up, scattering bones left and right, rushing blindly from this place of death and desolation, screaming. Even after his voice gave out, dwindling into a hoarse whisper, he kept on running and running through thorns and chaparral for mile after mile until finally he fell down dead himself, dead not from exhaustion but from sheer terror.

Western Jack and the Cornstalk

The cowpunchers around Clovis are dead set against planting, especially against planting corn. They tell you the reason why. The corn around there is better, and grows faster, than any other corn in the world. Also, it does very well in the poorest soil, even in desert sand.

There was a cowman named Kincaid, his wife, and their little boy, living on their modest spread somewhere west of Clovis. The boy accidentally dropped a kernel of corn on the ground and immediately a plant was shooting up. The boy grabbed it playfully, and before he knew what was happening, he was carried by it way up, so high that he was afraid to climb down but just clung tightly to the leaves, hollering for help. The father came running, but when he got to the cornstalk, his son was already more than a hundred feet up in the air. The frantic father hurried to get his ax and when he got back the kid was still up there, hanging on for dear life, but now he was at a height of two hundred feet. His father wielded the ax and made a cut in the stalk, but by then it had become as thick as the trunk of a big oak tree. The father was making another chop, but the first cut was already beyond reach way above him. His wife hurried to the scene to see what all the commotion was about, but by then the top of the stalk with the boy was above the clouds. The mother started weeping and wailing, but when a few teardrops fell to the ground near the stalk's base, it shot up twice as fast as before.

"He'll starve to death up there," lamented the woman, but for weeks and months corncobs fell down from the sky, piling up around the base of the stalk.

"He has lots of corn to eat up there, and lots of dew to lick up from the leaves to quench his thirst," said the father.

"But we'll never see him again," wailed his wife, "For heaven's sake, do something!"

Now there was a holy hermit living in a cave on top of the Twin Peaks, near Las Vegas, not too far from Clovis. This hermit was so saintly, and so beloved by God that whenever he wanted he could float up into the sky, all the way to the pearly gates, and have a chat with Saint Peter, and then float down again to his cave, to go on fasting and praying and mortifying his flesh.

The grieving parents went to see this holy one. On their knees they implored him to bring their little boy back.

"I'll see what I can do," said the hermit. He soared up to heaven, rang the bell, and Peter came out to greet him.

"Amigo," said the hermit, "there is a certain little boy who rode up from earth on a rather tall cornstalk. They think he is up here with you. They want him back."

"I wish he were, compadre," said the saint. "It's true, he passed by here, but with such terrific speed that, before I could grab hold of him, that cornstalk had already whizzed by me, carrying the boy way beyond heaven into the darkness of outer space."

"Can't you get the Boss to get him down to earth and his father's ranch. After all, He's almighty, isn't He?"

"Sure, sure, He's almighty all right, but this is a special case where even He is helpless. Probably a little trick played upon Him by you know who. I'm sorry, my friend."

So the hermit came home empty-handed.

Well, that's the kind of corn we have around here, and that's why we never try to raise any of it and stick to raising cattle.

Better Move That Drat Thing!

An old cowhand was sitting in the Seven Gables Hotel and Bar, Sheridan, Wyoming, his cheeks full of chawin' 'baccer, spitting his ambeer with perfect aim at the cat, into the vase with the potted palm, on the carpet, or hitting the fly crawling up the wallpaper. The porter, averse to that kind of shooting exhibition, placed a spittoon where he thought it might do the most good. The cowpoke ignored him, directing his juice at the navel of the undraped lady whose painting adorned the back bar. The porter moved the cuspidor in front of the bar, the cowboy propelled his ambeer into a nearby ashtray. Desperate, the porter placed the spittoon directly at the chewer's feet, who first stared at the porter, then at the brass cuspidor, and finally exclaimed: "Pardner, you better move that drat thing or, by God, I'm li'ble to spit in it!"

Being Afoot in Roswell

An old story tells of three young, rambunctious cowhands riding into a Roswell, New Mexico, saloon on their ponies, right up to the bar, downing their sneaky pete while remaining in the saddle. A traveling salesman from back East, imbibing his own phlegm cutter, complained of being crowded by all that horseflesh, saying that these goddam equines belonged in a stable and not in a barroom.

The boniface, an rugged old smoothbore, eyed the man from the East with disdain.

"Stranger," he finally unburdened himself, "what the devil are you doin' in here afoot, for chrissake?"

Outstunk the Skunk

Cattlemen, who hated the smell of sheep, were fond of ascribing a sheepy odor as well as a disreputable appearance to the men who tended sheep. The only legend that cowmen ever tell in mixed company has to do with a cowman, a farmer, and a sheepman who visited a carnival show. One tent bore the sign FIVE DOLLARS IF YOU CAN STAY IN THIS TENT FIVE MINUTES. The cowman swaggered in with assurance. In two seconds he was out, sputtering and coughing and urging the next man to try it. The farmer went in, and in half a minute he came hurrying out in discomfiture. Then the sheepman went in. The other two waited. One minute went by—two, three, four. Just as the cowboy and the farmer had made up their minds to go to the rescue, the tent's exhibit, a large, virile, and highly disgusted skunk, ran out from under the tent flap and made for the creek.

CHAPTER 9

Theッ Died with Their Boots On

Sometimes they did, but not always. Bat Masterson died at his desk writing a column for the sports section of the *New York Morning Telegraph*. Doc Holliday cashed in his chips on his bed, a victim of galloping consumption. Clay Allison broke his neck falling from his buckboard. Wyatt Earp began pushing up daisies at the age of eighty-one.

The Golden Age of the Gunfighter lasted from about 1850 to 1890. During this period of roughly forty years an estimated twenty thousand men died of "lead poisoning," from the Canadian border down to the Rio Grande, which comes to about five hundred victims per year in all this vast territory, comparing very favorably with the much greater number of annual homicides in any one of our larger cities today.

Shoot-outs occurred for two reasons: the snaillike westward march of the law and Mr. Colt's invention of the six-shot revolver.

God made some men big and some men small,
But Sam Colt made them all equal.

In the absence of law, certain men will take the law into their own hands. Some westerners did, but not nearly as many as legends would have us believe. Settling arguments by force of arms was an old, and generally accepted, American custom. Among our native heroes, Alexander Hamilton and Stephen Decatur died as the result of duels fought with pistols. These were stately affairs of honor, fought according to the strict code duello. The living bridge between the gentlemanly duelist and the unwashed western gunslinger was President Andrew Jackson, "Dean of Duelists," who fought no less than fourteen duels, though he managed to kill only one of his antagonists. Jackson's fights often degenerated into vicious brawls with knives and lead-headed canes, but then "Old Hickory" was a genuine frontier character from Tennessee.

"I always carried a gun," said Montana "Teddy Blue" Abbott, "because it was the only way I knew how to fight. If God Almighty'd wanted me to fight like a dog, He'd given me long teeth and claws."

The western shootist came in two varieties: the fellow who "fought fair" according to the gunslinger's unwritten code—barbaric, but a code all the same—and the low-down killer, who often shot his quarry in the back or from ambush with as little compunction as stepping on a cockroach. The unwritten law specified that one should not shoot a fellow with whom one had just shared a meal. One should not shoot a gent who was "not heeled"

—that is, carried no weapon—nor should one fire away without due warning. Even a rattler will give a warning before it strikes. Also, it was not cricket to smile while gunning a man down, as it might give him the notion that one was only joking. For a fair fight in accordance with such rules, there was no punishment.

The unsavory, unstable killer type often belonged to the genus "Kid," such as Billy the Kid, Kid Curry, or the Texas Kid:

> The genus "KID" wore his hair long, and in curls upon his shoulders; had an incipient moustache, and sported a costume made of buckskin ornamented with fringe, tassels, and strings of the same material—the dirtier the better. His head was covered with a cowboy's hat of phenomenal width of brim, having many metal stars, halfmoons, etc., around the crown. Upon his feet he wore either moccasins or very high-heeled, stub-toed boots, and an enormous pair of spurs, with little steel balls that jingled at each step. Buckled around his waist would be a cartridge belt holding two carefully sited revolvers, and a bone-handled bowie knife in his bootleg completed his dress.
>
> The "cayuse" was never far from his master, for when that gentleman wanted a horse he wanted him badly; either to escape from a worse man than himself, or to escape the consequences of having killed one.

Mythology and the movies have made heroes of some very bad hombres, of the James boys, the Daltons, Cole Younger, Billy the Kid, King Fisher, and similar gentry. That can't be helped.

> *But Western life ain't wild and woolly now;*
> *There is no daily gunpowder powwow;*
> *There are bunco games galore*
> *And the tourist dude holds the floor.*
> *But Western life ain't wild and woolly now!*

No-Head Joaquin and Three-Fingered Jack

Joaquin Murieta and "Three-Fingered Jack" García were the legendary bad hombres of the California Gold Rush days. They stood head and shoulders above all the other bandidos—after all, there are not many men who can boast of having their heads and hands exhibited in pickle jars of alcohol, for the price of two bits.

Leaving behind them a crimson trail of blood and death, the famous outlaws soon furnished gringo journalists the stuff for lurid legends that kept them busy for years. Every outrage, murder, and robbery was automatically laid at the door of the celebrated Joaquín Murieta and his band of desperadoes. To confuse the historians, there was a whole multitude of other cutthroats named Joaquín to make the life of gringo miners and prospectors miserable, such as Joaquín Bottilier, Joaquín Carillo, Joaquín Ocomorena, Joaquín Romero, and Joaquín Valenzuela. As a matter of course, the misdeeds of these Joaquíns, lumped together as one, were all blamed on Murieta, the top Joaquín of them all.

Legend made Murieta either into the most bloodthirsty and cruel pistolero ever to haunt the mother lode, or into a Mexican Robin Hood, the protector of his people, the widows' and orphans' friend.

No such ambivalence was involved in the Saga of Three-Fingered Jack, Murieta's chief lieutenant. All agreed that he was the ultimate throat slicer, doing his job so deftly that his victims were hardly aware of what had happened to them until after they were dead. One of Jack's chief amusements was to form a group of Chinese coolies into an outward-facing circle, tying all their queues together in the center, and then solemnly walking around the circle, methodically cutting their throats, one after the other. Jack was said to sometimes cut out and devour his victims' hearts. He boasted that he ate his meals with the same knife he used to slit throats and that it lapped up blood like a man dying of thirst laps up water.

This then is the Ballad of Joaquín Murieta. There lived in the verdant Valley of Sonora a gentle, handsome lad—our Joaquín. The valley was brightened by the presence of an angelic and most beautiful girl—Rosita Carmel Feliz. Joaquín and Rosita had been inseparable from earliest childhood. They were instructed together in the holy faith by the same padre, were confirmed together, danced the fandango at the same baile, and sang sweet songs to each other under the ancient cottonwood tree. Inevitably, like Romeo and Juliet, they fell deeply in love with each other while still in their early teens— the pure, chaste love of innocence.

There also lived in that peaceful valley a very important and powerful gouty, aged caballero, a hacendado and rico hombre, Don José Gonzáles. Don José's hacienda was so big that when people asked him, "Señor, does your hacienda lie in the state of Sonora?" he answered, "No, the state of Sonora lies within my hacienda." What Don José wanted, he usually got, and what he wanted was the lovely Rosita in her first bloom of budding womanhood. Only instant flight could save Rosita from the old lecher's clutches. Joaquín stole two blooded horses from among more than five thousand in Don José's remuda. The young lovers rode away as fast as their mounts would carry them. They did not stop until they had put a hundred miles behind them. Then they found a kindly priest who joined them

in marriage. They did not feel safe, however, until they had crossed the border into California, recently annexed by the United States.

In California, Joaquín and his Rosita lived happily together. Joaquín, a superb horseman, earned good money as a horse breeder and bronc buster. He searched for—and found—his older brother, Jesús Carlos, who had come to America a few years before him. Carlos had staked a claim in a gold camp called Hangtown, but the norteamericanos did not want "greasers" in the goldfields. They considered mining for precious ores a privilege of "the superior race." A bully called Lang jumped the claim. Carlos had the title and a friend, Flores, who had been a witness to the title registration. Joaquín, Carlos, and Flores set out to reclaim the property. Upon arrival at the gold camp, they found themselves confronted by an angry mob of gringo miners, egged on by Lang: "We don't want any goddam greasers here," they shouted. "Go back to Mexico where you belong! Git!"

Lang suddenly pointed at the mules on which Carlos and Flores were riding: "Them mules is stolen. I'd know 'em anywhar. Let's string them hoss thieves up!"

Instantly, Carlos and Flores were torn from their saddles, dragged to the nearest tree, and hanged. Joaquín was forced to watch his brother and friend dance the Dance of Death. He himself was tied to the hanging tree. The shirt was ripped from his back as the brutish Lang began to lash him cruelly with a huge bullwhip until the bones were laid bare.

"That's jest a lesson to teach you that greasers ain't welcome here," Lang said with an evil grin. "Ef you ever come back, you'll die of hemp fever like yer two amigos. Now git lost, you son of a bitch!"

Joaquín had endured his agony in silence, without uttering a sound. During his ordeal he kept his eyes fastened upon the faces of his tormentors until their features had been burned indelibly into his memory, swearing a silent oath to himself that they should pay with their lives for what they had done. Consumed with hatred, and determined not to be cheated of his rights to search for gold as the gringos did, he staked out a claim at a place called Saw Mill Flat, and there put up a small adobe house for himself and Rosita. He was savagely punished for his presumption. Six miners, occupying the claims next to his, burst into his humble home, yelling: "You bastard greaser, tryin' to horn in on white men's diggin's. You've asked for it!" Joaquín went for his bowie knife, but was knocked down from behind with the blunt end of an ax. When he came to, he found his Rosita naked, her clothes ripped from her body, tied to their bed, battered beyond recognition, victim of a fate worse than death. She was but barely alive. Joaquín cut her ties, covering her with kisses. She opened her eyes for a last time, whispered "Mi corazón," and with a deep sigh expired in his arms. He sat there for many hours as if turned into stone, clutching her body. In the morning he buried Rosita, who had not lived to bear his child. Then he spoke, though there were none to hear him: "By the blood of Christ, I will avenge you!"

Some time later the bodies of six prospectors were discovered lying in a ravine, their throats cut. They had been mutilated and their ears had been sliced off. They were the men who had violated and killed Rosita.

A dour, hollow-cheeked man opened a gambling saloon in Hangtown. Long black hair fell to his shoulders. Much of his face was hidden by huge mustaches and a bushy beard. His eyes glowed like coals with the ice-cold fire of hate. He was dressed like a typical gringo saloonkeeper. Nobody recognized in this disguise a formerly gentle, clean-shaven lad named Joaquín Murieta.

Soon uneasiness spread among the miners of Hangtown, nearby Saw Mill Flat, and Murphy's Diggings. Fear gripped the boozers in the saloons, the gamblers at their faro tables. Men were disappearing as if swallowed up by the earth. Later, their bodies, half-devoured by wild beasts, would be found in ravines and forest glens, sometimes floating facedown in mountain streams. All of them had their ears cut off.

A jolly drunk was seen staggering from a saloon to his nearby cabin. His friends heard him singing:

Hangtown whores are curious creatures,
They wind up by marryin' preachers,
Hitch up their skirts and show their features.
Hooraw, Hangtown gals!

He was found next morning at his cabin's door, his ears gone, his head nearly severed from his body, his teeth bared in a horrid grin.

A mule stumbled into Murphy's Diggings. Tied to its back was a miner's corpse, the ears sliced off close to the skull. This one did not have its throat cut. Looking at what remained of him, he appeared to have been lassoed and dragged, at full gallop, through thorns and brambles until his clothes and most of his skin was gone.

The denizens of mining camps within a radius of fifty miles took to staying home at nights, hardly daring to visit their privies after dark. If they had to venture from camp, they did so in the company of friends. Still, men kept disappearing as if by witchcraft. A party of miners were sitting in on a game of poker inside their favorite watering hole when one of them slammed down his cards on the table and exclaimed: "Boys, something jest occurred to me. Remember the necktie party Old Bill Lang organized fer two Mex hoss thieves, An' a third greaser got a whippin'? Waal, thar war thirty-one fellers in that party, an every man jack of them gents found murdered an' without his ears war one of 'em. So far, fourteen lost thar jug handles. That makes seventeen still to go." There ensued a long silence. The card game was not resumed.

Then occurred a great stampede of the seventeen who still had their ears left, but no matter how far they fled, the avenger found them—one at the Stanislaus, one in Vallecito, one in Cucumber Gulch, one in Washoe, Nevada. Thus Joaquín, soon referred to as El Tigre and El Rey de los Pistoleros, left a bloody trail of earless corpses. Sometimes, at night, out of the howling winds of the Sierras, came a song, "El Corrido de Joaquín Murieta," which froze the blood in the veins of the forty-niners:

Me he paseado en California
Por el año cincuenta;
Con mi pistola rajada,
Y mi canaña repleta.
Yo soy aquel mexicano,
De nombre Joaquín Murieta.

I was riding through California,
In the year of eighteen fifty,
With my pistol in my belt,
My cartridge belt full of bullets.
I am that Mexican
They call Joaquín Murieta.

As a poor little boy,
I was left an orphan,
My innocent brother they hanged,
And I was cruelly whipped.
My Rosita they ravished and killed.

The poor I protect with my weapons,
Put bread and meat on their tables.
Gringos I kill without mercy,
They tremble, hearing my name.
I am Joaquín Murieta.

On a cloudy night a gambler was riding along a mountain road when suddenly the clouds parted and the moonlight revealed the figure of a man, bent over a corpse, slicing off its ears. In the murderer the gambler recognized the black-bearded owner of Hangtown's gambling hall. In a flash Murieta was upon him, knife glinting in the pale light, cursing: "Gringo, you die!"

"Mercy," cried the gambler. "Spare me!"

"I spare no one," said Murieta. "Why should I spare you?"

"After they whipped you," said the gambler, "there was one who bathed your wounds, covering them with soothing balm. I am that man."

"For ten centavos worth of unguento, here is a bag of gold worth a thousand pesos. Va Con Dios."

Murieta left Hangtown before the gambler could expose him. He now appeared openly at the head of three hundred horsemen, raising havoc among the camps and towns of the Americanos. Astride his blooded black stallion, he rode splendidly attired in a black charro costume embroidered with silver and calzones lined with rows of silver buttons, and on his head was a black sombrero with a broad golden hatband. His heavy stirrups were of pure silver, with huge rowels. Stuck in his belt were two large horse pistols and an enormous, gold-handled bowie knife. Dangling from his saddle horn was a string of dried ears. Murieta never smiled. He had forgotten how to laugh. Among his followers were beautiful women, armed and attired like men. He took them to his bed sometimes, and then carelessly discarded them. He had lost the capacity to love. He and his bandidos killed a thousand men. They robbed the miners of a million dollars in gold. They robbed the Wells Fargo wagons carrying the precious yellow metal and killed the drivers. Posters sprouted on walls and fences offering a reward of five thousand dollars for his capture, dead or alive. With a piece of charcoal he scrawled on one of them: "Make it fifty thousand! Joaquín Murieta."

He had collected thirty pairs of ears from the men who had hanged his brother and whipped him, but not a pair from the thirty-first and last—Bill Lang. He knew that his archenemy was consumed with fear and hardly slept, drowning his terror in whiskey. He savored Lang's dread and was in no hurry to kill him, grimly enjoying playing cat and mouse with the trembling scoundrel. One night he rapped at Lang's window, crying: "I am Joaquín Murieta. Pretty soon I'll be coming for your ears!" Lang's heart stopped. He had been scared to death.

Joaquín was without pity, but for the sake of Rosita's memory he harmed no woman. He and his men came across a settler's wife with a wagon. She was alone. Her wagon's axle was broken. She had neither food nor money. He told her: "Young woman, you have heard of that Mexican who calls himself Joaquín Murieta. Perhaps you'll think that I am not all that bad. Once, I was a caring man with love in my heart. It is your people who made me into a wild beast without heart." He ordered his men to fix the wagon and gave the woman much food and a thousand dollars in gold.

Murieta and his band made travel in the goldfields impossible. All traffic stopped. The citizens were in an uproar. California's governor recruited a company of rangers, commanded by a captain named Love, to put an end to the depredations. On July 25, 1853, near Tulare Lake, the rangers ambushed Murieta and a handful of his followers. They riddled the King of the Pistoleros with bullets. Dying, he looked Captain Love in the eyes, saying; "It is enough. The work is done." Joaquín was twenty-three years old at the time of his death. It was said that with his own hands he had killed ten men for every year of his life. The rangers cut off his head and the hand of Three-Fingered Jack, and put their trophies into two glass jars filled with alcohol. Captain Love paraded the jars through the streets of San Francisco. They were sent on a tour of the state. It cost a quarter to stare at the head of the man some had called the "Terror of the Mother Lode." Eventually, the jar with Murieta's head wound up behind the bar of a San Francisco saloon from where it leered at

the aficionados bending their elbows at the bar, until it was finally destroyed in the great earthquake of 1906.

But this was not the end of the legend. There were many, including most of the Spanish-speaking folks of California, who said that the head in the jar did not belong to Murieta but to one of the lesser Joaquíns, and that the mutilated hand did not belong to Three-Fingered Jack but to some poor, no-account peon whose fingers Love had cut off to have proof of having killed the two famous bandits. Five thousand dollars was a lot of money—mucho dinero—and the rangers wanted the reward. For their purpose anybody's head and hand would do. The head was Murieta's and the hand Jack's because Love said so, and no ifs or buts about it.

The humble folk knew better. Had they not proof? Did hundreds of people not hear a black-caped rider sing:

Yo soy aquel mexicano
De nombre Joaquín Murieta . . .

I am that Mexican
They call Joaquín Murieta.
I am not dead, but live,
To defend my people,
To avenge their sorrows,
To care for the grave of my love.

And did not a black-caped horseman, every Sunday, place fresh flowers on Rosita's grave?

◇◇

The Headless Horseman of the Mother Lode

◇◇

Murieta was dead, but his ghost rode on. Many were the lonely travelers who on moonlit nights found themselves confronted by the headless specter of the great bandido astride a huge coal black stallion, draped in a black capote, his legs encased in black charro pantaloons edged with silver. And out of its headless trunk, like a deep rumble out of a bottomless well, rose an unearthly cry: *"Give me back my head!"*

One traveler, a fine gentleman, lately arrived from Boston, finding himself face-to-face with the headless phantom, died instantly of fright.

A California judge, dispensing justice at his court, saw the terrible specter walking toward him in broad daylight. It hovered before the trembling magistrate while out of its horrible pulsating neck hole gurgled the heartrending cry: *"Give me back my head!"*

Then the ghost vanished into thin air, leaving the judge, who had fainted, senseless on his seat. When the poor man came to, his mind was gone. He lived on for many years, his eyes unseeing, his ear unhearing, his lips drooling as, with a sickly grin, he repeated over and over again, a thousand times a day: *"I don't have it! I don't have it!"*

A young lady of good family and gentle upbringing, being then big with child, heard a hollow croaking before her window that froze the blood in her veins: *"Give me back my head!"*

Then and there, the poor lady had a miscarriage, giving birth to a stillborn son. Her husband, coming upon the scene, took a pistol and blew his brains out. The deranged woman spent the rest of her days in the madhouse, singing in an eerie voice: *"Do I have it? Do you have it? Does he have it? Do we have it? No! No! No!"*

When the poor lost soul died, the pallbearers, to their horror, heard her corpse singing in the coffin: *"I really don't have it! Hee! Hee! Hee!"*

A man who owned a cabinet of wax figures within a gallery of freak shows saw the headless demon flying in through his window, his serape fluttering like giant bat wings, his skeleton hands grasping a waxen head resembling Murieta's, screeching, *"Give me back my head!"*

Unfortunately, the ghost soon discovered that what he had seized was not his head, but a waxen replica. Furious, the phantom hurled the head into the owner's face with such tremendous force that it cracked the poor fellow's skull, so that he expired on the spot. The black-shrouded apparition then flew away with a piercing, inhuman laugh that shattered every window within a mile.

A group of jolly Irish immigrants encountered the demon amid thunder and lightning.

"Give me back my head!" howled the disembodied spirit, seizing the head of one among the group, an unfortunate fellow named O'Malley, and twisted it right off in front of his horror-stricken friends. The ghost kicked the head around for a while as if it were a

soccer ball but, after a short while, lost interest in his gruesome plaything, hurling it high into the clouds. O'Malley's head never came down, but stayed up there, in outer space, orbiting the earth. The evil apparition, on its phantom steed, galloped after O'Malley's head in the sky and could for some time after be observed dashing wildly back and forth over the firmament. The dead Irishman's friends were never the same again, condemned for the rest of their lives to reexperience the horrible scene again and again in an endless circle of nightmares.

Murieta's real head, preserved in alcohol, was kept in a pickle jar behind the bar of San Francisco's Golden Nugget Saloon. For the price of two bits the barkeep could be induced to remove the green-velvet covering to expose Murieta's ghastly countenance. The pickled head was a great conversation piece and attracted crowds of paying customers. But once each year, every August 12, the saloon was empty, because on that day, the anniversary of Murieta's death, the ghost was apt to come riding through the swinging door into the barroom, get down from his snorting steed, and try feverishly to pry open the jar's lid in order to reclaim the missing part of his anatomy. Frantically, the skeleton fingers would clutch the lid—always in vain. It was said that whoever had watched this unnerving scene would die within a year.

There was one who defied this dire prediction, an ancient befuddled drunkard and former prospector who had made the saloon his permanent abode. Always inebriated, wandering about in an alcoholic

WILL BE EXHIBITED
FOR ONE DAY ONLY!
AT THE STOCKTON HOUSE!
THIS DAY, AUG. 12, FROM 9 A. M. UNTIL 8 P. M.
THE HEAD
Of the renowned Bandit!
JOAQUIN!
AND THE
HAND OF THREE FINGERED JACK!
THE NOTORIOUS ROBBER AND MURDERER.

haze, suffering from delirium tremens, he cheerfully explained that he preferred the headless ghost to visions of pink elephants.

So on one August 12, punctually at the stroke of midnight, the ghost rode into the Golden Nugget. Despite having no head, and therefore no eyes, he got down from his horse and walked straight up to the grizzled tosspot, grasping him by the collar, screeching, *"Give me back my head!"*

"Sorry, old chap," said the undismayed lush, "I can't. But I'll give you a drink," and with that poured the contents of a whole bottle of whiskey down the phantom's gullet.

"Gracias, señor," gurgled the ghost, who then hiccuped and trotted off together with his horse.

On April 18, 1906, a monstrous earthquake shook the city of San Francisco. Thousands of buildings collapsed or went up in flames. The Golden Nugget's roof fell in, its walls crumbled. The jar containing Murieta's famous head tumbled to the floor amid a shower of broken glass, the preserving fluid forming a big puddle. The head was rolling about on the polished boards when suddenly the phantom, on its ebony stallion, swooped down upon it, placing it upon its shoulders. At once, the head opened its mouth wide, exposing two rows of brilliantly white teeth, and shouted over and over again: *"Mi cabeza! Mi cabeza! My head! I got it back! I got it back! I got it back at last!"*

With its head once more in its proper place, Murieta's ghost galloped off, through burning streets, smoke, and ashes, plunging finally into a huge crack made by the earthquake, never to be seen again.

◇◦◇

El Keed

◇◦◇

Henry McCarty, alias William H. Bonney, was a buck-toothed runt and juvenile delinquent best known by his nickname "Billy the Kid." Born on Manhattan's Lower East Side, he ultimately wound up in New Mexico. His first try at being a baddie was inauspicious—stealing dirty shirts and underwear from a Chinese laundryman—but he advanced his career by becoming a horse thief and cattle rustler. He was befriended by a tweedy English gentleman rancher named Tunstall, who was involved in the notorious Lincoln County War, a power struggle between various commercial and cattle interests in the region that led to some of the most spectacular shootouts in western history. Tunstall was dry-gulched, becoming the "war's" first victim. The Kid promptly went on a killing rampage, not only to avenge his late patron, but also for the fun and the money. The Kid's greatest claim to fame is that he killed a man for every year of his life—twenty-one. (Mercifully, he died young.) Arrested for murder, the Kid escaped and could have high-tailed it over the border into Mexico, but "nubile hips and pneumatic breasts" made him loath to leave. Eventually, the law caught up with him. His silhouette outlined against a moonlit window, he made a good target for Sheriff Pat Garrett, who sneaked up on him and blasted Billy into the misty beyond. The best that can be said about young Billy is that he was right handy with a gun.

Americans have the unique propensity, astonishing to foreigners, to make heroes out of brutal, unwashed killers, and Billy was no exception, as a veritable avalanche of legends extolled the callow youth, creating an idol—the handsome, bold, and death-defying, but pure and tenderhearted, "Keed."

◆　◆　◆

The sun was sinking over the Sierras as the cool breeze of eventide stirred up dust devils among the chaparral. A lone rider could be seen making his way across the malpais on a horse so worn and weary that it seemed on the point of collapse. The rider was a young and handsome lad, lithe and tall in the saddle, his face shaded by a large sombrero. Ever and anon, the youth looked back over his shoulder as if searching the horizon for unseen pursuers. His face was lit up by a broad smile as, in the growing darkness, his eyes discerned a light coming from the window of a low adobe building. Forcing his horse into a faltering trot, he reined in before the humble home, dismounted, tied his animal to the stump of a dead tree, and knocked at the door.

"Bienvenido," a voice welcomed him in Spanish. The stranger brushed the dust from his rawhide shirt, took off his sombrero, and entered. He was greeted by the comforting sight of a cozy, whitewashed room, the friendly glow from an adobe fireplace, the flickering light of a candle on a table beside a jug of water. An elderly couple, simple campesinos, were seated on a bench by the fire. At the table sat a strikingly beautiful girl, about seventeen years old, with glowing amber skin, cherry lips, and dark translucent eyes, combing her raven hair.

"Agua, por favor," the young stranger implored, his voice hoarse and cracking. The girl got up, poured water into a gourd dipper, and handed it to him. He drank deeply and greedily as one who had ridden far through the waterless desert.

The couple introduced themselves as José and Apolinara Padilla. Their daughter's name, they told him, was Pablita. After slaking his thirst, the young man answered with many words of politeness, but failed to mention his own name.

"Señor Padilla," he pleaded, "I and my horse are tired unto death, for we came a long way. I have not eaten since yesterday. Can you give me and my caballo shelter for the night, a little food for me, and the use of your pasture for my animal? I have money to pay for everything."

At the mention of money Don José stiffened. "Do not insult my hospitality, señor," he protested, "we do not have much, but whatever we do have is yours. Do not mention money again, por favor."

They motioned him to the table to eat as mother and daughter vied with each other to serve him. Pablita could not tear her eyes from the stranger. Flaxen-haired and blue-eyed, he was like no man she had ever seen. She thought him handsome beyond imagination. Fairy tales came to her mind, of saints and angels, knocking at doors, asking for a bed and a tortilla. testing the hosts' goodwill and open-handedness. Could this fine young stranger be such a saint?

The young man, in turn, feasted his eyes on the girl. He noticed that she was wrapped in a gorgeous flowery shawl with long fringes. He saw that her parents also were dressed as if going to a fiesta.

"Señor," her father told him, "make yourself at home. You may use my and my wife's bed to sleep on. I myself, my esposa, and my daughter must go to a baile."

At the word "baile" the young man's eyes lit up. "A dance!" he exclaimed. "I love to dance. May I come along?"

Don José frowned: "How can you think of that, tired and worn out as you are?"

"Thanks to your kindness, I have already regained some of my strength, and señor, I am never too tired to dance."

The host seemed embarrassed: "It would not be wise for you to go to this fiesta. I did not want to tell you this, but I see that I must.

The man who is giving this baile is as powerful as he is bad. He thinks he owns this town and all who live in it. He pretends to be a big ranchero, but his riches come from cattle rustling and his power from the pistolas of the gang of bandidos who assist him in his crimes. We would like to drive them out, but he kills all who stand in his way. His name is Policarpo Bonilla—a thief, a murderer, and a violator of women. There is no resisting him. His men will cut your throat at a nod from his head. We live in a no-man's-land here, without law and justice. This evil hombre is giving this baile, as he says, in honor of our little Pablita. He wants to possess and dishonor her as he has so many others. He says that if we do not come he will send his men to drag us there, by the hair if necessary. He vows that if we resist him, he will kill me and my good wife, and still force Pablita to come to him. It breaks our hearts, señor, but we are like little fledgling birds in the claws of a big cat. If you go there too, it will arouse his jealousy and will do us no good. He is sure to kill you and we do not want to have your death on our conscience."

At these words the girl began to weep. Her body was shaken by sobs, her face bathed in tears. "This monster says he wants to marry me," she cried, "but he only wants my body to toy with. He is as ugly as the devil himself, his face disfigured by scars. He has the eyes of a snake. His breath stinks of aguardiente. I will kill myself if he as much as touches me. I know this would be a great sin and that God would punish me for it, but I will do it rather than be his."

At this Señora Padilla burst into tears, crying aloud to the Holy Virgin of Guadalupe to save them from this evildoer. Her husband took a machete from the wall, concealing it beneath his poncho. "I shall kill the cabrón before I let him touch my daughter with his vile hands. Then we shall all die, but we shall die with honor. Stay here, señor, our troubles do not concern you."

"Va con Dios," said the young man as Don José and the weeping women disappeared into the darkness of the night.

The young man waited a short while until his hosts were out of earshot. He then went to his horse and from a saddlebag took a gunbelt with a Colt in each holster. He carefully examined his weapons and made sure that they were fully loaded. Then he vaulted into the saddle and rode toward the faint distant sounds of fiddles and guitars.

Inside Don Policarpo's big house the dancing was frenzied and the music overloud, just as the villain liked it. A dozen of his henchmen were there, acting as his bodyguards, all of them drunk, swearing, staggering, pawing the girls who had come only out of the fear of displeasing the bandits. Don Policarpo lorded it over everybody, swaggering, guffawing raucously, gulping down many shots of aguardiente. He was huge and muscular, but repulsive to look at. A large purplish raised scar seemed to divide his face in two. An enormous mustache was still not large enough to hide his harelip and the stumps of his yellow, rotten teeth.

At the sight of Pablita he swept off his sombrero and made an exaggerated bow: "Welcome, my little pigeon. Policarpo Bonilla will teach you what it is to dance in the arms of a real man of valor."

With a wolfish grin he grasped Pablita around her slender waist, brutally pressing her to him while trying to kiss the struggling girl. She battered the ruffian's chest with her small, delicate fists. He roared with laughter: "Ay, muchacha, this gives spice to the dance. I love a spirited wench!"

José Padilla watched the scoundrel abusing his daughter, gripping the machete beneath his poncho, fearful, yet determined to defend Pablita at the peril of his own life.

At that moment a voice rang out: "Villano, cabrón, stinking skunk, let her go if you want to live!"

"Quién es?" Without relinquishing his hold on Pablita's waist, Bonilla turned around to discover who was insulting him.

In the doorway stood the young blue-eyed stranger, a cold smile on his lips, his hands hovering carelessly above the butts of his pistolas.

The effect upon Bonilla was electric. He seemed to shrink into himself. Letting go of Pablita, he growled, "Ay, caramba! It is El Chivato, Billee the Keed!" and he let loose a frightful flood of the vilest curses.

"Yes, Billy the Kid, you dirty dog! Last time I saw your ugly mug, I horsewhipped you. I see you are armed. Try to outdraw me!"

"Don't shoot, Billee," the villain pleaded hoarsely. "Válgame Dios! I heard you was hanged in Lincoln three days ago."

"You heard wrong, you yellow-bellied skunk. Let's swap lead."

"No, no, Madre Santíssima, I don't want to fight you, Billee, are we not friends?"

"I'll give you five minutes to clear out of here," the Kid spat out disgustedly. "Vamoose and never come back if you know what's good for you, and take your rum-soaked friends along."

"Sí, sí, Billee, I am leaving. Don't shoot," Bonilla cringed. "Here, I drop my guns. I am going."

Bonilla turned as if leaving, slinking away toward the back door. The Kid relaxed.

"Mira, Billy, watch out!" cried Pablita, who had seen the brute whip a derringer from his vest pocket. Bonilla whirled around, aiming his weapon of last resort at Billy's heart. But the Kid was faster. His guns coughed in unison as Bonilla staggered backward, discharging his derringer harmlessly in the air, falling to the floor with a heavy thud. His body twitched once and then lay still.

"Está muerto," said the Kid. "He asked for it."

One of the desperadoes went for his pistola, but the Kid was not only the "Fastest gun in the West," but also the one who never missed. His gun belched fire and there was a shrill cry of pain as the ruffian's weapon was shot out of his fist.

"Que viva El Chivato!" cried Don José. "He is a sure shot whose bullets never miss their target!" There was no further resistance. The death of their leader had discouraged his band of outlaws. Drunk as most of them were, they got on their horses and were never seen again in the vicinity.

"Un millón de gracias, Billee," said Pablita, giving him a big beso, "you have saved me from this vile monster. You have saved us all!"

Doña Apolinara also kissed the young hero, while the men crowded around to give him heartfelt abrazos. Then the baile started in earnest, with joy, merriment, and great sighs of relief. The Kid and Pablita danced the whole night through, her admiring glances telling him that he had conquered her heart. Dawn came as the fiesta ended.

"It is time for me to go," said the Kid, "time to say goodbye."

"Why must you go?" asked Pablita, tears welling up in her eyes. "Why not stay here among the people who love you?"

"The law is after me, bonita. They would hang me if they could. The law is always after the wrong men. Justice will come some time to this part of the country, but not as soon as we wish."

"I shall always love you," sobbed the girl, "con todo mi alma, with all my heart. I shall never forget you. Va con Dios, mi corazón." He kissed her tenderly, mounted his horse, and rode toward the rising sun. She followed him with her eyes. He turned and waved his hat. Then he slowly disappeared from her view until she saw him no more.

El Chivato

Billy was a bad man
And carried a big gun.
He was always after greasers
And kept 'em on the run.

He shot one every morning,
For to make his morning meal.
And let a white man sass him,
He was shore to feel his steel.

The simple Spanish-speaking folks of New Mexico loved Billy the Kid. They called him "El Chivato." In their legends they made Billy into a Robin Hood and Sir Galahad rolled into one. They made up many songs about him and had only good things to say about the "Keed":

◆ ◆ ◆

Billee the Keed, ay! Es hombre muy valiente. Billee was kind and good. He cared for the poor. And he was brave. He was pequeño, a little muchacho, only so big, but his heart was as big as all of Nueva Mexico. He vanquished men twice his size. Sí, señor! And he was 'andsome, a tender lover. Válgame Dios! The leetle señoritas, they all try to catch El Chivato for their sweetheart, they all try to become his querida. And the Keed, he was a great lover, palabra honor. He could have the governor's daughter if he wanted. Ay, many pretty muchachas weep rivers of tears when he is keel. Pobre Billee! El amigo de la gente, the people's friend.

El Chivato, he rode a caballo negro of the pure Arabian sangre. An animal worthy of his valor. He was clothed as befitted a man like him, in a gold-braided suit and black buckskin calzones with rows of silver bells down the legs. His sombrero, with its heavy hatband of solid gold, I tell you, it was worth at least tres cien dólares! And Billee, he lived in a castle built for him by the gente, that even cannon balls could not penetrate. La pura verdad, señor. Yes, all the women were loco, crazy, about Billee.

Fair Mexican maidens play guitars and sing
A song about Billy, their boy bandit king,
How ere his young manhood had reached its sad end
He'd a notch on his pistol for twenty-one men.

The gringos, they don't like heem, they have no love for Billee. They say he is a cruel cabrón. Carajo! Here is one of the cuentos they tell about El Chivato. . . .

The Keed had worked for Old Man Chisum, more as a pistolero than a vaquero, if you understand my meaning, señor. It was war, guerra, a war about land and cattle and water, waged by the big rancheros against each other. Bueno. The Keed thought that Chisum owed him a thousand dollars for what he had done for him, but Chisum was muy mezquino, very stingy. He does not want to pay the Keed what was coming to him. So they have a big quimera, one big brawl, and Billee rode off muy enfadado, very angry. On the way he meets his old amigo, Tom O'Fallaher.

"I should have keel him, Tomás." "Kill who?" says Tom. "That sonuvabeech Chisum, that's who." "Kill him why?" asks Tom. "The tightfisted cabrón won't pay me what he owes me." "Is that all?" says Billee's compadre. "Does not this pícaro have thousands of cattle? Why not rustle a thousand dollars' worth of his ganado? De que te asustas? Or are you afraid?"

"Afraid, me?" says Billee. "Hombre, you must be crazy. Sure, let's do it!"

So Billee and his compañero get a gang together, very tough hombres, about ten of them, and they cut out three hundred heads from Old Chisum's herd. Bueno. The Kid and his amigos are driving the cattle through the malpais when Tom says, "Billy, do you see what I see?" And Billee looks back and sees about two dozens of Chisum's boys coming after them. Well, El Chivato es muy valiente, not afraid of the devil himself. So he finds a good place to make a big fight of it and makes his stand. The Keed's muchachos are well armed with Winchesters and double-barreled shotguns. Tom, he tells Billee, "Let's just scare 'em off. These buckaroos was once our good amigos."

"No," says Billy. "What do I care that yesterday they were friends? Today they are enemies. Let's kill them!" El Chivato was not in a good mood that day. Chisum's boys fired a volley, but the Kid had placed his men on low ground and the bullets passed over them. Then Billee and his outlaws returned fire and many of the

Chisum gang toppled from their caballos, and "Fuego!" cries the Kid again, and more of his pursuers are down. "Charge! adelante!" cries the Kid as they all charge the Chisum boys, coming on like an earthquake. You should have seen him, señor, thundering ahead of his men, on his fine pure-bred stallion, in his black, gold-embroidered charro outfit, firing his pistolas with their ivory handles and gold inlay, they were worth over a thousand pesos, es cierto, señor. And they killed all of those men of Chisum's, even the wounded. There was no mercy in El Chivato that day. And most of them he had killed himself—crack, crack, crack—every bullet scoring a bull's-eye, because Billy was the greatest gunfighter in the world. Palabra honor! It was the devil who gave him this gift. Maybe Billee had sold his soul to El Diablo for this gift of never missing. Quién sabe? Only God, the devil, and Billy himself know whether it is true.

Among the wounded was a muchacho named George Dye. He was a good amigo of the Kid. A bullet had shattered his leg and he was pinned beneath his dead caballo. Billee found him thus.

"Howdy, George," said Billee, with a right friendly smile. "Yore makin' a very fine target." He cocked his pistola and aimed it at the wounded man.

"For chrissake Billy, don't shoot," cried this pobre muchacho, "are we not pards? Haven't we bunked together and sparked the same gals?"

"No use talkin' of old times," said the Kid, "this is today, and you make too good a mark not to take advantage."

"Oh! Billy, Billy, you can't mean it! Have a heart!"

"Now, George," was the answer, "hold your head real still. I don't want to mess up that ugly mug of yours, and I don't want to hurt you more'n necessary. So hold still."

Then all the muchachos started to laugh and guffaw, and George smiled too, because they knew that it had all been a joke, a bad broma, maybe, but a joke all the same. El Chivato pointed his gun right at George's cabeza, and George said: "Making fun of me, Billy, as always." And then the gun exploded, and there was a neat little red spot right dead center between George's eyes, and George lay very still. "Finito," said the Kid, blowing the smoke from the barrel of his pistola. "Let's go to town, boys, and have ourselves some tarantula juice!"

Well, señor, this is one of the cuentos the gringos tell about Billee. But it is not true. Eso no es cierto. Billee was faithful to his friends, and kind, always. He did no such thing like killing an old amigo in cold blood. The gringos tell these tales because they do not like heem. It is because he took from the rich and gave to the poor. And the rich are always the gringos, and the poor, the pobres, are us, the gente who settled here long before the coming of the norteamericanos. It all depends on which side you are on, señor.

○○

He Rose from the Grave

○○

But one day Bill, he met a man
Who was a whole lot badder,
And now he's dead,
And we ain't none the sadder.

It was a moonlit night, but inside Pete Maxwell's bedroom it was as dark as dark could be. Billy the Kid, in his stocking feet, was groping his way toward the bed. He was dog-tired but in good spirits. He had evaded Sheriff Pat Garrett's posse. Tomorrow he would get over the border into Mexico and be beyond the law. He had cut himself a thick slice of meat down in the kitchen. He would eat and then sleep. He could not see the shape of a man, gripping a six-shooter, sitting on a chair in the corner, invisible in the utter blackness. As the Kid felt his way through the room, his body was momentarily outlined against the moonlit, weather-stained window. The Kid's ears picked up a slight noise, a mere rustle in the corner. He said, "Quién es? Who is it?"

The man in the chair recognized the voice. He knew at once that it was the Kid's. The room exploded in fire and smoke. The first bullet pierced the Kid's heart. A second crashed harmlessly into the wall. It was not needed. The Kid had not made a sound. He was lying dead on the floor.

Sheriff Pat Garrett went downstairs and told McKinney and Poe, his deputies, "I think I got the Kid."

"And I think you shot the wrong man," said Poe. "Some fellow was going to the bunkhouse over there, and though it was pitch dark, I'm sure it was our Billy. I'd recognize that runt anytime, light or no light."

"Nonsense," said Garrett, and then cried out loud, "Hurraw, I got the Kid!"

At this, all the women on the ranch came running with wild lamentations, filling the place with their anguished cries. Celsa Gutiérrez, one of the Kid's sweethearts, cursed Garrett, calling him a goddam cabrón, vowing to kill him. The Navajo woman, Delvina, offered to scratch his eyes out. Abrana García called down God's punishment upon the sheriff, shaking her fists in his face. Nasaria López, dissolved in tears, offered her soul to the devil if he would strike the slayer of her beloved Billy dead. Concepción Vigil was tearing her hair out in a paroxysm of grief. "Mi muchacho, mi pobre muchacho, mi corazón," cried Celsa. "I want to kiss his face in death as I kissed it in life."

McKinney brought two candles, and everybody went up the stairs to view the body. Billy was lying on his back, open-eyed, the blood drained from his face, but it was Billy Barlow, not Billy the Kid, who was stretched out on the floor.

"That's mighty embarrassing," said Pat.

"Barlow, that no-account saddle stiff," commented Poe. "He won't be missed."

"What do we do now?" asked McKinney. "By now the Kid's got a head start. I don't feel like starting to chase him all over the country again."

"I tell you what to do," said Pat Garrett. "I pronounce this here body to be that of William Bonney, better known as Billy the Kid, and propose to bury him at once before the flies get to him. Any objections?"

There were none. The sheriff and his deputies were determined to save their reputation and loath to go on another exhausting wild chase after the fugitive. Billy's friends were equally willing to give him a chance to get away and start anew somewhere else. His many sweethearts were likewise resolved, even at the price of never seeing him again, to save their beloved Keed from a necktie party. And so without further ado they put "the other Billy" under the sod and uttered a deep sigh of relief.

While this was satisfactorily accomplished, Celsa brought Billy's horse to him in the bunkhouse and planted one last tearful kiss upon his squirrel-toothed mug. And then the Kid rode into the darkness, leaving only his legend behind.

Of Billy's life during the next ten years or so the saga has little to tell. Some say that the Kid resurrected himself in the shape of a half-crazed vagrant known as Walk-Along, who roamed the deserts and sierras with a staff in his hand and a bundle containing his few belongings on his back, living like a wild animal in dens and caves. From time to time, this strange human would haunt lonely ranch houses, frightening women with his uncouth appearance, begging for a crust of bread or a glass of milk. This Walk-Along often hinted that he was none other than the one and only Billy the Kid, and some believed him and some did not. If he was indeed Billy, then he had wonderfully disguised himself, for his own mother would not have recognized him.

Some legends had it that Billy had become a gold miner in Deadwood Gulch, where he shot down another prospector in an argument over a claim. Later, it was said, he got together a gang of outlaws rustling cattle in Montana, one more time escaping the hangman by a hair. He had by then raised a luxurious mustache to hide his rodent-like front teeth, which were his hallmark.

Then a little luck came his way. He was hired by Buffalo Bill as a rootin'-tootin' cowboy in Cody's Wild West Show. He performed in London, where a titled, moneyed young lady took a shine to him. The Kid took her for his wife and, together with her money, took her to New York. He had been born in Manhattan, but had been taken west in early childhood. Now he was curious to explore the city of his birth. He bought a swank brownstone house in Chelsea and there he and his wife settled down. By then he had adopted the name of Henry McCarty, because this happened to be his real, original name by which nobody knew him. His wife taught him manners and savoir faire. They dined at Delmonico's, O'Henry's Old Steakhouse, and Lüchow's with its fine continental cuisine. They went to the theater and vacationed at Saratoga. Then his wife died in childbirth together with the baby.

He sold the brownstone, which had become too large for him, and moved into the Hoffman House Hotel. His wife had left him enough money to last his lifetime. He changed his mustache to a distinguished-looking "Prince of Wales" beard. One could watch him sitting near the Hoffman House bar, under the famous Bouguereau painting of naked nymphs and fauns, sipping bourbon while scanning the *New York Police Gazette*. He went to races, cockfights, dogfights, and boxing matches. He did some drinking, wenching and gambling. Most of the time he was unspeakably bored. The years went by, one by one. His hair turned white. In 1936 he celebrated his seventy-fifth birthday by going on a solitary drunk. A great yearning seized him to revisit the places that had seen him in his youthful glory. He was sure that after more than half a century nobody would recognize him. Certainly, the old charges against him must long have been dropped. He packed his valise, took a sleeper to Santa Fe, and from there took a bus to Lincoln, arriving there—a typical city slicker and tourist, toting a Kodak box camera.

Time had been kind to Lincoln. It had aged gracefully without much change. The Kid had a snort in the old whiskey mill in which he had killed a hombre or two. He gave a fiver to an old geezer who was cadging drinks at the bar, asking him to take him to the town's biggest attraction—Billy the Kid's grave. On the way they found their steps dogged by an old toothless crone, half-Indian by the looks of her.

"That vieja," his guide told Billy, "is a bruja, a witch. She was one of the Kid's queridas, not the only one, I assure you. She is loco. She thinks the Kid is alive and will come back to marry her."

"Remind me to give her a few dollars on the way back. I feel sorry for her."

"You are too generous, sir. She will only drink it up. This Celsa is just an old puta. Worthless. Don't waste time on her."

They stood before the grave with the old hag hovering in the background. The Kid studied the inscription:

THE BOY BANDIT KING.
HE DIED AS HE LIVED.

"Very nice," said the Kid. At this very moment he felt a giant fist gripping his heart, squeezing the life out of it. He writhed in pain. Daylight turned into night. He was twenty-one again, hearing faint footsteps, saying; "Quién es? Is it you, Pat Garrett, my old amigo?" But it was Death, not Garrett, who had finally caught up with him.

Thus Billy the Kid—El Chivato—died once more, this time for good. The old woman knelt down beside the Kid's body, bathing his face with her tears, covering it with kisses, sobbing, "Billee, mi corazón, mi amor, you have come back to me at last!"

A Whale of a Fellow with a Gun

The most bizarre of all gunfighters was Clay Allison, a man with the knack of inventing novel ways of killing his fellows. He was known as the "Corpsemaker," and his reputation was such that saloonkeepers closed shop when they saw him coming. He had a volcanic temper that erupted into insane violence whenever he had painted his nose. As one witness of Allison's anger put it; "Throw a drink into him and he's hell turned loose."

It is certain that he was not right in the head. One who knew him commented on a crazy light dancing in Clay's eyes that chilled the blood of even the toughest hombre. A Jekyll and Hyde type, Allison was forever seesawing between elation and brooding melancholy. When in a good mood, he could play the charming southern gentleman with an exaggerated reverence for sacred womanhood. In a jocular frame of mind he would often gallop up and down Main Street, stark naked, except for sombrero, boots, spur, and gunbelt, standing upright in his stirrups, shouting pleasantries to the ladies while waving the proof of his manhood at them. He usually ended his Lady Godiva act by inviting all bystanders to have their "phlegm cutters," at his expense, in the nearest watering spot.

Strangely enough, Clay looked upon himself as a solid citizen who would not hurt a fly unless in defense of law and order. When a Missouri newspaper ran an article about the death of his fifteenth victim, the deeply offended Allison wrote a letter of protest to the editor: "I have at all times tried to use my influence toward protecting the property holders and substantial men of the country from thieves, outlaws and murderers, among whom I do not care to be classed." When asked about his profession, he often replied simply, "I am a shootist." An acquaintance concluded that Clay "was a whale of a fellow with a gun."

Clay Allison was born in 1840 on a farm in Tennessee. A fanatic adherent to the cause of Secession, he enlisted in the Tennessee Light Regiment of Artillery at the outbreak of the Civil War, but his thirst for military glory remained unquenched. He was abruptly dismissed from the service on grounds of insanity. His discharge papers noted that "Clay Allison is incapable of performing his duties as a soldier, due to a blow on the head received in childhood. Emotional or physical excitement produces paroxysms of various character, partly epileptic and partly maniacal."

Notwithstanding, he later joined Nathan Bedford Forrest's raiders as a rebel guerrilla. After the war he went West to escape, as he said, the goddam Yankee bluebellies and carpetbaggers.

He punched cows along the Brazos River in Texas, raised hell in southern Colorado, and in 1870 acquired a ranch in Colfax County, New Mexico. He quickly gained notoriety for his many violently eccentric exploits. Once, at the end of a cattle drive, he arrived at Cheyenne, Wyoming, with a raging toothache. He hot-footed it to the nearest of two dentists in town. The luckless ivory puller drilled a hole into the wrong tooth, hitting the nerve. Without saying a word, Clay got up, went to the second dentist, had the cavity filled, and returned to the first practitioner. Pinning the poor fellow down in his own dentist's chair, Clay produced a pair of pliers and, at gunpoint, pulled one of his victim's teeth without benefit of anesthesia. He was trying to wrench out a second tooth when the "patient's" anguished cries for help drew a crowd, which made Allison desist in practicing vengeful dentistry. According to legend, Clay actually pulled three teeth, his victim being none other than the renowned "Doc" Holliday, the death-dealing, tubercular dentist, gambler, and shootist. It is, unlikely however, that a character like Doc would have tamely submitted to Clay's "three teeth for one" onslaught.

At Animas, Colorado, one of the rough new towns sprouting like mushrooms along freshly laid railroad tracks, swarming with gandy dancers, cardsharps, and "soiled doves of the prairie," Clay and his brother John made a nuisance of themselves inside a dance-hall saloon by tripping the light fantastic with six-guns strapped to their thighs against all regulations. Summoned by nervous customers, Marshal Charlie Faber invited the pair to drop their artillery and hand it over to him for safekeeping during the rest of the evening.

"Why us?" Clay objected politely, his hands poised over the butts of his peacemakers. "Why single us out when all the other boys in here are allowed to keep their guns?" He was grinning amiably, but the light was dancing in his eyes. Faber left quietly, only to return shortly toting a double-barreled "greener" loaded with 00 buckshot. Ordinarily, even the boldest pistolero paled in the face of this fearful

weapon, and Faber was sure that the mere sight of it would suffice to reestablish his authority. He could not have been more wrong. When the smoke lifted, the marshal was dead from two bullets, one from each brother, in his heart. John ended up with his right arm smashed by buckshot. Clay escaped unhurt.

For this little ruckus Clay was quite willing to have himself arrested and stand trial, but only on the condition that he could first see to it that his brother was properly cared for in the hospital at Fort Lyon, and that he himself would be neither handcuffed nor chained. There had been dozens of witnesses to the shoot-out, but, strange to say, not a single one of them showed up when the trial opened. Neither could twelve men, good and true, be found to serve as jurors. Case dismissed.

Bringing Clay to justice was a recurring and frustrating problem. Clay killed a Mexican, called Alvarez, seemingly just for the fun of it. Court was in session somewhere in Colfax County. The sheriff found Clay bending elbows at the bar of the St. James Hotel at Cimarron. He approached his quarry with trepidation: "Clay, the judge wants you for makin' that greaser die of lead poisonin.' "

"All right, but don't ask me to come unheeled."

Clay took his Winchester and his two Colt .45s and the two of them ambled off to the courthouse like old pals.

"That's a mighty nice hat you're wearing, marshal," Allison remarked casually. "Let me have a look at it."

The marshal obliged. Allison folded the brand-new imposing headgear three ways, tossed it high into the air, and put three bullets through it before it touched ground. "There, friend," he said, handing the poor man the hat that now resembled a sieve, "now you can say you've been under fire."

In court the clerk read the warrant while the judge contemplated Clay's armament, ordering: "Marshal, disarm the defendant!"

"Clay," the marshal pleaded timidly, "why don't you let me have your weapons for a while. I'll take good care of them."

"Well, now. I came here quiet and peaceably, but I'll be doggone if I give up my shooting irons."

The judge was growing impatient: "Marshal, disarm the prisoner. The dignity of this court must be upheld."

"Your honor, the prisoner don't like it."

"Goddamn it to hell, marshal, the defendant must and will be disarmed before I start hearing this case."

"Your Honor, if you insist, you've got to disarm him yourself. I'll be damned if I'll try. I've got a wife and kids."

"Under these circumstances, this court stands adjourned. Case dismissed!"

In 1870, swigging toothache medicine in an Elizabethtown, New Mexico, whiskey mill, Clay was accosted by a distraught woman, wailing that her husband had run amok, killing several people, and had wound up cutting the throat of his own baby daughter. Always willing to help a lady in distress, Clay, together with a drinking companion, broke into the jail where the presumed murderer was held. They dragged him to a nearby slaughterhouse and there hanged him from a projecting roof beam. Not yet satisfied, Clay cut off the man's head, impaled it on a stick, and with his ghastly trophy galloped thirty miles to Cimarron, where he exhibited it, among guffaws of maniacal laughter, to the customers of Henri Lambert's saloon. According to legend, the head's original owner had fallen victim to a false rumor. His widow was not pleased.

A bowlegged human named Mace Bowman was practicing fast draws in the backyard of Lambert's establishment. Bowman was supposed to be faster with a gun than Clay, who at once went to see whether this was true. The two of them engaged in a friendly contest, trying to outdraw each other, shooting at bottles, tin cans, chickens, and whatever else could serve as a target. It quickly became obvious that Bowman was a lot faster on the draw than Clay, who showed signs of getting riled.

"Let's you and me have a *real* shoot-out with no holds barred," Clay suggested. "Then we'll see if you can outdraw me."

"I've got a better notion," said the suddenly very apprehensive Bowman. "Let's go inside and see which of us can *outdrink* the other."

It was an offer Clay could not refuse. They tossed off one shot after the other neat until becoming booze-blind, when Clay proposed another kind of amusement. They took off their boots and socks, stripped down to their longjohns, and began firing away at each other, particularly at their feet, not to maim and kill, but "to make each other dance." The bardog bobbed and ducked all afternoon, "more than a hundred times," to avoid being hit by volleys of bullets. The fun lasted until the two hell-raisers' supply of ammunition was exhausted. Miraculously, nobody was hurt, but the damage to the bottled goods lined up on the backbar was terrific.

Clay Allison has been called a "man of grim originality"—not without reason. Take, for instance, his bizarre fight to the death with "Chunk" Colbert. Chunk was a gunslinger with fourteen notches carved in the handle of his revolver. Intent on adding a fifteenth, he came down from Colorado to Raton, gunning for Clay. He had no particular reason for it, except that he wished to enhance his reputation as a bad hombre. Clay ignored Chunk, neither trying to meet nor to avoid him. To everybody's stupefaction, because Chunk had made no secret about his intentions, he and Clay behaved like old pals when they finally bumped into each other. They caroused together for a day or two, painted the town red, frequented a couple of cathouses and entertained themselves with shooting out lamps and windows, all the time keeping a watchful eye upon each other.

"Let's you and me have a horse race," Chunk suggested.

"Why not?" said Clay.

Chunk had the faster horse and won the race, which instantly put Clay into his "sod-pawing" mood. They started arguing and Clay slapped Chunk across the face.

"We might just as well start killin' each other now," said Chunk offhandedly, rubbing his cheek.

"Good idea!" Clay agreed. "But let's do it in a special way to give the citizens a good show." He proposed having a shoot-out on horseback, specifying that he and Chunk should take their stations opposite each other, some two hundred yards apart, and at a given signal spur their horses into a dead run, firing at will as they came thundering on. They were just about ready to climb into their saddles when the bell inside the Clifton House summoned its customers to the table. "Let's put on the nose bag and eat first," said Chunk. "We ought to see that the dead one goes to hell with a full stomach." "Let's," Clay agreed. "I'm kind of gut-shrunk myself."

They went into the place and sat down at a table opposite each other, their six-shooters on their laps. They ordered a huge mess of ham, eggs, and potatoes, with coffee and whiskey on the side. One account has it that Clay ordered "coffee and pistols for two," but of course they had brought their artillery with them. They ate in silence, seemingly totally absorbed in filling their bellies, taking their time. They sat like this for almost an hour, lazily stirring the coffee with their gun barrels, always putting their Colts back on their laps, knowing that one, perhaps two, would never rise from the table. It says much for the Raton citizens' sangfroid that the place was full of other diners and gents painting their tonsils at the bar, intent upon watching the show, taking a big chance of being hit by a stray bullet once the shooting started.

Slowly and deliberately, Chunk laid down his fork and put his right hand under the table, seemingly fishing for his napkin, but it came up instead with his Colt .45. As he fumbled in a desperate hurry to beat Clay to the draw, his gun barrel got caught under the table's edge. The shot was deflected, the bullet whizzing harmlessly by Clay's head. Clay did not miss, neatly drilling a hold through Chunk's skull above the left eye. Chunk fell forward, his face coming to rest on his plate, settling among whatever was left of his order of "grunt an' cackle." Thus he expired "with egg on his face."

Clay went on eating as if nothing had happened, encouraging the fascinated onlookers to do the same. When he had finished, he pushed back his chair, rose, and addressed his audience: "Gentlemen, the proposed fight is now off, owing to an accident to one of the principals."

Clay's most famous, novel, and grotesque duel occurred as the result of an argument with a neighbor about the location of a fence. Clay's emotional Vesuvius erupted. A fight to the finish was in order. Clay specified the manner in which the duel was to be fought. The neighbor, obviously a citizen with his bark on, agreed. Both first uprooted an unmarked headstone from a nearby bone orchard, dragging it to the site of the proposed fight. They then dug a trench seven feet square. They stripped and jumped, stark naked, into the pit, armed with bowie knives of equal length. By mutual consent they battled savagely until one of them was killed. The fight was long and terrible, but at last Clay emerged the victor, though dripping blood from many wounds. Both combatants had agreed before the fight that the trench in which they struggled should become the loser's grave. Wasting no time, Clay covered his opponent's body with earth removed during the digging. Also according to their agreement, he set up the headstone above the grave—suitably engraved.

Those who expected Clay Allison to end his life as spectacularly as he had lived it were to be disappointed. On July 1, 1877, he was hauling sacks of grain on his heavy buckboard. As he started his team, one of the sacks began to fall off. Clay made a grab for it, lost his balance, and toppled from his seat. As he lay prone on the ground, one of the rear wheels rolled over him, breaking his neck, killing him instantly. He was thirty-seven years old and had, as well as can be determined, killed eighteen men. His mourners were few.

The King of the Pistoleers

A potpourri of contemporary quotations.

"Six feet one in his moccasins, deep-chested, with quiet gray eyes, clear and calm as a woman's, an almost womanly gentleness of expression, bright chestnut hair floating over his shoulders— it does not seem a promising picture to those who would hear of adventure. But that small, muscular hand had taken deadly aim at scores of men; before the gaze of that eye many a bold border spirit had quailed. He was the 'Magnificent,' Wild Bill Hickok, the terror of evil-doers."

Ladies found Wild Bill the handsomest man west of the Mississippi. His steely, piercing eyes could be the ruin of the chastest woman, turning to the glittering steel when faced with danger. "He is a naturally fine-looking fellow, muscular and athletic, as lithe and agile as the Borneo Boys of circus fame. Ah, Wild Bill, the Adonis of the Prairie!"

General Custer's wife, Libby, looked upon the "Knight Chivalric" as one of the finest specimens of "rugged American manhood." A Kansas lady vowed that she always thought John Wilkes and Edwin Booth the most beautiful men in the world—until she met Wild Bill.

HOWEVER...

"The man they call Wild Bill is an effeminate-looking fellow, his hair is falling in auburn ringlets over his shoulders like that of a girl. In contrast, his nasal organ is quite out of proportion. They call him the 'Human Ant-Eater,'' and the 'Cyrano de Bergerac of the Plains.' Hickok shot and killed a man for calling him 'Duck Bill.' "

WELL, BUT...

He was called the "King of the Pistoleers," the "Knight Chivalric," and the "Pistol Dead Shot." He once bagged two Indians galloping away from him at top speed, one riding behind the other, with a single bullet, coolly waiting until both horses and riders were perfectly aligned. His bullet never failed to find its target. No man in the whole wide world was as adept as our hero at wielding a six-gun. Inside a Kansas saloon Hickok performed a Homeric feat, never repeated since. Two ruffians, killers of ill repute, assailed him simultaneously from front and rear. Watching the ruffian behind him in the reflection of the barroom mirror with one eye, the other fixed on the assailant before him, the champion "triggernometrist" shot both of them through the heart with his brace of ivory-handled Colts.

As marshal in Hays City, Wild Bill had a row with Captain Tom Custer, brother of the famous general. Not wishing to face the "Sir Galahad of Pistols," the vindictive officer hired two murderous miscreants to kill the man who had humiliated him. They found Hickok inside the Free Soil drinking establishment. One of the soldiers tackled the bold marshal from the front, the other caught him from the rear. Hickok got one arm free, pulled his Colt, putting it over his shoulder, and killed the trooper behind him. Then he took care of the fellow in front with equally deadly effect.

To demonstrate his skill with his fabled ivory-handled "dragoons," Wild Bill tossed his wide-brimmed hat high into the air, using it as a convenient target. He shot an even-spaced row of holes along the outside of the rim as it was falling and before it touched the ground.

Hickok was able to hit the ace of spades, at fifty paces, with all six bullets, drive a cork into a bottle at seventy-five yards, and hit spinning silver dollars while racing his horse. He could hit a fly crawling on a wall.

HOWEVER...

"Old Bill couldn't hit the side of a barn at fifty paces. He was snail-like slow with a Colt. He was a successful killer because he shot the other fellow when he wasn't looking. He fired at a man sitting across from him at a table—and missed. As marshal Hickok had a fatal flaw, he often shot the wrong man, shooting a friend or harmless bystander instead of the bad hombre he was aiming at. When it came to telling an honest fellow from a felon, Wild Bill couldn't tell shit from honey."

It is said that on one occasion Bill pursued two murderers running away from him in *opposite directions*, up and down the street, sending them up the flume *simultaneously*, which he could have done if nature had fitted him with a *third eye* at the back of his head.

WELL, BUT...

"He was absolutely fearless. Fear was not a part of his make-up. He was afraid of no man, nor death, nor the devil and all his minions. Any man who by his own force and fearlessness beats the dark forces of savagery and crime, so that civilization may be free to take another step forward on her march to progress—is he not the greatest and truest type of the frontiersman? Such a one was Wild Bill."

Asked how many men he had killed, Hickok replied: "I suppose I have killed considerably over a hundred, but, by heaven, never without good cause. I was twenty-eight years old when I killed my first white man. I never included Indians in the list of those I sent to the far side of Jordan. This fellow was a cardsharp and counterfeiter. I was then in a hotel in Leavenworth, and seeing some loose characters around, and as I had some money about me, I thought it better to retire to my room. I soon heard men at my door. I pulled out my revolvers and bowie knife and held them ready, but concealed, and pretended to sleep. The door was opened and five men entered the room. One whispered, 'Let's kill the son of a bitch. I bet he has money.' I kept perfectly still until just as the knife touched my breast, I sprang aside and buried mine in his heart, and then used my revolvers on the others, right and left. One I killed, another I wounded, and then, gentlemen, I dashed from the room, and with the help of some soldiers, captured the whole gang of them—fifteen in all. Would you not have done the same?"

"Single-handedly, 'Magnificent Bill' wiped out McCanles' gang of Confederate cutthroats and robbers, no fewer than ten of them, with his trusty rifle, his silver-ornamented revolvers, and keen bowie knife. Remark our hero striking savage blows, following the devils up from one side to the other of the room into the corners, striking and slashing until all were dead. He had sent to the Nether World six of the desperadoes with his Dragoon Colts, and dispatched the other four blood-thirsty devils with his knife."

While traveling by rail one night, Bill had a narrow escape. Eight bloodthirsty bravos, determined to murder the marshal who had so often thwarted their evil designs, had secretly boarded the train. But Bill was on his guard. He left the car in which he was sitting, and with a pistol in each hand, went to that in which he knew he would find his would-be assassins. He threw open the door, and walked up to them, covering the gang with his pistols.

"Now, you scoundrels," Bill addressed them, "get out of this car, or I'll put a bullet into each of you. Leave the train instantly!"

His tone was so quiet that it would, of itself, have attracted no attention from bystanders, but they saw *shoot* in his eyes, and prudently retreated backward to the door of the car.

"Jump!" he commanded as they hesitated a moment on the platform, and the muzzles gleamed ominously in the flickering light of the next car. The train was rushing over the level prairie at a fearful rate, but death awaited them here, while that jump might give each a chance for life. Into the darkness then, each man leaped as the train sped onward; one was killed outright, three badly hurt in the fall; but if they had not jumped, there would have been none that escaped.

And then there was Wild Bill's famous fight with Conquering Bear. "Bill jumped from his hiding place, crying out defiance to the thunder-struck warrior: 'Defend yourself, you treacherous, lying red-skin!'

"Bill drew his pistols and tossed one to the savage chief. But Conquering Bear knew too well the deadly aim of his antagonist and refused to fight with pistols.

" 'If you don't fight, I'll shoot you like the good-for-nothing dog that you are,' Bill hissed from between his teeth, and the trembling Indian chose the bowie knife as the weapon to be used. The field of battle was prepared, but Conquering Bear stood motionless.

" 'Cowardly, stinking coyote! If you don't come and fight, I'll shoot you down in your tracks!'

"Aroused, the Indian leaped into the ring and the fight began. As the white man made a pass with his keen-edged blade, the Indian drew back as if to make a rush at him; now with a tigerish thirst for blood, each leaps upon the other, his left arm grasping his antagonist's body, his right hand holding his knife, the two blades edge to

edge. So they cling together, each striving to secure some advantage, however trifling; but in vain; they are too evenly matched. The gray eyes gleam like steel as they turn with every movement of the savage, and the dark orbs of the Indian are no less watchful. Then Conquering Bear again springs forward, and once more two flashing blades clash in the sunlight. Both by vigorous passes endeavor to surprise their enemy. At last Bill sees his opportunity and cuts at the Indian's heart, but a medal on the broad, tawny breast received the blow, and the knife glanced aside, though not without inflicting a deep gash in the Indian's side. But the thrust, so nearly successful, has exposed Bill's own body, and the savage makes a desperate lunge at the white man's heart. The scout's left arm, however, has served as a shield for the more vital part, and the flesh is stripped from the bone from the shoulder to the elbow. Still they fought on, though growing weaker every moment, as the blood flowed from their terrible wounds. Conquering Bear saw that victory must come quickly if it precede death, and once more made a pass at the scout's heart; but the blow was skillfully parried, and in another instant the keen edge of the white man's knife was drawn across the tawny throat; for a moment the swarthy form swayed in the air, the head thrown backward, then fell to earth, the blood gushing from the ghastly wound. So ended the fight. There was none braver than James Butler Hickok, known to the world as WILD BILL."

HOWEVER...

"It is disgusting to see the eastern papers crowding in everything they can get hold of about 'Wild Bill.' If they only knew the real character of the man they so want to worship! 'Wild Bill' is nothing more than a drunken, reckless, murderous coward, who is treated with contempt by true bordermen, and should have been hung years ago for the murder of innocent men. He shot an old teamster in the back for a trifling provocation, and was booted out of a Leavenworth saloon by a boy bartender—a fine example of his 'bravery.'

"And about that yarn of the Old Ant-Eater wiping out a dozen of McCanles' ruffians all by himself—he gunned down David Mc-Canles, who was unarmed, while hiding behind a curtain, shot the second man from behind a door, and shot the third fellow in the back while the poor sot was running away.

"The whole McCanles deal is pure hogwash. Wild Bill is depicted with his bowie knife up to the hilt in one bushwhacker's heart, with half a dozen men upon the floor in picturesque attitudes, two of the three remaining desperadoes have their knives puncturing his waistcoat, and the final one of the ten is levelling terrific blows at his head with a clubbed musket. We congratulate Bill on the fact that it is rather not true. It would have been too risky even for Bill, the 'Great Scout of the Plains.'

"One who knows says that Bill's brave deeds exist only in the fevered, prostituted brains of eastern scriveners. The farther away the writer is from the object of his veneration, the more heroic become the 'heroic deeds of Wild Bill, the "Achilles of the Western Prairies." ' "

WELL, BUT...

"No finer physique, no greater strength, no more personal courage, no superior skill with firearms, no better horsemanship than his —especially horsemanship. Admirers call him the 'Centaur of the Plains.' His fabled equestrian skills seem to fuse man and horse into one single living sculpture.

"His extraordinary black mare, Nell, was a noble animal with traits to match his own. Bill had trained her to perform tricks which would have put the most famous circus horse to shame. If Hickok slowly waved his hand over her head with a circular motion Nell would fall down as if struck by a cannon ball, and whenever the Great Scout would mention the precious mare's sagacity she would wink affirmatively to the great amusement of all present. Obeying Wild Bill's low whistle she jumped upon the billiard table of the Lyon House. One well remembered feat was Bill mounting Nell inside Hoff's saloon and with one bound, bursting through the batwing doors, alighting in the middle of the street."

HOWEVER...

"Old Nell was black, all right, but she was a 'He,' not a 'She,' a broken down old nag, blind in the right eye, and ripe for the knacker. As to Wild Bill's equestrian feats, they included frequently toppling from his horse, particularly if he had filled himself to the top with cheap whiskey. As for jumping in one bound from the interior of Hoff's whiskey mill, through the door, over a wide porch and over a five foot fence and boardwalk in front, some fifty feet in all, that's a tall fish story."

WELL, BUT...

"Bill was the darling of the weaker sex, whether virtuous matron or sporting woman. Withal, he was a model of comportment, a true gentleman in every sense of the word. His moral standards were high. He had none of the swaggering gait, or the barbaric jargon ascribed to him by the Beadle penny pamphlets. With his fine, handsome face, free from blemish, his light mustache, blue-gray eyes, and magnificent forehead, he was irresistible to the fair sex, yet never stooped low enough to perform a 'mean action.' And he was well-groomed always, affecting a black frock-coat and the finest, whitest linen shirts. His boots were made of kid, or the thinnest finest calf. He paid as much as fifty dollars for a pair.

"He kept house with his life-long love, Calamity Jane, but only after they were duly wed and received the blessings of an ordained clergyman. 'Oh, dearest Bill,' Calamity whispered in Wild Bill's ear, 'I love thee and will be thine forever. And I shall be to you a true wife. Do not believe the vile tales told about me. I am yet chaste and no gossip or scandal shall henceforth touch me. But let us keep our marriage secret. There are jealous men who would kill you for having won Calamity's heart, and there are jealous women who would poison me for having robbed them of the hope of winning your love.' 'It shall be so,' said Bill. When Calamity Jane finally shuffled off her mortal coils her last words were: 'Bury me next to my darling Bill!' "

HOWEVER...

Hickok's morals were much the same as those of Achilles, King David, Lancelot, and the Chevalier Bayard, though his amours were hardly as frequent as David's or as inexcusable as Lancelot's.

"He always had a mistress. I knew two or three of them. One I believe was a redhead to whom he gave twenty-five dollars to make her leave town. There was Nan Ross, but Bill told her he was through with her and she moved on. When Mrs. Lake, the widow of 'Old Lake of Circus Fame,' came to Abilene, she fell for him hard, fell all the way clear to the basement . . .

"He was a libertine and a rowdy, but the tales that Calamity Jane was his paramour, or even his wife, are pure horse manure. Whatever can be said against Bill, he was fastidious and picked his women for their looks. The idea of taking up with a drunken, foul-mouthed whore like Calamity, with that ugly mug of hers, is just plain humbug. One man said of Bill that his looks and movements were so feminine that some suspected him of practicing that vice which shall forever be nameless. They are wrong, but Bill is great lover?—that's ridiculous!"

WELL, BUT...

"Cat-eyed, he was. He slid into a room, keeping his back to the wall always, watching every man and every movement like a hawk. Not the slightest detail escaped him. He looked like a man who lived in expectation of getting killed. Nobody ever was able to tackle him from behind. Over the years he had developed the habitual alertness to shoot fast and to shoot first. Whenever Hickok sat down at a table, whether to eat or to play a game of cards, he always positioned himself with his back to the wall. This he did quite automatically. It had become second nature to him."

HOWEVER...

On August 21, 1876, Wild Bill sat in on a game of poker at Nuttal and Mann's saloon in Deadwood. He had settled down with his face to the wall and his back to the swinging doors. It was the first time he left his back uncovered and also his last. He was holding a pair of aces and a pair of eights, known ever since as the "dead man's hand."

A tinhorn gambler named Jack McCall came up behind him and shouted, "Take that!" and neatly drilled a hole through Wild Bill's cerebellum. The bullet passed through Hickok's head and came to rest, permanently, in the wrist of his poker partner, Captain Frank Massey. Frank later made it his habit to enter saloons with the exultant cry: "Gentlemen, the bullet which killed Wild Bill has come to town!"

The physician who inspected Hickok's body wrote: "I have seen many dead men on the field of battle and in civil life, but Wild Bill's was the prettiest corpse I ever saw."

A Western Duel

One cold night a stranger entered the Legal Tender Saloon, finding an assortment of gents warming their backsides at the chimbley fire. The newcomer shed his bear coat, jumped high in the air, clicking his heels, flapped his wings, and screamed like a painter. "I'm the Wrath of God," he yelled. "I'm the bad man from hellfire Creek who can whup his weight in wildcats. I'm the ring-tailed roarer spilin' fur a fight. Who want's to cut his wolf loose?" He looked expectantly from one man to the other but could find no takers.

After a long silence an old trapper, his cheek full of an oversized chaw of 'baccer, spoke up: "Stranger, we fight nothin hyar but Injins, but if yore so danged eager for a fight, let's have a spittin' contest. I bet you a prime beaver plew I kin outshoot you at ten paces."

"Stranger, yore a beauty," said the bad man from Hellfire Creek. "It's a deal. Let's see you do it."

They put up the pot, the ring-tailed roarer a five-dollar piece, the old trapper his beaver plew. They put a dime on the floor and measured off ten paces with a piece of chalk. The man who could whup his weight in wildcats bit off a chunk out of his twist of 'baccer and started chawin', and after masticating for a long spell gathered up the ambeer in his mouth and spat. His wad landed within an inch of the dime. The Wrath of God jumped high into the air, clicked his heels, and crowed like a rooster.

"Oldtimer," he said triumphantly, "beat this if you can."

The white-bearded trapper got down on his knees, sighted along his arm, using his thumb like a gunsight, and let fly, his wad landing plum center on the dime. The old man got up, bent down slowly, picked the dime out of the wad of ambeer, pocketed the dollars, and smiled his toothless smile.

"Is that how you do things around hyar?" said the ring-tailed roarer, putting on his bear coat again and disappearing out the door into the darkness beyond.

"This hoss sez the drinks are on me," announced the ancient beaver man, whose name was Old Bill Williams.

∘◦∘

The Nuptials of Dangerous Davis

∘◦∘

On the morning on which Adam Forepaugh entered the city of Laramie, and with a grand array of his circus's hump-backed dromedaries, club-footed elephants, and an uncalled-for amount of pride, pomp, and circumstance, captured the town, Dangerous Davis, clad in buckskin and glass beads, and ornamented with one of Smith & Wesson's brass-mounted, self-cocking Black Hills models, entered His Honor's office, and walking up to the counter where the Judge deals out justice to the vagabond tenderfoot, and bankrupt non-resident, as well as to the law-defying Laramite, called for $5.00 worth of matrimony.

On his arm leaned the fair form of the one who had ensnared the heart of the frontiersman, and who had evidently gobbled up the manly affections of Dangerous Davis. She was resplendent in new clothes, and a pair of Indian moccasins, and when she glided up to the centre of the room, the casual observer might have been deceived into the belief that she was moving through the radiant atmosphere like an $11.00 peri, if it had not been for the gentle patter of her moccasins as it fell upon the floor with the sylphlike footfall of the prize elephant as he moves around the ring to the dreamy strains of "Old Zip Coon." A large "filled" ring gleamed and sparkled on her hand and vied in splendor with a large seed wart on her front finger. The ends of her nails were draped in the deepest mourning, and as she leaned her head against the off shoulder of Dangerous Davis, the ranche butter from her tawny locks made a deep and lasting impression on his buckskin bosom.

At this auspicious moment His Honor entered the room, with a green-covered German almanac for 1852 and a copy of *Robinson Crusoe* under his arm, and as he saw the young thing who was about to unite herself to the bold, bad man from Bitter Creek, he burst into tears, while Judge Blair, who had adjourned the District Court in order to witness the ceremony, sat down behind the stove and sobbed like a child. At this moment William Crout, who has been married under all kinds of circumstances and in eleven languages, entered the room and inspired confidence in the weeping throng.

Dangerous Davis changed his quid of tobacco from one side of his mouth to the other, spat into his hands, and asked to see the Judge's matrimonial price list. The Judge showed him some different styles, out of which Dangerous Davis selected the one he wanted.

By this time about one hundred and thirteen men, who had been waiting around the court room during the past week in order to be drawn as jurymen, had crowded in to witness the ceremony.

After all the preliminaries had been gone through with, the Judge commenced reading the marriage service out of a copy of the Clown's Comic Song Book. When he asked if anyone present had any objections to the proceedings, Price, from force of habit, rose and said, "I object;" but Dangerous Davis caressed his brass-mounted Grecian bend, and Price withdrew his objection.

After the usual ceremony, the Judge put the bridegroom through some little initiations, instructed him in the grand hailing signs, grips, passwords and signals, swore him to support the Constitution of the United States, pronounced the benediction on the newly wedded pair, and the ceremony closed with an extemporaneous speech by Judge Brown and profound silence and thoughtfulness on the part of Brockway, as he reflected upon the dangers which constantly surround us.

Dangerous Davis mounted his broncho, and tying his new wife on behind him on the saddle with an old shawl strap, plunged his spurs into the panting sides of his calico-colored steed, and in a few moments was flying over the green plains, while the mountain breeze caught up the oleaginous saffron-hued tresses of the bride and in wild glee mingled them with the broncho's sorrel tail, and tossed them to the four winds of heaven.

Killing Off the James Boys

Now that a terrible mortality has again broken out among the James boys, it is but justice to a family who have received so many gratuitous obituary notices to say that the James boys are still alive and enjoying a reasonable amount of health and strength.

Although the papers are generally agreed upon the statement that they are more or less dead, yet in a few days the telegraph will announce their death again. They are dying on every hand. Hardly a summer zephyr stirs the waving grass that it does not bear upon its wings the dying groan of the James boys. Every blast of winter howls the requiem of a James boy. James boys have died in Texas and in Minnesota, in New England and on the Pacific coast. They have been yielding up the ghost whenever they had a leisure moment. They would rob a bank or a printing office, or some other place where wealth is known to be stored, and then they would die. When business was very active, one of the brothers would stay at home and attend to work while the other would go and lay down his life.

Whenever the yellow fever let up a little the Grim Destroyer would go for a James boy, and send him to his long home.

The men who had personally and individually killed the James boys from time to time contemplate holding a grand mass meeting and forming a national party. This will no doubt be the government next year.

Let us institute a reform. Let us ignore the death of every plug who claims to be a James boy, unless he identifies himself. Let us examine the matter and see if the trade mark is on every wrapper and blown in the bottle, before we fill the air with woe and bust the broad canopy of heaven wide open with our lamentations over the untimely death of the James boys. If we succeed in standing them off while they live, we can afford to control our grief and silently battle with our emotions when they are still in death, until we know we are snorting and bellowing over the correct corpse.

Theme and Variations

Old Slim is suspected of horse theft. An improvised court sentences him to be hung. The verdict is executed on the spot, a nearby tree coming mighty handy. Half an hour later a fellow appears leading the missing horse by the bridle. It has not been stolen. It merely ran away. The boys are scratching their heads, but erring is human. Smilin' Jack, known for his winning ways, is chosen to explain the situation to Old Slim's wife. He rides over to her house:

"Mrs. Mulligan, ma'am, I don't rightly know how to put this, but we hung your Slim for horse stealin'. Then we found out he didn't do it. I guess the joke's on us."

♦ ♦ ♦

Old Slim is hung for horse theft. His innocence is proven—post mortem. Smilin' Jack is appointed to gently break the news to Slim's old lady. He rides over to her place, determined to make it short:

"Are you the Widow Mulligan?"

"I'm Mrs. Mulligan, but I ain't no widder."

"Want to bet?"

♦ ♦ ♦

Old Slim is charged with having stolen a fine saddle horse. The boys are in a lynching mood. They put Old Slim on a horse with his hands tied behind his back. They lead the animal to a tree, put a rope around Slim's neck, and fasten the other end to a branch above him. Somebody slaps the animal's rump so that it runs off, leaving Old Slim dangling, kicking his heels for a while until he's dead. A little later the fellers find out they hanged the wrong man.

"This here little accident is kind of awkward," says the man who acted as the chief executioner. "Who's to tell his missus?"

"Let Smilin' Jack do it," is the unanimous decision. So Jack moseys over to Old Slim's place. "Mrs. Mulligan," he says, "there's been a slight mishap. Nobody's fault, really. Some darn fool said Slim was a hoss thief. Slim's a-sittin' on his pony, and they tied him up, and put the horse, with Slim on it, under the nearest tree, and placed a rope around your husband's neck, wrapping the other end around a convenient branch. They was about leading the pony from out under him when I says, 'Whoa, boys, let's not be hasty. This could be a mistake we don't want to be sorry about later. Let's talk this over.'

"So we all go over to the Legal Tender to resolve the matter over a jolt of sneaky pete and, natcherally, come to the conclusion that Slim couldn't have done it. So we all go over to where we've left him to bring him the good news, and I'll be damned, ma'am, if that fool hoss hasn't walked off, leaving Old Slim dangling in the air. We took him down and got some whiskey into him, but we was too late by a minit. It's a goddam shame, ma'am, but accidents will happen."

◆　◆　◆

They hung Old Slim for horse theft. Just a sad joke, really. The buckaroos deputized Smilin' Jack, on account of his savoir faire, to explain matters to Slim's old lady.

"Why me, always me?" Jack complained.

" 'Cause you're good at jawin'," they told him.

So Jack moseyed over to Slim's spread. "Mrs. Mulligan," Smilin' Jack says, "the boys asked me to tell you that some goddam dudes used your Slim to decorate a tree."

"Did he cash in his chips, at last?!" said the widow.

"It was like this, ma'am," Smilin' Jack explained. "Me, and the fellers, and Ole Slim, was bendin' an elbow at Nuttal and Mann's Number Ten."

"Boozin' and gamblin' and fornicatin' with the soiled doves, the hornswoggled son of a bitch!" said the widow.

"A sportin' man, Slim was, ma'am, a reg'lar fun-lovin fellow."

"By God! And what fun did I have?" complained the widow.

"Well, Old Slim, he tried his luck at the faro table and lost all his wampum, and then changed to blackjack and chuck-a-luck, and lost his watch and chain, and his stickpin too, come to think of it."

"His stickpin, you say? The low-down bastard! A diamond the size of a grape!" screamed the widow.

"Glass, really, ma'am, just plain glass," said Smilin' Jack. "Well, arter that, Slim sat in on a game of stud and lost his new boots, standin' there in his stockin' feet. Lost all his tail feathers, I'm afraid."

"The no-good son of a gun! I need a new pair of shoes and the sorry dog wastes his dineros that way!" complained the widow.

"W-a-a-l, Mrs. Mulligan, I thought to do him and you a favor. There were these rich dudes in our watering spot, city slickers from back East, tryin' to play the western he-man . . ."

"Come here to cure their ailin' lungs, the chicken-chested bastards," the widow interrupted.

" 'Xactly ma'am. Well, I told Ole Slim to get on his pony and ride off, and then I raised the devil, yellin' that Slim stole a hoss, and the dudes to make up a posse and go arter him. It made those gents swell up, all right."

"Makes no sense," commented the widow.

"Don't you get it, Mrs. Mulligan? I figgered Slim'd let 'em catch him and bring him back for a necktie party, and then hit 'em for damages, defamashiun of character, false arrest, and playin' posse without bein' properly deputized."

"For how much?" inquired the widow.

"I thought for 'bout five hundred smackeroos."

"You cheap son of a gun!" said the widow.

"W-a-a-l, ma'am, we saddle stiffs was waitin' for the dudes to come back, and back they came, but without Slim."

"It figgers," was the widow's comment.

"Where's Old Slim?" we asks.

"Died of hemp fever," said the chief dude. "We had a proper necktie party. No use wastin' time pussyfootin' around."

"Are you locoed?" says I. "You strung up an innocent man!"

"You figgered five hundred dollars for a false arrest. Hangin' Slim should be worth a hell of a lot more," said the widow.

"My feelins 'xactly. Me and the boys took them dudes straightaway over to the bank and made 'em shell out. I'm right sorry, ma'am, that my plan didn't work out, but the joke's on me."

"Never you mind," said the widow. "How much?"

" 'Bout five thousand bucks, near's I can tell. In gold too, no paper. I've got it right here."

"Come to think, Old Slim, he did have some good in him," said the widow.

◆ ◆ ◆

Old Slim is a compulsive gambler. He moseys over to Nuttal and Mann's Saloon Number Ten, at Deadwood, for a game of stud. One of the players, falsely, suspects Slim of cheating and shoots him dead. "Shucks," says one of the boys, "somebody's got to tell his missus." Smilin' Jack is elected. He rides over to Slim's and commiserates with the departed's wife:

"You know how it is, ma'am. Old Slim's got the gamblin' fever. So he goes to Nuttal and Mann's and tries his luck at faro, and he loses and loses—ev'ry cent he's got. So he tries to recoup his losses playin' three-card monte. He shouldn't have done it. That's a sucker's game. So he loses his gold watch and chain, and diamond ring too. Next he sits in on a poker game, and stakes his prize bull and, after he's gone, stakes his saddle horse and loses it. I reckon it warn't Slim's lucky day."

"That no-good husband of mine. That son of a bitch. I'll kill him!"

"Don't incommodate yourself, ma'am, somebody's already done that job for you!"

◆ ◆ ◆

Poor Old Slim got hisself shot over somethin' that wasn't any concern of his. "You was there, you've seen it," the saddle bums told Smilin' Jack, "you better go tell Slim's missus. You're good at that kind of thing. You've got a way with words."

"How you flatter me," says Smilin' Jack, but he hitches up his buckboard and drives over to Mrs. Mulligan, the brand-new widder woman.

"Life's one damn thing after another," he tells her.

"Ain't it the truth!"

"Ole Slim was playin' poker at the Number Ten Saloon."

"I know where he's at, the bum."

"Wild Bill is the sheriff right now. Those eastern writers call him the King of the Pistoleers. Between you and me, ma'am, we call him the Human Ant-eater, on account of his nose. Old Slim was there at the same time, also playin' poker. He's sittin' there with Deadshot Rube. Bill gets it into his head that Rube's dealing from the bottom and tells him so. Rube's insulted and throws down on Bill. They go for their artillery and swap lead. They're bangin' away at each other acrost the table. You know ma'am, that the King of the Pistoleers can't hit the side of a barn at twenty paces and Deadshot Rube can't hit the bottle in front of him. They keep missing each other, but they hit the bardog and poor Old Slim at the other end of the room. The bardog gets away with a flesh wound, but poor Slim gets it in the head and the heart and cashes in his chips right then and there."

"Tough luck."

"Well, Wild Bill and Deadshot Rube get tired shootin' at each other. They make up and shake hands. No hard feelin's. They are mighty sorry 'bout Old Slim. I suggest takin' up a collection—for you, ma'am."

"That's very thoughtful, Jack."

"Well, Wild Bill and Rube contribute handsomely, and all of Slim's many friends, all the ramrods and ranchers and cowpokes. The miners chip in too, particularly them what hit pay dirt."

"How much?"

"Bout three, four thousand smackeroos, I'd say, more than enough to give Old Slim the grandest funeral ever held in these here parts. More than enough to ease him down gently in a silk lined casket with silver handles, and lots left over for the handsomest head-stone in our boneyard, with a carved marble angel. And, natcherally, we'll have a band playin' the death march from Saul, and mighty fine preachin', and afterward a great fiesta in Slim's honor with plenty of good feed and booze for all comers."

"You make me weep, Jack, but it won't do. Poor Slim always told me: 'When I've gone up the flume, I want no do-funnies, no folderol, no fancy doin's. Plant me in the sod in a plain pine box, and put up a wooden cross, and have Smilin' Jack say an Our Father over me. He'll do it in style.' I'd sure like to do him up with a silk-lined coffin with silver handles, and all that, but we must respect the last wishes of our loved ones, who'll be lookin' down on us."

"What'd he do with a silver-handled casket anyhow? There's better ways of spendin' that money."

"Ain't it the truth!"

oooooooooooooooooooooooooooooooooooooooooooooooooooooooooooooooooooo

The Winchester Ghosts

oooooooooooooooooooooooooooooooooooooooooooooooooooooooooooooooooooo

There stands a strange, turreted and domed castle in California's Santa Clara Valley, exclusively inhabited by thousands of ghosts. It was, as a matter of fact, especially built for them by a guilt-ridden woman—Sarah Winchester, widow of William Wirt Winchester, the "Rifle King," owner of the great firearms factory at Hartford, Connecticut.

Petite, wasp-waisted, cheerful Sarah had been a doting wife and mother, relishing to the fullest a life spent in the lap of luxury. No amount of money, however, can protect a family, even a multimillionaire's family, from sickness and death. The Rifle King fell victim to consumption. On his deathbed, knowing that his daughter and only child, stricken by the same dread disease, would soon follow him to the grave, he told his weeping wife: "Dearest, this is God's punishment for the manufacturing and selling of instruments of death. Every time one of my repeating rifles kills a human being, I am committing murder—secondhand murder, maybe, but murder all the same. And you, my poor darling, are guilty too, because you enjoy the fruits of murder—our fine mansion, jewels, fashionable dresses, furs, and luxuries of every kind. The spirits of countless victims, slain by my famous rifles, are crying out for vengeance. It is their ghosts which are roaming without proper graves, hovering in limbo, their remains mouldering on lonely prairies and deserts, their bones scattered by wild beasts. My dearly beloved, soon I will shuffle off my mortal coil, but I will always be with you as a spirit. When my shade appears to you, be not afraid, it will tell you what must be done."

Having uttered his last words, the Rifle King turned his head to the wall and expired.

The daughter died soon afterward, leaving the widow bereft and in despair, but within a short time she felt her husband's spirit hovering near her, whispering, "Go West, dearest, make a home for the ghosts of the slain, appease their anger. The lost souls will haunt you, and give me no peace, until amends are made."

The poor woman did not know what to make of it, but every night her husband's shade entered her bedchamber, whispering, "For the sake of my salvation, propitiate the ghosts of those whose lives have been ended by death-dealing Winchesters. Go West, I implore you! Give the ghosts a home!"

And, shuddering, Sarah heard not only her dead husband's voice, but also the clamorings of numberless phantoms, pleading, "Give us a home!"

Sarah sold the fine house and left Hartford for California. She had inherited a fortune of twenty million dollars, which she resolved to use as her husband intended. She bought a thirty-acre estate that included a mansion of seventeen rooms, situated in the Santa Clara Valley, not far from San Jose. At once, in feverish haste, she began adding more and more rooms, keeping a whole army of workmen busy without regard for the costs. Turrets, domes, spires, and balconies sprouted like weeds, turning the mansion into a bizarre castle of mysteries.

For some superstitious folks thirteen is a number of ill omen. Not so ghosts, who consider it luck-bringing, as they whispered into Sarah's ears. And so she put to work thirteen carpenters, thirteen cabinetmakers, thirteen bricklayers, thirteen plasterers, thirteen house painters, thirteen parquetteers, thirteen glaziers, thirteen tile layers, and thirteen Japanese gardeners. Over the years her palace proliferated into a maze of a hundred thirty rooms, to which were added thirteen bathrooms, thirteen pantries, thirteen storage rooms under the roof and, in the center of it all, the Blue Room, the inner sanctum in which Sarah, dressed in splendid brocaded robes, surrounded by many priceless occult and magic objects, held séances and communed with her ghosts. And ghosts there were, by the hundreds. As soon as one more room was added, it was occupied by these specters, crowding upon each other, whispering, "Give us room, more room!"

Nothing was good enough for these phantoms which had been "Winchestered" into another world. Chambers with thirteen windows, reached by stairways of thirteen steps, were sumptuous beyond imagination. There were stairs made of Italian marble, stained-glass windows, inlaid wood panels, silver-ornamented doors, Tiffany lamps, gleaming multicolored mosaics, and bathtubs of sculptured bronze. The bathrooms had glass doors, or no doors at all. As the spirits were incorporeal, and therefore invisible, decency was not offended.

Sarah installed a ballroom in which ghostly waltzes and polkas were performed. She also added a music room and a billiard room. The mansion was replete with secret passageways, hidden stairways, underground tunnels, and trompe l'oeil doors that led nowhere—special features built to the ghosts' specifications.

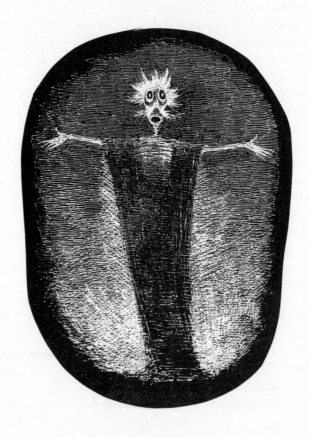

The castle stood amid huge trees, ornamental shrubs, and exotic plants. It was surrounded by thick, high hedges and almost completely hidden from view. Corporeal visitors were unwelcome, the castle being meant for the dead, not for the living. Those knocking at the door were discouraged by the haughty stern-faced butler, telling them, "Madame is unwell," or "Mrs. Winchester is not receiving today." Even President Theodore Roosevelt was denied admission, left to cool his heels before the great front portal. The only *living* person ever suffered to penetrate Sarah's inner sanctum was Harry Houdini, the famed escape artist and master of the occult, on account of his being an expert on ghosts and being on excellent terms with them. In time, the main entrance was simply boarded up, leaving a single door at the back for delivery of goods and victuals. Thus Sarah lived in splendid isolation, alone except for her thirteen servants and a multitude of spirits.

Every night at the stroke of twelve a great far-sounding bell from the mansion's tallest spire summoned the ghosts to come forth. At once the 130 chambers echoed to muted gunshots, the moans of the wounded, the curses of disembodied gunfighters, the war whoops of tribal warriors, the keening of Indian women, and the screams of their children, massacred at San Carlos, Sand Creek, the Washita, or Wounded Knee.

Every night the huge mahogany table was laid for thirteen diners —Sarah and twelve unearthly guests, the scene illuminated by a silver chandelier of thirteen lights. Here they feasted on dainties served on golden plates—on venison and glazed pheasant Souvaroff, caviar, quail Richelieu en gelée, bécasse Lucullus, truffles and lobster salad, washed down with noble wines, such as Château d' Yquem, Château Petrus, Château Margaux, *Premier Cru*, or Grand Vin de Château Latour, all decanted into goblets of the finest crystal. And, afterward, a bombe Marie-Antoinette, or a gateau régent aux marrons, finished off with a nipperkin of Hennessy or a brandy Napoléon. For phantoms with less educated palates, such as cowboys or Indians, there was an occasional steak or buffalo boudin served with a tumbler of home-brewed tanglefoot. What the spirits were unable to consume was eaten by the thirteen servants, who waxed fat on the ghostly fare.

All was not well, however, in the ghost palace. The lady of the house was troubled by premonitions of impending catastrophe. The increasing number of people killed by Winchesters, the spirits informed Sarah, called for condign punishment. She thought it might portend an all-encompassing deluge and promptly had her thirteen carpenters build a huge ark for herself and her invisible friends. She had guessed wrong. On April 18, 1906, the earth shook, Sarah's bed was upturned, and she herself was hurled violently to the floor. The ghosts had decided not on a flood but on an earthquake. As the ground split open and houses tumbled, the Winchester spirits broke into bloodcurdling, bone-chilling cheers. Unfortunately, the lesson was lost on the American people, who never guessed the real cause of this calamity. Sarah of course knew. She left her ghostly rabbit warren only once—through the back door—for her own funeral. At the moment of her death, there burst forth from a thousand phantom throats a great, eerie wailing and lamenting that could be heard for a hundred miles around. A local newspaper reported:

> Yesterday night, September 21, 1922, a tremendous melancholy noise was heard throughout the Santa Clara Valley and in numerous places along the coast. It sounded, in the words of Mrs. Betty-Lou Smith, a longtime resident of San Jose, "like the groans of a million women in labor." Mr. Carlos Martinez, a local wine grower, described it as "the howlings of all the devils in hell." As the night was clear and calm, and as nowhere in our state were perceived such natural phenomena as earth tremors or volcanic activity, the cause of this great, sorrowful noise remains a mystery.

CHAPTER 10

****

Bucking the Tiger

****

Gambling is as old as mankind. Painted pebbles and animal knuckle-bones, used as gaming pieces, have been found in Stone Age caves. Sumerians, Babylonians, Egyptians, Greeks, and Romans—all gambled. Gambling was the one vice the white man did not bring to the New World. Indians were passionate gamblers, playing the plum-pit, stick, pebble, moccasin, or hand games. The horse had hardly been introduced to the Plains when the "Red Knights of the Prairie" bet all they possessed on horse races. Mayan and Aztec priests and nobles wagered on the outcome of ceremonial ball games—games with high stakes, as the members of the losing team often had their heads cut off. The Founding Fathers played whist in their favorite taverns while quaffing hot buttered rum. Mountain men wagered their furs, horses, squaws, or even buckskin shirts at euchre. They bet on who could devour the most boudins—lightly roasted buffalo intestines. More men were gunned down inside saloons as the result of arguments over cards than for all other reasons combined. According to Colonel Frank Triplett:

> All men on the plains were gamblers, from the red savage, with his Indian poker, too complicated for a white man's brain, to the itinerant faro banker, with his broadcloth suit and his set of magnificent "tools." Gambling was the universal passion; some men hunted, some traded, some trapped, some ranched, some freighted, some drove teams, but all gambled. Here the

steady old veteran of three score and ten might be seen "chipping in" at a game of poker, there two youngsters, not counting more than two dozen years between them, engaged each other for small stakes at seven-up or euchre; in one place the Texan or Mexican bucked fiercely against a monte bank, while two or more stalwart sons of Africa gave way to the seduction of "craps."

Judges and clergymen gambled with the same abandon as bullwhackers or stagecoach drivers.

Many different kinds of games were the sucker's ruin—monte, chuck-a-luck, vingt-et-un, keno, roulette, euchre, craps, loo, banco, thimblerig, and a dozen others, but faro and poker, the latter introduced in its present form around 1830, were the preferred games. Gambling dens were aptly referred to as wolf traps, deadfalls, and skinning houses, run on the principle of never giving the sucker an even break. Every new gold strike brought to the scene whole flocks of cardsharps, bunco-steerers, and tinhorn gamblers with their many tricks for fleecing the little lambs. Theirs was a very remunerative, but also extremely dangerous, vocation, as tough Westerners considered it their birthright to kill the fellow whom they caught cheating.

Strangely enough, the macho world of the Plains gave rise to a number of gambling queens, such as Poker Alice, Simone Jules, Buckskin Alice, Minnie the Gambler, Kitty the Schemer, or Madam Moustache. "Occasionally Calamity Jane took a hand in a poker game or attempted to manipulate a faro box, but she was much more adept at another business even more ancient than gambling."

The great part gambling played in western history is shown by the way gambling terms became part of our everyday language. Faro contributed "getting down to cases" and "coppering a bet." To poker we owe "bluff," "kitty," "pot," "ante," "showdown," "four-flusher," "call," "jackpot," "raise," "freeze-out," and others. "In a nutshell," of course, came from the old flimflam game.

A Hard Head

In most all of the many fights that I have been engaged in, I made use of what I have called "that old head of mine." I don't know (and I guess I never will while I'm alive) just how thick my old skull is, but I do know it must be pretty thick or it would have been cracked many years ago, for I have been struck some terrible blows on my head with iron dray-pins, pokers, clubs, stone coal, and bowlders, which would have split any man's skull wide open unless it was pretty thick. Doctors have often told me that my skull was nearly an inch in thickness over my forehead. They were only guessing at it then, of course, but if my dear old mother-in-law don't guard my grave, they will know after I am dead, sure enough, for I have heard them say so.

For ten to fifteen years during my early life, sporting men tried to find a man to whip me, but they couldn't do it, and finally gave it up as a bad job. After they gave up trying to have me whipped, and they knew more about my old head, they would all go broke that I could whip or kill any man living, white or black, by butting him. I have had to do some hard butting in my early days, on account of the reputation I had made for my head.

I am now nearly sixty years of age, and have quit fighting, but I can today batter down any ordinary door or stave in a liquor barrel with "that old head of mine"; and I don't believe there is a man living (of near my own age) who can whip me in a rough-and-tumble fight. I never have my hair clipped short, for if I did, I would be ashamed to take my hat off, as the lines on my old scalp look about like the rail road map of the state in which I was born.

During the winter of '67 or '68, John Robinson's circus was showing in New Orleans, and they had with them a man by the name of William Carroll, whom they advertised as "the man with the thick skull, or the great butter." He could outbutt anything in the show except the elephant. One night after the show Al and Gill Robinson were uptown, and their man Carroll was with them. We all met in a saloon and began drinking wine. While we were enjoying ourselves, something was said about butting, when Gill spoke up and said Carroll could kill any man in the world with his head. "Dutch Jake," one of the big sporting men of New Orleans, was in the party, and he was up in an instant, and said: "What's that? I'll bet $1,000 or $10,000 that I can find a man he can't whip or kill either."

I knew what was up, and as we were all friends, I did not want to change the social to a butting match, so I said: "Boys, don't bet, and Mr. Carroll and I will come together just once for fun."

The Robinson boys had great faith in Carroll, and so did Dutch Jake have in me. I was at least fifty pounds heavier than Carroll, and I knew that was a great advantage, even if his head was as hard as my own. It was finally agreed that there would be no betting, so we came together. I did not strike my very best, for I was afraid of hurting the little fellow; but then he traveled on his head, so I thought I could give him a pretty good one. After we struck, Carroll walked up to me, laid his hand on my head, and said, "Gentlemen, I have found my papa at last."

He had the hardest head I ever ran against; and if he had been as heavy as I was, I can't say what the result would have been if we had come together in earnest.

Poor fellow! He is dead now, and I know of no other man with as hard a head, except it is myself. My old head is hard and thick, and maybe that is the reason I never had sense enough to save my money. It is said of me that I have won more money than any sporting man in this country. I will say that I hadn't sense enough to keep it; but if I had never seen a faro bank, I would be a wealthy man to-day.

Indians Can Play Poker

The year I was in St. Paul they paid off a lot of Indians a short distance from town. I was told that the Red Man was a good poker player, and was always looking for the best of it. They paid them in silver, so I got some of the hard money, hired a horse and buggy, got some whiskey, and started out to give them a game, more for the fun and novelty of the thing than to win their money; for I had the old keno game running, and she was a good provider. When I got among the savages, they were having a war dance. After the dance they smoked the pipe of peace and drank my whisky, and I smoked their pipes. After the friendly smoking was over, they started in to play poker. They invited and insisted on me changing in, so at last I sat down and took a hand. One of the old bucks soon began to cheat. He had an old hat in front of him, and inside the hat he had a looking-glass, so that on his deal he could see every card he dealt out. I knew he was after me, so I told him to put the hat away and play fair. He saw I was no sucker, so he put it away. We played for some time, and it was all I could do to keep even by playing on the square with big "Injins," as I found them very good card players. I held out a hand, but had to wait for some time for the "wild man of the forest." At last there was a big "blind and straddle," and I kept raising it before the draw. They all "stayed," and drew two or three cards (I do not remember which). I took one, and when we came to "show down," I was the lucky fellow. This was too much for the bucks, so three of them dropped out, and left an old chief and myself single-handed. As I was over $150 ahead of the game, I played liberally, to draw the old chieftain on; and as he had one of his bucks walking around behind, and talking "big Injin" all the time, he was getting the best of me. I knew that my hands were being given away, but I did not let them know that I was on to their racket. I waited my chance, and clinched on to four fours and a jack. I kept "going blind," until the chief got a big hand, and then he came back at me strong. We had it hot and heavy. I let the buck see my hand until it came to the draw, and then I shifted the hand, and came up with the four fours and the jack, but the warrior did not get to see *that* hand. I then made a big bet. The old chief called his squaw, and she brought him a sack of silver. He then "called" me. We showed down; the money was mine; and then you should have seen the fun. The buck that had been giving my hand away started to run. The old chief jumped up, grabbed his tomahawk, and lit out after him. I jerked off my coat, dumped all the silver into it, jumped into my buggy, and lost no time getting out of that neck of the woods. As I was going at a 2:40 gait, I looked back and saw the buck and the old chief going through the woods. I never knew whether the old man caught the buck or not, but I do know he did not catch me.

Jim Bowie Takes a Hand

It happened in 1832. A young southern gentleman from Natchez went to St. Louis on his honeymoon. To defray the expenses thereof, he transacted some business, such as collecting fifty thousand dollars on behalf of several cotton planters from his area. Unfortunately, he fancied himself quite a cardplayer, sitting in on a number of high-stake games at the best hotel in town. A local cardsharp figured the young honeymooner for an easy mark. He formed a consortium with two others of his kind to relieve the greenhorn of his considerable fortune.

When the young gentleman and his bride boarded the splendid new side-wheeler *New Orleans* for their return journey downriver, the three sharpers were waiting for him. One of them posing as an eastern merchant and cotton buyer, the other two claiming to be Louisiana planters, the trio made themselves agreeable to the newlyweds and promptly engaged the mark in a number of friendly poker games over a glass of the best. After first letting their victim win a few hundred dollars, the sharpers pulled out all stops and took the poor innocent for forty thousand dollars in greenbacks. While the young man was frantically trying to recoup his losses, Jim Bowie happened upon the scene. Being an old hand at the game, Bowie saw immediately that the crooks were "dealing from the bottom." After a few more hours, the young gentleman from Natchez had bet and lost his last dollar.

Maddened by remorse and his guilty conscience at having lost not only his own money, but also that which his friends had entrusted to him, the young man rushed to the ship's side to throw himself overboard, where Bowie just managed to grab him by the scruff of his neck, barely saving him from a watery suicide. Taking the distraught greenhorn firmly by the arm, Bowie forcefully conducted him to his cabin, putting his bride as a guard to watch over him.

Bowie then sauntered back to the bar where the wicked trio were celebrating their success with a bottle of Moët & Chandon. Bowie bellied up to the bar, casually exposing a bulging purse. The sharpers saw no reason why they should not crown their success by adding the seemingly wealthy, well-dressed gent to the list of their victims and, after a few minutes of polite conversation, suggested a game of poker, which Bowie said was a splendid idea. Again, as when suckering in the young man, the three "gulls" let Bowie win a few pots and then moved in for the kill. One of the "planters" dealt Bowie a hand such as comes only once in a lifetime and upon which even the most cautious poker player would go the limit. The "planters" threw in their hands after a few bets, but Bowie and the "cotton buyer" kept raising each other until the pot had grown to seventy thousand dollars. At last, Bowie spied what he had confidently expected: the sharper's agile fingers dipping into his sleeve. Quick as a flash, Bowie gripped the cheat's wrist while at the same time producing from beneath his coat a wicked-looking knife.

"Let's see your hand," Bowie shouted. "If it holds more than five cards, I'll cut your goddam throat with this!"

The sharper tried to tear himself loose, but Bowie twisted his wrist so that he had to drop his cards—four aces, a jack, and a seven.

"I think I will take the pot," Bowie pronounced with an icy smile, "holding four kings and a queen you yourself dealt me."

"Who the hell are you?" asked the gambler, furtively groping for his derringer.

"I am James Bowie, at your service."

"The voice was like velvet," says the legend, "but it cut like steel into the hearts of the chief gambler's confederates and deterred them from any purpose or impulse they might have had to interfere. They shrank back from the table, smitten with terror by the name. Bowie softly swept the bank notes into his large slouch hat and lightly clapped it on his head."

One of the cardsharps got up enough nerve to try to stab Jim from behind, "but Bowie drew his pistol and shot him off the wheelhouse, just as the great orb of the sun, like a golden cannon ball, sank into the waters of the Father of the Rivers."

Chivalrous, kindhearted Jim gave the young man two-thirds of his winnings, keeping the rest as his own spoils of war. With tears welling up in his eyes, the innocent from Natchez vowed never to play poker again, while his bride planted a chaste kiss on the cheek of him who had saved her young husband from ruin, dishonor, and suicide. Whether the young man kept his promise the saga does not tell.

The Curly-Headed Little Boy

"Make your bets, gentlemen, Come down, gents! All down, gents?"

"Hold on!" exclaimed a shrill, puerile voice, as if coming from under the table. Everyone looked down, and there was apparently a curly-headed boy, whose mouth was little above the level of the bank. He cautiously, coolly, and methodically thrust forth a small hand and laid down two dimes upon the ace. Everyone laughed—all but the dealer, who with the same placidity thrust back the dimes and dampened the little fellow's ardor by observing; "We don't take dimes at this bank."

But no, the little fellow had spunk; he was not so easily dashed. Picking up his dimes, his hand suddenly reappeared, this time holding a very weighty buckskin bag apparently filled with the yellow dust. This he tossed upon the ace, exclaiming, "There, I guess you'll take that. Six ounces on the ace!"

Everyone was astonished. All looked around to see if he had any relatives or friends in the crowd. He appeared to be entirely alone and a stranger to everyone; but the play began—and, strange to say, the ace won!

"Good, bully! Lucky boy!" were the exclamations on every side.

The fortunate little gambler pocketed his bag and placed upon the deuce the six ounces he had just won. Wonderful to say, the deuce won! He was now the gainer by twelve ounces. He was the hero of the table. All eyes were upon him; and it was seen that he was not as young as he seemed—an old head upon a child's shoulders! For the remainder of the deal old players regulated their bets by his, and he carried them along upon the wave. The bank looked a little sickly from this bleeding.

The deal being out, the banker, the same cool imperturbable figure, chose another pack of cards, and shuffled and cut and reshuffled and recut until the patience of the crowd was almost exhausted. It was the boy's cut, and a layout was made.

"Twenty-five ounces on the deuce," said the little man, piling all his winnings around the card. But few other bets were made; the older hands were afraid this sudden luck would change, and they all held back. The plucky lad was pitted against the man of fifty— youth, enthusiasm, and dare-all luck arraigned against the craft and cunning of the experienced gambler! How our sympathies were warmed by the fearlessness of the boy! The play began, the deck was faced; and, as I live, the deuce was in the door! The boy won the full amount of his bet.

The successful urchin was the least excited person in the room. He hauled in his winnings as carelessly as if those stacks of dollars were only chips. Another shuffle, and another layout was made. The field was now given up entirely to the two antagonists. The ace and the five were the cards; against all our hints the boy staked his fifty ounces on the five. We were breathless with fear; the dealer himself paused a little before drawing the card—but at length the deck was faced, and slowly and cautiously the cards were drawn, one by one— deuce, tray, king, queen, and seven appear in succession—and then —the five! The boy was again victorious; his fifty ounces were now one hundred. The last round made a huge chasm in the appearance of the bank, and the table in front of the little hero was absolutely covered with money.

The banker was as cool and methodical as ever; taking a fresh deck, he shuffled it carefully, and made another layout. The boy bet his hundred ounces and was again victorious! Two hundred ounces were now piled up before him. We advised him to desist, not to tempt his luck too far; but he coolly replied: "I'll break the bank or it'll break me!"

Did any one ever hear of such determination, even in a man? He increased in our estimation, and we liked him all the better for his grit. More than half the bank was his already, a fortune in itself! But the little, round, gray eyes of the boy were not upon his winnings, but were feeding eagerly on the money that was not yet his.

"Queen and tray, come down!" said the dealer.

"How much have you in the bank?" asked the boy.

"A hundred and fifty ounces."

"I tap the bank upon the queen."

This would decide the game. A stillness of death was upon the crowd; our breath was hushed; our very hearts almost ceased to beat; the suspense became painful; even the banker paused and wiped the cold drops from his brow.

The deck was faced at last, and calmly, steadily, and without hurry the cards were drawn, one by one. One—two—three—four—five—he had lost! The queen had thrown him; and his entire winnings were swept away by the sharp croupier beyond.

Dizzy and sick with the result, we turned our eyes upon the loser; he bore himself bravely and did not seem to feel the loss as sensibly as ourselves. He looked about with a stern, defying air, as if to chide us for our sympathy. As yet he had lost nothing. His large buckskin bag was still intact. Laying it upon the table, with the air of a Caesar, he put his all upon the throw, defying fate to do its worst! Our pity was suddenly changed to admiration. We felt that he was lost; but we were sure he would die game.

The cards were again shuffled and cut. The seven and the king were laid out; the boy chose the king. The cards were drawn. At last the seven appeared and the game was ended. He saw his well-filled purse stowed away along with many others within that Chinese box and, whistling "O Californy," turned his back upon the scene. The crowd parted sympathetically to let him through; and he strutted out with all the importance of a noted hero.

I passed out silently after him and joined him in the street. He looked at me furtively with one eye, without ceasing to whistle. I took his arm, leading him around the corner of the house, begged to know the amount of his loss, and if he had any money on which to come and go. He did not cease his whistling, but planted himself firmly before me and looked up. I took out my purse and offered him a part; the whistling instantly ceased; his face swelled out into a broad and homely grin. Looking cautiously around for fear of being overheard, he whispered: "Mum's the word; I believe you're a good egg! You want to know how much was in that bag? Well, I'll tell you; just four pounds of duck-shot mixed—and—nothing more; what a swarin and a cussin' when they open it!" and the little imp laughed till the tears were in his eyes.

The game in question, if anybody is interested, was faro.

Shall We Have a Drop?

Two men were observed playing poker in Tombstone's luxurious Birdcage Saloon. On the stage can-can girls threw their legs high up into the air, exposing waterfalls of rustling frou-frou unmentionables, while a "Turkish" odalisque, straight from Brooklyn, did the hootchy-kootchy, clad only in striped silk pantaloons, writhing like a rattlesnake about to give birth. The players paid them no mind. They took poker seriously and had Venus, the goddess of love, risen out of the ocean foam before their eyes, floating in glorious nakedness on an iridescent seashell, they would not have honored her with a single glance.

One of the two men was a stout, dandified fellow with a black goatee, dressed in a brown velour jacket with black cuffs over a brocaded vest. His silken cravat was fastened with a stickpin whose diamond was just a trifle too large to be genuine. The magnificent jacket had suspiciously wide sleeves.

The other gentleman was likewise fastidiously dressed—not as flamboyantly as the first, but in the best of taste, to wit: a well-tailored black broadcloth suit, a snow white "b'iled" shirt, and a black string tie. He was a keen-eyed, long-legged individual, thin as a rail, with corn-colored hair and sweeping mustachios. This citizen as could have been guessed by the description of his person, was none other than the "King of Gambling Men," also known as the "Dangerous Dentist," namely "Doc" Holliday—gamester, cardsharp, dental surgeon, and notorious gunslinger.

"Shall we start the ante at a hundred dollars, sir?" inquired the velvet-cuffed gent, whose accent betrayed a hint of New Orleans's Vieux Carré.

"Suit yourself," agreed Doc, a slender cigarillo dangling from his lips. "The sky's the limit."

They played for a while with varying success, Lady Luck frequently changing sides from one man to the other. To those watching the game, it was apparent that both gentlemen were most accomplished at cheating, which, one might say, made this a "square" game.

"Shall we have a drop?" Doc interrupted the action. "Poker needs brandy like a cock needs hens."

"I second the motion," said the goateed dandy, "let's liquor. Garçon, a couple of brandies, if you please."

The drinks arrived. Doc moved the flickering candle to one side, knocked down his snort at one gulp, and slammed the glass down upon the table, spilling a few drops of the "good creature."

"I really should refrain from both strong waters and the use of tobacco,'" he said offhandedly, "but what is a gent to do in this godforsaken desert?"

"What indeed, but, voilà, here we are."

"I out of sheer necessity," sighed Doc, "to cure a pair of bad lungs. Dry air is good for them."

They continued to play, and from that moment on Lady Luck was unashamedly on Doc's side. A small mountain of silver began to grow before the sometime dentist. Soon his opponent was out more than a thousand dollars. The velvet-cuffed one seemed momentarily sunk in thought as he contemplated his shrinking pile of gold. Losses sharpened his wits. He noticed that, when dealing, Doc held the cards lightly at the edges, manipulating them in such a way that they were reflected in a drop of brandy illuminated by candlelight. His eyes fixed on the drop, the eagle-eyed dentist could read every card reflected in it.

The goateed fellow went for his gun then, but already Doc's "gambler's friend," a small, ivory-handled derringer was staring him in the face.

"Sir," sputtered the goatee, rising with whatever dignity he could muster, "you are a low-down cheat. I thought I was dealing with a gentleman."

"So did I, stranger," was Doc's answer, "until I saw that extra ace up your sleeve. Please keep your hand off that cannon—I assure you that I am much faster on the draw. You wouldn't have a chance. Don't look so sad. There's a multitude of green horns around here for you to recoup your trifling loss, which may I say, is but a small tutoring fee. Never take on a fellow who tells you that he won't play poker until 'he gets a drop.' With that I bid you adieu."

Colonel Tubbs Strikes It Rich

The Golden Nugget gambling saloon at Whoop-Up was the mining camp's classiest joint. Here prospectors, speculators, greenhorns, bullwhackers, officers from the 7th Cavalry, cardsharps, railroaders, adventurers, and their attendant bevy of "cyprians," rubbed elbows at the gaming tables, where roulette, faro, vingt-et-un, monte, poker, keno, and other games of chance were played beneath tinkling crystal chandeliers whose lights were reflected in silver-dust mirrors imported from France.

Here the click of the roulette wheel mingled with the noise of dice rattling in their boxes, and the raucous voices of the dealers, shouting: "Come down! Come down! Come down on the red! On the black! Make your pile, gents! Make it quick! Why work? The money's here! The money's yours! Walk up, gents, walk up! Get it while it lasts! Step up! Step up! Step lively!"

Here the reek of cheap rotgut mingled with the aroma of choice liquors, the enticing odor of fine perfumes with the smell of patchouli, with which the lowest of the "soiled doves of the prairie" bedaubed themselves—all of this blending with a cloud of smoke from a hundred cheroots. Here a pound of gold dust was wagered upon a throw of the dice.

This unvarying scene of wickedness, sin, triumph, and dejection was presided over by the Golden Nugget's owner, Countess Eleanor Dumont, whose presence had once graced the halls of French châteaux and the palace of Napoleon III, but whom a stranger fate had brought to Whoop-Up Gulch.

Beautiful and alluring she was, this sometime mistress of kings and revolutionaries, the sweetheart of the mighty, the rich, and the famous of this world. Her ivory skin glowed in the soft light shed by flickering chandeliers, her ruby lips smiled a welcome to one and all, while her limpid, flashing eyes turned sober-minded gents into madmen at her feet. Her raven hair was crowned with a small circlet of diamonds, her tiny waist was girt by an emerald-studded belt, while upon her alabaster bosom rested a golden locket whose lid was never lifted and whose contents no man durst behold. It was rumored that within it rested a miniature of the French emperor. In contrast with such splendor stood the vile stogie on which she puffed with evident gusto, and the large tumbler of raw whiskey ever at her elbow.

But our tale today is not concerned with the notorious gambling queen but with "Colonel" Joseph Tubbs, the grizzled old galoot of a gold miner who has struck it rich more than a dozen times, only to repeatedly lose it all at cards and in the fruitless search for the "great mother lode," which like a mirage evermore kept eluding him. Where and how old Tubbs acquired his epithet of "colonel" was an unsolved mystery from which he had never lifted the veil.

Tubbs was a short, stubby old fellow, with a genial face and bulbous nose, reddened somewhat by long exposure to the sun, and more so perhaps by a love for the miner's favorite, "tarant'ler juice." His merry visage was framed by a large, untamed beard, stained with tobacco juice. His equally primeval junglelike hair fell down over his shoulders, while his mighty "stummick" seemed to burst the somewhat worse-for-wear flowered vest that was his hallmark. Such was the big-hearted, eccentric old codger, a living legend of the Black Hills, the Golden Nugget's foremost habitué, who never laid by a cent. It was the self-same Tubbs who had founded the town and composed its doggerel anthem:

The world was made in six days,
The seventh was for booze an' grub,
We named the town in one day,
The next we Whooped her Up.

The colonel used to boast: "That's a fact, stranger, I war the originator of this here gleeorious town o' Whoop-Up. I war the fust mortal who ever diskivered auriferous ore in these parts an' staked his claim, an' made this pile, yer bet, by gum!"

Now, as I said before, old Tubbs had hit pay dirt and then had lost it all at gambling and prospecting. He had given up "lookin' for that pizen called gold." He was living in a dugout at the lower end of the gulch. He asked no favors. He had his own proud but peculiar way of earning his square meal a day, his plug of 'baccer, and his jolts of tanglefoot. He showed up punctually every evening at dusk in the Golden Nugget in order to place his daily bet.

Tubbs had his own unique system of winning at roulette. From his once-considerable fortune he had saved exactly sixty-two shiny silver dollars, which constituted his entire gambling stake. Invariably, he plunked himself down at the roulette table, placing a single simoleon on the red. Should black come up, he simply doubled his bet. If it came up again, he once more repeated the doubling. If the little silver ball, upon whose whim his life depended, came down on black six times in a row, he would have staked his whole capital. If it stopped at black seven times, he would be ruined and faced with starvation. Therefore, he did not so much bet on the red as on black never coming up more than five times in a row. Should the red come up at the first turn of the wheel, he would simply pocket his winnings, always one dollar, and never more, then wander over to a table, permanently reserved for himself, to treat himself to a good meal, a Havana seegar, and a generous tumbler of his preferred brand of poison.

Luck, so far, had been with Tubbs. The longest he had ever had to wait for the red was five whirls of the wheel. His unique kind of betting constituted his only fixed income—one dollar per day. Even had he stacked all his sixty-two dollars, his winnings would have been only one lone smackeroo. But that was all he wanted. The little clicking ball coming to rest on the red was the daily bread that sustained his 250-pound corpus.

On the evening in question, the cherry-nosed colonel, as always, strode into the Golden Nugget, ignoring the hectic gamblers busy at their various games of chance, ponderously settling down at the roulette table, greeting the croupier with a genial: "Good day ter ye, Pierre. Jest hand me the brandy, for et's a scandalous fac' thet I heven't hed more'n half a dozen snorts this hull blessed day."

With a great amount of fuss he emptied the heavy bag, containing all he owned in the world, spreading the the coins out before him, and then stacking them up in six neat, precisely aligned columns. Then he placed a single silver dollar on the red, propped his elbows on the table, cupped his chin in his hands, and said: "Jumpin' crockerdiles! Give her a whirl!"

Other players made their bets. The croupier exhorted one and all: "Come down, gents, come down! Make yer play! Odds or even, red or black, manque or passe! Make a fortune on yer fav'rite number! Come down! Come down! Rien ne va plus! Here we go!"

The wheel began to turn, fast at first, and then slowing down, until the little ball came to rest—on the red!

Tubbs watched impassively, Contrary to his usual practice, he let the bet stand, not picking up his two dollars. There was a slight murmur. Nobody had ever seen old Tubbs do this before. The wheel whirred around once more, and again the red came up. Tubbs's expression did not change. Four dollars now were lying before him. And he let them stand. Then the incredible happened. Against all odds, against all the rules of mathematical probability, the red came up, again and again, ten times in a row. Not a muscle in Tubbs's face moved. Not the slightest twitch betrayed his emotion. He let his bet stand as before. His winnings had increased by leaps and bounds. The coins before him had grown into a glittering mound. Still he sat there, stolidly, without blinking, chin in hands, oblivious to the mounting excitement around him. And still one more time the little ball stopped at the red. Now all was absolutely quiet inside the Golden Nugget. One could have heard a pin drop. A crowd had gathered around the roulette table, watching in awe. Madame Dumont had descended from the high seat from which she surveyed all that was going on within her gambling emporium. She talked to the croupier, who examined his machinery to see whether it had been tampered with and who also checked the wheel's alignment. But everything was working properly. If Tubbs was offended by this scrutiny, which implied suspicion, then his face did not betray it. He just kept sitting there as if rooted, making no move to rake in his loot.

Word got around that the old coon was on an unbelievable winning streak. Whoop-Up was in an uproar. Denizens of the Golden Nugget rushed to witness the miracle, among them Tubbs's old and trusted friends Deadwood Dick and Calamity Jane.

"Whoopee!" the famous Wildcat of the Plains shouted as she took her place beside the red-nosed child of fortune. "Whoopee! I'm Calamity Jane and the drinks are on the house. Hooraw fer the cunnel. Let her rip!"

Before Tubbs now rose a veritable Pikes Peak of coins—fifty, sixty, seventy thousand dollars or more.

"Yer tarnal old fool," Deadwood Dick whispered into the old miner's ear, "take yer money an' run afore the black comes up, an' come up it will, or ye can hang me up fer grizzly meat!" But Tubbs ignored him. Once more the little clicking ball rested on the red. Madame Dumont stood up, waving her beringed hands, and announced in a loud, ringing voice: "Gents, messieurs, ze bank, it is broken. Rompu, bustaid. Mon Dieu, je suis desoleé, and sorry, but zee Goldain Nuggette, she eez closed until I shall get monnaie from ze bank in Deadwood. In ze meantime, mesdames et messieurs, you are all invited to belly oop to ze bar. Champagne for everybody. Champagne on ze house!" There was no question—La Belle Dumont had class.

"Com'on, ye old galoot," Deadwood Dick admonished Tubbs, "take yer loot. I'll get a wheelbarrow to help ye carry it off."

"Yea, let's go, old hoss," Calamity chimed in, nudging the old fellow. Then the dreadful and unexpected happened—Tubbs toppled from his seat, all 250 pounds of him, landing with a resounding thud on the sawdust-sprinkled floor. He was lying there, belly up, glassy eyes wide open, with an odd smile on his ruddy face. For a while everybody kept staring silently at the old man lying on the floor. Deadwood Dick bent down, slid his hand under Tubbs's frazzled shirt, and felt for a heartbeat. He found none. The horrible truth dawned upon him that Tubbs had gone to play roulette in a better

world. The ancient miner had finally cashed in his chips. "He's dead," Deadwood Dick said at last, stumbling over the words.

"His heart must've stopped when he made his fust bet," Calamity exclaimed, tears streaming down her face. "That's why he didn't simply take his two dollars and quit. That's why he let his bets stand."

"Pore old hoss," Deadwood Dick added, "to miss his greatest strike. To have finally hit the mother lode an' never know it! But it was a nacheral way for him to go. I'll shore miss the old galoot."

"Zee monnaie," inquired Madame Dumont, "zeese zousands of dollairs, vot shall vee do viz zem? Who are Monsieur Tubbs's heirs?"

"He had no heirs," said Calamity. "Ole Tubbs here was all alone in this world."

"Quel malheur! Vot shall vee do?"

"Thar's plenty folks around hyar who're down on their luck," said Calamity. "Women whose men got their hair lifted by the red varmints, kids whose fathers were plugged by road agents. Poor suckers whose claims have been jumped by thimbleriggers. Old down-and-out painted cats who cain't find a feller to give 'em a tumble. I suggest distributin' this whole caboodle among them. Old Tubbs would have wanted it that way."

"Old Calam here has hit the bull's-eye, as always," said Deadwood Dick, ending the discussion.

✛✛✛

Good for Our Entire Assets

✛✛✛

A story, supposedly true and often embroidered, tells of a Denver bank teller faced with three worn-out-looking citizens when he opened the bank one morning, one of them clutching an envelope to his breast.

"I want to negotiate a loan," declared the man with the envelope.

"Upon what collateral?" asked the teller.

The man explained that he had sat in at an all-night poker game with the other two. There were almost five thousand dollars in the pot with everybody holding a good hand. He had run out of money and been given half an hour to raise five thousand dollars to "see" the others. He wanted to get the loan on his hand, which was in the envelope. The teller could have a peek, but of course not his fellow players, who had come along to watch that the cards in the envelope were not monkeyed with.

"What an idea, my dear sir," objected the bank clerk, "we don't lend money on cards."

"But you ain't goin' to see me raised out on a hand like this," moaned the gambler, letting the teller have a peek at his cards—four kings and an ace. "These gents think I'm bluffing, and here I could clean them out!"

"That's too bad," said the teller. The sad gambler was about to leave when the bank's president walked in and inquired about his lamentations. Being shown the cards, he immediately authorized a bank loan of five thousand dollars.

"Don't you have any sense?" he lectured his cringing employee. "Don't you ever play poker?"

"No, sir,"

"Ah, I thought so. If you did, you'd know what good collateral was. Remember now, four kings and an ace are always good in this bank for our entire assets, sir, our entire assets!"

+++

The One-Eyed Gambler

+++

A little game of draw was in progress in Omaha, and among its participants was a one-eyed man. He was playing in rather remarkable luck, but no one could very well find fault with that. Presently, however, there came a jackpot, and it was the one-eyed man's deal. He opened the pot, and while he was giving himself cards a certain bellicose gentleman named Jones thought he detected the one-eyed man in the act of palming a card. Quick as a flash, Jones whipped out a revolver and placed it on the table in front of him.

"Gentlemen," he said decisively, "we will have a fresh deal; this one doesn't go."

The players were surprised, but as none of them had bettered his hand save the opener, who made no sign of disapproval, they willingly consented.

"And now that we started on a new deal," pursued Mr. Jones, carelessly toying with his revolver, "let me announce that we are going to have nothing but square deals. I am not making any insinuations or bringing any charges, and I will say only this, that if I catch any son of a gun cheating I will shoot his other eye out."

CHAPTER 11

Lady Wildcats of the Plains

It is said that the female of the species is deadlier than the male, and while the shady ladies of the West could not compete with the likes of Billy the Kid or Joaquín Murieta in the killing business, not a few of them were as handy with a gun as with a pair of loaded dice, or a branding iron used on other men's heifers. Some combined prostitution with various forms of banditry and were the type, at least in their youth, of which Mark Twain said that he would rather behold their nakedness than General Ulysses Grant in full dress uniform with medals.

There was pretty Jenny Stevens, known as "Little Britches," a four-foot-nine bundle of violence who, together with "Cattle Annie" McDougal, joined the Doolin gang of holdup men, cattle rustlers, and train robbers.

There was Belle Starr, the "Bandit Queen," who on her forty-third birthday was wafted into eternity by a blast from a double-barreled shotgun.

Nor should we forget "Cattle Kate" Maxwell, who ran a "hog ranch" and had unorthodox ways of increasing the size of her herds, resulting in her demise due to "hemp fever."

Mention must be made also of Pearl Hart, the "Pearl of Arizona" and "Queen of Lady Road Agents," who held up stagecoaches and, as a highly respectable elderly lady, showed up in Yuma, Arizona, to visit once more the cell in the local calabozo in which she had languished for two long years.

And there was glorious Lola Montez, long-time mistress of King Ludwig of Bavaria, who lavished his country's treasures upon her and was, as a consequence, forced to abdicate. Known as "the Countess," because her royal paramour designated her "Gräfin von Landsfeldt," a somewhat faded Lola wound up entertaining California miners and gamblers with her famous "spider dance."

And a toast to the lady gamblers, such as "La Belle" Siddons, also known as Madame Vestal, the "Goddess of Chance," who gained fame as a Confederate spy and cashed in her chips in that place of legends—Deadwood.

Another gambling queen was cigar-smoking "Poker Alice" Ivers who, after having learned manners and diction in an English ladies' academy, won and lost fortunes at poker in the American West. Her favorite curse was "You cheatin' bastard, I shoot you in the puss," a threat she carried out on at least one occasion. Prudish to the last, she ran a bagnio in which her established rule was "Never on Sunday."

Alice had a rival in Simone Jules, alias Eleanor Dumont, who won immortality under the moniker "Madame Mustache," because of a superfluity of hair on her upper lip. As owner-operator of a gambling den, she killed two men, not without reason. When her mustache finally became too luxuriant, she ended it all with a draft of prussic acid.

Also deserving more than just a footnote is "Big Nose" Kate Elder, soiled dove of the prairie and bedmate of Doc Holliday, dentist, gambler, and shootist. Kate came to an untimely end in a Bisbee, Arizona, saloon, the unintended victim of a drunken shoot-out.

The most famous of all lady wildcats is, of course "Calamity Jane" Cannary, the "Beautiful White Devil of the Plains," a professional live tourist attraction and fairy-tale character. Legends about her are like grains of sand on a beach, still proliferating in books, poems, plays, and movies.

Born Before Her Time

Martha Jane Cannary, better known as Calamity Jane, became notorious for wearing pants, smoking, drinking, skinny-dipping, being sexually promiscuous, and telling all to whoever would listen, which would not make headlines today, but was enough in the good old days to make her into a fabled frontier character and dime-novel heroine—"The Beautiful White Devil of the Yellowstone." She lived according to her motto: "Never go to bed sober, or alone, or with a red cent left in your pocket."

She was, or rather claimed to be, a bushwhacker, mule skinner, Pony Express rider, Indian fighter, army scout, stagecoach guard, nurse, angel of mercy, and the West's foremost femme fatale. She doubled as a part-time prostitute and could drink most men under the table. But more than anything else "Calam" was a self-promoting tourist attraction. She was "married" several times, had many lovers, and children in and out of wedlock. This seems surprising, as she had a face like a horse, skin like sandpaper, and a body resembling that of a down-and-out wrestler. Her popularity with the opposite sex is, however, easily explained by the fact that during her heyday, men in the West outnumbered women by about twenty to one. Early photographs show her in a slouch hat, coarse pants, and a stained, fringed buckskin jacket, rifle in hand, a bowie knife stuck in her belt, chomping on a big cigar.

Calamity Jane was born in 1852, on a Missouri farm. Her family moved west while she was still a child. The "undeodorized lass" progressed from Independence to Julesburg to Cheyenne to Virginia City and to Blackfoot, Montana, where her mother opened a joyhouse called the Birdcage. Her foremost days of glory, however, were spent at Deadwood, South Dakota, where she acquired her reputation for drinking, brawling, gambling, swearing, and whoring. Eastern fabulists loved her because "she was so colorful," climbing the very heights of imagination in the process. Dime-novel writers made her a heroine in the East among aficionados of penny dreadfuls. On her own home ground she was considerably less admired. The editor of the local Deadwood paper complained: "As far as real merit is concerned, she is a fraud and a dead giveaway. A hundred waiter girls or mop squeezers in this gulch are her superiors in everything; her form and figure are not only indifferent but repulsive. It makes me tired to see so much written about such a woman."

She was, however, good copy. What a scoop it must have been when one journalist discovered that she had joined the Indian-fighting army disguised as a soldier until, one hot day, she went skinny-dipping with the boys. An officer passing by noticed that one of the bathers had "two things too much and one thing too little," which abruptly ended her military career. She made a habit of striding into saloons, firing her pistol at the ceiling, banging on the bar, and shouting raucously: "I'm Calamity Jane and the drinks are on the house. I sleep where, when, and with whom I want. Let her rip!"

In a Tucson cathouse, the irrepressible "Calam" opened fire with her cap 'n' ball at "greasers" for aspiring to obtain her favors. Her body was for white Anglo-Saxons only. She also unloosed her artillery inside Denver's famous Windsor Bar, whose boniface refused to "serve whiskey to a lady." She smoked up a Bozeman, Montana, saloon whose bardog, who had served her enough booze to sink a battleship, refused to let her have any more because, in his opinion, "she had more than enough."

On the other hand, "she was generous when sober, which wasn't often," bought candy for kids, nursed soldiers and miners suffering from smallpox back to health and, when in the mood, entertained barroom customers with her own rendition of "It's a Hot Time in the Old Town Tonight."

In Deadwood she shared the spotlight with another living legend —Wild Bill Hickok, King of the Pistoleers. She always talked about what close friends they had been, hinted that she had shared his bed, even that she was married to him. By the time she spun these yarns, he was already dead, gunned down at Nuttal and Mann's Number Ten Saloon, and therefore unable to contradict her. She also claimed to have personally arrested and brought to justice Hickok's murderer, Jack McCall, in a butchershop, subduing him with a meat cleaver, because she had absentmindedly left her six-gun at home. A bibulous writer improved upon this by claiming that Calamity had once saved McCall from being hanged, but after the low-down varmint had shot her darling Bill, she personally placed the halter around his neck, saying, "I gave ye yer life oncet, I'll take it back now!"

She went on a so-called "lecture tour" at the 1901 Pan-American Exhibition, where she got "ramsquaddled" and claimed to have killed Crazy Horse. Her last years were spent in an alcoholic haze. She got the better of a clergyman who rebuked her for being drunk and wanton, by shouting at him, "Shucks, you can kiss my butt, yer holiness, I don't take preachin' from an old billygoat I've slept under the same blanket with for more'n a dozen times."

She died on August 2, 1903, at Terry, South Dakota, on the twenty-seventh anniversary of Hickok's demise. Her last words, it is said, were: "Bury me next to Bill."

In the words of Duncan Aikman: "The Joan of Arc of the Indian Wars, the angel of mining camp mercies, the tragic bearer of an erotic nemesis, the imp spirit of the frontier's female wilderness, she was becoming folklore."

And here is the legend of how Calamity Jane got her name.

How Old Calam Got Her Name

Some say "Old Calam" got her moniker because her life was one calamity after the other. Others say with conviction that she got her name because, shortly after making her acquaintance, gentlemen were stricken by a venereal calamity. Not so, say the dime novels written in her honor.

◆ ◆ ◆

In the year of 1873, if an observer could have gazed upon the Goose Creek Valley of Wyoming, he would have seen a thrilling sight. Far ahead over the vast plain a fugitive white man was flying on his swift, foaming steed, enveloped in a cloud of dust. Behind him galloped a score of savages, their painted, gleaming visages distorted with the passion of exultation, vengeance, and the lust for scalps, their warbonnets streaming after them in the wind. Whipping up their ponies, they yelled like all the devils in hell, their strength pressed to the utmost limits. But even though the red fiends whip their horses until crimson flecks of foam spurt from their nostrils, they cannot gain upon him who wears the uniform of a captain of cavalry, riding erect on his magnificent charger, scorning his pursuers. It is Captain "Pat" Egan, the gallant cavalier, who is riding for his life.

But, egad, what is this? His horse flags as a lone slim figure, watching from a hilltop, spies the arrow shafts imbedded in the noble animal's flanks. And behold, the horse is faltering, slowing to a labored walk as the savage foes come nearer.

The valiant Egan glances back: "I will sell my life dearly! God help me!" he utters prayerfully, but it seems that Satan himself is helping his red disciples. The foremost warrior looses his whirring arrow. It flies true and lodges between the shoulder blades of the stalwart officer. A loud report, and he is hit in the thigh by a bullet from a gun a vile, money-grubbing trader sold to the bloodstained miscreants in defiance of the law. Egan sways in the saddle. His steed sinks to its knees, its noble head touching the ground. Unafraid in the face of death, Egan confronts his foes. The chambers of his Colt are empty now, except for a last bullet he saves for himself. With triumphant howls, like coyotes circling a campfire, the savages surround the wounded soldier, giving a wide berth to his "arme blanche." They want him alive, savoring in advance the fiendish tortures they mean to inflict upon him. He cannot escape. Nothing can save the brave captain. Death stretches out its bony hand to seize him.

But hark! Do you hear the thudding hoofbeats, the crack of a repeating rifle! IT IS THE BEAUTIFUL WILD JANE TO THE RESCUE!

Swift as lightning Jane Cannary came dashing down the hill from which she had surveyed the scene, a living sculpture astride her little black Mexican cayuse Trick, the animal running at the top of its speed, vaulting over every obstacle in its path—still the daredevil Wildcat of the Plains retained her seat as if glued to the animal's back, her tresses flowing wildly back from beneath her slouch hat, her eyes dancing with excitement, every now and then her lips giving vent to a ringing whoop, which was credible in imitation, if not in volume and force, to that of a full-blown Comanche warrior.

Twice more in succession the trusty rifle cracked and each unerring bullet dropped its man, either dead or wounded, from his pony. A second more and she was by the captain's side, heedless of the surprised and awed savages milling around in confusion, helping the wounded Egan to mount up behind her. One more exultant yell burst forth from her throat as she spurred Trick into a full gallop, and thus rescuer and rescued sped away as fast as the wind. They were not followed. The savages had learned to fear the daring maid's marksmanship, seemingly a miracle of the whites' Christian God. Discouraged, they gave up the chase.

When Jane and Egan arrived at the fort, the captain for the first time had a chance to thank and to gaze upon her who had saved him. Jane Cannary was the possessor of a form both graceful and womanly, and a face that was peculiarly handsome and attractive, though upon it were lines drawn by the hand of hard usage. The lips and eyes still retained in themselves their girlish beauty, the lips their full, rosy plumpness, and the eyes their dark, magnetic sparkle, and the face proper had the power to become stern, grave, or jolly in expression, wreathed as it was in a semiframework of long, raven hair that reached below a faultless waist.

Her dress consisted of buckskin trousers, met at the knee by fancifully beaded leggings, with moccasins of dainty pattern upon her feet; a velvet vest and a flowered shirt, open at the throat, partially revealing a breast of alabaster purity; a short velvet jacket, and Spanish broad-brimmed hat, slouched upon one side of a regally beautiful head.

She had dismounted and Egan feasted his eyes upon her with wonder and more than just thankful admiration. She smiled at the gallant officer: "Jane Cannary, at your service. But let's take care of that cussed arrow first."

"It's nothing much, miss, and the leg, too, is only a scratch not worth making so much fuss about, or getting your dainty hands bloody. It's all in a day's work for us fellows in this man's army. You saved my life. How can I ever thank you?"

"Oh, shucks, don't mention it. Here's my paw. Put her there. I'm as glad to see yo're not badly hurt as a b'ar is to hug a human." Calamity lightly vaulted back into the saddle.

"Hold on!" Egan protested. "Shall we not meet again, Jane?"

"Probably, as I'm gen'rally around. Whar there's mischief, there you'll find me."

"I shall call upon you presently," he said with a smile, making light of the pain his wounds caused him. "You are quite a woman. Were you a man, I am sure you would have risen to be a general. Jane, you are a wonderful little woman to have around in a calamity. I name you Calamity Jane, the Heroine of the Plains!"

And as Calamity Jane she was known from that day onward.

Calamity Jane Meets a Long-Lost Lover

Calamity Jane left the town, and riding up the gulch, turned off among the mountains, through a dark, lonesome ravine, through the bottom of which a small creek dashed noisily, and where but little of the light of day ever penetrated.

She was mounted on her thoroughbred cayuse, which had few rivals in the Hills, and well-armed with a sixteen-shot Winchester rifle, and a brace of holster revolvers, besides those she wore in her belt. Every bit of a mountain knight she looked, as she rode along, scanning everything around her with a sharp gaze.

Ahead of her, around an abrupt bend, came clear and sharp the ringing thud of hoof-strokes—then a fierce shout that echoed around the hills with clanging reverberations.

"Hello! Someone coming this way, I reckon!" Calamity muttered, wheeling her horse to one side, just behind a clump of manzanita bushes. "Either red-skins or road-agents, I predict, after some lone pilgrim."

She had not long to wait to learn that her prophecy was correct.

A single horseman came dashing around the bend, with his horse running at full speed, while sitting with face backward; he was grasping a rifle in his hands, ready for use.

He managed to retain his seat with as much ease as though he occupied a fronting position, which evinced superior horsemanship.

From her position, Calamity could do no more in the way of a glance than to make him out as a young man—his face she could not see. Nearer and nearer he came; then a band of five horsemen burst forth into view around the bend, yelling like so many Comanche red-skins.

They were road-agents, all armed with carbines of Winchester pattern, and were in hot pursuit of the lone fugitive, whose easy riding so attracted Calamity's admiration, that she wheeled her cayuse out into the ravine with a ringing shout.

"Let 'em have it, pilgrim—plug et to 'em like blazes, an' I'll back ye! Hurra! Whoa up thar, you imps o' Satan, fer ef ye buck ag-in' Calamity Jane yer bound ter get snagged ag-in' an earthquake!"

The words were loud enough to be heard by the pursuers and pursued; then the girl dare-devil raised her rifle to her shoulder, and sent a death-dispatch with unerring aim into the road-agents, killing one outright, and wounding a horse.

Seeing that he was re-enforced, the fugitive opened fire, also dropping one of the desperadoes from the saddle, although the wretch was only wounded. Three others were left, and they came on with furious oaths and curses, beating their animals with the carbines to increase their speed, and then firing wildly.

One chance bullet struck the fugitive's animal in the ear, and penetrated to the brain. Instantly, the poor brute began to stagger, then stumbled and dropped dead a few feet from where Calamity had taken her stand. Luckily, the rider was prepared, and he leaped lightly from the saddle, and escaped injury.

At the same instant Calamity's rifle again cracked twice in succession and each unerring bullet dropped one stage-robber, either dead or wounded, from his horse; seeing that he now had no chance, the remaining outlaw turned his mount abruptly around and took the back trail, urging on his animal in mad desperation, with both spurs and voice. Bound to finish the victory, Calamity fired the remaining thirteen cartridges in her repeater, but only succeeded in wounding him, as he disappeared from view.

Then she turned to the rescued fugitive, who was standing by his dead horse, and gazing at her in admiration and wonder.

He was a man of some five-and-twenty years, with supple, handsome form, and a light, jovial face, which, while it possessed no particular beauty, was a good-naturedly, good-looking face, with perfect features, dark brown eyes and hair, and a slight dark mustache. He was attired in a gentleman's garb, and armed with a rifle and a pair of revolvers.

Clearly, he was astonished at his sudden rescue, for he stood gazing at Calamity as if she were something more than mortal.

And she laughed in her cool way, as she crossed one shapely limb upon the neck of her horse, and returned the gaze in genuine Black Hills fashion.

"Guess you war purty nigh glad to get away frum them agents, pilgrim, warn't ye?" she demanded at length, while she lit a cigarette.

"Indeed I was!" the man replied, with enthusiasm. "I had all the road-agent experience I care for, since I've been fighting the devils for the last half hour. There were twelve of the fellows when they commenced the chase, a couple of miles back."

"An' ye dropped 'em all, eh?"

"All but the three you fetched down and the fellow that escaped."

"Wal, then, you're a brick—thet's all! Couldn't a-done better myself. Reckon you're a fresh 'un in these diggins, eh?"

"I am. I only arrived at Deadwood yesterday, and, purchasing a horse, set out for a ride to Whoop-Up, wherever that may be, having no idea the distance was so great. But excuse me, please, you're a woman, are you not?"

"Well, yes, I reckon I am in flesh, but not in spirit o' late years. Ye see, they kinda got matters discomfuddled w'en I was created, an' I turned out to be a gal instead of a man, which I ought to hev been."

"Indeed? There is something in your face which reminds me of a girl I used to know six years ago, before I went East, from Denver. What is your name, ma'am?"

"Calamity Jane, at yer service."

"What? Janie was my little sweetheart's name!" the stranger exclaimed. "It cannot be that YOU are indeed Jennie Forrest—the same I once knew. She left Denver for Virginia City a couple of years after, since when I have never heard from her."

"Yes, I am Jennie—she that was Jennie Forrest," Calamity replied, slowly, "but who can you be?"

"I am Charley Davis—don't you remember me? Six years ago, on your sixteenth birthday, you promised to wait for me and become my bride!"

"YOU Charley Davis?" the girl exclaimed delightedly; "then thar's my paw—grab it! I'm as glad to see you as a heifer is to see a bull."

The stranger eagerly accepted the proffered hand and shook it warmly, while he gazed admiringly into the face of the girl-scout.

"You have greatly changed, Jennie, but it is for the better, excepting your attire. Why dress thus, when the attire of your own sex is more becoming?"

"I don't allow ye ken beat men's togs much fer handy locomotion an' so forth, an' then, ye see, I'm as big a gun among the men as any of 'em. An' ef ye're goin' to Whoop-Up, let me advise you in one respect; snatch off yer b'iled shirt, an' put on a flannel caliker. Reckon they'd set you up as a swell ef ye war to go in that way."

"Oh, I'll run the risks. But, Janie, isn't your attire unmaidenly, considering your sex?"

"Maidenly—unmaidenly?" Calamity muttered, staring hard at him. "Charley Davis, when you left me, with a betrothal kiss clinging to my lips, I was a maiden, and as modest as they make 'em. But terrible changes have come since then. I am now a world's dare-devil, people say. Ask me nothing, for I tell yer the same measure—nothing. In Whoop-Up—this trail takes you there, by turning to your left at the canyon below—in Whoop-Up you may by chance hear all that the world knows of the story. Go hear, and then you will not be surprised."

She spoke with a fierce earnestness that was thrilling, and then drew up her bridle as if to go.

"Hold on, Jennie, shall we not meet again?" Davis exclaimed, very anxiously—"very soon, I hope."

"Probably. I'm not hard to find," saying which the girl dare-devil rode on up the ravine, leaving the stranger to pursue his way on to Whoop-Up afoot.

CHAPTER 12

The Man Who Never Was

Calamity Jane was about one-quarter fact and three-quarters fiction. Closely connected to her in legend was Deadwood Dick, a character who existed solely in penny dreadfuls written by Ed Wheeler, a Brooklyn city slicker. Real or not, thousands of his readers steadfastly believed that Deadwood Dick was a real live western hero. Does it matter?

Deadwood Dick

Calamity Jane, Wild Bill Hickok, and Buffalo Bill gave pleasant employment to dozens of pen-pushers grinding out a never-ending stream of dime novels in which the three famous frontier characters lent their names, unwittingly and unwillingly, to the most improbable yarns ever spun in western literature. A New York brownstone dweller by the name of Ed Wheeler, a so-called "penny-a-liner," intended to horn in, but was in great need of a chief character. After searching long and diligently, but in vain, he decided to let his imagination run amok by simply inventing his own hero, "The Man Who Never Was"—Deadwood Dick! Wheeler cranked out a flood of dime novels featuring his mythical hero, using real Wild West characters, such as Calamity Jane, for a supporting cast. His readers were convinced that Deadwood Dick was a living person of flesh and blood, and soon the Man Who Never Was took his place among such folk heroes as Hickok and General Custer.

In 1926, when America celebrated its 150th birthday, Deadwood, South Dakota, celebrated "Black Hills Days of '76," glorifying Old Yellow Hair, Sitting Bull, Wild Bill, and such like. The trouble was that they were all dead. Nobody knew what had happened to the great Deadwood Dick. Could he possibly be still alive? A frantic search uncovered an old geezer named Dick Clark, found shoveling manure inside a Deadwood stable. Smelling free drinks and bundles of green frogskins, the manure shoveler confessed that he, indeed, was the long-lost one-and-only Deadwood Dick. Well, his name was Dick, and he was a native son, and he was willing to let his hair grow and wear a buckskin jacket and a "hogleg" in his belt. Deadwood Dick alive! The news spread like wildfire. The nice old fellow was the hero of the hour, the willing centerpiece of the big celebration.

He even was brought to Washington to shake hands with President Calvin Coolidge. In no time he had convinced himself that he was what he claimed to be, cadging drinks at the old Nuttal and Mann Saloon, regaling the patrons with stories which invariably began: "Waaal, one time, when I an' Calamity an' Buffalo Bill was scouting fer Gen'ral Custer . . ."

Deadwood Dick and the Grizzly

Deadwood Dick was in a fix. He had accidentally run into the biggest, meanest, most ferocious bear that ever tried to hug a human being. The terrifying beast was enraged to find Dick on what it considered to be its own private trail. Dick climbed to the top of a stone outcropping, surrounded on two sides by smooth, vertical, towering cliffs, and on the two others by a yawning abyss. If he had hoped to be rid of his pursuer, he was to be quickly disappointed.

Dick's was a situation few men could wish to find themselves in. There he was marooned upon the plateau, with the positive assurance that he must enter battle with the huge grizzly who had followed him with growls that were anything but music to Dick's ears. The bear fixed Dick with malevolent eyes in evident contemplation of a fine meal, while Dick faced bruin, not sure how to handle this antagonist. He had his two six-guns, but these were puny weapons, sure to fail to penetrate the thick matted fur and layers of hide and fat of the mighty beast.

Dick accordingly drew his Green River knife and edged out into the center of the plateau, near the ugly brute. He had no wish to be crowded off the plateau into the bottomless abyss below. As he advanced, the grizzly reared up on his hind legs, towering over the fearless westerner, and came on with a reverberating growl that would have chilled the blood of everyone but our gallant Deadwood Dick. The man braced himself. He knew that he faced a life-and-death struggle, and he set his teeth together, determined to sell his life as dearly as possible.

On came the monster, with his frightful jaws wide open, Dick feeling its hot, foul breath upon his face. He sprang forward, plunging his knife deep into the bear's breast, but before he could dodge, Dick received a tremendous blow from one of the grizzly's paws that sent him reeling halfway across the plateau. Instantly drawing one of his Smith & Wesson revolvers, Dick fired, in quick succession, six bullets into the yawning wound he had opened with his knife. His heart was pounding as he was seized by a strange excitement, close to elation. The bullets had staggered the huge brute, and blood was spurting from the wound in a sickening stream; yet the maddened giant attacked once more with a mighty roar that seemed to shake the hill to its foundation.

Deadwood Dick drew his other six-gun, standing there like a rock. When the enraged beast was but three yards off, he fired two shots with unerring precision—one bullet in each eye of his ponderous enemy.

With a terrific roar the grizzly rushed on, with blood streaming from its eyes and totally blinded—rushed on, straight over the edge, crashing helplessly down into the canyon below.

"Attaboy! I couldn't have done better myself! I war jest gettin' ready to dispatch the brute myself with my Winchester!" exclaimed a voice, and, looking up, Dick beheld a face peering down at him from a ledge far above. "Reckon you dispatched him jest in time afore it got too dark fer straight shootin'."

"I guess so. That was a close call. But how's feller to get down or up from here, I'd like to know."

"I'll give you a hand. I'll lower one end of my lariat and you can climb up to here. Once on my ledge. I'll warrant I can get you safely down this cussed mountain."

Slinging his rifle to his back and securing his revolvers, Dick got hold of the lasso, and up he went with a monkey's agility, pulling himself up to the ledge where his rescuer welcomed him with a hearty "Glad you made it, pilgrim!"

"Calamity Jane!" Dick ejaculated involuntarily, for in the features of the stranger he recognized a description he had obtained of the young female daredevil.

"At yer service, sir!" was the reply, accompanied by an amused laugh. "You stare at me as if I were a critter from another world."

"Yes, well, excuse me," Dick stuttered with embarrassment. "You see, I've heard so much about you. You will pardon me, and—"

"Heard about me? You bet your boots! But, by Ned, pardner, you did remarkable execution with that cussed b'ar. I don't believe thar's another galoot in Whoop-Up as could do the job in quicker time, or a more scientific manner. Didn't get nary a tear?"

"No. I was doggone lucky," Dick replied, marveling, while he spoke, at the wild beauty of the girl before him. "I got away with only a cuff on the side of my head."

"Which did you more good than a pint of patent medicine. It aroused the fight in you. It's all the medicine a man wants to brace him up. Men need a slap an' women a slight, to wake 'em up. Anyhow, that's my logic. Shall I conduct you down the mountain, or can you make it alone? Let's go, pilgrim. Nuttal and Mann's saloon, where we're headed, serves a powerfully good brand of coffin varnish."

Deadwood Dick to the Rescue

The Sturgis–Deadwood stage was creaking along a rutted Black Hills trail, enveloped in a cloud of dust, carrying, besides a drummer and an Indian trader, a precious burden—beauteous Polly Anderson, chaperoned by her aunt Milly, on the way to meet the radiant girl's fiancé, gallant Captain Tom Calhoun of the United States Cavalry, stationed at the fort, still a bone-rattling seventy miles away.

Up on the driver's seat, gruff old Pat Mayotte cracked his whip, humming a song to himself. Perched beside him sat his "shotgun" rider, Slim McIvers, dozing, swaying to the coach's rhythm. Inside, the drummer longed for a snort from the bottle hidden in the deep pocket of his duster, while the trader yearned to light a cheroot from his ample supply, but both gentlemen refrained, conscious of being in the presence of ladies.

"Hope to God, ma'am, we're not running into Chief Red Wolf's band of Sioux miscreants," said the drummer in order to make conversation. He was interrupted by the loud blast of a rifle shot, shattering the stillness of the forest. On the roof, McIvers toppled from his seat, dead with a bullet hole between his eyes.

As if dropped from nowhere on the road by an evil spirit, the tall figure of a man stood pointing his sixteen-shot Winchester straight at Pat, growling: "Whoa, stop right thar or I'll blow yer noggin' off!"

Having no choice, Pat obeyed. Fear gripped the passengers inside. The drummer, peering timidly out from between the coach's window curtains, had seen the stark figure with the Winchester.

"A road-agent, by Jove!" he whispered hoarsely. "Don't move, and pray."

The menacing figure standing in the road was clad in a long black coat that reached below the knees, black boots with huge spurs, and a black, wide-brimmed Mexican hat, and his face, except for the malignant, evil-glowing eyes, was hidden by a black kerchief. Close by, half-hidden by a large pine tree, Pat Mayotte discerned a huge black stallion, champing at the bit. The blood in Pat's veins turned to ice. By the robber's outfit he knew who they were up against—it was Snake-Eye Sam, the fiendish, pitiless stagecoach robber, lately come to the Hills from the California Sierras where, so rumor had it, he had killed more than forty men, ravishing at knife point any female passenger who took his fancy.

"Have a pity, Lord," Pat muttered under his breath, "for Snake-Eye Sam will have none."

"Get down, pilgrim," Snake-Eye ordered, and Pat obeyed. One more shot, fired point-blank, and the poor driver was on the ground, weltering in his blood, a death rattle reverberating from his throat.

The robber yanked open the door of the coach. "Everybody out!" he ordered in a tone that brooked no resistance. "An' be quick about it ef ya know what's good fer ya!"

The passengers alighted, trembling and ashen-faced, certain that their lives were forfeit.

"Behave yerselves!" Snake-Eye told the two men, whose teeth were chattering, "an' keep your hands up!" Expertly, he relieved them of their wallets, gold watches, and all other valuables. Then he turned to the women, snatching the older lady's purse, tearing from her throat a pearl necklace, brutally wrenching from Polly's finger her diamond engagement ring.

"That'll fetch a good price," he muttered with a fiendish grin, leering at Polly with malevolent eyes in the same way a horse trader might appraisingly contemplate a fine specimen of horseflesh.

"Ye're a looker, by gum!" he hissed, "How'd ye like to git better acquainted with a real hombre?" and with brute force he grabbed the girl around her slender waist.

"Unhand me, foul villain!" she cried, her innocent young face pleading more eloquently than any words.

Snake-Eye Sam laughed heartlessly at her tender pleas, and dragged poor Polly, sobbing with fear and revulsion, to his horse. The girl swooned and fainted as the robber hoisted her seemingly lifeless form onto his horse and mounted up behind her. Mercifully, Polly was no longer conscious of her plight, of the fate worse than death that the human devil incarnate intended to inflict upon her.

"For the love of God and your immortal soul," her aged aunt pleaded, with hands uplifted, as in prayer, "let her go. She is betrothed and about to be wed!"

"Sorry, ma'am, but the groom will hev to wait a while longer. Hasta la vista!" And in an instant he was galloping away with his fair captive.

"Woe is me!" her aunt cried in desperation. "All is lost!"

"Hark!" exclaimed the drummer, turning his ear to the distant hills. "I hear hoofbeats!" Suddenly, his face lighted up and he cried: "Fear not, madam, for all is not lost! There is but one man in all the West who rides a great white stallion such as the one that approaches so swiftly! It is Deadwood Dick to the rescue!"

The drummer had spoken true. Deadwood Dick it was who presently reined in his horse beside the stagecoach, contemplating the crimson scene of carnage. His form was stalwart and iron-cast, with strength delineated to the critical eye in every curve and muscle. His face was plain, yet rather attractive, with its firm mouth shaded by a heavy yellow mustache, eyes of a dusky brown, and hair light and worn long down over the shoulders. A face it was which a lady might admire, and a gentleman envy. His attire was plain, consisting of a buckskin suit, knee boots, and a gray-felt slouch hat. He carried no weapons but his trusty rifle and a single cap-and-ball pistol. Around his saddle horn was coiled a lasso of prodigious length.

"I know this for Snake-Eye Sam's diabolical work," said Dick gazing sadly at the lifeless bodies of Pat Mayotte and Slim McIvers, "the wretch who did this must be brought to justice!"

"For God's sake, dear man," sobbed Aunt Milly, "justice, as you say, but first and above all my niece must be delivered from the hands of that devil. She's about to be wed. Save her, save her, dear man, and all I own in this world shall be yours. Save her before, before . . ."

"Deadwood Dick at your service," answered the stalwart horseman. "Say no more. I understand your fears, but all shall be well. But speak not of reward, my dear lady. Rescuing a damsel in distress is all the reward I could wish for. But there is no time to lose. I must be off!"

And with those words Deadwood Dick took his leave, urging his steed into a thundering gallop.

Through canyons and dense forests, over rushing streams and dizzying heights went the wild hunt. "Faster, faster, Snowstorm," (for that was the white stallion's name), Dick urged on his horse, "we must and we shall free that young girl whose life and honor are at stake! It's up to you and me!"

The proud animal redoubled its stride as if it understood what was at stake. Ahead, and unaware that Deadwood Dick, like an avenging angel, was hot on his trail, Snake-Eye reined in his horse at a small stream to let him drink. Polly was draped across the animal's back like a freshly slain deer. A deep moan escaped from her lips.

"Comin' to, my beauty?" the vile caitiff muttered under his breath with a wolfish grin. "We're close to an abandoned miner's shack I know of. Mebbe we'll stop thar fer a bit an' get chummy."

Polly shuddered, pretending not to hear. "I'll hurl myself from the nearest cliff before I let this fiend touch me!" she silently vowed.

Something made Snake-Eye Sam look back. On the trail, a mile behind him, he spied a flash, a brightness. It was a sunbeam playing upon the silver fleece of Deadwood Dick's great white stallion. The robber instantly recognized it for what it was. A foul curse burst from his lips. "Deadwood Dick! Hell and damnation! I'll slit yer throat, gal, afore I let him take ye from me!" He spurred his mount into a dead run.

Deadwood Dick too had gotten a glimpse of his enemy. "Fly, fly like the wind, Snowstorm!" he urged on his stallion, who needed neither whip nor spur to do his beloved master's bidding. Speedy, the robber's black horse, was fast as lightning, but even swifter was Snowstorm, not laboring under a double burden. Snake-Eye could hear his thundering hoofbeats coming closer and closer.

"Damn ye, Deadwood Dick!" he cried. "I'll salt ye down fer winter meat!" He whipped out his pistol from its holster, turning in the saddle to fire at his pursuer and paying no heed to his fair captive. Wide awake now, Polly, quick as a flash, grabbed the ruffian's arm and sank her teeth into his hand, making him drop his weapon. At the same instant, the loop of Deadwood Dick's lasso tightened around the villain's neck, jerking him from his saddle. Momentarily stunned, the robber lay flung to the ground, fighting for breath, his malignant eyes bulging from his head. Faster than the eye could follow, stalwart Dick threw the rope's other end over the sturdy limb of a nearby tree, refastened it to his saddle horn, and swiftly guided Snowstorm a few yards farther, thereby lifting up the road-agent until he was dangling from the branch, writhing in his death throes.

"Deadwood Dick at your service," the bold rescuer told Polly. "Don't look now, miss. The villain's getting his just deserts, earned a thousand times by his foul misdeeds. But it's not a sight for tender eyes."

He could have spared himself saying this. Polly had fainted again. Dick carried her limp form to the nearby brook and bathed her face with cold water from his cupped hands, loosening her blouse at the throat and partially exposing a heaving bosom of snowy purity, even whiter than Snowstorm's silver coat.

Polly opened her eyes and beheld him who had saved her from a fate too terrible to contemplate. Deadwood Dick gazed at her in awe and admiration. Never before had he found himself in the presence of such radiant beauty. The girl was a splendid specimen of young womanhood. He could hardly turn his eyes from a face so alluring.

"You risked your life to deliver me from this devil," whispered Polly. "How can I ever thank you?"

"To bring you back, alive and well, to your loved ones, miss, is all the thanks a man could ever wish for. I shall get the horses. In two hours you shall be snug inside the Indian Queen Hotel in Whoop-Up. It's not much of a town, miss, but the hotel is tolerably clean and the food is good. I'll make sure that your aunt is there too."

To himself he thought: "And to think that I went to all that trouble to deliver this singular example of beauteous womanhood to another man. Well, what's a fellow to do? It's all in a day's work."

Behind in the lone forest, Snake-Eye Sam was left suspended, a warning to all murdering outlaws.

CHAPTER 13

OAOAOAOAOAOAOAOAOAOAOAOAOAOAOAOAOAOAOAOAOAOAOAOAOAOAOAOAOAOAOAOAOAOAOAOAOAOAOAOAOAOAOAOAOAOAO

An' That's My Roolin'

OAOAOAOAOAOAOAOAOAOAOAOAOAOAOAOAOAOAOAOAOAOAOAOAOAOAOAOAOAOAOAOAOAOAOAOAOAOAOAOAOAOAOAOAOAOAO

In the Old West all manner of men, including saloonkeepers, served as judges. In many god-forsaken places they received neither salaries nor regular fees, but operated on "hope"—that is, covered their expenses through the fines they imposed. Men who upheld the law during those long-forgotten days were untrammeled by a knowledge of the law and of Latin, which could only have gotten in the way of common sense. Their rulings were often highly eccentric and biased, since they ran courts as they damn well pleased. If a law was needed, they promptly enacted one. If a law got in their way, they ignored it. They followed no precedent and allowed no appeals. A judge might be functionally illiterate and yet exhibit good horse sense, dealing out justice honestly, after his own fashion, thereby gaining the respect and affection of his fellow citizens. Such a one was Major Barry, the "Texas Bantam Cock," who held court inside a California saloon during the gold-rush days. Barry knew how to put a recalcitrant, obstreperous lawyer in his place. As he himself put it down in his own inimitable spelling:

> H. P. Barber, the lawyer for George Work insolently told me there were no law fur me to rool so I told him that I did not care a damn for his book law, that I was the Law myself. He jawed back, so I told him to shetup but he would not so I Fined him 50 dolars and comited him to gaol fur 5 days fur contempt of Court in bringing my roolings and disissions into disreputableness and as a warning to unrooly citizens not to contredict this Court.

A newspaper in Manzano, New Mexico, recorded a dialogue between a similarly erudite judge and the defendant:

JUDGE: There is on the docket a case against you for ARSENY. Guilty or not guilty?

PRISONER: Guilty, Your Honor.

JUDGE: The sentence of this court then is, that you pay a fine of two hundred dollars or marry the girl!

Some judges tempered justice with mercy. Others, such as "Hanging" Judge Isaac Parker, the "Law West of Fort Smith," sentenced no fewer than 160 men to death and was mighty vexed to see half of them slip through his fingers due to the shenanigans of softheaded lawyers. Seventy-nine "evildoers," however, died of sudden "throat trouble" brought on in workmanlike fashion by George Maledon, Parker's "neck-stretcher," who, on special occasions, transported half a dozen unlucky citizens to the netherworld simultaneously by means of an oversized common trapdoor. George's grim boast was: "I never hanged a man who come back to have the job done over ag'in."

By and large, justice in the early days functioned according to the motto that there was more law in a Colt six-shooter than in all the nation's lawbooks. Of all the highly unorthodox western judges of the last century, the most famous was Roy Bean, the "Law West of the Pecos."

The Law West of the Pecos

Roy Bean had never read the law. He sprang from Justitia's head like Athena from the head of Zeus, styling himself "judge" and "justice of the peace" by virtue of his possession of a single tattered and fly-specked volume of the *Revised Statutes of Texas, 1879*. Other lawbooks, sent to him from time to time, were used to light his stove, or their torn-out pages were stacked between the seats of his two-hole privy. Bean was unkempt in appearance, sported a scraggly, tobacco-stained beard, and had a shiny, bulbous nose, reddened by imbibing huge quantities of beer and forty-rod. He could generally be seen on the porch of his saloon-cum-courthouse, wearing a wide-brimmed sombrero, an ever-present cigar clamped between his teeth. He always wore a collarless seldom clean shirt, baggy pants, and a much stained and bespattered vest, buttoned only at the top to give room and ease to his Falstaffian belly. He was a fraud and a joke and a holy terror, as, on rare occasions, he condemned men to hang on the flimsiest evidence, having the sentence executed on the spot. He came down hard on Mexicans, Indians, blacks, and Chinese, but was tenderhearted in the case of Irishmen and former Johnny Rebs, particularly if they happened to be paying patrons of his establishment.

Born about 1825 in Kentucky, Bean killed his first man in Mexico at the age of twenty. In 1850 he got thirty days for launching a fellow man into glory during a "duel" in the then tiny town of Los Angeles. He almost died of hemp fever when he started an affair with a comely señorita betrothed to a Mexican officer who was not amused. During the ensuing encounter the luckless fiancé came up second-best. His amigos waylaid Bean, strung him up from the nearest tree, left him dangling, and rode away. His inamorata, who had watched the scene from behind a clump of bushes, promptly cut him down while he was still alive. He carried the mark of this misadventure, a deep red scar around his throat, until the day he died. His neck remained permanently stiff, "like an iron bar," so that he could not turn it. He later claimed that his neck had been stretched like that of a "goldurn jeeraff" and that it had taken him months to bang it back into its proper length. In his youth Bean gloried in being a mean barroom fighter. He once slowly and deliberately shoved a burning cigar up his opponent's nose.

In 1861 Roy arrived at Mesilla, New Mexico. A partisan of the southern rebellion, he organized a band of rapscallions to fight the Yankee Bluebellies. They called themselves the Free-Rovers, possibly because they were too free with other peoples' property. Otherwise known as the Forty Thieves, they did no fighting but were a menace to Mesilla's chicken population.

For a while Roy roosted among a jumble of shacks he had dubbed "Beanville," near San Antonio, Texas. He married a teenage muchacha named Virginia Chávez, who presented him with two boy and two girl Beans. The marriage was not a success. The couple fought like cats and dogs. On one occasion Roy found his señora in bed, presumably not alone. He snatched a burning stick from the fireplace and applied it vigorously to her derrière, whereupon she vanished from his life.

In 1882, "bearded, rum-soaked, and fat," Bean arrived in the hamlet of Vinegaroon with his copy of the *Revised Statutes of Texas*, a fierce passion for liquor, and an even greater one for his unattainable idol, the actress Lillie Langtry, a picture of whom he always carried in his wallet. He set up a saloon and was soon known as Old Vinegaroon, though Spanish-speaking folks simply called him Frijoles. A short time later Roy moved to the tiny jerkwater town of Langtry, of which he claimed to be the name-giver, and there set himself up as the "Law West of the Pecos" in his combination of saloon and courthouse, called, slightly misspelled, Jersey Lilly in honor of the actress he adored. It was situated within a stone's throw of the whistle-stop on the newly built San Antonio–El Paso line. The Jersey Lilly was a sort of ramshackle bungalow with signs proclaiming: JERSEY LILLY, JUDGE ROY BEAN, NOTARY PUBLIC, LAW WEST OF THE PECOS, JUSTICE OF THE PEACE, ICE AND BEER. As one of the ballads about Roy had it:

He was born one day at Toyah,
Where he learned to be a lawyer,
And a teacher and a barber and a mayor.

He was a cook and old-shoe mender,
Sometimes teacher and bartender,
And it cost two bits to have him cut your hair.

The old rascal was about sixty years old when he established his
rule at Langtry, and it was only at that historic moment that the
Legend of Roy Bean had its beginning.

○▲○

Ah Ling's Hommyside

○▲○

Judge Roy Bean of Vinegaroon
Held his court in his own saloon,
Fur a killin' or a thievin, or other sech fracas,
Bean was the Law West of the Pecos.

An article in the *Saturday Evening Post* of 1931 concluded that
"as a matter of cold legal fact Roy Bean was no more a justice
of the peace than the first jackrabbit he met in the Big Bend brush."
Such criticisms never bothered the old scalawag, who had soaked up
a lot of courtroom jargon during many trials in which he figured as
the defendant. He usually started proceedings with a solemn "Hear
ye, hear ye! This honor'ble court is now in session an' if any galoot
wants a snort afore I start tryin' this case let him step up to the bar
and name his pizen."

Roy's temple of justice was his saloon, his judge's bench the bar.
Behind it was a chair on which he used to sit when dealing monte,
and for dispensing justice he placed the weighty *Revised Statutes of
Texas* on the chair and took his seat upon it, which enabled him to

look over the counter at the defendants before him. The jury box consisted of a dozen beer barrels on which the panel of tried-and-true men took their seats.

In performance of his duties Judge Bean was self-important, scurrilous, high-handed, and outrageously profane. He allowed no appeal. The presence of lawyers was discouraged. Objections to his rulings were squashed by the display of a pair of oversized shooting irons. Thus with a booming voice that brooked no contradiction, Roy tried cases, passed sentences, performed marriages and divorces, leveled fines, and played coroner. His most famous inquest, the story of which has been told and retold in a dozen different versions, involved a murdered Chinese laundryman named Ah Ling. The defendant was an Irish gandy dancer who, as the only witness, testified on his own behalf. His Honor looked with favor upon the Sons of Erin because they were good customers, and the accused was one of the best. By contrast, he detested the "pigtailed heathen Sons of Heaven," who never spent a cent on his wet goods.

Roy got out the *Revised Statutes* from under his ample hindquarters, placed the heavy tome on the bar, and pretended to study it.

"This here book, which is a Texas lawbook," he finally ruled, "says that hommyside is the killin' of a yooman, male or female. Thar's innum'rable kinds of hommyside—murder, assasinashion, shootin', knifin', pizenin', killin' in self-defense, plain hommyside, negl'cent hommyside, an' praiseworthy hommyside. Thar is three kinds of yoomans—white men, niggers, an' greasers. It stands to reason that ef a Chinee was yooman, the sendin' of him up the flume would come under praiseworthy hommyside. It says nowhere in this here book of statutes that killin' a Chinaman is onlegal. The prisoner at the bar is discharged on condition that he pays for havin' this pigtailed heathen buried."

In another version of the same tale, the Irishman, Paddy O'Shaughnessy, swore that he had merely intended to frighten Ah Ling for not doing a good job with Paddy's laundry: "Faith, yer Honor, them divilish infidel Sons of Asia is worse than Orangemen, begorrah! May God give me mercy in the last days. It wasn't murder. 'Twas the Chinee's own fault. If I'd had a shillelagh I'd jest given him a good knock on his bean, ef this honor'ble court pardons the pun. Not 'avin' a shillelagh, I shot at the bastard wid a gun, but, by the Mither o' God, I told that dirty bodach to duck an' he didna duck, the pig-tailed sonuvabitch. 'Twas his aun fault, as I said afore. He did it out o' malice. That's as true as the sun, bedad!"

Judge Bean put his specs on his rosy proboscis and consulted his statutes, cleared his throat, took a nip of the good creature, and pronounced: "Paddy O'Shaughnessy, you stand before this bar of justice charged with murderin' one oriental named Ah Ling. Murder, Paddy, is a serious crime, special serious for the galoot who got killed. These here revised statutes of Texas say that the killin' of a citizen is punishable by death, but, by gob, it don't say a word about killin' sech a sorry specimen of the animal kingdom as a goddam Chinee. An' it is my roolin' that this was a justifi'ble case of hommyside an' that Paddy here, a powerfully good customer of your Honor, stands acquitted of all charges. I pronounce him innocent, an' I'll fine any gander-eyed galoot who sez different. The drinks, however, are on Paddy. This honorable court stands adjourned. What'll it be, gents?"

In still another version it is Roy's dim-witted factotum, Oscar, who sent Ah Ling to join his ancestors with a rusty saber left behind by a besotted cavalryman. The proceedings went like this:

"Hear ye, hear ye, boys, this honorable court is now in session, an' if any of you saddle-stiffs wants a shot afore I use my gavel, let him specify his brand of coffin varnish an', gentlemen of the jury, make sure of bein' well lubricated, fur this trial here may take some time. Wall, you all know the defendant here, Oscar, who stands accused of the orful crime of murder. Oscar shore is a puny, pitiful specimen of the yooman race. But we're mighty fond of him all the same. Who would clean out the spittoons, an' wipe the floor an' put sawdust on it, if it warn't for good ole Oscar here.

"Waal, yore honor'ble jedge is a square shooter, an' no bottom dealer, an' ef Oscar is guilty this court'll hang him higher than Haman, by ned! But have another snort afore I go on. Waal, here's the book, the Revised Statutes of the Great State of Texas, the Lone Star State, my friends, the State of Davy Crockett an' Jim Bowie, an' Sam Houston. An' it's all in here, boys, from the Alamo clear to this here Year of our Lord, eighteen eighty four, yessir. An' supposin El Stupido here is guilty I'll wrap it to him as if he was a stranger, by gob!"

Whereupon the judge proceeded to read the statutes from cover to cover, wading through Texas law from "alienation of affection" to zapping "zorillas in a zanja." After reading for some three hours, interrupted by frequent recourse to the Jersey Lilly's stock of strong waters, Bean closed the book and roused his comatose jury:

"And thar she is, gents, the full unabridged an' unexpurgated law of the Great State of Texas, from soda to hoc. An' thar ain't a single goddam mother-violatin' line in it nowhere makin' it a crime to kill a Chinaman. Tharfore my roolin' is that the defendant is discharged. My further roolin' is that all present are fined one dollar legal tender fur fallin' asleep while yer honorable jedge was readin' the law, the money to be fer buryin' the slant-eyed Son of Heaven. Court stands adjourned. Belly up to the bar, boys!"

○▲○

Fining the Deceased

○▲○

A red-haired drifter of whom nothing was known except that his first name was Mike, got more than commonly soused and, tottering across Myers Canyon Bridge, went over the side, breaking his neck on the rocks below. The body was loaded on a buckboard, driven to the Jersey Lilly, and there laid out on a table. Bean went through the dead man's pockets and came up with a revolver and forty-one dollars in cash. He empaneled a jury and proceeded to hold an inquest:

"Members of the jury, this here down-on-his-luck galoot met his Maker due to nacheral causes, to whit, fallin from a bridge while in a state of intoxicashun. An' that, amigos, is all there is to it. This here hombre's gone belly up an' he cain't tell us why he carried a six-shooter which, in the court's opinion, is a good gun. An' he cain't tell us how he came by these dineros. He's already flappin' his wings up there some place, this court shore hopes. This ain't no business of the court. But it is its business that this feller was carryin' about his pusson a concealed weapon, which is agin' the law. The court is obleeged to fine the deceased forty dollar for this misdemeenoor, to be employed in plantin' this poor sot proper-like in the boneyard. The forty-five, which, as the court opined, is a damn good gun, yer honor'ble jedge retains as a sooveneer to keep it out of reach of childers an' sech like innocents who could endanger themselves with it. An' that, folks, is my roolin'."

"Thar's one dollar left, jedge," one of the customers interjected. "What's that for?"

"That, you cross-eyed lunkhead, feedin' off yer range, is fur buyin' your hon'rable judge a drink."

Bean, who could extract simoleons from a rock, loved inquests because there was money in them. A Mexican was found dead in an arroyo with a bullet drilled neatly and plumb center between his eyes. Roy first robbed the corpse of a small golden cross hanging from its neck, as well as of a silver belt buckle, and then held an inquest, concluding solemnly:

"I rool that this hombre cashed in his chips as a result of bein' shot by a person unknown who was a damn good shot."

The Hanging of Carlos Robles

This story has been told so many times and in so many versions that one almost blushes to relate it. It is probably the figment of an eastern writer's imagination, but to hell with debunkers!

A Mexican was brought before Judge Bean on a charge of cattle rustling. Roy brought down his gavel with a bang, roared "Silence in court!" and proceeded:

"Hear ye! Hear ye! This hon'rable court is now in session, an' if any buzzard wants to whet his whistle, let him step up an' name his brand. Now, who's the rantankerous cuss before me. Oscar? Speak up, featherhead!"

"Carlos Robles, Your Honor."

"All right. Carlos Robles, it is the findin' of this here court that yore charged with the heinous an' despic'ble crime of cattle rustlin', which is an outrage agin' the Great Sovereign State of Texas an' the peace an' dignity of this court, This scurvy atrocioosh crime is punishable by death. How do you plead?"

"No hablo inglés."

"Court accepts yore plea of guilty. The jury will now deliberate; an' if any of you spavined saddle stiffs bring in a verdict short of hangin', the court will find you in contempt. Boys, have you arrived at a verdict?"

"We have, Your Honor. Guilty as charged."

"Thank you, gennelmen. Rise, Carlos Robles, an' receive yore jedgement. You got anythin' to say why sentence shouldn't be passed upon you?"

"No comprendo, señor."

"Carlos Robles, you've been tried by yore peers, but not by yore equals, as they are as high above you as an eagle is above a cockroach, an' they found you guilty as hell."

"Carlos Robles, soon the icy winds of winter will have passed. Soon spring will come with its wavin' green grass an' flowerin' trees. Gentle zephirs will stir the tresses of loverly maidens, as silver rivulets will come hop-scotchin' down the mountains an the benev'lent sun will kiss all the lil' pink an' white buds. Then will come the scorchin' summer, an' the grain an' corn will ripen from which good

hombres will make sourmash an' ever-glorious white lightnin'. An'
then fall will come to brighten leaves into shinin' gold under the
glowin' sun, an' apple trees will be bearin' apples to turn into applejack. Yessir. An' then we'll have winter agin, an' this Great Sovereign
State of Texas will be mantled in snow, an' the white mountaintops
will glow pink in the sunset an' the boys will be congregatin' around
the glowin' stove, a-sippin' red-eye, playin' poker, monte, an' euker.
But you won't be here seein' any of it, Carlos Robles, not by a damn
sight, 'cause it's the roolin' of this court that you be took to that
majestic cottonwood yonder an' hanged until yore too dead for to
skin. An' may God have mercy on your no-account soul, you mud-
skinned sonuvabitch! Oscar, let the prisn'er have a snort afore the
boys decorate the tree with him.''

Roy Bean's Pet Bear

Roy Bean had a pet bear, and it was beautiful to see how the two of them got along. Some say the old griz's name was Bruno, others made it Sarsaparilla, but that's neither here nor there. Roy had a cage made for the bear, but Bruno never saw the inside of it. The ferociously friendly critter was kept right next to the Jersey Lilly, tied to a tree by a chain long enough to give Bruno ample space to exercise his legs.

Bruno was good for business. Roy taught him to drink beer and the bear took to it like a bock-beer–weaned Bavarian. Roy would toss a bottle at Bruno, who would catch it between his huge paws, pull out the cork with his teeth, and empty its contents with one mighty swallow. Travelers passing through Langtry would leave their train to watch Bruno perform, buying bottle after bottle to have the show go on.

Roy also enlisted Bruno in the cause of justice. His Honor developed a habit of punishing drunks who had passed out after refusing, or being unable, to pay for their coffin varnish, or low-down characters who had made a ruckus while being booze-blind, by tying them to Bruno's tree with a chain just long enough to be out of the bear's reach. Waking up from their binges and contemplating Master Bruin standing erect, fangs bared, and his huge claws mere inches from their anatomy, not only sobered them up in no time, but also instilled in them a new respect for the law.

It is said that few men ever got the better of Roy Bean, but a drummer by the name of Sam Betters did. Roy had a wonderful racket going that produced for him an ever-flowing stream of greenbacks. The Jersey Lilly was the only saloon within a hundred miles. Whenever a train stopped at Langtry, all male passengers, as a matter of course, alighted to make a beeline for Roy's liquid refreshments. They had about fifteen minutes to quench their thirst before the train pulled out. Sam Betters was such a traveler. He ordered a beer at Roy's outrageous price of one dollar per bottle and paid with a new crisp and crackling twenty-dollar bill, unaware that the judge never made change. Roy put the note in his till with an absentminded look, yawing on a glass to give it some polish.

"This beer's as warm as piss," Betters complained. "Don't you keep it on ice?"

"Boys, did you hear this? The tenderfoot wants ice in July! That's a good one."

Roy never kept ice, despite the fact that his sign proclaimed "ICE, BEER, AND CHOICE LIQUORS." Sometimes he put a special lump of glass in the tumbler of a favorite customer just to make him feel good.

The train's whistle emitted a loud blast. Betters inquired, "Hey, where's my change?"

Roy smiled with a faraway look, chomping on his cigar.

"Goddam it, man, the train's leaving. Gimme my change. Hurry up!"

Roy continued to smile beatifically, gazing at the distant mountains shimmering in the haze. It dawned upon Betters that Roy had no intention of making change. The train's whistle sounded a last warning.

"You goddam money-grubbing, theiving old fart," yelled Betters, "I want change for my twenty!"

"Ye infinitismal pismire a-crawlin' up my pants leg," Roy answered good-naturedly, "this court fines you twenty bucks fur aboosin' yore honor'ble judge an' usin' profanity. The beer's on the house."

The train started pulling out slowly. Betters barely managed to get back on it. He was leaning out the window, shaking his fists, yelling like the devil: "Bean, you cheating son of a bitch, some day I'll get even with you!"

Roy waved back, grinning from ear to ear.

One or two years later Roy was in El Paso on business, bending his elbow at the bar of the Ruby Saloon. As fate would have it, Betters was there too. "Howdy, Judge," said the drummer, patting Roy on the back, "that was quite a joke you played on yours truly a while back at Langtry. Well, I've got a great sense of humor. No hard feelings, Bean. Let me buy you a drink."

"Sir," said Roy, "yore speakin' the language of my tribe."

They downed quite a few and got jolly, calling each other by their first names. "Say, Roy," said the drummer, "I just come from your place. That bear of yours is dead."

"What?!" screamed Roy, deeply shocked, spilling his drink. "It's onpossible. Bruno was fine when I left him a week ago."

"Gone over the range, I tell you. I saw him laying there. Poisoned, they told me."

"Pizened!? I'll kill the skunk who done it, kill him with my own hands."

"Tell you what, Roy. Seeing you was so fond of the brute, wouldn't it be grand to have him stuffed, so you could still see him standing by the swinging doors, drawing customers even in death?"

"You have a p'int thar, Sam. It would be a nice touch. An' he would bring in customers, like you say."

"There you are. Why not send a telegram to forward his skin. I know a great taxidermist. Cheap too. It could be done while you're here in town. Then you could take him home with you, nice and stuffed."

Roy sent a telegraphic message:

> OSCAR
> LANGTRY TEXAS STOP AT THE JERSEY LILLY
> STOP SKIN BRUNO AND SEND SKIN TO JUDGE
> BEAN AT RUBY SALOON EL PASO STOP

Oscar never questioned an order by his master. He put two double-O charges of buckshot into the poor bear, skinned it, and sent off the hide with the next train.

Roy returned with a magnificently stuffed, erect Bruno. His first words to Oscar were "I want to get my hands on that varmint who pizened my bear."

"Whaddayamean?" exclaimed Oscar. "He warn't pizened. I shot him like you told me."

"Like I told you, you addle-brained bastard?!"

"Like you said in your telegram."

"In my telegram, you locoed feather-headed nitwit!?"

"Shore. I couldn't skin him afore he was dead, could I?"

Slowly, the awful truth sank it. Fortunately for Sam Betters he never ran into Roy again.

This story is contradicted by an equally suspicious one, namely that Roy Bean on his deathbed bequeathed an alive-and-well Bruno to his idol, Lillie Langtry. And lo and behold, it came to pass that the famous actress traveled from El Paso to San Antonio to play Desdemona to a local Othello, and that her train stopped at Langtry, and that she alighted from her compartment in all her finery to visit the abode of her late lamented admirer. And lo, Bruno was entrusted to her to love and to cherish. But bears were not the haughty actress's cup of tea and coldhearted Lillie took Bruno far out into the wilderness, and there left him amid the chaparral, mesquite, and creosote bushes, then hitched up her skirts and ran like hell to catch the next train before Bruno could catch up with her. And for years the cowboys in their bunkhouses, trembling with fear, could hear the bear's ghost howling, howling, howling, crying for his beer.

○▲○

Judge Barker, Old Zim, and the One-Eyed Mule

○▲○

Jim Barker, a well-known character of the mountains, whose latchstring hangs out at the head of Blue Lizard Gulch, was duly elected a justice of the peace of El Paso County at the September election, and Mike Irving, a companion of Jim's, was empowered to officiate as the executive officer of his court. Last week Jim convened his first court, to hear the complaint of Elder Slater, a traveling missionary, who had caused the arrest of Zimri Bowles, a resident of the foothills, upon the charge of stealing the elder's one-eyed mule. Zimri had been arrested by Irving, the constable, while in the act of easing the descent of the mule down Mad Gun Mountain, with his lariat fastened to the tail of the animal. The proof against Zimri was conclusive. Accordingly, the Justice, after much legal perplexity of mind, proceeded to sentence Zimri to one year's confinement in the Territorial penitentiary, which sentence he concluded as follows: "An' now, Zim, seeing as I'm about out of things to eat, an' as you will have the costs to pay, I reckon you'd better take a turn among the Foot Hills with your rifle, an' see if you can't pick up some meat before night, as you can't start for the Big Canyon before morning."

Which marketing duty was performed by Zim, bringing in one blacktail fawn and a rabbit within the time prescribed as a postscript to the sentence.

On the following morning, the constable, mounted on his broncho, accompanied by the prisoner astride of the mule which the Elder kindly loaned him, started through the mountains for the penitentiary, where they arrived the second day out, their animals loaded with a deer, two antelopes and a small cinnamon bear, which they sold to the warden of the prison. After dividing the money the Constable proceeded to hand over Zimri on the following mitimus which is carefully preserved and may be seen in the possession of the warden:

> To the hed man of the Colorado prison, down at the foot of the Big Canyon on the Arkansas.—Take notice:—Zimri Bouls, who comes with this here, stole Elder Slater's one-eyed mule, and it was all the mule the Elder had, and I sentenced Zim officially to one year in the Colorado prison, and hated to do it, seein as Zim once stood by me like a man when Injuns had me in a tight place an arter I sentenced Zim to one year for stealing the Elder's mule, my wife, Lizzy, who is a kind o' tender-hearted critter, come and leaned her arm on my shoulder, and says she, "Father, don't forget the time when Zim, with his rifle, covered our cabin from Granite Mountain, and saved us from the Arapahoes, and Father, I have heard you tell that arter you was wounded at Sand Creek, an helpless, it was Zimri's rifle that halted the Indian that was creeping in the grass to scalp you." And then there was a tear fell splash upon the sentence I was writing and I changed my mind sudently as follows: seeing the mule had but one eye, an warnt mor'n half a mule at that, you can let Zimri go at about six months, an sooner if the Injuns should get ugly, an, furthermore, if the Elder shud quiet down and give in any time, I will pardon him out instanter.

> Witness my official hand an seal,
>
> James Barker, J.P.

El Cuatro de Julio

"Stand up, Señor Don José," said his Honor. "You stand charged with having filled your ugly corpus with tanglefoot whisky, willfully, deliberately, and from a premeditated design to disturb the peace and quiet of a day that is held sacred by every patriotic American."

"Los Americanos son carajos," interrupted the prisoner.

"Shut up your ugly mug," said the Judge, "or you will be committed for contempt. You got drunk, and kicked up a row on the Fourth of July, and then finished spreading yourself out on the street to broil, and started a barbecue for blue-tailed flies, do you consider that a proper way to celebrate the glorious Fourth?"

"El Cuatro de Julio no vale nada, que viva Guadalupe Hidalgo."

"Five dollars and costs," said his Honor.

"Broke es de Banke," replied José, as he sorrowfully took up his line of march towards the jail.

A Drink's Worth of Punishment

Yesterday we were informed of a "muss" that took place in one of our fashionable saloons. A man called for a drink and swallowed it before going down in his pockets to see whether he had the wherewith to pay for it. He didn't find it, after a careful search, and told the man behind the bar to "mark down on the slate." This the bar keeper refused to do on the ground that he "didn't do credit business," whereupon the honest customer "skinned off" his clothes and passed them over the counter to be held as security for the drink until morning, when he promised to call and redeem them. The tumbler wrestler became very angry at this, swore he didn't keep a pawnshop, and finally jumped the counter and kicked the poor fellow out, following him to the sidewalk and part of the way home, laying on vigorously all the time. The abused man took it all without a word or an attempt at resistance, until he thought he had received about a drink's worth, when he turned round and gave the enraged saloon keeper one of the most exhaustive thrashings that ever human frame was subjected to!

CHAPTER 14

Sky Pilots

Many of the West's early missionaries and preachers were as eccentric and uneducated as the early judges. Often they were handier with a shooting iron than with a sermon. Some were itinerant horsemen or mule riders, trotting from one tiny settlement or helldorado to the next, spending a day or two at a single log cabin or sod house, preaching the Lord's Word in return for a square meal, a rasher of bacon, or a scrawny chicken. In the words of the famous pioneer preacher Peter Cartwright: "We had little or no education, no books and no time to read or study them if we could have them. We had no colleges, even a respectable school within a hundred miles of us. . . . We could not, many of us, conjugate a verb, or parse a sentence, and murdered the King's English almost every lick."

As the saloon was always the first building to be put up in a new mining camp or cow town, so it also served initially as church, courtroom, and schoolhouse, Sermons were held, eulogies delivered, and marriages sanctified in many a whiskey mill.

The mule-riding "gospel sharks" and "sin-busters" were fierce specimens of devil-rasslers, with strident, earsplitting vocal cords, preaching the Word not only with their lips, but with their whole bodies, writhing in holy ecstasy, waving their arms, dancing on their tiptoes, sometimes giving the impression of suffering from epileptic fits. As Abraham Lincoln once said, in order to get the attention of his rustic flock, a good preacher should look as if he were fighting bees.

Religion in the Wild West had its own distinctive flavor. Often the preacher exhorted his flock during his hellfire-and-brimstone sermon: "Get down on yer knees, sinners, and yell!" And yell they did, making the windowpanes (if there were any) rattle and the floor shake. At Las Vegas, New Mexico, two itinerant gospel sharks, accompanied by two lady missionaries, invaded Close and Paterson's drinking establishment, turning, with the owners' consent, the bar into a pulpit, sermonizing and baptising fifteen hurdy-gurdy girls and three cardsharps. The twice-born sinners were led to the bar-altar by two "soiled doves" named Lazy Liz and Nervous Jessie. Amid the hurrahs of an enthusiastic crowd of alcoholic onlookers, the penitent salvation seekers vowed to forsake "King Faro, Prince Stud Poker, Bacchus, Gambrinus and lustful Queen Venus, for the Prince of Heaven." Religion, in the Old West, was like the men and women who inhabited the new land—rugged, ebullient, and highly individualistic.

Preachin' One Can Understand

Cowhands ain't much fer goin' to church, mostly 'cause they can't understand all them fancy sermonizin' words. Saddle stiffs ain't got much savvy outside of cows. But thar war one gospel shark they loved listenin' to, 'cause he spoke their lingo. He'd been a cowman oncet, as square a cowman as ever crossed leather, but then the Lord had lit into him like a blast of buckshot. He'd seen the lite, and had been granted a revelation, an' turned preacher man. As I mentioned afore, he could explain things to the buckaroos like nobody else. Take, fer instance, how he made palatable to 'em the story of King David an' Bathsheba.

◆ ◆ ◆

Dearly beloved, cowboys an' cow gals. Thar's allus a lot of sinnin' an' furnicashiun goin' on. You knows it. I knows it. I done some of it myself. But the Lord has pity an' forgives the sinner providin' he repents. Yea, brothers an' sisters, the Lord forgiveth all, 'xcept cattle rustlin' an' hoss stealin'. He knowest we are only hooman. Yea, even the great men in the Bible do a heap of sinnin', yea, even a feller like King David hisself.

Waaal, Ole Davy, he war the bossman, the top dog in Israel, had himself a ranch at a place called Jerusalem, a million acres, thousands of longhorns, dozens of buckaroos doin' the herdin'. Joab war the ramrod and a feller called Uriah war the segundo. This Uriah was a feller like a forked stick with britches on, but he had himself a wife, beautiful to behold, and her name war Bathsheba.

An' it came to pass that Bathsheba took a bath in the creek an' Ole Davy chanced to come a-ridin' on his palomino an' he saw Bathsheba frolickin' thar in the water, mother-nakkid, an' the sight hit him like a mule's kick, like a 'Pache arrer in the heart an' below whar he felt a mighty stirrin'.

Boys, you all know what I mean. A right purty gal mother-nakkid! It does somethin' to a feller, even unto King David, even unto a sky pilot like yours truly. Natcherally, it's wrong. Whaffer do we have sech feelin's? We have 'em for to marry, an' beget, an' be frootful in holy wedlock, an hon'rable estate an' pleasin' in the eyes of the Holy Bossman up thar, but it don't allus work out that way.

Boys an' gals, Ole Davy, he sinned. He committed addleterry. He coveteth his segundo's wife an' dealt from the bottom of the deck like a common kyardsharp. And it was so. Now Davy was a most handsome gent. Kain't no wummin get away from him. He had a soft curly baird an' when he bussed a gal, an' she felt that soft baird acrost her cheek, her legs started saggin' under her an' one thing led to 'nother.

An' Davy could play the harp. Larned it from an old Mex. He could play "Turkey in the Straw," an' "Barb'ry Allen," an "The Gal I Left Behind Me." A wummin nary resists a good harpist or a sweet-singin' sedoocer.

An' don't forget: Ole Davy was the bossman, the ranchero, the gent who owned the big house with the pianner, an' all that cattle. He was the man with the mucho dinero. Wimmin go for that. Ole Davy held the winnin' hand. An' when he saw Bathsheba's naked-ness, it smote 'pon him like a slingshot of great potency. An' he plumb adores her. He goes loco o'er that li'l woman's blue eyes. He goes ravin' mad at the thot of her cute li'l behind. He watches her frolickin' an' swimin' an' splashin. He sees her goin' home to a low-slung 'dobe house.

Arter that he ast Joab, his ramrod: "Wist thou who's livin' thar in that li'l 'dobe?"

An' Joab sez: "Verily, it is Uriah, thine segundo."

"An' doth that Uriah keep a purty li'l heifer in thar?"

"His wife, Bathsheba. She's a looker, for shore."

"Has Uriah got his brand and earmarks on her?"

"They wuz married in church, proper-like."

"I wish I'd-a run my brand on her," sez Old Davy, her bein' married hittin' him hard. He rassles with his conscience an' the con-science loses out. He starts coyotin' 'round that li'l 'dobe whenever Uriah is out brandin' calves or roundin' up steers. It war remarkable how many things Davy could think up fer Uriah to do, mostly jobs that kept him way out on the range, farthest from the 'dobe house. An' Davy is like a rooster arter a hen. He allus manages to run into Bathsheba, accidentally like, an' gets acquainted. I reckon he ropes at her more'n a dozen times. He rides his pony to death jest to have a look at her. She's like sunshine in the woods fer him. He gets so loco o'er that wummin, he takes to makin' po'ms on her:

> *Your eyes are beautifool like those of a longhorn.*
> *You'se the purtiest gal ever born.*
> *Like slim cornstalks are your legs,*
> *An' for a li'l kiss I begs.*
> *Yore bosoms are as white as snow,*
> *The nicest ones I ever saw.*
> *An' from yore rose-red ruby lips,*
> *Bushels an' bushels of honey I sips.*

He had a gift for makin' po'ms, Old Dave had, a fact born out by his psa'ms in the Good Book. He was hankerin' after Bathsheba 'til his tongue hung out like a calf rope. She drove him to talkin' to hisself.

And it came to pass that Joab, his ramrod spake unto him: "I might be feedin' off my range, boss, but I gotta ask, what aileth thee?"

An' David answered unto him: "That lissome lassie Bathsheba got me locoed. I jest got to drop my rope o'er her. But that goldurn Uriah is in the way."

Joab sez unto him: "Patrón, I'll send Uriah out visitin' line camps, way out yonder, an' I'll bring that corral bunny unto you." An' it war thus.

Ole Davy pretended to make friends with Uriah, an' called him pard an' compadre, an' made him a present of a barrel of the finest bug juice. An' that chucklehead Uriah wuz blind as a snubbin' post, an' fell for it, an' got as drunk as a blind hawg, an' arter that went out to the line camps. An' Joab, Davy's ramrod, brung Bathsheba unto him. An' she lay with David an' he knowed her carnally. They went at it like jackrabbits, oncarin' that it war onpleasin' to the Lord.

An' Uriah never wist that Ole Davy war hornin' in on his pasture. He never could read David's kyards. An' Bathsheba got big with child an' it warn't Uriah's.

An' it came to pass that David jined unto him Joab, his ramrod, and spake unto him thus: "Next cattle drive, don't make straight for

Dodge or Abilene by the Chis'm Trail, but make thee a li'l detour through 'Pache country an' mebbe you'll run into them red fiends. Iffen you do, set ye Uriah in the forefrot of the hottest battle, an' retire from him, that he may be smitten and die. Thar'll be a nice fat bonus in it for thee."

An' Joab an' Uriah an a dozen buckaroos gat themselves up, an girded their loins, to drive cattle to Abilene. An' neither did Joab take the Chis'm Trail, nor the Goodnite Trail, but cut acrost 'Pache country. And it was so.

An' Joab, the ramrod, had Uriah ride p'int far ahead, while he and the buckaroos tarried behind, an' the 'Paches got to Uriah. An' the red varmints smote Uriah with their tommyhawks, an' let fly at him with their cap'n'balls, an' made a pinchusion outa him with their arrers, an' Uriah was daid.

An' Joab an' his men turned back to the Chis'm Trail and sold David's cattle at a profit in Abilene. Wherefore they rioted in the streets of that town and did what war onseemly within the gates of the city, an' made a noosance of theyselves in the dance halls an' cathhouses. An' arter they had drunk all the saloons dry, they returned to their boss David.

"Camest ye to tell me some news?" Ole Davy ast Joab.

"Thar's good news, an' thar's bad news," sez Joab. "We got the longhorns to Abilene an' sold 'em at a nifty figger an' brung you bags of shekels, but Uriah, thine segundo, got hisself an Injin haircut an' lost his topknot. Uriah, thine servant, is daid."

"It happens to the good an' the bad, the old an' the young, the rich an' the poor, fer the sword devoureth one as well as the other. Uriah's lucky to have left this vale of tears an' we must go on as well as we can 'til we jine him in the ever-after. Set yerself down, Joab, an' have a drink."

An' they downed a few shot glasses of hard stuff, the kind that can draw a blood blister on a rawhide boot. It came to pass that Ole Davy handed Joab, his ramrod, a fat envelope an' winked at him, an' Joab got himself up and winked back.

An' Bathsheba jined herself unto David an' borned him a son whose name war Solomon. An' Solomon grew up into a smart kid an' got to be king arter Ole Davy. God war wrothy at David for havin' dry-gulched Uriah but, by-m-by, calmed down an' forgave him. Brothers an' sisters, sinnin' is human an' you cain't avoid it altogether, but don't overdo it, lest you burn in hellfire everlastin'. Iffen you chance 'pon a purty wummin frolickin' nakkid in the creek, avert yer eyes an' run like hell. An' that goes fer you gals too. If you chance 'pon a feller scratchin' the topsoil off of him in the river, look ye not at his nakkidness lest you go blind, but bid him put his britches on or, leastwise, kivver his self with his Stetson whar it'll do the most good.

As to Solomon, strictly speakin' he war a bastard. This didn't bother the Children of Israel none. He was their king an' mighty above men, an' a very smart cookie. Wharfore, dearly beloved, if it came to pass that yore paw or maw waren't properly hitched, don't let it worry you, but thinketh ye of Solomon. Amen.

The Parable of the Prodigal Son

Now, there was a certain man who had two sons.

And the younger of them said to his father, "Father, give me the portion of the goods that falleth to me."

And he divided unto him his living, and the younger son purchased himself an oil-cloth grip-sack and gat him out of that country.

And it came to pass that he journeyed even unto Buckskin and the land that lieth over against Leadville.

And when he was come nigh unto the gates of the city, he heard music and dancing.

And he gat him into that place, and when he arose and went his way, a hireling at the gates smote upon him with a slung-shot of great potency, and the younger son wist not how it was.

Now in the second watch of the night he arose and he was alone, and the pieces of gold and silver were gone.

And it was so.

And he arose and sat down and rent his clothes and threw ashes and dust upon himself.

And he went and joined himself unto a citizen of that country, and he sent him down into a prospect shaft for to dig.

And he had never before dug.

Wherefore, when he spat upon his hands and lay hold of the long-handled shovel wherewith they are wont to shovel, he struck his elbow upon the wall of the shaft wherein he stood, and he poured the earth and the broken rocks over against the back of his neck, and he waxed exceedingly wroth.

And he tried even yet again, and behold! the handle of the shovel became entangled between his legs, and he filled his ear nigh unto full of decomposed slate and porphyry which is in that region round about.

And he wist not why it was so.

Now after many days the shovelers with their shovels, and the pickers with their picks, and the blasters with their blasts, and the hoisters with their hoists, banded themselves together and each said to his fellow: Go to! Let us strike. And they stroke.

And they that strake were as the sands of the sea for multitude, and they were terrible as an army with banners.

And they blew upon the ram's horn and the cornet, and sacbut, and the alto horn, and the flute and the bass drum.

Now it came to pass that the younger son joined not with them that did strike, neither went he out to his work, nor on to the mine lest at any time they that did strike should set upon him and flatten him out, and send him even unto his home packed in ice, which is after the fashion of this people.

And he began to be in want.

And he went and joined himself unto a citizen of that country; and he sent him into the lunch room to feed tourists.

And he would fain have filled himself up with the adamantine cookies and the indestructible pie and vulcanized sandwiches which the tourists did eat.

And no one gave unto him. And he fainted from lack of proper nourishment.

And when he came to himself, he said, How many hired servants hath my father on the farm with bread enough and to spare, and I perish with hunger.

And he resigned his position in the lunch business and arose and went unto his father.

And when he was yet a great way off, he telegraphed to his father to kill the old cow and make merry, for behold! he had struck it rich, and the old man paid for the telegram.

Now the elder son was in the north field plowing with a pair of balky mules, and when he came and drew nigh to the house, he heard music and dancing.

And he could't seem to wot why these things were thus.

And he took the hired girl by the ear and led her away, and asked her, Whence cometh this unseemly hilarity?

And she smote him with the palm of her hand and said, "This thy brother has come, that was dead and is alive again," and they began to have a high old time.

And the older brother kicked even as the government mule kicketh, and he was hot under the collar, and he gathered up an armful of profanity and flung it among the guests, and gat him up and girded his loins and lit out.

And he gat him to one learned in the law, and he replevied the entire ranch whereon they were, together with all and singular the hereditaments, right, title, franchise, estate, both in law and in equity, together with all dips, spurs, angles, crooks, variations, leads, veins of gold or silver ore, millsites, damsites, flumes, and each and every of them firmly by these presents.

And it was so.

Lissen to the Heavenly Poker Player!

Dearly beloved! Heed the Great Faro Dealer up thar in heaven! He can look into yore kyards (yore hearts) an' take a gander at what kinds of kyards yore holdin'! Lissen to what the heavenly poker game teaches us:

The "Ace" reminds us that thar's but one God in Heaven.

The "Deuce," that God made Adam and Eve sinless.

The "Trey," of the three Wise Men, guided by the Star of Bethlehem.

The "Four," of the four Evangelists.

The "Jacks," who remind us of the false prophets of the Amalekites.

The "Queens," of the Queen of Shebah, Esther, Abraham's Sarah, Pharaoh's daughter, an', above all, of the Queen of Heaven.

The "Kings," of King Saul, David, Solomon, and Herod.

Yes, dearly beloved. I let ye have a peek into the devil's hand. Ye kin see that yore sittin' in on a rigged game, playin' against the hellish bottom-dealer, the cussed sharper whose name is Lucifer, attended by his shills and minions, the fallen angels, whose names are Bunco Steerer an' Thimble Rig! Yea, brothers an' sisters—(Female voice from the crowd: "I ain't a sister to no man.") Shet up, ye scarlet harlot. Waal, brothers an' sisters, what kind of dough have ye chipped in? What's yore ante? Your very souls, I tell ye, that's what! An' Satan's a-sittin' thar, starin' ye in the face. He's got an ace up his sleeve, an' his minions play with marked kyards an' loaded dice. Snake Eyes comin' up fur ye ev'ry time. An' Lucifer cold-decks ye an' sweeps up the pot, takin' yer flutterin', squeakin' souls down into the fiery skinnin' house, into the hellish deadfall whar thar's howlin' an' the gnashin' of teeth forever an' ever. Yea, brothers and sisters— (Voice from the crowd: "Don't you 'sister' me!") Shet up, ye Whore of Babylon!

(Voice: "You usta call me yer little sweetie, reverend!")

Shet up, ye soiled dove! Brothers an' sisters, partickerlarly ye fellers, resist them blandishments of the devil's shills sech as them Jezebels yonder, whose names are Fornicashiun an' Uncleanliness. Copper yer bets, sez I! Come on, boys! Put yer money down. Place yer bets on yore Heavenly Father who runneth a square game. Don't play the devil's game, which is as crooked as a dawg's hindleg! Stick with Christ, who'll deal ye a full house! When the great showdown comes on Jedgment Day, an' the Heavenly Dealer "sees you," O brothers an' sisters, I pray ye come up with the right hand, with all the four Aces—Faith, Hope, Charity, an' Repentance. Then call out loud: "Keno!" an' rake in the heavenly pot, an' live in eternal bliss from Soda to Hoc!

Hear What the Great Herd Book Says!

Hear what the Great Herd Book says; "When the Son of Man (or the Great Herdsman of Life) shall come in His glory and all the holy angels with Him, He shall sit upon the saddle (throne) of His glory and before Him shall be gathered all nations, and He shall separate them from one another as a shepherd divideth his sheep from his goats." Now, when the herd is cut, the tailings are allowed to drift at will to be the prey of the cattle thief. But the cattle which have an owner will be cared for, taken into green pastures, and fed through the cold, stormy weather. Hear the great stock-owner: "Then shall the King say to them on His right hand, Come ye blessed of my Father (or ye of my father's brand), inherit the Kingdom." But hear what is to become of the tailings of that great roundup: "Then shall He say to them on His left, depart from Me, ye cursed, into ever-lasting fire prepared by the devil and his angels" (or the great cattle thief of human souls). Boys, if you are in the old thief's pasture, just jump right through the fence and run like hell out into the sunlight of God's pasture green!

A Funeral Oration

Brothers and sisters. We come here to pay our last reflect, I mean neglect, to our discarded brother Tom. Old Tom, he died of lead pizening. Got hisself ventilated by a citizen with his bark on, durin' a game of kyards. Gone up the flume he is. Cashed in his chips. It's a goddam shame. Old Tom, he was a very constipated gennelman, a Civil War veterinarian, I mean vegetarian, I mean venereal. Heck, you all know what I mean. He fought for the Union and the five cent cigar. He was a churchgoer for sure, always a-comin' down the aisle with his New Testicle in his hand, always studyin' it. Knew his Ole Testicle too. Old Tom, he come from a fine famblee of extinguished descendants. He was dealt the dead man's hand by his Predator, I mean Cremater, tarnation, you know what I mean. He's gone to the great behind to shake hands with Saint Peter, playin' a game of stud with the angels. He's gone to the great behind for sure, a sittin at the footstool of the Lord. Old Tom, he warn't 'xactly a totateeter, what I mean is a meadow-yaller, goddam, you all know what I mean, but Tom had only a li'l nip here and there, nary more'n five or six a day. He was a shinin' rectangle, I mean rectum, hell, you know what I mean. He was a fine sample to the whole consternation, I mean constipation, to the whole congestion, hellfire and brimstone, you know what I mean, pards. Wall, it's time now to plant Ole Tom in this here boneyard. He was a good, upstandin' buckaroo, coveted his neighbor's wife or girlfriend only oncet or twicet, but always made a good job of it. Oh, well, what the heck! Let us pray.

A Black Hills Sermon

From Deadwood? Well, yes sir, I reckon; I've been a year on the
   tramp.
Not missin' a railroad excitement, or skippin' a good mining camp.
I've sampled the country all over, and took in the "diggings" all
   'round.
And at last I've fetched up with the "Web Feet" way down here on
   Old Puget Sound.

Yes, Deadwood is dead, sure enough, sir; as we say—"Too dead for to
   skin"—
And there's not an old timer remainin', except a few stiffs that's
   snowed in.
But there was a time in that country, when everything was in full
   bloom,
When licker was sold for a quarter a throw, and minin' was all on the
   boom.

It was just about then that Tom Miller was grinding his little "Show Mill."

With that partner of his, Billy Nuttall, that the knowing ones called "Lanky Bill."

It was thar, in their "show shop" one Sunday, that I heard a quaint sermon begun—

The preacher "an old reformed gambler," and the text he gave out, "The Prod Son."

The Prodigal Son was intended to call all these sinners to God,

But the preacher warn't partial to diction, so he just cut it down to "The Prod."

And you'll find that the "Gospel Shark" dealin' this game is not present to-day,

And he asked me to "shuffle a hand up so all of you suckers could play."

"And right here," he continued, "this racket's a new game to me in this town.

So just play it through; there's no limit, you'll never be told to take down.

But you'll find that the 'Prod Son' was a 'Young Kid' whose Ole Man was pretty well heeled

He had plenty of 'Stuff' in his 'leather,' and long horns and sheep in his field.

It occurred to the kid that he'd tackle the old man for his little bit,

And he would pack up his grip sack and quietly get up and git.

He asked the old man just to give him a portion of what he had got.

And he wouldn't stay home there a waitin' till Death opened up a 'jackpot.'

And the old man did give him his divy right down to an old postage stamp.

And the kid hollered 'over the river,' and ducked for the first mining camp.

And he gathered the gang all around him, all the boys and girls he could see,

And every one of 'em got loaded, and they had a great blow out and spree.

They played the thing up to the limit, and took in each snoozer and bloke,

Until they had run all the gamut, and the 'Prod Son' of course he was broke.

The Good Book don't say, nor does history state, the game that he played in that place,

But it's safe to suppose, my itinerant lambs, that 'his Prodship' got steered agin brace.

Be that as it may, it just bust him, and bust him right down to the dogs.

And the very next thing we hear of the 'Prod,' he is livin' on husks with the hogs.

It occurred to him then that his racket was hardly a one that he could win,
So he thought he'd go back to the old man, and try to blow him in agin.
Now perhaps some of you unbelievers don't think he welcomed his son,
You may think he unchained the bull-dog, and just double-shotted the gun.

But he didn't; he just killed a yearling to feed this durn ungrateful scamp,
And he bought him the best sheeney suit of new clothes to be had in the whole minin' camp.
And he got up a blow-out and shindy, and everything went off slam-bang.
He invited the boozers and snoozers, the hobos and all of the gang.
And the wine and the whiskey flowed freely and they danced 'till the gray break of day,
And the 'Prod Son' stood solid again, boys, and further the Good Book don't say."

Just then a big gambler, uprising, remarked, "Now, my friend, by your leave,
There's a part of the 'Prod Son' racket, that I cannot hardly believe;
For there ain't in this camp a two-dealer, or man that will shake chuck-a-luck,
If a sucker goes broke agin either, they won't give a case for his chuck.
So that place in your sermonizing which says, 'He went down to the dogs,
And when he was needing a squarer, he had to eat husks with the hogs,'
Don't seem to me just orthodoxy, and unless you say you was there,
I don't mind telling you cold, pard, your yarn isn't on the dead square."

The preacher just straightened himself up, and said, "Then you think that I'm preachin a lie."
And a forty-five cracked in a minute, and the big gambler's turn came to die.
There were many old "blood purifiers" and "expectorators of lead,"
And when quiet was restored some fifteen or twenty were dead.

The preacher resumed, "Thar'll be preachin' next Sunday at just ten o'clock.
We're goin' to run scripture teachin, right thro' here from Soda to hoc.
My text is the first Lord's commandment, and this is the rule I've laid down,
To run this game easy and quiet, if I kill every sucker in town."

CHAPTER 15

Critters

The animals of the Great West were strange to the immigrants and excited their imagination, furnishing the subject of many tales and legends. The most numerous stories were those about snakes, bears, and horses, in that order. Snakes, it was believed, never die before sunset. Horsehairs put into water turn into snakes. Rattlers sneak into barns to steal cow's milk. A serpent will hypnotize a rabbit by staring at it so that it cannot run away. As for horses, the story of the Great White Stallion of the West is remembered in dozens of local variations. It is thought that if a man meets a white horse a redheaded girl will make love to him, but if a young bride and groom ride in a carriage drawn by a pair of white horses, the marriage will end in tragedy. As far as bears were concerned, newcomers to America were told that bears were born as little lumps that the mother had to lick into shape, that Master Bruin sucked his paws for nourishment while hibernating, that some Alaskan bears, out of a bad conscience for stealing a farmer's honey, brought him a dozen big salmon in return as a token of appreciation, and many stories tell of a fellow who, during a dark night, wrestled a man in a fur coat barring his way—a bear, as it always turns out.

Some legends deal with ogres and fabulous monsters rather than with real-life animals, as for instance the windigo or wandingo, a fiendish man-eating creature that preys on wanderers who have lost their way, or the loup-

garou, the werewolf of the French-speaking trapper and voyageur, often a bad man, who never went to mass, and turned into this horrible cannibalistic "varmint." A subspecies of this ogre, the loup-garou de cimetière, specializes in digging up corpses from churchyards in order to devour them. Finally, the high ranges of the Rockies were said to be inhabited by a ten-foot-tall hairy, apelike creature called Big Foot, seemingly a close cousin to the Abominable Snowman.

The Valley of Headless Men

High up in the Canadian northland, just below the Arctic Circle, where the Yukon and Northwest territories meet the jagged end of British Columbia, lies a beautiful valley. Though surrounded by a forbidding country of blizzards and ice storms, this valley is filled with lush forests and luxuriant plants, with meadows covered with wildflowers and miles of berry patches. There fawns gambol in the sun, birds chirp and warble, while bright-colored butterflies flit among blossoms replete with sweet nectar. The valley's earth is warmed, and the climate rendered mild, by innumerable boiling and steaming hot springs, nature's own subterranean heating system. Also, by the whim of some strange local god, gold is to be found here, gold by the handful and by the bucketful.

And yet there are no human beings to be encountered in this beautiful valley trying to escape the harsh climate of the region. This earthly paradise is shunned by the nearby Indians, and not only because its beauty is marred by an all-pervading reek of sulphurous vapors. To the natives this is the Valley of Headless Men, the Vale of the Nakoonis, hairy demons resembling giant bears, who suffer no human being to enter their balmy realm and who punish unsuspecting trespassers with death.

In 1904, during the aftermath of the Klondike Gold Rush, three brothers—Charlie, Willie, and Frank McCleod—ventured into the Valley of Headless Men in search of the shiny, precious yellow metal that has kept mankind spellbound since the dawn of history. In Edmonton the brother named Charlie had encountered a grizzled old prospector wearing around his neck a rawhide thong from which dangled a large gold nugget.

"I found it inside that devil's cauldron they call Headless Valley," the man explained, "up there, north of Fort Liard. There's lots more of that stuff where this came from."

Asked why he had not stayed to help himself to all that gold, the oldtimer said, "There's critters there you don't want to monkey with, big as Kodiak bears and so covered with hair that they seem to be wearin' fur coats. They're apt to tear you apart with their huge claws, then gobble you up like candy. The gold's there for the pickin', but it lies among heaps of human bones. One of them ungodly beasts, the Injuns call 'em Nakoonis, almost had me for breakfast. It got so close I felt its hot stinkin' breath upon my neck. No, friend, you don't want to go there, not for all the gold in the world."

Charlie told his two brothers: "There's more gold up there than they ever got out of the Klondike. That old coon tried to scare me off with his tales of huge hairy monsters. That's only to keep out the competition. He wants it all for himself."

Charlie got a good job with the Hudson's Bay Company and did not pursue the matter further, but Willie and Frank caught gold fever and, together with an Australian prospector named Wilkerson, set out for the land of the hairy Nakoonis—and were never seen alive again.

When two years went by without his brothers coming back, Charlie got worried. He quit his job with the Hudson's Bay Company and went on a one-man expedition to find the missing men. After a long, bone-wearying trek, he finally reached the Valley of Headless Men and soon stumbled upon an old dogsled to which had been tied a faded message: "We've hit pay dirt." He began searching the area and, after three days, found Frank's and Willie's remains—two skeletons in union suits, one stretching out its bony hands for a rusting rifle. Both skeletons were intact, except that the skulls were missing. Of the Australian there was no trace. It was later rumored that Wilkerson had showed up in Olympia with bags of gold dust, boarding a ship bound for Sydney, but this rumor could not be verified.

Charlie questioned a few Indians living near the valley. They told him: "It was the Nakoonis. They kill all who dare to go into that bad place. They tear their heads off. That's why we call it Headless Valley." That was all Charlie could get out of them, but he was scared. He buried his brothers' remains and then left quickly, haunted by the memory of two headless skeletons in woolen underwear.

All this did not discourage a Swedish gold-seeker named Ole Jorgensson. "The Australian did it, that's obvious," said Ole. "And he cut off their heads and hid them somewhere to make it look as if the Indians had murdered those two brothers, or, maybe, to prevent superstitious men from going there. He probably wants to come back for more. It doesn't scare me. Indians, Australians, or hairy bear people, it's all the same to me. I have a good rifle and a six-shooter. I'm ready for them."

At Fort Liard, Ole ran into a storekeeper called Fields who grub-staked him for a half share in whatever the Swede might find. Ole disappeared into the wilderness. Two years later a Ntlakyapamuk Indian appeared at Field's store with a letter from Jorgensson. Ole had found the mother lode. "Come quick, my friend," he wrote, "and bring plenty of supplies. We will both be rich!" Enclosed in the letter was a map indicating the spot where the Swede had built him-self a cabin by a lake.

It took Fields a few weeks to get the supplies together, load them on a mule, and reach Headless Valley. He found Ole's cabin burned to the ground. Nearby he discovered Jorgensson's headless corpse, skeleton hands still grasping a Winchester from which two shots had been squeezed off—at whom or what he could not guess. This time two red-coated Mounties arrived to investigate, but they found nei-ther clue, nor head, nor a trace of gold. There were unnaturally large bearpaw prints all over the place, looking strangely human.

The Indians shrugged, saying: "We told you, white folks, not to go in that valley, told you the Nakoonis would get your heads. But the white man has no ears to listen."

Three other men with no ears to heed a warning arrived in the Valley of Headless Men. It is not known who they were or what they were called. It is only known that they told all and sundry that the Australian was still in the valley killing intruders venturing into his domain. They were not afraid, because they outnumbered him three to one and were heavily armed. Their headless skeletons were found a year later, by a river, still in their bedrolls. One skeleton was clutch-ing a piece of fur. The Mounties gave it to a naturalist for identifica-tion. He told them that the pelt fragment belonged to a creature unknown to zoology.

Twenty years later three prospectors, named Kilroy, Hayes, and Hall, went into the valley, lured by old tales of gold. They were not worried about an Australian assassin, saying, "Whoever murdered all those fellers they tell about must long be dead."

Hall left camp one morning to look over a promising mountain slope which he thought contained veins of gold. When he did not return, Kilroy and Hayes went in search of him, but they didn't find a single bone, or shred of clothing, or anything else that belonged to Hall. What they found was a huge, curved, solitary claw covered with dried blood. A paleontologist later insisted that it belonged to a long-extinct cave bear.

Years later a trapper named Powers ventured into the valley, not for gold, but because he was sure that this lush, temperate area must be swarming with fur-bearing animals—silver fox, marten, sable, ermine—a treasure in pelts. When twelve months went by without Powers coming back, the redcoats at Fort Liard said to each other: "Time to look for a lost head again." They found Powers' moldering remains, a ghostly index finger curled around the trigger of his Colt, whose cylinder had been emptied. What he had shot at could not be determined, but there were gigantic footprints which one Mountie said must be from the biggest Kodiak bear ever. His captain was sure they belonged to a ten-foot-tall fellow who never clipped his toenails.

The next victim was a man called Shebbach who went into the valley to trap as well as look for that phantom gold. Of him only heaps of scattered bones were found, of course without a skull. The Mounties could not even be absolutely sure that the bones were Shebbach's. Among them they discovered a single small nugget, not much larger than a pea.

More men went into the valley to lose their heads—in 1936, 1938, and 1941. A rumor spread that during the war a Japanese Zero had crashed in Headless Valley. The plane and the pilot's body had been recovered, but the whole incident had been hushed up by army intelligence and the FBI. As to be expected, the pilot's head was missing. A huge, crescent-shaped bite, the size of half a watermelon, had been taken out of his side, cutting the knight of Bushido almost in half.

And so it went. The last man to lose his head in the valley (up to now) was an adventurous bardog from Nome who was relieved of that so necessary part of his anatomy in the fall of 1976. One anthropologist studying Indian languages in the area was determined to get to the bottom of the mystery. Carrying a large backpack, he set out on skis, because the season was advanced and snow had arrived unusually early. He was about to make his camp on top of a high mountain pass, just outside Headless Valley, and was in the process of taking off his skis when, in the bright moonlight that made the snow look like glistening silver, he made out the shape of a huge, terrifying, fur-covered creature—half-animal, half-human—running with awkward strides but great speed toward him. Quick as lightning, he snapped his bindings back into place, grabbed his poles, went into a deep crouch, and tore hell-bent down the steep slope in a race for dear life with the horrible creature. He was a champion skier, but the monster, hurtling down the mountainside, kept pace with him. Already it was stretching out its giant paws with long, razor-sharp claws, to grasp him by the neck, but just in the nick of time the Nakooni stumbled, fell, and instantly became enveloped in a great ball of snow. The snowball quickly grew into an avalanche the size of a big house, gathering speed as it came thundering down, rolling, rolling, rolling, splintering trees on its way, crashing at last into the forest, far, far below.

The thoroughly shaken anthropologist did not escape altogether. He lost three toes to frostbite on the way back to Fort Liard, where he arrived more dead than alive. After having recovered he said that the Nakoonis must be Yetis, a subspecies of the Abominable Snowman. Others maintained that the anthropologist was a well-known alcoholic who had seen giant white mice and pink elephants, but no abominable Yeti or Nakoonis. Whatever he saw, the moral of the story is: *Don't lose your head looking for gold in the Valley of Headless Men!*

A Loup-Garou, or a Windigo, or Maybe a Carcajou

There was once a joli garçon, a voyageur, by the name of Baptiste. In 1825 he joined a party of fellow coureurs de bois as a trappair libre, a free trapper and mountain man, to go after beaver. Being a half-breed, part French voyageur and part Chippewa, he was as much at home in the prairies on the far side of the Missouri as was a catfish in the waters of the Big Muddy.

Civilized he was not, this Baptiste, neither in mind or body. A fierce son of nature, he was a wolfish-looking cuss, his face framed by a forest of unkempt black hair, his luxuriant beard covering almost all of his broad chest. He had no need of possessions, save what was needed to trap Frère Castor. He owned a shaggy, razor-backed horse; a dog that was three-quarters wolf; a Hawken rifle whose heavy ball could stop a charging buffalo bull in its tracks; powder, ball, and flint; a strike-a-light and tinderbox with sun-dried punk; a skinning knife; a twist of 'baccer; a fast-dwinding supply of whiskey; and, most important, five heavy steel traps. That was all except the tattered buckskin shirt and leggings that he wore until they disintegrated from wear and tear.

Baptiste was as solitary as a badger and as averse to company as a grizzly. In his vast domain, somewhere between the Platte and the Medicine Bows, he lived like a hermit in caves, dugouts, or lean-tos. He thrived on whatever his Hawken could bring down. And he was not choosy. He devoured everything from gopher to buffalo. A lightly roasted rattlesnake was deemed a delicacy. Whatever ran, hopped, crawled, swam, or flew was très bon à manger, by gar! Painter meat didn't shine, but he ate it anyway. A feast of boudins—buffalo intestines filled with deliciously fermented grasses, roasted on a bed of hot embers—was bliss. He fought Rees and the terrible Pied Noirs and, once, argued over a fresh kill with a famished grizzly bear, winning the argument. For months at a time he did not see another white man.

His rutting season reoccurred every half year or so, usually coinciding with his rotgut and 'baccer running out. Whenever that happened, Baptiste was seized by restlessness, getting antsy, emerging from his lair like a hibernating beast, wild-eyed and gamy, setting out with his bundles of beaver plews, his "hairy dollars" as he called them.

First, Baptiste made it to the nearest fort to haggle with the despised bourge-way, the trader in charge of the fort's store, swapping pelts against a new six-month supply of provisions, particularly foofaraw, such as beads, small mirrors, and vermilion paint to charm a willing squaw into sharing his blanket. The bourge-ways always took outrageous advantage of Baptiste on the one-plug–one-plew system—that is, selling him a twist of chawin' 'baccer, worth two bits, for a six-dollar beaver plew.

"Enfant de garce!" Baptiste complained on these occasions, "Bougre, zees ees brigandage. Vous êtes robbairs. Sapristi! Vous take avantage de pauvre Ba'tiste!"

"Wagh," was the usual answer, "that's the way the stick floats. Take it or leave it."

He took it. The bourge-ways always got the better of the free trappers. With a new supply of whiskey and chewing tobacco, his possible bag and parfleches bulging with foofaraw, "pour l'amour," Baptiste put the spurs to his old pony, making tracks for the big rendezvous on the Popo Agie. On the way a snake slithered across his path while a huge horned owl hooted at him.

"Sacré bleu," he muttered, "it ees a mauvais augure, a very bad sign." He crossed himself, spat three times over his left shoulder, and gave the evil-eye sign to the unimpressed owl, because, like all his fellows, he was very superstitious.

Arrived at the grand rendezvous des trappairs, Baptiste immediately sought out his vieux compagnons—Antoine, a fellow voyageur; Gouge-Eye Luke, a beaver man out of Kaintuck; and Igmoo Tanka, the Panther, a gigantic fellow part-Sioux and part-Irishman.

"Mille tonnères!" exclaimed Antoine. "Here is ze man raisin' ze diable!"

"Hallo, old hoss," Gouge-Eye Luke chimed in. "This child is glad to see your ugly mug. Here, have a swig of old towse."

"Hau, welcome, you consarned corn dodger," added the Panther. "I thought you wuz rubbed out. Have some mni suta!"

They had not seen each other for more than a year and enjoyed their rare get-togethers. Thus the friends settled down to an orgy of

drinking, fighting, gambling, and wenching, making up in three days for a half year of hardship and loneliness.

"Old hoss," Gouge-Eye Luke remarked as Baptiste emerged wobbly from the tepee he shared with two dusky 'sposas, "there's a citizen over there braggin' he can eat more boudins faster'n any other mother's son. Why don't you take him up on it?"

"Quoi?" said Baptiste. "Zat miserable bougre ovair zere? Parbleu, scalp my old tête if it ees not the vieux sarpint Pierre Frozen Toes. I shall beat 'eem mangeant les boudins. I shall bet ten dollars 'pon it."

"Wagh, Ba'tiste, you cussed devil," said Pierre when challenged to perform, "voici mes dix dollars. Hyar goes for meat."

Eager trappers placed roughly ten feet of coiled buffalo boudins on a mound of hot raked ashes after having tied a strip of red trade cloth plumb center on the sausagelike mess.

"Enfant de garce," said Baptiste. "Zut alors. Maintenant nous mangeons. Allez oop!"

"Hyar's brown skin a-comin'," shouted the Panther on a run to witness the affair. "I'll be dogged if I miss this!"

"Moi aussi," added Antoine. "This child is bettin' on Ba'tiste."

Each contestant took an end of the boudins between his teeth and, at a signal from Gouge-Eye Luke, started to wolf them down. So began a mighty chawin' and swallowin'. Pierre had barely managed to get down a measly two feet when Baptiste was already past the center knot and going strong. After gobbling down another foot for good measure he stopped, exclaiming, "Moi, je suis le vainqueur, by gar!" He accepted his prize, immediately converting the dollars into a keg of "Injin whiskey," raw red-eye spiced with three rattlesnake heads for flavor and a handful of gunpowder to give her a kick.

The friends now went on a stupendous blowout, a frenzied bout lasting all of three days. After that they passed out, not emerging from their tepees or bedrolls for another three days. Coming to and getting the cobwebs out of their heads took another day. Sobered up somewhat, Baptiste exclaimed: "Diable! Mes amis, I feel a leetle queer. J'ai faim. I'm wolfish for meat. My feet, dey feel like dancin', like runnin', like goin' on a chasse. I smell strong meat, by gar! Somezin' powerful, mes amis, somezin' peut-être wiz a heap big pelt. O là là, I can smell 'eem. Mes pieds, zey are already beatin' the rataplan. Je suis bewitched, nom de diable. Je m'en vais!" With that Baptiste ran off with great leaps and bounds.

"Comme un fou," said Antoine.

"His gourd's out of whack," said Gouge-Eye Luke.

"Lila witko, out o' his mind," said the Panther. "He'll dry out. He'll be back in no time at all."

But Baptiste did not come back. Three days passed and his friends grew uneasy.

"What can de mattair be?" said Antoine. "Pauvre Baptiste. Peut-être he has gone ondair?"

"It's those Blackfoot devils," said Gouge-Eye Luke. "They've rubbed him out at last."

"Maybe a grizzly chewed him up," said the Panther. "We must find him. Git up! Hiyupo! Let's go!"

Luckily, it had not rained and the Panther was the best tracker on the Plains. He had no trouble making out Baptiste's footprints on account of the hole in the sole of Baptiste's left moccasin. They tailed him for some seven miles and then noticed that Baptiste's tracks were followed by others, unnaturally large, unlike any they had ever seen, halfway between the tracks of a huge bear and a catamount, but with seven monstrous toes, or rather claws, on each paw.

"Mon Dieu!" exclaimed Antoine. "C'est le maudit loup-garou, de wairwolf! Pauvre Baptiste. Il est perdu!" Antoine was shaking like an aspen tree.

"Holy Mother of God!" said Gouge-Eye Luke. "I'm mighty skeered. This ain't the loup-garou, it's that cussed varmint the windigo. I can read his sign."

"It ain't the loo-garou nor the windigo," said the Panther, "it's the ghost carcajou, the Wanagi Huhatopa, maybe even the Unktehi, the Great River Monster. That's poor doin's for sure. Hurry boys, afore it's too late!"

They hastened on. After another seven miles they were terrified to see Baptiste's footprints changing, getting bigger, the toes coming out of the moccasins—five toes, six toes, seven toes on each foot, changing into claws.

"Vite, vite!" cried Antoine. "Le loup maudit. Nous sommes foutus! Le bougre ees makin' pauvre Ba'tiste into a monstre like 'eemself!"

At last, the three friends came upon a horrid scene. They beheld Baptiste, who, from his waist down, had already been changed into a loup-garou, complete with a bushy tail. Over the poor voyageur towered a monster with a bestial body, the face of a man-devil, a tiger's fangs, and wicked eyes glowing like coals. The infernal creature was howling and cackling frightfully, turning the men's veins into ice.

"Le loup-garou!" screamed Antoine.

"The windigo!" screamed Gouge-Eye Luke.

"The ghost carcajou!" screamed the Panther.

"Windigo, loup-garou, what does it mattair?" cried Baptiste. "Help! Help à moi, mes amis, au secours! I'm goin' ondair!"

"Boys, run!" Gouge-Eye Luke yelled, beside himself with fear. "Run for your lives or the dratted thing will get you too!"

"Non, non, non!" cried Antoine. "Je suis a sinner, a fornicator, a no-good drunkard, but once j'étais un étudiant for de priesthood and I still have zees," and he drew from the bosom of his greasy buckskin shirt a silver cross, holding it aloft, admonishing the werewolf: "Apage Satanas! Away wiz you, unclean demon, damned mauvais diable! Allez-vous-en, monstreux loup-garou! Vamooze!"

The monster bared its fangs, foamed at the mouth, snapped at the cross, and howled frightfully, but it retreated step-by-step. Antoine now also produced a tattered Bible from his possible bag, hitting the evil beast over the snout with both the cross and the Good Book. This somewhat amateurish exorcism worked. The monster whimpered. The light in its eyes dimmed. It cowered, it retreated and, finally, fled with gigantic leaps, leaving only its ungodly sulphurous stink behind.

"Victoire!" exclaimed Antoine. "Nous sommes sauvès! Grace à Dieu, le loup-garou has vanished. Il est disparu!"

"Hooraw! The windigo is gone! Wagh! We spooked him fo' sartin!" shouted Gouge-Eye Luke.

"Washtay!" shouted the Panther. "The ghost carcajou, we hornswoggled him for sure."

"Loup-garou, windigo, carcajou be damned!" Baptisted cried angrily. "Parbleu! Je suis foutu! Look at me!" He hopped clumsily on his hair-covered wolf's legs. "Look at me! Mes jambes, mes pieds! What jolie fille will give me a tumble now!"

"Il faut prier," said Antoine, "we must pray to God an' all de saints."

"Wagh, that's the way of gettin' out of a skunk hole," said Gouge-Eye Luke. "I hain't done it for years, but this old coon is prayin': God, Ba'tiste got hisself in a fix. Do somethin'!"

"Wakan Tanka, onshimala ye!" prayed the Panther, "Ba'tiste here is in a bad way. Grandfather, pity him!"

Muttering incantations in French, English, and admittedly poor Latin, Antoine passed cross and Bible up and down Baptiste's animal legs while Luke and the Panther continued praying, and, lo and behold, slowly, before their eyes, the wolf's legs became human again. Baptiste jumped for joy and clicked his heels, but the very tips of his toes remained furry for ever and his nails resembled claws for the rest of his life.

"Eh bien," was Baptiste's comment, "it could have been worse, n'est-ce pas?"

The Call of the Wild

An old legend circulating in the high country of Montana tells of a band of gray wolves that were relentlessly and remorselessly on the hunt for human babies. They ate boy babies, but girl babies were carried off and raised along with their wolf cubs. There was a rancher and his wife, Zach and Betty, who were running cattle in the Beartooth Range. They had a tiny one-year-old-daughter, named Angie, with nut brown curly hair, hazel eyes, and dimples. One moonless night they were roused by a frightful howling around the ranch house. "Them's wolves," said Zach. "They're after the newborn calves, I guess. I think I'll get myself a wolfskin for a rug."

He got his double-barreled shotgun down from the wall, made sure it was loaded, and went out into the night. It was so dark that he could not see anything at all. Now and then, for a fraction of a second only, he had a momentary glimpse of a pair of wolf's eyes reflecting the light in his window, but always the points of light disappeared before he could aim his gun. He felt himself surrounded by the snarling, growling pack, felt the wolves' bodies touching his own. There was a snapping of teeth and a sharp pain as wolf fangs fastened upon the calf of his right leg. He tore himself loose and blindly fired one barrel. There was a howl of pain, followed by a whine and a whimper. Zach had enough. His feral foes did not act like normal wolves; they were somehow different, more like human fiends.

Zach felt their hot breath, heard their panting and slavering. He fired the second barrel, not so much to hit the unseen brutes, but to scare them off. Then he ran back inside the house, slamming the door behind him. He heard them scratching and howling at the door, heard his child scream. Zach went into the bedroom, wiping the cold sweat from his brow.

"I heard Angie cryin'," he told his wife. "Maybe you should look in on her."

"She's teethin', that's why," said Betty, "poor little thing." She went into the small chamber next to the bedroom, where they kept the crib. Zach heard his wife cry out in anguish. He rushed into the tiny room and found his wife sobbing as if her heart was about to break. The crib was empty, Angie gone. The window had been left open to let the air in, because the day had been hot and sultry. Once more Zach loaded his shotgun and ran out into the night, gripped by fear as he remembered the rumors about demon wolves carrying away human babies. His teeth were chattering in spite of the heat. He made out a light in the bunkhouse. The cowhands there had been wakened by the commotion. There was nothing anyone could do in the inky, impenetrable blackness.

There was an old hermit trapper, living some ten miles off, said to be a good tracker. "Don't fret yerself," he told Zach. "If she's alive, I'll git her fer you."

Zach, his cowpunchers, and neighbors followed the old recluse in search of the missing child. They found numerous wolf tracks, but they all led into a windswept wilderness of bare rocks in which the tracks petered out. The searchers returned with dogs that took up the scent. They followed the eager, yelping dogs to a rushing river. There the dogs lost the scent. A single tuft of wolf's hair, caught in a thornbush, was the only reward for their pains. Zach and his companions scoured the whole country round about in ever-widening circles —all in vain. Angie was gone. Years went by. Zach and Betty had other children—twin boys. They had to console themselves with that. But the anguish and uncertainty over what had become of Angie gnawed at their innards and soured life for them.

But later there were rumors, strange, disturbing, and hard to believe. Now and then some lone line rider, prospector, or a Cheyenne Indian or two, came out of the mountains saying that they had caught a glimpse of gray wolves in the distance, elusive shadows darting in and out of trees and boulders, their glowing eyes reflecting the setting sun. Among the pack, so they said, they had seen, or thought they had seen, a naked white girl with long brown hair. Such rumors grew more and more frequent.

"I don't believe any of it," Zach told his wife. "It's a case of too much whiskey and a runnin' mouth! I'm sure it's nothin' but a heap of damn lies. But it keeps me awake at night. I can't rest till I find out for myself whether there's somethin' to it."

"She would be fifteen by now," said Betty.

This time Zach hired an old Sioux Indian, a hunter, trapper, and yuwipi man, meaning someone who had the gift to find lost things. His name, strangely enough, was Wolf Running. The old man, looking more like a shriveled mummy than a human being, his face resembling an oversized, wrinkled walnut, wore a small rawhide bag around his neck.

"Shunka manitou pejuta," he explained, "wolf medicine."

The old fellow came and went, sometimes in company with other elderly Sioux men. Frequently, he brought back a chunk of venison, or maybe a fox skin. Whenever he heard a rumor that the naked girl had been seen at one or another place, the yuwipi man went there to search. One day he came back to Zach in a great state of excitement, waving his arms, mumbling and stammering.

"Me saw the winchinchala without clothes," he said. "She sat on a stone suckling a wolf pup. It was just moonlight, but I saw. The wolves too. Then, suddenly, all gone!"

At once Zach got together some two dozen riders—his own cowboys and others from nearby ranches. The old Indian led them to the spot where he had seen the naked girl. They brought a lamb with them for bait, tethering it to a tree. Then they waited. All of a sudden the night's silence was shattered by the howls of wolves and the lamb's pitiful bleating. Some of the cowboys lit their torches. In the flickering light they saw that the wolves were huge and watched one of them drag the bleating lamb away. They also saw the girl, naked as a jaybird, running with the wolves, long hair streaming behind her. This time the searchers managed to hang on to their prey, torches lighting their way. Dawn came, making their task easier. The girl flew before them like a will-o'-the-wisp, almost as fast as the men's horses. On and on went the wild hunt. At last, one of the riders got his rope on the girl, jerking her off her feet.

Zach had not seen Angie since she had been a baby, but he recognized her at once—nut brown hair, hazel eyes, dimples. Zach cried out, "Angie!" and imagined he saw a flicker of remembrance in her eyes. He was wrong. The wolf-girl snarled and sank her teeth into the flesh of his palm. It took two men to pry her jaws apart. They lifted her onto a horse's back, her ankles tied by a rope under the horse's belly, brought her to Zach's house, and locked her in a room. Betty wept, tried to caress her long-lost daughter, saying over and over again, "Angie, Angie, dear Angie," the girl glowering at her without understanding.

Whenever Zach and Betty came into her room, Angie would cower in a corner, in a state of rage and fear. Sometimes she attacked them with tooth and nail. She accepted no food save raw meat. She howled like a she-wolf. Sometimes, with the help of friends, they forced clothes upon her, but she tore them off as soon as she was alone.

Months passed. Angie had calmed down. She no longer fought her parents or twin brothers. She understood a few words and could speak some. After a year she no longer tore her clothes off. She accepted, and learned to like, cooked food. A few months later she joined the family at the table. She began playing with the twins, learned to ride, to sew, and to work at her spelling. At eighteen she had become a ranch girl like her neighbor's daughters. She made friends, went to dances and hoedowns.

She met Bill, a rancher's son, a strapping, handsome lad. He and Angie took a liking to each other. They walked hand in hand, sat together on the swing that Zach had put on the porch. They touched, they kissed. Bill knew next to nothing about her past. Zach and Betty thought that the less he knew, the better. The wedding day was set and a house made ready to receive them.

Angie looked radiant in her white wedding dress. The young couple enjoyed the wedding feast, the fiddling, and the dancing. They laughed at seeing some of their friends get tipsy. It became time for the guests to depart. Bill carried his bride into the bedroom and set her down. They embraced. He said, "I love you, Angie." "And I love you, Bill," she answered back.

At that moment, there was an uproar outside—snarling and howling, the furious barking of dogs, the neighing and stamping of horses, a heifer's desperate bellowing.

"I've got to see what's goin' on out there," said Bill.

"Don't leave me," pleaded his young bride.

"I've just got to," Bill insisted, "I'll be back soon."

"Don't be long, love, don't be long."

Outside, a life-and-death struggle was in progress between dogs and wolves, and Bill found himself in the middle of a snarling pack, emptying his six-gun at the indistinct, raging shapes, hoping to hit the wolves and not his dogs. Just as suddenly all was quiet again, the wolves gone, the dogs whimpering, licking their wounds, the heifer dead. "Get some sleep," Bill told a few cowboys who had rushed to his help. He went back into the house, anxious to join his bride. When he reentered the bedroom, Angie was gone. Her wedding gown lay crumpled on the floor. A breeze blew through the open window, stirring up the curtains. Angie was never seen again. And that is the end of the story.

The Windigo

The windigo is a fearful creature, the most horrible that ever was. To look at it is to go blind. To hear its unearthly growl is to become deaf. To get a whiff of its rank odor is to lose one's sense of smell. To come into bodily contact with it means becoming lame, but no one who is touched by the windigo survives longer than seven days.

The windigo has long, sharp teeth, but no jaws. It has eyes out of which shoot lightning, but it has no face. It has a shaggy fleece, but no body inside it. It has no feet or paws, but large, terrible claws like curved daggers. To cross its path is sure death, but its tracks are easily recognized because they are over twelve inches long.

The windigo can be killed in only one way. One must have a rifle made by a pious man who prayed over it three times a day while working on it. Such a rifle must be loaded with a silver bullet into which the sign of a cross has been scratched. The silver bullet has to be rammed down with a patch made from a page of the bible. Not any page will serve, but only one with the Lord's Prayer on it. The hunter must go to church on Easter Day and recite a psalm forward and backward without making a single mistake. Then the hunter must go to a crossroad and be there at the stroke of twelve on a moonlit night, in which case the windigo will appear. And if the hunter does not turn to stone with fright, and if his eyes do not fail him, and if his hands do not tremble with fear so that he cannot aim his weapon, then the hunter might, just might, succeed in killing the windigo. But if the hunter does not do everything exactly as described, the windigo will eat him up in three bites.

The Great White Stallion of the West

Nor the team of the Sun, as in fable portrayed,
Through the firmament rushing in glory arrayed,
Could match, in wild majesty, beauty and speed,
That tireless, magnificent, snowy-white steed.

The phantom horse of legends was known under many names— the Ghost Horse of the Plains, the Snow White Pacer, the Stallion of Solitudes, the Deathless White Mustang, Gray Lightning, the Milk-White Steed of the Prairies, and Equus Superbus, to mention only a few. Hunted by many, but never caught, the Great White Stallion became the symbol for men's yearning for the unattainable. As such, the Super Horse of the Rockies furnished the topic for innumerable related legends.

The first rumor of the phantom horse to reach readers in the big eastern cities was contained in a passage from *A Tour of the Prairies*, Washington Irving's account of his 1832 trip to the Arkansas and

Cimarron river country: "We had been disappointed this day in our hopes of meeting with buffalo, but the sight of the wild horse had been a great novelty, and gave a turn to the conversation of the camp for the evening. There were several anecdotes told of a famous gray horse, which has ranged the prairies of this neighborhood for six or seven years, setting at naught every attempt of the hunters to capture him. They say he can pace or rack faster than the fleetest horse can run." Thus was born the legend of the Ghostly White (sometimes Gray) Steed.

When Don Francisco Coronado, so the legends have it, crossed the Rio Grande into the land of the pueblo dwellers in his futile search for the fabled golden cities of Cibola, one stallion and one mare broke loose from the expedition's horse herd and vanished into the wilderness. These two wonderful animals became the ancestors of the Great White Stallion of the West. This phantom steed was marvelous in every respect. Gleaming white, almost iridescent, his silky coat shone like silver in the sunlight, dazzling the eyes of the beholder. Noble was his delicately formed head, regal and full of fire his sparkling eyes. His beauty defied description. When in motion, the ripple of his powerful muscles was likened to the flow of swiftly poured milk.

The white stallion moved with extraordinary grace, yet also with great force. His speed and endurance seemed supernatural. He moved with a king's dignity, never at a trot or gallop, but eternally, majestically pacing or ambling, full of disdain for the horses of his pursuers, cantering after him at a furious pace, stretched to the limit, their bellies almost touching the ground. No matter how fast, they could never catch up with him, as the white steed mockingly kept them at the same distance without ever breaking his stride.

He was the solitary ruler of the prairie. Seldom glimpsed from afar, he was almost always alone, scornful of the company of other horses. Only once during his lifetime did he assemble a harem of sleek, untamed, never-roped mares to bequeath his seed to a new generation of starbright mustangs. Never caught, he seemed immortal. He was said to have the power to reproduce, to recreate himself in his exact likeness, grace, and strength, and only when a new Great White Stallion, resembling him in every aspect, was ready to take his place, would he consent to give up his ghost in a hidden, never-to-be-discovered spot, perpetuating his own legend of eternal life.

There were many who hoped to conquer, possess, and ride the phantom horse, but all of them failed. The one who came closest was

Don Alonso, a rich hacendado, obsessed with the love for fine horses as well as for woman flesh, yearning to see the Caballo Miraculoso tethered inside his corral, tamed, ready to submit to its rider. To capture the uncatchable, Don Alonso took twelve vaqueros with him, each with three of the fleetest horses, also his best roper and a marksman said to have the ability of "creasing" his elusive prey—that is, shooting at the great mustang so that the bullet merely grazed the animal's neck close to his spine, momentarily stunning and immobilizing him so that he could be approached and lassoed. Don Alonso promised a thousand gold pieces to whoever could put the Great White Stallion in his power.

The twelve vaqueros were born to the saddle, superb riders, who lusted after their master's gold. Whenever one of their horses tired, driven to the very limit of endurance, they left it to die of exhaustion, switching to a fresh mount. But effortlessly, seeming to float phantomlike before them, the white steed outdistanced them, never letting the marksman come close enough to shoot, or the man with the reata close enough to rope him; but maddened with his obsession, Don Alonso would not give up. A year or two after every failure, he would call his best riders together to try again. And one day, remembered forever, he had it in his power to make his dream come true. He came upon the Great White Stallion, not alone as was his wont, but protecting his seraglio of mares against a pack of ravenous timber wolves. Unmindful of the human predators, the stallion put himself between his mares and their attackers, darting, lightning-swift, to every point of danger. With flashing eyes and flaring nostrils, he struck again and again with his hooves, crushing to death one wolf after the other. Now and then one of the lobos managed to fasten his fangs into his flesh, reddening his neck and flanks, but always he tossed it aside like chaff, breaking its back with his whirling hooves. After the last predator had been disposed of, the phantom horse neighed triumphantly, standing defiant, motionless as a statue, looking straight at Don Alonso as if wishing to challenge him.

At this supreme moment Don Alonso broke into tears, waving back his roper and his marksman. "This archangel of a horse," he told his vaqueros, "God has not meant him to be ridden by mortal man. Let us go."

Don Alonso gravely doffed his sombrero, waving it high, saluting the phantom steed. The Great White Stallion neighed in reply.

Some versions of this tale have a sad ending. The noble steed is driven into the waterless desert. Weakened by thirst, he finds a waterhole and drinks greedily—as much as he can swallow. Heavy with liquid, and therefore slowed down, the king of the mustangs is finally caught and dragged into a corral from which there is no escape. With water, grass, and buckets of oats all around him, he refuses to eat or drink, preferring death to captivity. Untamed and unconquered, he dies on the twelfth day.

Until Judgment Day

There were once two fellows, Jack, the Gamblin' Man, and the Kaintuck Kid. They met at a gambling saloon called the Bucket of Blood. Jack won over a thousand dollars at the faro table. Bucking the same tiger, the Kid lost everything he owned in this world, including his gold-plated watch and his saddle horse.

"I dunno what to do now," said the Kid. "I'm cleaned out for good. A feller without his hoss, a feller afoot, is lower than a chinch bug."

"Cheer up," said the Gamblin' Man. "I always had a dream, a mighty yen to catch me the Great White Stallion of the Prairies. I've sworn to myself that if ever I got ahold of some money, I'll spend whatever time it takes to get him. I need a partner. How about it?"

"Might as well," said the Kid. The Gamblin' Man bought the two finest horses he could find for himself and the Kid—deep-chested, fleet, and of great endurance—also a couple of pack mules, and supplies of whatever they might need for a long chase.

"We'll ride the prairies until we find that horse," he vowed, "if it takes us till doomsday!"

They hunted the Plains from horizon to horizon, all over the Great Ocean of Grass, the Llano Estacado, the southern deserts, along the foot of the Shining Mountains, from the Big Muddy to the Rockies, from the Pecos to the Yellowstone, and beyond, into the Plains of Canada. They lived on whatever game fell victims to their rifles, using the earth for their bed and the sky for their blanket. They ventured into wild country where there was no trace of humans, white or red. Doggedly, they followed even the faintest signs of wild horses. They sighted many herds of wild mustangs and, here and there, a solitary stallion. Time and again the Kid would point excitedly at one particularly superb, light-colored steed, exclaiming, "There, there, it's him! What a horse! Let's go get him!"

But always Jack restrained him with a sobering "No, no. That's not him, not by a long shot!"

Spring turned into summer, summer into fall, flocks of birds darkening the sky on their way south. Winter arrived among flurries of snow. The old cottonwood trees along ice-covered streams were splitting asunder with loud cracks in the flesh-numbing cold.

"My bones will soon be makin' the same kind of noise, crackin' apart in this goddam cold," complained the Kid. "For chrissake, let's go back to a real town, with a real hotel, with a real bed, and a real live woman to warm it up. Let's go to where a man can get a drink. Right now I'd go for a mug of white ligntnin' rather than for a white stallion."

"Go back, tenderfoot, go and rock yourself to death in a rockin' chair on some crumblin' porch," said Jack who seemed oblivious to cold or heat, hunger or thirst, oblivious to a anything but the quest for the phantom horse. "Go back and warm your arse by some old woman's stove. I've sworn to get what I'm come for, and if I don't get him, I'll go on after him until Judgment Day!"

They were worn to the bone—Jack, the Gamblin' Man, and the Kaintuck Kid. The skin of their faces had changed to a dark, cracked parchment. Their eyes glowed with a strange fever. Their bodies had shrunk; their ribs were sticking out like those of a starving wolf. Their horses were in a like state. One of the mules had broken down and died. There was nothing now for them but to ride, on and on, ride on like puppets on a string whose farthest end was hidden in nothingness. They rode wordlessly now, grimly, their silence broken only by the cry of an eagle or a coyote's howl in the night.

One day they stumbled upon the tracks of a wild horse, small hooves set wide apart, the tracks of a mustang with a marvelously long stride.

"Look at that!" exclaimed the Kid. The Gamblin' Man said nothing but rode on with redoubled fury, teeth clenched in an insane grin.

Night came. They lay down on the bare earth, rolled up in their ponchos. A full moon was rising, bathing the prairie in its ghostly glow. Somewhere an owl hooted. A horse neighed. Jack was up in a flash, flinging his poncho aside. He had glimpsed a silvery shape wrapped in moonlight.

"There, there, it's him at last!" he shouted. "Oh God, how beautiful!"

He spoke true, because a hundred yards off stood the Great White Stallion, motionless, as if carved from marble, looking straight at them.

"Hurry, hurry, *h-u-r-r-y!*" screamed the Gamblin' Man, more a long drawn out animal's howl than a shout, as he jumped on his horse's back, not bothering with saddle or rein, the Kid tearing after him.

The White Stallion moved at last. Effortlessly, he kept his pursuers at the same distance, pacing, striding. The wondrous animal seemed to glide rather than pace, like a boat sailing before the wind, or a soaring bird. A picture of grace and liquid motion, the stallion seemed to move slowly, but still he easily outpaced his pursuers, coming after him at a dead run. Thus the chase went on, interminably, in the pale eerie light of the moon. At last, there was a faint hint of dawn. The hunters' horses were close to collapse, their nostrils streaming blood, their mouths and necks flecked with foam. They no longer responded to shouted urgings, to spurs dug into their flanks, to the touch of the whip.

"Stop, Jack, stop!" shouted the Kaintuck Kid. "It's no use. We can no more catch him than catch our own shadows. This is the devil's work. I'm scared!"

"Stop if you want, you good-for-nothin' son of a bitch!" Jack screamed back. "I'll follow him into the jaws of hell, until Judgment Day!"

On and on went the wild chase, the riders getting a last ounce of effort from their frantic mounts. Far ahead, the Kaintuck Kid discerned a black line. A mile further he recognized it for what it was— a huge crack in the earth's crust, a yawning mile-deep chasm. He cried out in anguish: "Watch out, Jack, watch out! There's a canyon!"

The Gamblin' Man paid him no mind, leaving his friend behind. The Kid got a glimpse of the White Stallion hurling himself into the air with a mighty leap, saw the Gamblin' Man and his mount leaping after. The Kaintuck Kid reined in his horse at the last moment. It stood at the chasm's rim, its legs trembling, covered with foam, eyes rolling with terror. Slowly, it sank to the ground, its rider jumping aside. Trembling himself, the Kid looked down it the gaping abyss. Far, far beneath him he made out the tiny shapes of Jack, the Gamblin' Man, and his horse, crumpled, broken, lifeless. Of the Great White Stallion of the West not a hair could be seen.

El Diablo Negro

Just as there were many tales of the Great White Steed of the West, so we have also the stories of El Diablo Negro, the ebony-colored, man-eating stallion of the desert. Already Washington Irving heard marvelous accounts of a black horse, sixteen hands high, which could outpace the Phantom White Mustang of the Plains. The norteamericanos knew him as the Black Devil, the Blue Streak or, simply, the Raven. Indian storytellers called him the Black Death. Among the Sioux he was known as Wanagi Shunka-Wakan Sapa, the Black Ghost Horse.

The Devil Stallion was wondrous to behold, bigger than any other horse known to man. Not as graceful as the White Phantom Steed, he inspired terror by his supernatural strength and ferocity. Beautiful he was, proud and splendid as Lucifer, the Fallen Angel among equines. He was sleek as oil, his skin like obsidian, reflecting the rays of the sun. His body was broad-chested, his hooves hard as flint, his neck an arched bow, his mane rippling silk, his eyes glowing coals.

El Diablo Negro was invulnerable. Arrows and bullets rebounded from his glassy coat. In combat he shrieked like a panther, turning the blood in many a man's body into ice. While the Indians feared him as a man-killer, they eagerly hunted his offspring, begotten upon ebony-colored mares, as black as their sire. Such sons or daughters of El Diablo were not only arrow- and bulletproof, but also rendered their riders impervious to all man-made weapons. But the most wonderful thing about the Black Devil was his power of human speech. He could talk, if only to one chosen man.

Once a large war party of Arapahoes penetrated deep into the southwestern country, planning to raid the Comanches' horse herds, but lost their own ponies instead, as well as the life of one of their braves. Having picketed their horses for the night and gone to sleep, they were awakened by a great commotion, neighing and whinnying. The din was caused by a monstrous black stallion that had gnawed through the hobbles of the Arapahoes' mares and was making off in triumph with his newly acquired harem. Some of the mares' owners followed in pursuit on whatever mounts they had left. El Diablo turned on the foremost rider, tore him from his pony, and carried him off between his enormous teeth just as a cat might carry off a mouse. His friends came upon the Black Devil and his band the next day. He had killed their companion with tooth and hoof, and, horror-stricken, they watched as the monster animal tore pieces of flesh from his body and devoured them. The Arapahoes did not try to recover his remains or their mares, but fled in terror, spreading far and wide the tale of the man-eating horse.

The Buffalo Soldiers, a regiment of colored troopers, knew him as the Ole Black Debbil. He raided their horse herds as he had ravaged those of the Arapahoes. An army scout following him was torn from his saddle and stomped to death. The man-eater would have devoured him too had not a whole troop of cavalry driven him off.

Two experienced mustangers had caught a wild, spirited, dun-colored stallion and placed him in their corral together with a dozen mares. At midnight they were roused by the shrieks of fighting horses. Hastening to the corral, they saw, by the light of their lanterns, their own stallion and the Black Devil locked in mortal combat, the black brute's teeth dripping with blood. As the awe-struck mustangers watched, El Diablo literally tore the dun to pieces, tearing big bites of flesh from its quivering flanks. Looking up from its deadly work, the devil horse glimpsed the two watching men and instantly made for them. They fled in terror, barely getting back to their dugout, where they barricaded themselves behind the stout log door. All night long, until dawn, the black monster battered with his hooves against the thick door, finally splintering it but finding the narrow opening not wide enough to let him through. After trying again and again to squeeze himself through, squealing with rage at his inability to do so (and with the two mustangers cowering within, petrified with fear), El Diablo finally gave up and ambled off, not without the mustangers' mares. Though being left afoot, and limp with exhaustion, the intended victims praised God and all His saints for having saved them from this horse of perdition.

And yet there was one being, and a human at that, whom El Diablo loved after his own fashion—a Mescalero Apache named Buffalo Hawk. He was a medicine man. The whites called him a sorcerer. Besides performing strange rituals and healing ceremonies, he was also a fierce fighter and an avenging Angel of Death. In his youth the band of Mescaleros to which be belonged had been invited to a

fiesta by Mexican villagers. Plied with pulque and aguardiente, the Indians had laid down in a befuddled sleep when their treacherous hosts fell upon them with gun and knife, killing all the men and carrying off the women and children into slavery. In this way the Mescalero shaman lost his entire family. Having not touched any of the proffered liquor, and in command of all his faculties, he had been the only one to escape, the last of his band. He had only one thing to live for—revenge!

A lone assassin, shunning the company of men, he roamed the desert and mountains like a solitary panther in search of human prey. He spared no Mexican who crossed his path, neither man, woman, or child. It was no wonder that Mexicans dubbed him El Diablo Rojo —the Red Devil. One night the shaman was huddled before his campfire when he heard hoofbeats and a mighty snorting. Looking up, he beheld a black horse of monstrous size—the man-eating stallion. For the first time the four-legged devil spoke in the human tongue.

"You diablo, I diablo," he told the shaman. "You hate Mexicans, I hate Mexicans. The faintest whiff of the chili smell from their bodies drives me mad with the urge to kill them. Be thou my master. Let us team up to avenge ourselves upon this accursed breed. Together we can kill more than we can slay by ourselves."

The Mescalero shaman was the acknowledged champion of all horsemen among the southwestern tribes. He exulted to feel the mighty stallion's body under him, gloried in the terrific speed with which the Black Devil carried him wherever he wished to go. The stallion's swiftness, its teeth and hooves, together with the Apache's stealth, his lance and death-dealing bow, made a fatal combination, a killing machine spreading terror throughout the Rio Grande border country. So welded seemed man and horse that the campesinos believed themselves the victims of a satanic centaur, killing them by the dozens and by the hundreds, transforming a whole region into a wasteland. Villages and fields were abandoned, roads stretched untraveled as a whole population fled to escape the avenger's fury.

A few rich hacendados got together. Something had to be done or the two diablos would make their whole district uninhabitable. There was a bandido in the calabozo, awaiting death by hanging. El Tigre was his nickname. He acknowledged no other. He was sly as a fox and strong as a bull. For many years he had terrorized high and low, evading capture again and again. A woman's betrayal had finally landed him in jail in the gallows' shadow. She had lured him to her bed, had given him a sleeping potion, called in the rurales while he lay unconscious, and collected the reward.

"Let us not hang this cabrón," said the rich rancheros. "Of all the bandidos this El Tigre knows his trade best. Of all the assassins he is the deadliest. Let us offer him life and riches in exchange for ridding us of the two diablos, the two-legged and the four-legged one."

El Tigre was pleased. To go after the two diablos was dangerous, but preferable to being hanged. Also, the reward was commensurate with the risk. Besides, there was nothing El Tigre was afraid of. Thus began a deadly game—hunter pursued by hunter, killer by killer. The cat-and-mouse game went on for month after month. The bandit turned bounty hunter was skilled at his task. Stealthy, tireless, the human bloodhound and unshakable shadow followed the trail of the shaman and his devil horse. At last El Tigre came so close to his prey that in his mind he could already feel the reward money weighing down his pockets. Too close, as it turned out.

Noiselessly, in the dark of the night, the bounty hunter crept toward the shaman's campsite, a knife clenched between his teeth, a pistol stuck in his belt. Not the rustling of a leaf or the breaking of the tiniest twig could be heard as, inch by inch, unseen and inaudible, El Tigre moved stealthily toward his intended victims—unseen and unheard, but not unsmelled. While the shaman slumbered, the demon horse picked up the faint odor of chili. El Tigre's having wolfed down a big plate of chili con carne before setting out on his murderous endeavor became his undoing. With flaring nostrils the Black Devil followed the hated scent carried to him by the wind. Before the luckless bandido knew what had hit him, steel-hard hooves were pounding him into a bloody mass while huge teeth tore chunks of flesh from his body.

The shaman was up by then, hurrying to the scene of carnage. Mad with blood, screaming in his colossal fury, the stallion turned upon his master whom, in his frenzy, he no longer recognized. There was only one place of safety for the man—on the enraged animal's back. The Mescalero vaulted onto it, his thighs and heels digging into the great horse's flanks, his fists gripping the mane, holding on for dear life. The demon steed bucked, skydived, plunged, and reared as no other horse before. He leaped six feet into the air. He tried to sideswipe his rider, to scrape him off against some tree. The stallion rolled over on his back to crush the shaman beneath his immense weight, but the Apache was off his back in a flash and, just as swiftly, was in his seat again as soon as the Black Devil was on his feet. The stallion turned his head back as far as he could to fasten his teeth upon the bold rider, who managed to remain barely out of reach. Thus the finest rider of the Southwest and the mighty demon horse matched strength against strength, remaining in deadly combat all through the night. The Black Devil employed every trick in his repertoire in vain, as the Apache remained stuck to his back, so that man and horse fused into one and together crashed, plunged, and thundered over the trembling ground. With dawn exhaustion overcame them. They grew faint and fell. Panting, they lay side by side.

Daylight came, and in the rays of the rising sun the Black Devil recognized his rider. Then the demon steed addressed the shaman for the second and last time with a human voice: "Master, I love you, but only an hour ago I would have torn you to pieces in my fury. This must never happen again. There has been enough killing. Whatever wrong has been done to us has been avenged a hundredfold. I know of a faraway high mesa, covered with lush grass, with a great waterhole in its center that never runs dry. There I shall end my life among my willing mares. You, my master, return to your tribe, henceforth to live in peace, rearing a family to replace the one you have lost."

"It shall be so," replied the shaman.

Snake Yarns

A settler was driving along in his horse and buggy when a large diamondback struck his wagon tongue, which immediately began to swell up. Fortunately, the driver had his ax with him and with great presence of mind chopped the wagon tongue off at its root, thus saving the rest of his buggy. The same snake, or more likely, one of its descendants, struck a telephone pole that immediately swelled up to twice its width. People on the line complained of static noises which at times were so loud as to drown out the conversation. One customer said that the noise reminded him of the sound of a large diamondback's rattles. One lady customer, who was constantly on the phone and who had a habit of pressing the receiver tightly against her right ear complained of pain in that particular organ, which swelled up and turned purple. That snake's poison was very potent.

◆　◆　◆

The roadrunner is New Mexico's state bird. Its diet consists of snake meat, particularly that of rattlesnakes. In a duel between rattler and roadrunner the bird invariably wins. Deftly evading the furiously striking fangs, the bird pecks the snake to death, devouring it with great gusto.

A certain campesino named José got drunk every Saturday night. One time he got so very besotted that he fell down unconscious on his way home. There he was lying in the middle of the road, snoring, with his mouth wide open. A small rattlesnake slid down his throat, all the way down into his stomach, where it curled up contentedly. José was so soused that he noticed nothing. He must have been very drunk indeed.

José awoke with a great commotion going on inside his stomach. He at once sought help from a curandera, a bruja, a witchwoman with a great reputation of being able to cure the most outlandish diseases. The curandera knew at once what was causing the commotion inside José's body.

"Pobrecito," she told the bewildered patient, "you have a live culebra de cascabel inside your stomach. Listen, don't you hear it rattle?"

The curandera knew just what to do. She warmed up a pitcher of milk and held it close to José's mouth. The culebra smelled the milk and instantly came up to get its share, rattlesnakes being inordinarily fond of warm milk. As soon as the rattler stuck its head out of José's mouth, the curandera grabbed it by its neck, pulled it out of José's gullet, and flung in into her backyard, where she kept a pet roadrunner. The bird eagerly killed the culebra and gobbled it up.

"Amigo," the curandera told José, "you owe me a sheep, a fat one. And stop drinking!"

◆　◆　◆

A Texas cowboy once came upon two rattlesnakes that had each other by the tail. He sat down to watch. The snakes swallowed each other up until only their heads were left. "Never saw anything like it," the cowboy later told his friends.

There is one nonvenomous species of snake which lives on a diet of other snakes, including rattlers. It swallows them whole, beginning at the head, being impervious to the venom.

A Rolling Snake Gathers No Moss

His ax on his shoulder, a young man was walking across a field toward a stand of timber to cut some wood. He heard a rustling noise and saw that he had almost stepped on a large rattlesnake. He took his ax and chopped the snake into three parts. The rattler's head kept on moving, hissing, looking at him. Then he saw something that made the blood curdle in his veins. Out of the grass rose the snake's wife. She was enraged because he had killed her husband. She was a full six feet long and slithering toward him at full speed. Her mouth was open, showing her big fangs dripping yellow poison. The young man threw his ax away and began running for his life, looking all the time over his shoulder to see if he was gaining on the venomous serpent. Then he noticed something that made his hair stand on end: the snake took her tail into her mouth, making herself into a hoop. It was rolling along like a wagon wheel, faster and faster. The young man ran on in a cold sweat. His teeth were chattering. No matter how fast he ran, the hoop snake kept right after him. He jumped over a brook, the snake rolled over it. He leaped over a fence, the snake leaped after. He thought he could outrace it by running uphill, but the hoop snake rolled up, up, up behind him. The young man's lungs were about to burst. His heart was beating so fast he

thought it would jump out of his chest. Blood spurted from his nostrils. His legs were giving out under him. But then, with great presence of mind, he remembered what his grandmother had once taught him—the only way to get rid of a hooper. With a last great effort he jumped to the side just as the rattler was about to bump into him, and as the living hoop passed by, he quickly jumped through it and ran in the opposite direction, the one he had come from. The snake wife was rolling so fast she couldn't stop. The hoop rolled on and on, down a steep slope, plunging finally into the river. In that river lived the greatest catfish ever. It was at least fifteen feet long, endowed with a mouth like a gaping barn door. It took one look at the hoop snake and swallowed it whole with one bite.

Hoop snakes are just about the worst critters a fellow can bump into, especially if they have taken a dislike to him.

The White Snakes

The German settlers of Missouri, Iowa, and the Dakotas tell snake stories that might be partially of European origin.

In the last century there lived a young pioneer who had taken up his homestead of 160 acres in the new land west of the Missouri. He was very much in love with his beautiful wife, whom he cherished in every way. In the crawl space beneath his cabin two white snakes had taken up their abode. They were as white as snow and had sparkling eyes as red as rubies. The young settler had become used to these uninvited guests, and actually grew fond of them. Every evening he put out a cup of milk for them, which was always empty in the morning.

One day the young man's wife caught a fever, sickened, and died. Her husband was beside himself with grief and would not be consoled. He said that he wished to die too and be buried with his one and only love. As his wife's body was laid out for a last viewing, the two white snakes suddenly crept up to the bier. One of them carried three sprigs of a special kind of sage in its mouth. The snakes placed one sprig each on the dead wife's lips and eyes and, at once, she opened her eyes, was breathing again, and sat up. In a short while she was well again to the excessive joy of her husband, who had not words enough to praise the white snakes that had brought his wife to life again.

Alive she was, but a change had come over her. She no longer loved her husband but conceived a passion for their neighbor, an unmarried, unprincipled rake. The unsuspecting husband stood in the way of their wicked desires and the guilty pair resolved to kill him. One day while he was working in the field, his neighbor crept up behind him and stabbed him in the throat so that he fell down dead. The bad wife told all the folks around that her husband had died of an accident. "He stumbled and fell onto his scythe," she said, lamenting loudly so that all pitied her. Many people came to the wake, because the young husband had been liked by all the folks in his part of the country. Among the mourners was the murderer, who said over and over again how much he had liked the dead young man who had been such an ornament to the community. So there was much weeping—genuine and pretended. While the wake was in progress the two white snakes suddenly appeared. They slithered up to the open coffin and one of the serpents placed sprigs of sage on the victim's throat and eyes. Instantly, his death wound closed and he opened his eyes. As he came alive again, the first thing he did was point at his wife and say, "I loved and cherished her, and yet she connived at my murder." He then pointed at his wicked neighbor, exclaiming: "My death was no accident. This man treacherously stabbed me in the throat. Behold my murderer!"

Before those present could seize the guilty pair, the two white snakes were gliding toward them. One snake stung the wicked wife in the leg, the other struck her lover. They fell down and died in agony.

In good time the revived young man fell in love, remarried, and raised a fine family. He died of old age, happy and contented. The white snakes survived him because their kind lives for hundreds of years. They might still be there, in the crawl space beneath the old cabin, provided it still stands.

A Pair of Fine Boots

This story, in many variations, is told throughout the Southwest.

Dōna Inez was a most handsome woman, vivacious, small-waisted and high-bosomed, with sparkling eyes of black obsidian. She was married to a wealthy ranchero who owned some hundred thousand acres on which he ran several thousand longhorns. This husband of hers was also active in politics and involved in a number of businesses besides cattle raising. The marriage had been arranged between the two families concerned. The ranchero was twenty years older than Doña Inez. He was often absent on business—for days, even for weeks.

The ranch was managed by a ramrod called Miguel, a tall, swaggering, good-looking fellow with a go-to-hell grin, gleaming teeth that seemed artificial but were not, a sweeping mustache, and luxurious sideburns. In the husband's absence Miguel often came to the main house with its many-columned porch to discuss ranch business with Doña Inez. He usually stayed for dinner and a glass of wine or a copita of aguardiente. Their discussions of ranch business often lasted for a considerable time.

Whenever Miguel went up to the big house to make his reports, he dressed with great care. He combed his mustache, donned a fine silk shirt, and put on his special visiting boots. His pride and joy, these boots were hand-tooled, richly carved with the images of eagles and roses, and outlined with tiny bits of silver. Of solid silver also were his jingling spurs, equipped with enormous rowels. Thus ensplendored from head to toe, the eternal cigarillo dangling from his lips, Miguel set out to discuss business with Doña Inez. He always chose the finest-looking horse for these visits, with a saddle and bridle to match the magnificence of his clothing.

Riding from his own place to the big house, Miguel had to cross an arroyo that was at all times pervaded with a foul, oppressive odor, the stench, it was said, of a giant diamondback, La Reina de las Cascabelas, the Queen of All Rattlesnakes. Fabulous and frightening stories were rife about this monstrous serpent that had not been seen for years but was believed to be still living in a cave deep inside the arroyo. Wise folks made a wide detour around this evil place, but not Miguel, who was not afraid of any snake, however large.

One night, having taken care of ranch business with Doña Inez while her husband was away, Miguel mounted his noble steed to return to his own dwelling. In the darkness the horse stepped into a gopher hole and broke its left foreleg. There was nothing to do but put the animal out of its misery. Not given to hesitation, Miguel unholstered his six-gun and shot the horse between the eyes, not without profound regret. He took off the ornate saddle and, sadly, continued on foot. In the uncertain light of an early dawn, Miguel made out what seemed to be a tree trunk and sat down upon it to rest. This was a fatal mistake because the tree trunk turned out to be the Queen of Cascabelas, about a hundred years old, some fifteen feet long, with a back the width of a dog's, and very much alive. The mammoth diamondback reared up into a coil and struck, its enormous fangs penetrating Miguel's wonderfully ornamented boots, stabbing into the ramrod's ankle. Miguel's leg swelled up instantly and turned blue. As the sun rose, Miguel died, unshriven and unconfessed. Vaqueros found his body with the odor of rattlesnake still pervading the air all around.

At Doña Inez's suggestion, her husband gave Miguel a magnificent funeral. He ordered for his deceased ramrod an impressive headstone with the carved likeness of a cowboy boot encircled by a snake, held up by an angel, the whole surmounted by a fluttering dove. As was fitting, Miguel was laid to rest in his finest charro costume, but with his plain instead of his ornamented visiting boots on. These had been appropriated, with all the vaqueros' consent, by his best friend, Maclovio. The boot that had been struck by the monster cascabela had burst at the seam because of the dead man's leg having swelled up enormously, and even so it had taken two strong men to pull it off. The busted seam was easily repaired. Maclovio was happy with his newly acquired fancy footwear.

Now this Maclovio succeeded Miguel as the ranch's manager. He too was tall and handsome, and had an extraordinary set of gleaming teeth that he exposed in a hell-for-leather grin. It was not long before he also went regularly up to the big house to discuss the state of the cattle and related matters with Doña Inez in her husband's absence. Like his predecessor, Maclovio also spruced up before these visits— combed his mustache and put on his dead friend's gorgeous boots. On one of these visits Maclovio had taken his boots off. Why he had done such a thing nobody could imagine. Taking his leave, Maclovio put on his boots again with a flourish and great force. Doing this, he let out a cry of pain and jerked the right boot off again. Looking at his ankle, he saw imbedded in it one of the huge fangs of the Queen of Rattlers. It had remained, undetected up to that moment, stuck in the boot. The fang still contained a great deal of deadly venom. Maclovio's leg turned first yellow, then green, and finally black. It swelled up and caused Maclovio unendurable pain. In a panic Doña Inez tried to suck out the poison with her ruby lips. Now Inez had been created, by god or the devil, depending on how one looked at it, with an absolutely perfect body, the body of a goddess made for love, a body like those one admires on the canvases of Titian or Goya. It had only one single small blemish—a rotten tooth, invisible, far in the back of her sensuous mouth. The baneful toxin found this weak spot. Doña Inez and Maclovio expired in each other's arms. The patrón sold his ranch and moved elsewhere. Don Ignazio, the village priest, saw in this calamity the finger of God. Now nobody dares to go anywhere near that arroyo in which the monster snake is supposed to live, or to have lived, because all this happened a long time ago and the Queen of all Rattlesnakes must surely be dead by now. But one never knows. It is better to be careful.

According to experts on the subject, the fang of even a very large diamondback cannot penetrate a thick cowboy boot. Also, a single fang can no longer do much harm. The severed head of a recently killed rattlesnake, on the other hand, can still bite and inject a lethal dose of venom.

The Young Man Who Wanted to Be Snakebit

There was a young man whom everybody called Whiskey Johnny on account of his fondness for strong drink. He lived in a tiny settlement at the edge of the wilderness. A single road connected it to the rest of the world. It was hardly more than a deer track. The French were on the warpath. The whole country swarmed with hostile Indians. The settlement was cut off and supplies were running low. Strong liquors were not to be had anywhere, not even at the tavern. The hamlet had neither school nor church, but it had a doctor in residence who also doubled as apothecary, leech, barber, and tooth-puller. It was rumored that he kept a keg of whiskey for medicinal use. Whiskey Johnny sauntered into the physician's house, slammed two bits on the table and said, "Give me a drink!"

"This whiskey is for curative purposes only," said the doctor, "and for emergencies, such as snakebite."

The next day Whiskey Johnny appeared again, with a swollen cheek, his head swathed in a dirty towel. "This is an emergency, Doctor," he stammered, "my rotten tooth is driving me mad. I can't stand the pain. Give me a shot of the hard stuff!"

"A toothache is no emergency. My whiskey is for snakebite only."

Soon after, Whiskey Johnny appeared again, limping pitifully, a bloody rag wrapped around his left leg. "This is truly an emergency. The ax slipped and went into my shin. Whiskey, for pity's sake!"

"A superficial wound," said the doctor, "this is no emergency either. Whiskey is for snakebite. How often do I have to repeat it?"

A few days later, as he passed a spot called Rattlesnake Hill because it harbored a den of those venomous reptiles, the physician noticed Whiskey Johnny, barefoot and with his pants legs rolled up over his knees, madly stomping through the grass and heather.

"Johnny, Johnny," cried the doctor, "what do you think you're doing?"

"What I'm doing, you damned old fool," Whiskey Johnny shouted back. "Can't you see that I'm trying to get snakebit?"

The Peg-Leg Cat

Jacob Schutz, the hunter of the Great White Hart, owned a cat. No ordinary cat would do for him. As Jacob was a mighty hunter among men, so his tomcat, Tiger, was a mighty hunter among felines. No run-of-the-mill barnyard tabby was he, hunting for mice and rats in kitchen and cellar. Tiger was a fearful outsized member of the whiskered tribe, the offspring of a real wildcat and some lovesick grimalkin. His mewing was more like a cougar's roar, his claws terrifying curved daggers. So fierce was he that none but Jacob dared to come near him, and then only with his leather mittens on. Even Jacob's huge black dog, Wacker, beat a hasty retreat when faced with this formidable feline. This mighty puss disdained the ordinary diet of the peaceful mouser. Staying out in the forest most of the time, even in the coldest winter, Tiger consumed only what he himself had caught—squirrels, gophers, rabbits, groundhogs, and such like. Birds above a certain size (he ignored the smaller ones) were snatched out of midair. Likewise the pike from the stream.

Once Tiger had been out of sight for many days, vanished without a trace. "He's met his match in a catamount or lynx," thought Jacob, but he stumbled upon Tiger with a foreleg caught in a bear trap. He was in the process of biting it off and had almost succeeded. The leg could not be saved. It had been gnawed through until only shreds of sinew and muscle remained. Jacob released Tiger from the trap. The feral cat sensed that the feral man was trying to help him. He allowed Jacob to take him home. Hunched before the fireplace, the ravenous Tiger accepted a proffered chunk of venison, for once eating something he had not caught himself. While he devoured the meat, Jacob whittled a wooden leg for him. It was not easy to figure out how to fasten the artificial limb to the stump. In the end, Jacob tied wooden leg and stump together with wet rawhide. As the hide dried and shrank, the peg leg remained fixed in place as if welded to the stump. For extra measure Jacob also fashioned a sort of harness that bound the artificial limb to Tiger's body as well. Happy to end his enforced stay in Jacob's rude cabin, the tom went thumping along, seemingly well satisfied. He purred, sounding like a dozen grinding stones. Then he sauntered off into the forest, taking up his accustomed life, obviously doing all right. Waxing fat and sleek, he soon

seemed to be his old self again. Soon word spread throughout the region about this remarkable peg-legged animal.

On one of his infrequent forays to the village for provisions, Jacob ran into an old acquaintance who inquired, "It wonders me, friend, how does it go with thine Kater?"

"Ach, sehr gut, very well, better than afore."

"And he can hunt wiss his Holz Bein, his peg leg? How does he catch his prey?"

"Ach, friend, I vil tell you. I saw him de other day catch a rabbit viss one paw, like so, and hit him aufn Kopp, beat its brain out, viss his wooden leg!"

CHAPTER 16

Mostly Lies

And here is proof, if proof be needed, that the American frontier produced some of the biggest liars in the world.

Somebody in My Bed

I just dropped in at a comfortable-looking inn, where I concluded to remain a day or two. After a good substantial meal, I lit a "York County Principle" (the like of which sell in these regions at the rate of four for a penny), and seated myself in the ring formed around the barroom stove. There was a brawny butcher, the effeminate taylor, a Yankee fiddler, two horse dealers, a speculator, a blackleg, the village Esculapius, and "the captain," who in consequence of being able to live on his means, was a person of no small importance, and therefore allowed to sit before the firestove with the poker to stir the fire—a mark of respect granted ONLY to persons of standing.

Yarn after yarn had been spun and the hour for retiring had arrived—the landlord was dozing behind his bar,—and the spirit of the conversation was beginning to wane when the doctor whispered to me that if I would pay attention, he would "topp off" with a good one.

"I believe, Captain," said the doctor, "I never told you about my adventure with a woman at my boardinghouse, when I was attending the lecture?"

"No, let's hear it," replied the individual addressed, who was a short, flabby, fat man of about fifty, with a highly nervous temperament, and a very red face.

"At the time I attended the lectures, I boarded at a house in which there were no females but the landlady and the old colored cook—" (Here the doctor made a slight pause, and the captain, by way of requesting him to go on, said "Well.")

"I often felt the want of female society to soften the severe labors of deep study, and dispel the ennui to which I was subject—"

"Well," said the captain.

·· *395* ··

"But as I feared that forming acquaintances among the ladies might interfere with my studies. I avoided them all—"

"Well."

"One evening after listening to a long lecture of physical anatomy, and after dissecting a large negro, fatigued in body and mind, I went to my lodgings—"

"Well," said the captain.

"I went into the hall, took a large lamp, and went directly to my room, it being then after one o'clock—"

"Well."

"I placed the light upon the table, and commenced undressing. I had hardly got my coat off when my attention was attracted to a frock, and a quantity of pettycoats lying on a chair near the bed—"

"Well," said the captain, who began to show signs that he was getting deeply interested.

"And a pair of beautiful small shoes and stockings on the floor. Of course I thought it strange, and was about to retire—but then I thought it was my room, I had at least the right to know who was in my bed—"

"Exactly," nodded the captain. "Well!"

"So I took the light, went softly to the bed and, with a trembling hand, drew aside the curtain. Heavens! What a sight! A young girl—I should say an angel, of about eighteen, was in there asleep—"

"Well!" said the captain, giving his chair a hitch.

"As I gazed upon her, I thought that I had never witnessed anything more beautiful from underneath a little nightcap, rivaling the snow in whiteness, curled a stray ringlet over a neck and shoulders of alabaster—"

"Well!" said the excited captain, giving his chair another hitch.

"Never did I look upon a bust more perfectly formed. I took hold of the coverlid—"

"Well!" said the captain, throwing his right leg over his left.

"And softly pulled it down—"

"Well!" said the captain, betraying the utmost excitement.

"To her waist—"

"*Well!*" said the captain, dropping the poker and renewing the position of his legs.

"She had a nightdress, buttoned up before, but softly I opened the first two buttons—"

"Well!" said the captain, wrought to the highest pitch of excitement.

"And then, ye gods! What a sight to gaze upon—a Hebe—pshaw! words fail me. Just then—"

"*Well!!!*" said the captain, hitching his chair right and left, and squirting his tobacco juice against the stove that it fairly fizzed again.

"I thought I was taking a mean advantage of her, so I covered her up, seized my coat and boots, and went and slept in another room."

"IT'S A LIE!" shouted the excited captain, jumping up and kicking over his chair. "It's a lie! I'll bet up to fifty dollars that you got into the bed."

The Weather

A tenderfoot said to an Arizona cowman: "This would be a fine country if it had water." "So would hell," was the reply.

◆ ◆ ◆

Sandstorms in the Southwest can be trying. After a particularly violent one, a saddle bum was riding across the desert when, in the middle of nowhere, he came upon a bowler hat resting on the desert floor. He dismounted to pick it up and found a head under it.

"Godalmighty," he said, "The 'Paches cut a tenderfoot's head off, but where, in hell, is the rest of him?"

To the cowpuncher's horror the head, which turned out to belong to an English traveler, began to talk, very politely: "I say, dear chap, would you lend a hand? I happen to be buried alive up to my chin by this infernal sandstorm of yours."

"Amazin'," said the local citizen. "What in tarnation are you doin' afoot in the middle of the desert?"

"Hurry please, dear fellow, because I am deucedly uncomfortable. And get a shovel. I am not on foot. I have my horse under me."

◆　◆　◆

On the exceedingly rare occasions when it does rain, the whole Southwest turns into a sea of mud. A traveler noted in his diary: "Ten inches of dust by measurement." The next day he noted that knee-deep mud prevented him from crossing the street. A man making his way gingerly on the boardwalk in front of a Bisbee, Arizona, saloon after a sudden rainfall, slime already oozing below the swinging doors into the bar, noticed a head sticking out of the mud in the street, asking for a drink. The good Samaritan obligingly produced a shot glass of red liquor and inquired if he could be of further assistance.

"No, thanks," answered the head, "I'm in the saddle and as soon as my horse gets its second wind, we'll work ourselves out of this."

◆　◆　◆

General William Tecumseh Sherman once said, apropos the southwestern climate, that if he owned both Texas and hell, he'd sell Texas and, with the proceeds, buy himself a home in the other place.

It Gets Mighty Cold Around Here

I'm telling you, stranger, come winter it gets mighty cold around here. The first real cold night I heerd an orful noise like thunder, arthquake, floods, and cannon fire all ramsquaddled together. In the mornin' I take a peep out o' my winder and where there had been a mighty forest, there was nothin'. Not a single tree was standin'. They had all been cracked to flinders by the frost lying about for miles an' miles an', I'm telling you, stranger, the cold had petrified 'em and turned 'em into glass, an' when there was a breeze, it made a tinklin' so loud it split my eardrums. An' overhead, you can hang me up for bar meat, ef a flock o' birds didn' freeze in flight and came down on me like hail. Waaal, stranger, thinks I: "This will make a fine wild chicken pie," an' with that I gathered up a few bushels o' them thar birds, an' took 'em into the cabin an' lit a fire. Strike me dead, stranger, if the flames didn't freeze into icicles. I broke 'em off, right an' left, and sold 'em to some Yankees on their way to a place that was just a bit warmer. Yessir, I made good money on the deal. I was sittin' by the chimbley when suddenlike, the whole roof crashed down on me. You can call me a lyin' skunk ef'n the smoke risin from the chimbley hadn't frozen to a height of a hundred feet an' the weight had caved the whole roof in. Yessir, the wind blew so cold that my feet all froze up. I put 'em in a tub of bilin' water an' it froze up faster than a greased fart on a lightnin' rod, an' there I was with my feet stuck in a tub of ice. I had to chisel 'em out, bit by bit. Yessir. An' when I stepped out, the air was frozen solid an' I had to chop it up fine afore I could breathe. Sez I to myself, "Tom, old hoss, let's go over to the tavern whar it might be warmer." Call me a dead chicken ef it war not colder than the darn cabin. The fiddler sawed at his bow with his mittens on, but not a sound came out of it. I had a mind to cheer him up with a song, but it froze in my mouth. The boniface was yellin', makin' a lot of chin music, but that was frozen. He was wavin' his arms like a windmill, excited like, pointin' to the winder, and, stranger, strike me dead, ef it waren't a cussed Injun standin' thar drawin' a bead on me with his rifle. I grabbed hold of a kettle o' bilin' water an' chucked it at him, a-knowin' that it would turn to ice, an' so it did. That thar chunk o' ice went right through the winderpane and hit that red varmint on his noggin, strikin' him dead on the spot. To keep warm I was chawin', beaverlike, on a twist of 'baccer, an' when I spit out the ambeer it turned into ice too an' hit the boniface in the mouth an' knocked out three of his front teeth. Come spring, an' I don't lie to you, friend, when I woke up heering fiddling an' singin' comin' out o' the tavern. I was ramsquaddled. Fiddlin' and singin' on a Sunday mornin'? But, sure enuff, I heerd myself singin' to the tune of a fiddle. My song an' the fiddler's sawin' had come unfrozen, an', to tell the truth, it was almost too loud to bear. I'm tellin' you, stranger, winters are mighty cold around here.

Texican Liars

Two characters met at a San Jacinto River crossing and sat down by a campfire regaling themselves with these tall tales:

◆ ◆ ◆

I see that war no help for it. so I took my feet outen the stirrups, threw my saddlebags over my shoulder, and in me and my mare went.

We war in a awful tight place for a time, but we soon landed safe. I'd jest got my critter tied out, and a fire started to dry myself with when I see a chap come ridin' up the hill on a smart chunk of pony.

"Hoopee! stranger"—sings out my beauty—"How d'ye? Kept your fireworks dry, eh? How in thunder did ye get over?"

"Oh," says I, "mighty easy. Ye see, stranger, I'm poerful on a pirogue; so I waited until I see a big log a-driftin' nigh the shore, when I fastened to it, set my critter a-straddle on it, got into the saddle, paddled over with my saddle-bags, an' steered with the mare's tail."

"Ye didn't so, by Ned!" says he, "did ye?"

"Mighty apt to," says I, "but arter ye've sucked all that in and got yer breath agin, let's know how *you* crossed."

"Oh!" says he, getting his pig's eyes on me, "I've been a-ridin' all day with a consarned ager, an' orful dry, and afeard to drink at the prairie water holes; so when I got to the river I jest went in fer a big drink, swallered half a mile of water, and come over dry shod."

"Stranger," says I, "ye'r just one huckleberry above my persimmon. Light and take some red-eye. I thought ye looked green, but I were barkin' up the wrong tree."

CHAPTER 17

Miracles, Saints, and Witches

Tales of the Hispanic Southwest are in a category by themselves. There are so many of them that nobody has counted them yet. They came up across the Rio Grande together with the conquistadores, with Don Juan de Oñate and, later, Don Diego de Vargas. They came to New Mexico, aptly called the Land of Enchantment, as early as 1598. They came from Spain via Mexico. Unlike the stories and fairy tales of Anglo-Saxon America, Hispanic legends have a strong Old World flavor, telling of kings and dukes, princes and princesses. The immigrants peopling the province of Neuva México were profoundly Catholic, which gave a unique color to their "cuentos," with emphasis on miracles, on Santa María and the Holy Child, on saints, priests, and witches.

During many centuries of history Spain has been home to many different peoples—Iberians, Celts, Basques, Phoenicians, Carthaginians, Greeks, Romans, Visigoths, and Arabs. Out of their multi-cultural myths grew the folklore of Spain. Travelers from western Europe, crossing the Pyrenees, brought with them bits and pieces of their own mythology. Gypsies contributed their part. In Mexico, Hispanic elements mingled with Aztec, Mixtec, and Mayan traditions and, north of the Rio Grande, the Pueblo Indians and the Hispanic newcomers influenced each others' dances, songs, and festivals. Thus the Spaniards brought to the Southwest the Mattachine Dances, of Moorish origin, and the Fiesta del Gallo, or Chicken-Pull, which have become part of certain Pueblo festivals. On the other hand, some Indian sacred clown rituals have infiltrated the Hispanic fiestas.

From Europe too came the stories of "brujas," witches, and of ghosts. The belief in witchcraft is still strong today, being shared by both Pueblo Indians and Navajos.

In the mountain villages of New Mexico, Spanish is the universal language, an old-fashioned, seventeenth-century Spanish. It has been said that the Catholic faith can be worn like a brilliant silken mantilla or like a hair shirt. The villagers wear it both ways, at their patron saint's colorful fiesta and on Good Friday, when the Penitentes scourge themselves with whips to atone for their own and the world's sins. In such places not only are the old stories still told, but new ones are born time and again. Here saints still appear to the devout. It is the Land of Enchantment, the Land of Legends.

The Three Lost Daughters

Don Manuel Juarez was a rico hombre, the wealthiest rancher in the San Luis Valley, where he owned the finest hacienda, thousands of acres, and large herds of horses, cattle, and sheep. Don Manuel, a proud Castilian, was a widower. He lavished all his love and affection upon his three daughters, one more beautiful than the other, and all of the pure blood of Spain. He also had a beloved son, Fernando, an accomplished young caballero, the finest horseman in the valley, admired and respected by all.

One accursed day, when Don Manuel was far away in Santa Fe on business, and all his vaqueros were out in the pastures busy with their varied tasks, a band of roving Apaches attacked the ranch. Only young Fernando and the three daughters were at home at the time. Fernando defended himself and his sisters with the courage of desperation, killing two of the raiders before succumbing to the greater number of his savage foes. Having done their bloody work, the Apaches set fire to the ranch and seized Don Manuel's wailing and sobbing daughters, threw them across their ponies' backs, and thundered off toward the west. When Don Manuel returned from Santa Fe, he found his vaqueros and peons, aroused by the smoke and flames, assembled around the smoldering remnants of his rancho. Within its ruins the disconsolate father discovered the pitiful remains of his only son.

After the hurried burial of his heir, Don Manuel gathered all his men around him. Together they swore a solemn oath to recapture the abducted daughters and avenge Fernando's death, or die in the attempt. Reinforced by a large caballada of his fellow ranchers, well armed and well mounted, they took off after the Apache war party. They caught up with the Indians within a day near Saguache Lake, a body of water which for generations had been the topic of many dark and somber tales. Facing overwhelming odds, the Apaches did not stand and fight, but galloped helter-skelter toward the lake, still holding their three wailing captives firmly in their grasp. Thus they plunged into the lake and were instantly swallowed up by its swirling waters. When Don Manuel and his vaqueros reached the spot, it was as if the Indians and their three victims had never existed. No matter how carefully the frantic father and his companions searched, not a trace of the kidnappers or the three girls could be found—then or later. The disconsolate father and his retainers had become the victims of an evil, unexplainable miracle which, the vaqueros said, was the devil's work.

There had always been rumors that the lake contained in its depths a maelstrom that pulled everything within its orbit into the vortex of a swift-rushing subterranean channel whose entrance and exit were known to only a very few Indian shamans. It was also said that, by holding his breath, a man, falling or thrown into the lake at this particular spot, could survive, being rushed in mere minutes beneath the lake's bottom to be ejected somewhere outside through a secret opening in a cliff wall. In this fashion an Indian raider who knew the secret could make the watery passage unharmed, if wet, and escape his pursuers. For many a day a distraught Don Manuel and his men searched for this hidden exit from the lake, but they never found it. They returned home in utter dejection. Don Manuel's remaining days were clouded by the uncertainty of not knowing whether his daughters had perished or whether they had emerged from their ordeal alive only to be forever captives of savage tribesmen. Don Manuel died within the year—a prematurely aged and broken man. This is the sad saga of Saguache Lake and the three lost daughters.

The Two Witches

One time there were two man witches and they make a bet. This a long time ago. They say they change themselves into a horse, and run a race. The witch that lose the race, he stay a horse all the time. So they run a race and one witch lose the race, he have to stay a horse because of his bet.

So the other witch takes this horse and sell him to a man. But he say, "Don't you ever take the halter off of this horse, or else it be too bad." Now one day a little boy take this horse down to the river for water and a priest come by. This priest say, "What you water a horse with the halter on? That horse can't drink; you take off the halter." So the boy take off the halter, and the horse change right away into a fish.

Now that bad witch is flying around like a hawk, and he see what happen, and he change hisself into a big fish. That little fish see this, and he change into a bird. The bad witch change into a hawk again, and this little bird fly, fly, until he too tired, and he see a princess sitting in a garden. Quick he fly to this princess and hide hisself in her lap. She take this poor little bird and put it in a cage, no one can get him now. He too happy, this bird, and sing all day long.

Now something wrong with this princess, she too sad all the time, never laugh. This witch change into a physician and he come along and say he can cure her, but he need the blood of that bird. All right, the king give him the bird, and he cut its throat. But when the blood

run out, it change to seed. That witch change into a hen and eat up the seed, but when he come to the last seed he can't find it, and that seed change into a coyote and eat up that hen!

There's a man sees that coyote and take him home to mind his store. A witch woman comes along and she wink at that coyote. She see that coyote a witch. So that night the coyote think to go to her, and he take a big leg of mutton from the store, put it on his shoulder, and go to see her. But the town dogs they smell him when he go by, and they jump on him and tear him all apart. That the end of those two witches.

The Owl Witch

Don Ramón's family was bothered by a big tecolote, a big owl. This bird of ill omen stole the chicks, carried off the pigeons, and even made off with a little kitten. Whenever there was a new moon, the owl appeared at one of the windows hooting and screeching and flapping its wings. Always after that happened, a horse went lame, or cutworms got into the beans, or a child took sick, or grandfather Miguel came down with a bad cough.

"Madre de Dios," said Don Ramón's esposa, "this tecolote must be a witch, an evil bruja!"

So Don Ramón got out his shotgun, and when there was a new moon again, he was waiting at the open window with his arma de fuego. Around midnight he heard loud screeching, and hooting, and wing flapping. Though it was too dark to see, he fired a shot in the direction of the noise. Then all was quiet.

In the morning Don Ramón looked out the window and saw on the ground before it the dead tecolote. Its right wing had been shot off and its left eye was missing.

Later in the day one of Don Ramón's neighbors dropped in and said: "Have you heard the horrible news? That old woman who lives among the dead cottonwoods across the stream was found murdered. Her right arm was torn off and her left eye shot out. There was much blood. It was a horrible sight. Who could have done such a thing?"

"I could make a guess," said Don Ramón.

San Isidro and the Angel

As everybody knows, San Isidro is the patron saint of all who work on the soil, who sow and reap. San Isidro is a down-to-earth saint. He doesn't give himself airs. He is not afraid to get his boots muddy or to get calluses on his hands. He works his little ranch near Velarde, New Mexico. He grows beans and chili peppers and other good things. He is that kind of a saint.

Naturally, Isidro's wife, Santa Rita, is also a saint. She is a curandera. She helps those who are sick. Being a saint, she is also a very good cook, the best in all New Mexico. How could anyone be better? Every day at noon Santa Rita goes out into the fields with a big basket full of food for San Isidro, sometimes enchiladas and posole, or burritos and tamales, or maybe, fajitas and pollo adobo. Bringing lunch to her esposo, Santa Rita has to cross a little stream. That is no problem for her. Whenever she arrives at that brook, the water parts for her, some of it flowing upstream, and some of it flowing downstream. The water does this out of respect for her, because she is a saint. A saint shouldn't get his feet wet. So San Isidro and Santa Rita have a very good marriage. In their case, how could it be otherwise?

One day San Isidro was plowing his bean field. It happened to be the fifteenth of May. As everybody knows, the fifteenth of May is San Isidro's feast day. As he was plowing along, driving his big red ox before him, San Isidro heard footsteps behind him. He turned his head and saw that an angel was walking in his furrow.

"What on earth are you doing, Isidro, working on your own feast day?" said the angel. "Don't you know that nobody is allowed to work in the fields today? Don't you know any better? You are setting a very bad example. God sent me to make you stop working at once."

"Señor Angel," answered Isidro, "tell God he knows nothing about farming. I have to plow my beans now while the weather is good and before it is too late. Tell God to mind his own business."

"He won't like this," said the angel, and left.

After a while the angel was back telling San Isidro: "You are a very insolent and sassy saint. God wants you to stop working at once. If you don't obey, God will send a hailstorm or, maybe, a belated blizzard to ruin your crops in order to teach you a lesson."

"It's my own feast day, so I don't have to obey Him," said the saint. "Let him send hail or blizzards. I can manage them. Am I not a saint?"

"You will make Him very angry," said the angel, and left.

In no time the angel was back: "Isidro, God is really upset with you. He ordered me to tell you that He'll send down a blight on your fields, locusts and cutworms to ruin your crops."

"Let Him," answered Isidro. "I know how to deal with such pests." The angel shook his head and left, only to return on the double.

"Isidro," he said, "God will send you a very bad neighbor, a drunkard, a troublemaker, a lecher, an Anglo, a Protestant even, a cabrón who will drive his cattle into your field and steal the peaches from your trees."

Instantly, San Isidro stopped what he was doing. "Señor Angel," he said, "God has got the better of me. Hailstorms and cutworms I can manage, but not a bad neighbor. God always wins."

◆◆◆

A Riddle

◆◆◆

There once was a cruel king who squeezed out of his people the last drop of blood in the shape of taxes. He had many armed men at his beck and call. They wore armor and wielded weapons of steel. What could a poor campesino do against them? The cruel king did not like the people to complain against him because, as he said, complaints lead to rebellion.

Yet a poor man, by the name of Pedro, did complain. "The king's men," he said, "have taken all my grain, even the seed corn. They took my goats and they took my lambs. They not only stole my last chicken but even took the last egg. They call it taxes. I call it robbery. So I am starving, living on roots and the wild fruits of the forest like an animal."

The king heard about this and exclaimed angrily: "I'll teach him what it is to starve. I'll make him eat his boots, if he has any!"

The king's men went to Pedro's humble hut and took him prisoner. They loaded him down with chains and cast him into a dark, dank dungeon. They did not feed him, because the cruel king wanted him to starve to death for having dared to complain. Poor Pedro had a daughter called Juanita. She carried a little baby boy at her breast. Her breasts were overflowing with milk. She loved her father dearly and shed many tears over his sad fate. In the dungeon's wall was a small hole. Through it Juanita nursed her father, keeping him alive with her mother's milk.

The cruel king had one weakness—riddles. He loved riddles to distraction. There was not one riddle in the whole wide world he could not solve. He made it known throughout his realm, by town crier and trumpeter, that if any person could pose him a riddle he could not solve, then this person could make a wish, and if it was in the king's power to grant it, then he would do so.

The poor prisoner's daughter heard it. She boldly went to the king. She told him: "I have a riddle for you. I give you three days to solve it."

Antaño fui hija, hoy soy madre.
Un hijo que tengo fué marido de mi madre.
Aciértala, buen rey, y si no, dame a mi padre.

I used to be a daughter, but now am a mother.
I have a son who is my mother's husband.
Solve the riddle, good king, or give me back my father.

The king racked his brain to find the answer to this riddle. He did not sleep a wink during all the three days and nights. He gave up. He had Juanita brought before him. "Tell me the answer to your riddle!" he commanded.

"And you will grant me a wish?"

"You have my royal word."

"Well, then. I was once a daughter, good king, but I nursed my father with the milk from my breasts. Thereby, I became his mother. But of course, being my father, he is my mother's husband. It is so simple, king, a child could have guessed it."

The king commanded Pedro to be taken from jail and brought into the royal presence. Pedro was brought before the throne. The king told him: "Because I could not solve your daughter's riddle, I let you go free, but if you ever complain about me in public again, I shall have your head cut off. Here, take this bag containing one hundred gold maravedis for yourself and your daughter, because it was a very good riddle."

To his henchmen the king said: "This is my order: Do not collect taxes from this man or from any member of his family. This is my royal command. Yo el rey! I the king!"

The Many-Times-Killed Young Man

There once was a sixty-year-old man, Don Policarpo, who owned a cantina somewhere between Belen and Socorro. He had a pretty esposa, Doña Inez, who was thirty-five years younger than her husband.

There was also a certain young, no-good muchacho named Jesús María, a lover of other men's wives.

Don Policarpo was a busy man. Tending bar at his cantina kept him up until the wee hours of the night. Much of the time Doña Inez was left alone at home with nothing to do. Jesús María was a lazy ne'er-do-well who somehow managed to get along without working. The devil, always on the watch for souls to catch, will find some mischief to do for idle hands. One night Don Policarpo, tending bar in his cantina, suddenly felt sick. His body was sore. His head ached. His stomach rumbled. His nose ran. His ears kept ringing. So he asked his customers to leave, closed up shop, and staggered home two hours earlier than was his wont.

When Don Policarpo arrived home, he found his place in the marital bed already occupied by that young wastrel, Jesús María. In righteous anger the injured husband grabbed a sharp knife from the table and stabbed Jesús María—once, twice, thrice—until this naughty young man was dead. He then turned to his wife, slapping her face and beating her with his fists, screaming, "Puta, whore, mujer sucia, slut, adúltera! Look, what you made me do!"

"It's your own fault, capón!" she screamed back at him. "Never at home, never doing what every good husband should to keep his wife happy! You have killed him! Madre de Dios! The gringos don't understand about passion and honor. They will sentence you to hang!"

"Válgame Dios! Evil woman, for once you are right. What am I to do?"

"Estúpido! What an idiot the devil induced me to marry! Drag the body over to our vecino, our neighbor, and leave it on his porch. Let him figure out what to do. Take care that nobody sees you." Don Policarpo hoisted Jesús María's body onto his back and, bent under the heavy burden, waded across the little stream to the house of his neighbor, Vigil, the saddlemaker. There he propped the corpse against the door, muttering, "Adiós, cabrón, dissolute, adulterous son of a mangy he-goat. May you rot in hell!" After unburdening himself in this manner, Don Policarpo crept home to administer another beating to his wife, who gave him a black eye in return.

Pilar, the wife of Vigil the saddlemaker, was awakened by the noise of Jesús María's body being dumped on her doorstep. She nudged her husband: "Mi esposo! I think there is somebody at the door. I'm afraid. It might be a robber. There are many bandidos around. Be careful."

Vigil grumbled, got up, took his pistola out of the drawer, made sure it was loaded, and in his nightshirt went out the back door, tiptoed around the house, and peeked around the corner to see what had caused the noise on his front porch. In the uncertain light of a pale moon, the saddlemaker discerned the shape of a man leaning against the door—surely a bandido trying to break in. Without hesitating, he fired off his pistola at the intruder. The body crashed down with a great clatter. Doña Pilar was screaming: "Vigil, love of my life, are you all right?"

"I think I killed this ladrón," answered Vigil. "Get me a light."

Doña Pilar, also in her nightshirt, appeared with a lighted candle.

"Ay de mí!" exclaimed the dumbfounded saddlemaker. "This is no bandido! It is Jesús María, the dissolute skirt chaser. He is carrying on with Doña Inez, the esposa of our neighbor, the cantinero. This evil young man must have been drunk to confuse our house with theirs."

"Santíssima Madre!" wailed Doña Pilar." You have murdered an innocent man. They will put you in the calabozo for the rest of your life. What will become of pobre Pilar then?"

"Stop cackling like a clucking hen," said the saddlemaker. "Pull yourself together. Help me carry this unfortunate one over to the place of the ranchero, half a mile that way. He is an Americano with about a dozen vaqueros, I mean cowboys. This will confuse the policía. And you, querida, mi corazón, you have seen nothing, heard nothing, and know nothing about this."

It was heavy work for them to haul the body to the rancher's place. "Look, husband," said Doña Pilar, having a sudden inspiration, "that evil-smelling privy I can just make out, over there. Let us put him on the seat. People will think he died of a sudden colic."

They dragged the corpse to the outhouse and propped him up on the seat. "Gracias a Dios," whispered Vigil, "it is done and over with. Vamos!"

"Bufón, idiot!" hissed his wife. "Have you not forgotten something?"

"Forgotten what?"

"To take down his pants, estúpido! Or do you expect me to do it?"

Don Vigil did as told while his esposa modestly averted her eyes. Then they hastened away without having been seen.

In the uncertain light of a dawning day a cowboy approached the privy to ease himself but found the place already occupied. Impatient, he admonished the occupant: "Come on, man, don't take all day!" The occupant did not answer. The cowboy became fidgety: "Seems I've been talkin' Chinese to a pack mule. Get off the pot, Rube, or do I have to kick you out?" Again there was no response. At that the desperate cowboy got into a horn-tossing mood, kicked in the door, grabbed the corpse by the scruff, yanked it from its seat, giving it a mighty clout on the head, yelling, "You damn son of a bitch! I'll teach you to try to make a fool out of me!"

The corpse slumped to the floor. The cowboy took a closer look and exclaimed: "Goda'mighty! Good nightshirt! I've killed the feller. It's only a no-account Mex, I reckon, but it could get me into trouble. I've got to get rid of him."

After making sure that nobody was watching, the buckaroo carried the body to an empty wagon and tossed it in. "I've got to get hold of a hoss," the cowhand muttered to himself, "and dump him into the nearest canyon. They'll think he was murdered by some badmen." He wrapped the body in an old horse blanket, tied it up with a rope, and went off in search of a horse.

After the cowpoke was gone, a drifter came riding up on a spavined pinto and spied the big bundle in the wagon. "Wonder what could be inside?" he mused. "Could be somethin' valuable." Quickly, he hoisted the heavy bundle behind him on his horse and rode on as fast as his sorry nag could carry its double load. When the drifter thought he was far enough to be safe, he rode into an arroyo surrounded by cottonwoods. There, out of sight, he eagerly untied and unwrapped the bundle. "Holy Moses!" he exclaimed. "It's a stiff! They'll think that I've done him in. With my record I wouldn't have a chance. I must get this hombre far away and cover my tracks." The drifter rewrapped the corpse and rode on all day until he came to a small cowtown. He once more unwrapped the body and dragged it into the nearest saloon, pretending to be a staggering boozer supporting his drunken pal. He propped his burden against the bar, made his inconspicuous exit, and rode off without looking back.

Inside the saloon, bellying up to the bar, was the "Texas Keed," a buck-toothed juvenile gunslinger. The Keed eyed the corpse with suspicion: "Stop starin' at me, if ya know what's good fer ya. I don't like to be stared at."

The corpse leaned on the bar, saying nothing. "I'm the human tornado loaded with chain lightnin'! I'm the admiration of all wimmin and the terror of their husbands. I'm the walkin' death and not one to be fooled with, stranger. I won't say it a third time—stop starin' at me!"

The corpse, grinning disdainfully, remained silent. Beside himself with rage, the Texas Keed whipped out his six-gun and let fly, ventilating the corpse with a hail of bullets.

"You've blown out his lamp, by Ned!" the bardog accused the Keed. "He warn't armed. This warn't a fair fight. This calls fer a necktie party."

"Hell," said the Texas Keed, "I only winged him. He ain't daid, he jest fainted with fear. I myself'll get him to the pillroller." He dragged the body out and plumped it on his horse, telling the bystanders, "I've only nicked him. The sawbones'll fix him up awright." The Keed trotted off.

Part way out of town, he encountered the stagecoach coming in from Tularosa. It was empty, except for the driver. With a sudden inspiration, the Keed hurled the body under the wheels of the stagecoach, yelling at the driver, "You dumb bastard! Why don't ya watch what yer doin'! You've run this feller over. He's crow meat fer sure. Yep, he's gone up the flume, awright."

"It ain't my fault," protested the driver. "He jumped right in front of me. He musta been drunk."

"You're supposed to look out fer drunks," said the Keed, spurring on his horse.

"Jesus, this could lose me my job," said the stage driver to himself. He propped up the corpse beside him on the driver's seat, making it look natural. In town he took on three passengers for Socorro—one soiled dove of the prairie, one drummer, and one cowman. Then he proceeded on his round.

"What's the matter with him?" inquired the soiled dove, pointing at the corpse.

"Drunk as a b'iled owl," said the driver, "dead to the world, ma'am. You know how these fellers are. Once they start, they can't stop. I've got to get him home to his old lady."

"She'll give him what-for, I bet," said the cowman.

They rolled on for some time. In the dark of a starless night the driver could barely make out the shape of a lone 'dobe house along the way. It gave him an idea: "This is the place," he said. "Come on, you old booze hound." He halted the stage, got the corpse down from its seat, draped it with one arm over his shoulder and dragged it to the house. He propped it against the door, and went back to the coach. Back upon his lofty throne he remarked to his passengers, "These drunks sure are a pain in the ass, if you pardon the expression."

"That's no way to talk to a lady," said the soiled dove.

Inside the adobe, Doña Inez shook her husband awake: "Mi esposo, did you hear it? There's someone at the door."

"Maybe another one of your lovers, mujer sucia, every night another one! It was only the stage passing by."

"No, no, husband, there is someone at the door. And how can you be so cruel as to remind me of what should be forgotten. Go and see what it is."

"Madre Santíssima, how you plague me," grumbled Don Policarpo. He lit his lamp and went to the door. He had to push it open against the weight of the corpse, which fell down with a plop on the porch's wooden floor.

"Eeegh!" the cantinero screamed in terror. "Holy Mother, protect us from evil!" Trembling with fear, his teeth chattering, he told his wife: "That cabrón, your dead lover, he's come back to haunt us. Válgame Dios! It is witchcraft. We are lost!"

"It seems we'll have to inconvenience our good neighbor Vigil the saddlemaker one more time," said Doña Inez.

The Caveman of the Hermit Peaks

In 1860, at Las Vegas, New Mexico, Don Manuel found himself host to a holy man, forbidding, even fear-inspiring, yet kindly mannered. The visitor from out of nowhere had long-flowing white hair and a scraggly beard. He was clad in a black robe that enveloped his body from the neck down to his bare feet. A curiously carved belt encircled his waist. From it dangled a rosary, made by himself out of wood, nuts, and leaves. His face was broad but cavernous, his mouth but a thin slash across his face. His eyes were hollow, but consumed with an inner fire. Some said that his gaze was like an auger boring into their minds and hearts.

The stranger called himself a solitary wanderer, a pilgrim who had roamed the world from one sanctuary, shrine, and holy place to the next in his endless search for salvation. He told his host that in between wanderings he had lived for years at a time as a world-shy hermit in caves or grottoes, beneath overhanging rocks, or on windswept mountaintops, amid wild animals, shunning the company of his fellowmen. He revealed himself as a Carthusian monk, bound by his vows to a life of prayer, silence, chastity, and self-denial. Don Manuel also discovered that beneath his black robe, his only garment, the stranger wore a girdle of spikes and thorns to mortify his flesh and, perhaps, atone for sins, real or imagined.

The visitor was known by many names—Fray Francisco, Don Juan Castellano, or Don Agustín. Some who were uncomfortable in his presence dubbed him the "mad anchorite." Those to whom he had done some kindness, and they were many, called him El Santo Ermitaño, or even Señor Jesús. He later told Don Manuel that his true name was Giovanni d'Agostini and that in 1800 he had entered the earthly vale of tears at Rome, the Eternal City—a son of sunny Italy. He added that he had made many pilgrimages to Santiago de Compostela, Lourdes, Trier, Canterbury, and to the Black Madonna of Czestochowa, in Poland, whose wonder-working image shed real tears, once every year, on the day of the Savior's Crucifixion.

In 1840 he had received a revelation. The Virgin had appeared to him in a dream, commanding him to travel to the New World to preach and spread the teachings of Bruno, the founder of the Carthusian Order. Thus he had sailed across the ocean to Mexico, South America, and the Caribbean Islands, sometimes reviled and imprisoned, as the Church eyed him with suspicion, even, on occasion, accusing him of practicing forbidden arts. A further vision had drawn him to the Shrine of the Holy Virgin of Guadalupe and, hence, to New Mexico.

At Las Vegas the common folk revered the hermit, convinced that he had the gift of healing, as well as many herbs, known only to him, to cure diseases regular doctors were powerless to heal. A girl named Concepción, coughing up blood, her body ravaged by consumption, came to him for help. He had given her a potion made from twelve different herbs, and she had gotten well. Her pale, sunken cheeks grew ruddy. Her wasted body put on flesh. Her ugliness turned to beauty. She married a good man.

Pablo, a santero, who could no longer carve his wooden images of saints because an opaque film covered his eyes, asked the ermitaño to give him back his sight. The Carthusian put a salve on Pablo's eyes, the film dissolved, and the joyful woodcarver went back to his God-pleasing work. As word of the hermit's healing powers spread, Don Manuel's home was besieged, day and night, by crowds of the lame, the halt, and the blind, wishing to be cured.

"I thank you for your hospitality," the monk told his host, "but I must leave you to seek the life of solitude that is ordained for me."

On his bare feet Don Giovanni ventured into the mountain wilderness, some thirty miles from Las Vegas. On Cerro Tecolote, the Hill of Owls, he discovered a cavern in a canyon wall that he chose for his abode. He stuck nails, pointing inward, into his cave's entrance, so that he should painfully bump into them, reminding him thereby to tell his beads and say his prayers. Once a month the saintly hermit emerged from his cave to wander down to Las Vegas, where he exchanged beautifully carved crucifixes and rosaries for cornmeal and salt. From his grotto's ceiling, moisture dripped, drop-by-drop, into a hollowed-out spot on the cave floor. From there he got all the water he needed. The people said that three drops of this water, caught at the top of one's tongue, would make a person tell the truth, and nothing but the truth, but nobody was ever able to catch more than two drops. Only for the hermit did the water drip with any sufficiency. That is why some people in Las Vegas remained liars all their lives. Some folks chanced upon him in the woods at the foot of his mountain. He was talking to animals, like Saint Francis, and the wild beasts answered. This, the watchers swore, they had seen with their own eyes.

Even on Cerro Tecolote the hermit's cave was besieged by many people clamoring to be doctored or to receive a blessing. The Santo Ermitaño felt that his solitude was overwhelmed by these visitors and withdrew to another, higher, more remote cave in the Organ Mountains, three hundred feet below the eastern summit of the great twin peaks dominating the landscape for many miles around. These peaks were bare of all vegetation, with a smooth, naked surface of gray rock glittering in the sunlight. Here too he was searched out by his admirers, though less numerous than before. These good folks put up a wooden shelter for him, which he never used, and erected three large crosses for his edification on the very top of his peak.

Visitors returning to their villages below told of the hermit's God-given power to perform miracles. There was no water on the peak to quench their thirst, but the holy one had struck the side of a cliff with his wand and forthwith crystal-clear water gushed from a crack in the rock wall. Others related that three does came and showed him where to strike the cliff and said that this water had a healing magic in it, because the hermit bathed a blind woman's eyes with it and she could see. To feed his visitors, the Carthusian always had a huge pot ready, filled with delicious chili stew, and the pot always remained full to the brim no matter how many people ate from it. Once twelve

men came to see the hermit. He had only half a handful of mush in his cave but, miracle of miracles, it fed them all. His devotees also swore that the saintly man was able to read their minds.

The solitary cave dweller predicted his own death. Every night as darkness fell he lit a bonfire that could be seen clearly in the valley below. Comforted by its warmth and the light shed by its flames, he prayed and chanted sacred songs. One day in April 1869 he told a visiting priest, "Tonight there will be no fire."

When the villagers noticed that on this evening the fire, whose flames had become for them a beacon of faith, was missing, they crossed themselves and said to each other, "The Santo Ermitaño is dead."

A party of men who had loved him made the arduous ascent to discover what had become of Don Giovanni. To their horror they found the old man in his cave, murdered, a dagger thrust through his heart. Don Giovanni's premonition had turned out to be true. There were rumors that not a dagger but many Apache arrows had killed him, that the Indians, without his knowing it, had hated him for establishing his sanctuary at a site sacred to them. Still others maintained that he had been hacked to pieces with swords and machetes by bandits who hoped to find golden church treasures inside his trunk, which was so heavy that two men could not lift it.

The hermit's death has remained a mystery to this day. After his murder an old woman said that she had overheard him talking to a one-eyed stranger, saying, "I know you are the man who has come to kill me."

A few old people still pray to him and tell of miracles resulting from such invocations. The twin mountains on whose summit he sought refuge have been known ever since as the Hermit Peaks.

The Miracles of Chimayo

Every Good Friday the roads to Chimayo, twenty-five miles north of Santa Fe, are crowded with pilgrims on their way to the miraculous Shrine of Chimayo, where they hope to be cured of whatever ails them. Some come by car or motorcycle, others on horseback; but many come on foot, ten, twenty, even thirty miles to make it hard on themselves, some run, and a handful even go so far as to make the journey on their knees. El Santuario de Chimayo is New Mexico's Lourdes, where miracles of healing occur and the happily cured leave their canes and crutches behind, hanging at the shrine's wall, mute testimony to the shrine's curative powers.

It all started during the semana santa, Holy Week, in the year of our Lord 1823. Don Bernardo Abeyta, a pious and God-fearing man, belonging to the Brotherhood of Penitentes, was mortifying his flesh on a lonely hill. He was scourging himself with a whip studded with nails and thorns, crying fervently: "Yo penitente pecador—I am a repentant sinner." Thus he atoned for his sins, which in his case were mere trifles. As he prayed and lashed himself, he beheld a wondrous light emanating from a nearby hole in the ground, close by a little stream that runs through the Chimayo Valley. Weak though he was from fasting and torturing himself, his legs crippled by rheumatism, Don Bernardo hobbled over to the shining light as fast as a deer and began digging in the ground with his bare hands. As he scooped out the earth, he came upon a crucifix bearing the carved image of Our Lord of Esquipulas. Now Esquipulas is a place of veneration in faraway Guatemala and how Nuestro Señor came from this far land to New Mexico is a great mystery, but then for a saint nothing is impossible and he can perform many miracles where and how he wishes. Don Bernardo fell upon his knees to worship the santo, offering a prayer to it. He then brought the image to Father Sebastián de Alvarez, the village priest, who took the saint to the Church of Santa Cruz, where he placed it in a niche of the main altar. But the next day the miraculous cross and image was back in its hole in the ground where it had been found.

"Some foolish trickster has done this, bringing the santo back here," complained Father Sebastián, "but I will put things right." So the priest took San Esquipulas back to Santa Cruz and put him into the same niche again. But the following morning the saint was back in his old hole.

"Santa Cruz and Chimayo are such tiny, no-account places, not fitting to be the abode of a saint as great as this," said Don Bernardo. "I am sure he wants to be in the big church of our capital city of Santa Fe."

Whereupon Don Bernardo got on his old mule and took the saint to the big church, where he put him right next to the altar. But the unbelievable happened—next morning the Lord of Esquipulas was back where he wanted to be.

"I think the saint wants to stay here with us," said Don Bernardo.

His wife began to grumble: "Mi esposo, this santo is just a piece of carved wood. You neglect your fields, your sheep, and me, your wife, for the sake of this wooden image. I shall burn it up!"

She had hardly uttered these evil words when she became crooked and hunchbacked, with her mouth pulled out of shape, making her hideous to look at.

"See what you have done, foolish mujer," Don Bernardo told his wife. "Let us kneel and pray to the saint to make you as pretty as before."

They prayed and Señora Abeyta took on her old shape again.

Don Bernardo still suffered agonizing pain from his rheumatism. One evening he was sitting on a hill overlooking the valley, admiring the sunset, when the Lord of Esquipulas appeared to him, standing by the little stream, enveloped by a heavenly light. Don Bernardo hastened to venerate the saint, but when he got there, lifting up his

folded hands, the vision disappeared. Don Bernardo fell upon his knees on the very spot where the saint had been standing and was instantly, and forever, cured of his rheumatism. In gratitude for this wonderful blessing Don Bernardo built a santuario with a splendidly carved and painted altar at the very place the santo had indicated. He enshrined El Posito, the sacred spot from which he had dug the crucifix, in a small square room to the left of the altar. There too he placed the cross with its saint, and it is said that once, during Holy Week, it sprouted branches and green leaves. From time to time, the santo gets down from the cross and takes on human shape, journeying far and wide to perform good deeds. On such occasions he travels so fast and far that he wears out his shoes. So people who believe in him are forever busy making new boots for him. Whenever the santo leaves the santuario, he does it in the middle of the night, because he does not want to be seen changing himself into a living man. From the six-foot-deep hole in the center of the little room, pilgrims take the miraculous earth that cures the diseases of all who truly believe in its powers. And no matter how much of holy earth they dig up, there is always more.

For half a century pilgrims arrived from everywhere to adore the cross and bring back to their homes some of the blessed earth, but then another great miracle occurred. Don Bernardo had a neighbor, Don Severiano Medina, who was also suffering grievously from rheumatism. To this Don Severiano appeared in a dream the Holy Child of Atocha, which has its shrine at Fresnillo, Mexico, indicating that if he turned to it for help he would be cured. Don Severiano began to pray fervently and earnestly to El Santo Niño. One day he was walking in the fields with his little daughter when they both heard church bells ringing somewhere in the ground below. They dug and found the image of the Holy Child sitting in an upright position, with a pilgrim's hat and staff. They reverently knelt down before El Santo Niño to adore it, and at once Don Severiano's rheumatism vanished, never to return. Overjoyed, the grateful worshiper built a private chapel to house the miraculous image, which without wasting even a minute began to bestow blessings of many kinds upon those who prayed to it.

But that was not all. Soon another Santo Niño was found in the same hole from which the holy cross had emerged. This Niño was installed in its own shrine inside a third room of the santuario. Some say that it is the Holy Child of Prague. This image also wears a wide-brimmed pilgrim's hat surmounted by a golden crown. It also wears out its shoes by going out at night doing good works. It is given gifts, not only of fine little shoes, but also of new clothes, which is why its high-collared silken cape is sometimes red and sometimes white, and his camisa is sometimes white and sometimes blue. This Santo Niño helps barren women to conceive and finds lost children, giving them water to drink and showing them the way home. Some say it is not the little image itself but the faith it inspires that brings about these blessings. There is no end of miracles at the Santuario de Chimayo.

The Miraculous Staircase

Bishop Lamy of Santa Fe was a Frenchman. It was his heart's desire to build a chapel in the City of the Holy Faith that was to be a replica of the Sainte-Chapelle in Paris, that wonderful medieval edifice whose slender ribs of stone are merely the frames for the magnificent glowing stained-glass windows, that cause the chapel to be filled with otherwordly multicolored light. Of course, Santa Fe being a much smaller city than Paris, its chapel would be proportionately smaller than the Sainte-Chapelle.

Another cherished dream of the good bishop was to install a convent where well-educated nuns would teach the boys and girls of the town's old families comportment, grammar, music, and all the other arts that go into the making of a civilized person. He therefore sent for a group of Sisters of Loretto to come by way of the old Santa Fe Trail. Theirs was a hazardous and exhausting journey, for travelers were still subject to raids by bandidos or hostile Indians. After their harrowing trip the sisters duly arrived, safe and sound, and founded their Academy of the Sisters of Loretto. Logically, the name Bishop Lamy intended to give the future church was the Loretto Chapel. At first, things did not work out as the good bishop had hoped. He had brought over from Europe an architect, Antoine Mouly, who went blind when the building was barely begun. The bishop engaged Antoine's son, Projectus Mouly, to continue his father's work of drawing up plans and designs. The problem was that, whereas the father's eyesight had been bad, the son's was too good, because his glance fell upon the sultry wife of the bishop's nephew and he began visiting the lady whenever her husband happened to be absent. The husband did not like this and he sternly forbade Projectus to set foot in his home, likewise forbidding his wife to receive him, whereupon the lady left his bed and board to live with the charming young architect at the Exchange Hotel. The outraged husband got himself a large-caliber Colt, waylaid the seducer as he emerged from the hotel, and shot him dead. In consequence, poor Bishop Lamy found himself without an architect and with a nephew in jail. As one of the sisters wrote in her dairy: "Mr. Lamy prefers to be left alone and brood over the loss of his domestic felicity . . . my impression is that His Grace knows of the tragic act—but knows nothing of what has caused it." Which is to be doubted, as His Grace was a Frenchman and intelligent.

In the absence of skilled local stonecutters and carvers, the bishop had imported a number of craftsmen from Italy. They built everything symmetrically with help from an architect—one door on the left, and an identical one on the right, so and so many windows on one side, and an equal number on the other. They finished the job, but when they took down the scaffolding it was found that there was no stairway leading up to the choir loft. Worse—there was in the whole chapel no room anywhere for a staircase. The Mother Superior, whose name was Madeleine, was very unhappy. After all, what good is a choir loft if there is no way to reach it? And so the black-robed sisters began searching for a skilled artisan to find a way of building the missing staircase. Many carpenters came, looked things over, and shook their heads. All of them said that there was simply not space enough to squeeze in a staircase.

The sisters of Loretto were desolate. The Mother Superior wept. What were they to do? One of the sisters, Blandina by name, had an idea. She took up her rosary and started praying, and telling her beads, for someone to come and solve the problem. Watching her, Mother Madeleine exclaimed, "Sister Blandina is right. Only prayers can help us. We must make a novena to Saint Joseph who, being a carpenter himself, will sympathize with us. We will get up one hour earlier than usual every morning and assemble in the chapel to pray to him."

The sisters held their novena and at its end, on the ninth day, a gaunt, white-bearded man leading a burro knocked on the convent's door. One of the sisters opened the door just a little bit and asked what he wanted. "I wish to speak to your Mother Superior," answered the stranger. He was brought to Mother Madeleine, who inquired, "Why have you come?"

"I have come," said the man, "because I am a carpenter and I will build the staircase you so badly need."

"That is very good of you," said the Mother Superior. "Let's see if you can do it."

The stranger went to work with a will. At first, the sisters were skeptical, because he had no tools except a hammer, a saw, and an old T-square, but as they observed how quickly and wonderfully the work progressed, they congratulated each other, saying, "This is indeed the right man for the job, whom God has sent us in answer to our prayers."

Whenever the sisters came into the chapel to pray, the carpenter discreetly made himself scarce, to return immediately after they had finished. He toiled long hours with a speed and skill that seemed more than human. It was also strange that he always had a good supply of hardwood at hand though nobody ever saw him buying wood of any kind. And no matter how hard and long he labored, he never tired in spite of being obviously a very old man. From time to time, Mother Madeleine brought up the subject of payment, not only for his work, but also for the materials he used, but the stranger always said that money was of no use to him and, please, not to bother him with such mundane matters.

As the work progressed, the nuns were amazed to discover that their carpenter was making a spiral staircase, something that had never before been done in Nueva Mexico and, being obviously a very pious and God-fearing man, he made the staircase of thirty-three steps—one for every year of our Savior's earthly life. At last, the work was finished. It was a truly great and splendid work of art, wondrous to behold, soaring in a double spiral upwards to the choir, seemingly without any visible support. Not a single nail or any other thing of metal had been used in its construction. All was held together with wooden pegs.

Mother Madeleine was at first speechless as she looked upon the finished stairs. "This is perfection," she exclaimed at last, her eyes filling with tears of joy, "perfection in its whole and in its smallest part."

She called for all the sisters to meet with her. "My heart is full of gratitude for this wonderful craftsman," she told them. "We must prepare a special feast for him as a sign of our appreciation for the wonderful thing he has done. Dear sisters, each and every one of you must prepare your favorite dish. We will set our best table for this good man, with silverware and candelabra, and, perchance, a bottle of His Grace's finest would not be amiss."

And so the sisters vied with each other roasting, boiling, frying, and braising, but when the meal was ready to be served, the carpenter was nowhere to be found. He was gone, having taken his burro and his tools with him. He had simply disappeared without asking for his pay or saying goodbye. Nobody had seen him leave either the chapel, the convent, or the city. He had gone without leaving a trace.

"Do not ask who he was, or where he has gone," said Mother Madeleine, "because he who built this wonderful escalier in answer to our prayers was none other than Saint Joseph himself, and from now on, and evermore, the wonder he has wrought shall be known as the Miraculous Staircase.

◆◆

The Hitchhiker

◆◆

This story occurs again and again in different places all over the West. The places, names, and details vary, but the plot is always the same.

Two young men, Eddie and Carl, from the University of Colorado, were driving their old Chevy home to Walsenburg. They were in a good mood, drinking "Purple Jesus," the collegian's delight. Vacation had come. The night was pleasantly cool and the stars were out. On both sides of the road the black shapes of towering mountains were silhouetted against the silvery sky. They drove around a bend to a corner dominated by a huge cottonwood seared by lightning. Caught in their headlights was a young, very pretty blonde in an organdy dress, sitting on a rock, a piece of luggage by her side. She was waving frantically for them to stop, and stop they did. She went up to the driver's side, where Eddie had the wheel, saying with a big smile of relief, "I'm sure glad to see you guys. I've been stuck here for hours. Can I hitch a ride with you?"

"You bet," said Eddie. "Hop in."

The girl pointed to a faded sign with an arrow saying SILVER CITY, and to a narrow dirt road leading off into the mountains: "That way, fellows. Silver City. You can't miss our place, an old Victorian house, full of turrets and balconies and curlicues. It's a real landmark."

"But we are going to Walsenburg," Carl objected.

"Gee, fellows, it's only twenty miles. You wouldn't leave me here alone in the middle of the night. Please. Mom will have coffee for you and her own special cherry pie she's famous for. Please."

"Cherry pie sounds real good," said Eddie while Carl put the blonde's bag in the trunk. The girl settled down in the backseat.

"I'm Daisy," she said. "We even have a pond in case you guys want to go for a swim."

"Eddie and Carl, pleased to meet you."

They drove on in silence, savoring the scent of pine and sage. The road was steep, winding, and full of potholes.

"This must be a hell of a drive in winter," said Eddie over his shoulder. There was no answer.

"I guess she has fallen asleep," said Carl. Ahead of them they saw a pole with a bright light. It belonged to a neglected-looking clapboard house whose white paint was peeling—an old-fashioned combined grocery and gas station. In front stood two ancient rusty gas pumps with white glass globes on top. A sign read GAS, ICE, SODA POP. In the window a red and blue neon sign blinked BUDWEISER.

They drove another mile and came to the imposing ruin of a large wooden house, half burned and half fallen in, with a faint acrid smell of ashes still clinging to it. One gaunt turret was still standing, together with parts of a gingerbread porch showing a lot of scrollwork. From the turret came the hooting of an owl. They drove on for another mile and came to a dead end. Carl leaned over into the backseat, saying, "Daisy, wake up! We need directions. We're lost." He stopped abruptly: "Hell, she isn't there. She's gone!"

"That's insane," said Eddie. "How could she have gone?"

"She must have jumped out without us noticing it. Not the first crazy dame we've run across. A pothead, probably, stoned out of her mind. Jesus, why us?"

They backed and filled till they got the car turned around on the narrow path. They stopped back at the gas station and knocked at the door. A sleepy old man in long johns appeared, grumbling, "I'm closed."

"We just want to ask directions. We're lost. We're looking for Silver City."

"This is it."

"This is what?"

"Silver City. My place. That's all there is to it."

"Well, maybe you can give us some advice. We picked up a girl about twenty miles back. She said her name was Daisy and that she lived in Silver City. In a big house. We couldn't miss it," said Carl. "She was in the backseat and now she's gone. We don't want to get into any trouble about her."

"Good nightshirt!" exclaimed the old man, exposing the stumps of his remaining two teeth, "She's done it agin!"

"Again? What the hell do you mean, again?" Eddie asked.

The old-timer scratched his head: "Her name was Daisy Rutter. Died some nine or ten years back in a car wreck at the corner where you picked her up. She was with two young fellers, jest like you. They had been drinking. Crashed into that big cottonwood. Car went up in flames. They were torched. It sure wasn't pretty. Her folks were well off. Owned a big place a mile further on. Nothing much left of it now. You see, she was their only child. So after she was gone the place soured on them and they left. Never came back. But she does, Daisy does. Once in a while she plays this trick on college boys like you, like the fellers who died with her. Then they come whining to me, asking 'What shall we do?' To tell the truth, I'm sick of it."

"Her bag is still in the trunk."

"I wouldn't bet on it. Can I sell you fellers some beer, nice and cold?"

"Thanks, but we must be getting on," said Eddie, shuddering. "It's still a long way to Walsenburg."

"Suit yourselves, boys."

Source Notes

Foreword

"Professed to give my narrative": *The Life of Colonel David Crockett, the irrepressible backwoodsman, written by himself* (Philadelphia: Porter & Coates, 1865), pp. 7–8.

"If it be objected": D. M. Kelsey, *Pioneer Heroes and Daring Deeds* (Philadelphia: Scammel & Co., 1882), p. v.

"This is true, us men pursued": Farley Mowat, *West Viking* (Boston: Little, Brown & Co., 1965), p. 270.

"Freydis, big with child": Ibid., pp. 256–57.

Chapter 1 • OHIO FEVER

"Disowned in an age of scepticism": Samuel Adams Drake, *New England Legends and Folklore* (Boston: Roberts Brothers, 1883), p. v.

"I ask you to look": Emerson Hough, *Frontier Omnibus* (New York: Grosset & Dunlap, 1907), pp. 7, 11, 19.

The Devil and Major Stobo: My own rendition of a story told by my wife, Jean, born and raised in Lancaster County, Pennsylvania.

The Cheater Cheated: This was told to me by Tom Cook, a Mohawk friend.

"The English manner of carrying on trade": Lewis Evans, quoted in Frederic May, Jr., *The Allegheny* (New York: Farrar & Rinehart, 1942), pp. 38–39.

The Wild Hunt: My own version of a story told by my wife's family.

Dreams: Funny Stories; or, The American Jester (New York: At the shop of Christian Brown, 1804).

The Skeleton Hand: I got this tale from my wife, Jean. This is my own version.

The Wild Hunter of the Juniata: From various sources, such as Augustus Lynch Manson, *The Pioneer History of America* (San Francisco: Bancroft & Co., 1883), and Charles McKnight, *Our Western Border* (Philadelphia: McCurdy & Co., 1876), pp. 109–11. The quoted passage is from Manson, pp. 168–69.

The Consequences of Not Letting a Man Have His Drink: My own version of several old tales.

The Laughing Head: My own retelling, inspired by an old Pennsylvania tale told me by my wife.

Chapter 2 • THE LONG HUNTERS

Tarzan Boone: My own version. I coined the name "Tarzan Boone" because of Boone's propensity for swinging from vines.

Swallowing a Scalping Knife: McKnight, *Our Western Border,* pp. 289–89.

That's John's Gun! Ibid., pp. 716–17.

A Clever Runner: My own version.

A Damn Good Jump: My own version. The quoted passage within the text is from Kelsey, *Pioneer Heroes and Daring Deeds,* pp. 190–91.

The Warrior Woman: Manson, *Pioneer History of America,* pp. 402–4.

The Corcondyle Head: My own version.

Chapter 3 • BACKWOODSMEN

"The instant I enter on my own land": Henry Tuckerman, *America and Her Commentators* (New York: Charles Scribner's Sons, 1864), p. 92.

The Irrepressible Backwoodsman and Original Humorist: All quotations are from *The Life of Colonel David Crockett.*

Grinning the Bark off a Tree: From *Sketches and Eccentricities of Col. David Crockett* (New York: J. & J. Harper, 1833), pp. 125–27.

David Crocket on the Stump: Joseph S. Williams, *Old Times in West Tennessee* (Memphis, Tenn.: W. G. Cheeney, 1873), pp. 175–76.

The Drinks Are on Me, Gentlemen: My own version of this often-told story.

Gouging the Critter: My own version.

Jim Bowie and His Big Knife: My own version, incorporating the following quotations:

"When the oncoming hordes": Colonel Frank Triplett, *Conquering the Wilderness* (New York: N. D. Thompson & Co., 1883), p. 698.

"Two Mexican Officers": Kelsey, *Pioneer Heroes and Daring Deeds,* p. 348.

Won't You Light, Stranger?: Slightly abridged, from T. C. Haliburton, *The Americans at Home; or, Byways, Backwoods, and Prairies* (London: Hurst & Blackett, 1854), vol. 2, pp. 237–39.

Ohio Poem: An early nineteenth-century folksong, one of many versions.

Chapter 4 · RING-TAILED ROARERS OF THE WESTERN WATERS

"They resembled—those unwieldy vessels": Seymour Dunbar, *History of Travel in America*, 4 vols. (1915; reprint ed. in 1 vol., Westport, Conn.: Greenwood Press, 1968), p. 272.

"He was of the restless type": Ibid., p. 292.

A Shooting Match: David Crockett Almanac, 1840, vol. 2, quoted in Walter Blair and Franklin J. Meine, *Mike Fink, King of Mississippi Keelboatmen* (New York: Henry Holt & Co., 1933), pp. 133–35.

Did Such a Helliferocious Man Ever Live? My own version, a distillation of a dozen different accounts.

Like Father, Like Daughter: David Crockett Almanac, 1853, quoted from "Sal, the Mississippi Screamer," in Jack Conroy, ed., *Midland Humor* (New York, 1947), pp. 9–10.

She Fought Her Weight in She-B'ars: My own version.

He Crowed and Flapped His Wings: Montgomery Bird, *Nick of the Woods* (Philadelphia: Carey, Lea & Blanchard, 1837), vol. 1, pp. 58–59.

A Fight Between Keelboatmen Averted: My own version, from a combination of several others.

Stranger, Is This a Free Fight?: Harper's Monthly Magazine, December 1855.

The Screaming Head: My own version.

Stopped Drinking for Good: There are several versions of this story. I drew upon them for my own version.

Chapter 5 · MOUNTAIN MEN

"The rendezvous is one continued scene": George Frederick Ruxton, "Adventures in Mexico and the Rocky Mountains," *Blackwood's Magazine*, 1848, quoted in Glen Rounds, *Mountain Men* (New York: Holiday House, 1966), p. 6.

"The fur trader, trapper, or mountain man": Robert Glass Cleland, *This Reckless Breed of Men* (New York: Alfred A. Knopf, 1950), p. 5.

Little Big Man: My own introduction.

"Discharging his rifle and pistols": Emerson Bennett, *The Prairie Flower* (1849), quoted in Kent Ladd Steckmesser, *The Western Hero in History and Legend* (Norman: University of Oklahoma Press, 1965), p. 37.

"Among the men congregated": De Witt C. Peters, *The Life and Adventures of Kit Carson* (New York: Clark & Co., 1859), pp. 98–101.

Kit Carson and the Grizzlies: Ibid., pp. 82–86.

Run for Your Life, White Man!: My own version.

Old Solitaire: My version, incorporating the following quotations. "Williams always rode ahead": Ruxton, "Adventures in Mexico and the Rocky Mountains," quoted from George Frederick Ruxton, *In the Old West* (Cleveland and New York: Macmillan Co., 1915), pp. 184–85.

"When with a large party of trappers": Ibid., p. 187.

"On one occasion": Ibid., p. 189.

"A party of trappers were crossing": Charles H. L. Johnston, *Famous Frontiersmen* (Boston: Page Co., 1913), pp. 221–22.

"Old and gray, marked with the scars": Triplett, *Conquering the Wilderness*, pp. 430–31.

Pegleg Smith and Headless Harry: My own retelling.

Mind the Time We Took Pawnee Topknots? Lewis H. Garrard, *Wah-To-Yah and the Taos Trail* (1856; reprint ed., Palo Alto, Calif.: American West Publishing Co., 1968), pp. 153–54.

Lover Boy of the Prairies, Including the Saga of Pine Leaf, the Indian Amazon: My own version, gathered from many sources. Some quotations are from Thomas D. Bonner, *The Life and Adventures of James P. Beckwourth* (New York: Harper & Brothers, 1856). This work was reprinted many times, by several publishers—Alfred A. Knopf in 1931, the University of Nebraska Press in 1971, and various British publishers in the late nineteenth century.

Putrefactions: Ruxton, *In the Old West*, pp. 32–36.

The Injin Killed Me Dead: My own rendition of a many-times-told tale.

Heaven According to Old Gabe: My own story.

Damn Good Shootin': My own retelling, from many fragments.

Uncle Joe, the Humorist: Abridged, from Frances Fuller Victor, *The River of the West* (San Francisco: Bliss & Co., 1870).

Ba'tiste's Nightmare: Slightly abridged, from George Catlin, *The Manners, Customs, and Conditions of the North American Indian* (London: Henry G. Bohn, 1866), vol. 2, pp. 178–80. My own copy curiously bears the stamp of the Allahabad Light Horse Regimental Library. How it got there and hence to New York is a mystery.

Song of the Voyageur: William Henry Drummond, quoted in Grace Lee Nute, *The Voyageur* (New York: D. Appleton-Century Co., 1931), p. 262.

Chapter 6 • TIMBER!

Paul Bunyan and His Little Blue Ox: My own version.

Paul Bunyan Helps to Build a Railroad: My own retelling.

Kidnapped by a Flea: My own story.

Thunder Bay: James Stevens. *The Saginaw Paul Bunyan* (New York: Alfred A. Knopf, 1932), pp. 141–46.

Chapter 7 • GOLD! GOLD! GOLD!

Tommy-Knockers: My own version of a number of variations of this story.

It Had a Light Where Its Heart Ought to Have Been: My own version.

He Ate All the Democrats of Hinsdale County: My own retelling, from a dozen sources.

A Golden-Haired Fellow: My own rendition of an anecdote many times told.

Treasures of Various Kinds: My own version.

The Missing Chest: My own version of a supposedly true happening.

Chapter 8 · GIT ALONG, LITTLE DOGIES

"For the matter of a week": William Savage, quoted in Alfred Henry Lewis, *Wolfville Days* (New York: Grosset & Dunlap, 1902), pp. 7–15.

The Saga of Pecos Bill: My own version.

The Taming of Pecos Bill's Gal Sue: My own version.

Coyote Makes a Texas Cowboy: My own story.

The Heart-Shaped Mark: My own version.

The Skeleton Bride: My own version.

The Western Jack and the Cornstalk: My own version.

Better Move That Drat Thing: My own version, out of very many.

Being Afoot in Roswell: My own version of an old anecdote, many times told.

Outstunk the Skunk: Winifred Kupper, *The Golden Hoof* (New York: Alfred A. Knopf, 1945), p. 77.

Chapter 9 · THEY DIED WITH THEIR BOOTS ON

"The genus 'KID' wore his hair long": James Cabell Brown, *Calabazas* (San Francisco: Valleau & Peterson, 1892), pp. 25–26.

"But Western life ain't wild and woolly now": Howard Thorpe, *Songs of the Cowboy* (Boston: Houghton Mifflin Co., 1908), p. 86.

No-Head Joaquín and Three-Fingered Jack: My own retelling.

The Headless Horseman of the Mother Lode: My own retelling.

El Keed: My own version.

El Chivato: My own version. The verses quoted are from John A. Lomax and Alan Lomax, *Cowboy Songs* (New York: Macmillan Co., 1938), pp. 140–41.

He Rose from the Grave: My own version.

A Whale of a Fellow with a Gun: My own retelling.

The King of the Pistoleers:

"Six foot one in his moccasins": Kelsey, *Pioneer Heroes and Daring Deeds*, p. 474.

"He is a naturally fine-looking fellow": *Manhattan Independent*, October 26, 1867.

"The man they call Wild Bill": From contemporary local newspapers.

"Old Bill couldn't hit": From contemporary local newspapers.

"He was absolutely fearless": William E. Connelley, *Wild Bill and His Era* (New York: Pioneer Press, 1933), p. 17.

"I suppose I have killed": Ibid.

"Singlehandedly, 'Magnificent Bill' ": George Ward Nichols, "Wild Bill," *Harper's Magazine*, February 1867, pp. 273–85.

" 'Now, you scoundrels' ": Kelsey, *Pioneer Heroes and Daring Deeds*, p. 505.

"Bill jumped from his hiding place": Ibid., pp. 493–95.

"It is disgusting": Nyle H. Miller and Joseph W. Snell, *Great Gunfighters of the Kansas Cowtowns* (Lincoln: University of Nebraska Press, 1967), p.110.

"Bill was the darling": Miller and Snell, *Great Gunfighters of the Kansas Cowtowns*, p. 113; Eugene Cunningham, *Triggernometry* (Caldwell, Ohio: Caxton Printers, 1952), p. 266.

"He always had a mistress": Peter Lyon, *The Wild, Wild West* (New York: Funk & Wagnalls, 1969), p. 46.

A Western Duel: My own version.

The Nuptials of Dangerous Davis: Bill Nye, *Bill Nye and the Boomerang* (Chicago: Belford & Clarke, 1881), pp. 250–53.

Killing Off the James Boys: Ibid., pp. 48–49.

Theme and Variations: My own version.

The Winchester Ghosts: My own retelling.

Chapter 10 · BUCKING THE TIGER

"All men on the plains were gamblers": Triplett, *Conquering the Wilderness*, p. 336.

"Occasionally Calamity Jane took a hand": Herbert Asbury, *Sucker's Progress* (New York: Dodd, Mead & Co., 1938), p. 356.

A Hard Head: George Devol, *Forty Years a Gambler on the Mississippi* (New York: George Devol, 1892), pp. 267–68.

Indians Can Play Poker: Ibid., pp. 20–21.

Jim Bowie Takes a Hand: The quotations are from Asbury, *Sucker's Progress*, pp. 207–8.

The Curly-Headed Little Boy: Abridged, from Charles B. Gillespie, "A Miner's Sunday in Coloma: From the Writer's Journal, 1849–50," *Century Magazine* 42 (1891).

Shall We Have a Drop? My own tale.

Colonel Tubbs Strikes It Rich: My retelling of a long yarn in one of the Deadwood Dick dime novels of 1888.

Good for Our Entire Assets: Richard Erdoes, *Saloons of the Old West* (New York: Alfred A. Knopf, 1979), p. 161.

The One-Eyed Gambler: Eugene Edwards, *From "Jack Pots: Stories of the Great*

American Game" (Chicago: 1900), p. 321. Also quoted in Asbury, *Sucker's Progress*, pp. 352–53.

Chapter 11 • LADY WILDCATS OF THE PLAINS

Born Before Her Time: My own introduction.

"As far as real merit": *Deadwood Daily Champion*, quoted in Watson Parker, *Gold in the Black Hills* (Norman: University of Oklahoma Press, 1966), p. 168.

"The Joan of Arc of the Indian Wars": Duncan Aikman, *Calamity Jane and the Lady Wildcats* (1927; reprint ed., Lincoln: University of Nebraska Press, 1987), p. 110.

How Old Calam Got Her Name: A potpourri from old dime novels, with missing parts rendered in the same Victorian style.

Calamity Meets a Long-Lost Lover: From a dime novel by Edward Wheeler, *Deadwood Dick on Deck* (New York: Beadle's Pocket Library, 1887).

Chapter 12 • THE MAN WHO NEVER WAS

Deadwood Dick: My own introduction.

Deadwood Dick and the Grizzly: After 1880s dime novels.

Deadwood Dick to the Rescue: From various fragments of dime novels in the author's collection.

Chapter 13 • AND THAT'S MY ROOLIN'

"H. P. Barber, the lawyer for George Work": Quoted by Evelyn Wells and Harry C. Peterson, *The Forty-Niners* (Garden City, N.Y.: Doubleday & Co., 1949), p. 209.

The Law West of the Pecos: My own introduction.

"He was born one day at Toyah": Charles J. Finger, *Frontier Ballards* (Garden City, N.Y.: Doubleday & Co., 1927), p. 277. One of fourteen verses.

Ah Ling's Hommyside: One of a dozen versions, beginning in 1899. This one is from C. L. Sonnichsen, *Roy Bean, Law West of the Pecos* (Old Greenwich, Conn.: Devin Adair Co., 1968), p. 121.

"Judge Roy Bean of Vinegaroon": Omar Barker, "The Ballad of Roy Bean," in Everett Lloyd *The Law West of the Pecos* (San Antonio, Texas: Naylor Co., 1936), quoted in Finger, *Frontier Ballads*, p. 276.

Fining the Deceased: My own version.

The Hanging of Carlos Robles: My own version. There are many others.

Roy Bean's Pet Bear: My own version.

Judge Barker, Old Zim, and the One-Eyed Mule: From *Greeley Tribune* (Colorado), 1875. Reprinted in *Colorado Magazine*, November 1937.

El Cuatro de Julio: From the *Mesilla Independent,* July 7, 1877.

A Drink's Worth of Punishment: From the *Weekly New Mexican*, September 1872.

Chapter 14 · SKY PILOTS

"We had little or no education": Strickland and Cartwright, *Autobiography of a Backwoods Preacher* (New York: Harper & Brothers, 1856), p. 6.

Preachin' One Can Understand: My own reconstruction from several fragments.

The Parable of the Prodigal Son: Nye, *Bill Nye and Boomerang*, pp. 87–90.

Lissen to the Heavenly Poker Player! My own version. The quotation "The 'Ace' reminds us" to "David, Solomon, and Herod" is from James Cabell Brown, *Calabazas* (San Francisco: Valleau & Peterson, 1892), p. 831.

Hear What the Great Herd Book Says! From a manuscript in the New Mexico State Library.

A Funeral Oration: Contributed by Robert Burnette, twice chairman of the Rosebud Sioux tribe.

A Black Hills Sermon: William DeVere, *Tramp Poems of the West* (Tacoma, Wash.: Cromwell Printing Co., 1891), pp. 21–22.

Chapter 15 · CRITTERS

The Valley of Headless Men: My own version.

A Loup-Garou, or a Windigo, or Maybe a Carcajou: There are innumerable windigo and loup-garou stories. I have made one out of many.

The Call of the Wild: My own version.

The Windigo: My own version.

The Great White Stallion of the West: My own version, except for the quotation from Washington Irving, *A Tour of the Prairies*.

"Nor the team of the Sun, as in fable portrayed": J. Barber, *U.S. Magazine and Democratic Review* (New York), 1843.

Until Judgment Day: My own version.

El Diablo Negro: This is my own version, combining several "demon horse" tales.

Snake Yarns: My introduction.

A Rolling Snake Gathers No Moss: My own version. There are innumerable others about the legendary hoopsnake.

The White Snakes: My own rendition.

A Pair of Fine Boots: Again, my own version.

The Young Man Who Wanted to Be Snake-Bit: One of my wife's old stories.

The Peg-Leg Cat: Again, my rendition of a childhood story of my wife's.

Chapter 16 • MOSTLY LIES

Somebody in My Bed: From *The Spirit of the Times,* December 13, 1845, vol. 20, p. 518, quoted in Thomas D. Clark *The Rampaging Frontier* (Indianapolis: Bobbs-Merrill Co., 1939), pp. 112–13.

The Weather: Simply a bunch of old anecdotes.

It Gets Mighty Cold Around Here: My own rendition, from many different versions.

Texican Liars: Samuel Hammett, *In Piney Woods; or, Sam Slick in Texas* (Philadelphia, 1858).

Chapter 17 • MIRACLES, SAINTS, AND WITCHES

The Three Lost Daughters: My own version.

The Two Witches: Helen Zunser, "A New Mexican Village," *Journal of American Folklore,* vol 48 (1935), pp. 125–78.

The Owl Witch: My own version.

San Isidro and the Angel: My own version.

A Riddle: Maria Leach and Jerome Fried, eds., *Funk and Wagnalls Standard Dictionary of Folklore, Mythology, and Legend* (New York: Funk and Wagnalls, 1950), vol. 2, p. 1070. These riddles occur in the Southwest.

The Many-Times-Killed Young Man: My own version.

The Caveman of the Hermit Peaks: This is supposedly a true story. I composed my version from various accounts and tales dealing with this hermit.

The Miracle of Chimayo: My own rendition.

The Miraculous Staircase: My own version.

The Hitchhiker: My own version.

Bibliography

Aikman, Duncan. *Calamity Jane and the Lady Wildcats.* 1927. Reprint ed. Lincoln: University of Nebraska Press, 1987.

Applegate, Frank. *Indian Stories from the Pueblos.* Philadelphia: J. B. Lippincott Co., 1929.

———. *Native Tales of New Mexico.* Philadelphia: J. B. Lippincott Co., 1932.

Asbury, Herbert. *Sucker's Progress.* New York: Dodd, Mead & Co., 1938.

Barker, Ruth Laughlin. "New Mexico Witch Tales." In J. Frank Dobie, ed., *Tone the Bell Easy.* Austin: 1932, pp. 62–70.

Blair, Walter, and Frank J. Meine. *Mike Fink, King of Mississippi Keelboatmen.* New York: Henry Holt & Co., 1930.

Blair, Walter, and Frank J. Meine, eds. *Half Horse, Half Alligator.* Chicago: University of Chicago Press, 1956.

Bonner, T. D. *The Life and Adventures of James P. Beckwourth.* New York: Harper & Brothers, 1856.

Botkin, B.A., ed. *A Treasury of Western Folklore.* New York: Crown Publishing Co., 1951.

Brown, Charles E. *Whisky Jack Tales.* Madison, Wis.: State Historical Museum, 1940.

Brown, James Cabell. *Calabazas.* San Franciso: Valleau & Peterson, 1892.

Catlin, George. *The Manners, Customs, and Conditions of the North American Indian.* 2 vols. London: Henry G. Bohn, 1866.

Clark, Thomas D. *The Rampaging Frontier.* Indianapolis: Bobbs-Merrill Co., 1939.

Clough, Ben C., ed. *The American Imagination at Work.* New York: Alfred A. Knopf, 1947.

[Crockett, David.] *The Autobiography of David Crockett.* With an introduction by Hamlin Garland. New York: Scribner's, 1923.

De Vere, William. *Tramp Poets of the West.* Tacoma, Wash.: Cromwell Printing Co., 1891.

Devol, George. *Forty Years a Gambler on the Mississippi.* New York: George Devol, 1892.

Dobie, J. Frank. *Coronado's Children: Tales of Lost Mines and Buried Treasures of the Southwest.* Dallas: Southwest Press, 1930.

Dorson, Richard M. *America in Legend*. New York: Pantheon Books, 1971.
———. *Davy Crockett, American Comic Legend*. New York: Rockland Editions, 1939.
Ellis, Amanda. *Legends and Tales of the Rockies*. Colorado Springs: Denton Printing Co., 1954.
Erdoes, Richard. *Saloons of the Old West*. New York: Alfred A. Knopf, 1979.
Erenhart, Perry. *Treasure Tales of the Rockies*. Denver: Sage Books, 1961.
Espinoza, José Manuel. "Spanish Folk Tales from New Mexico." *Memoirs of the American Folk-Lore Society* 30 (1937): xvi–xvii.
Favour, Alpheus H. *Old Bill Williams*. Chapel Hill: University of North Carolina Press, 1936.
Fuller, Frances. *The River of the West*. San Francisco: Bliss & Co., 1870.
Garrard, Lewis H. *Wah-To-Yah and the Taos Trail*. Glendale, Calif.: Arthur H. Clark Co., 1938.
Hallenbeck, Clive. *Legends of the Spanish Southwest*. Glendale, Calif.: Arthur H. Clark Co., 1938.
Lawrence, Eleanor. "Horse Thieves on the Spanish Trail." *Touring Topics*, 23, no. 1 (January 1931).
Lewis, Alfred Henry. *Wolfville Days*. New York: Grosset & Dunlap, 1897.
Lovelace, Leland. *Lost Mines and Hidden Treasure*. San Antonio, Texas: Naylor Co., 1956.
McDaniel, Ruel. *Vinegaroon*. Kingsport, Tenn.: Southern Publishers, 1936.
Meine, Franklin J., ed. *The Crockett Almanacs*. Chicago: Caxton Club, 1955.
Nye, Bill. *Bill Nye and the Boomerang*. Chicago: Belford & Clarke, 1881.
Patterson, Paul. *Pecos Tales*. Austin: Texas Folklore Society, 1967.
Peters, DeWitt Clinton. *Pioneer Life and Frontier Adventures*. Boston: 1884.
Pike, Albert. *Prose Sketches and Poems*. Boston, 1834.
Porter, Clyde, and Mae Reed Porter. *Ruxton of the Rockies*. Edited by LeRoy Hafen. Norman: University of Oklahoma Press, 1950.
[Porter, William Sydney.] *Complete Works of O. Henry*. New York: Garden City Publishing Co., 1937.
Randolph, Vance. *Ozark Superstitions*. New York: Columbia University Press, 1947.
———. *Sticks in the Knapsack and Other Ozark Folk Tales*. New York: Columbia University Press, 1958.
Reader's Digest. *American Folklore and Legend*. Pleasantville, N.Y.: Readers Digest Assn., 1975.
Russell, Carl P. *Picture Books of the Fur Trade History*. Reprinted from the *Missouri Historical Society Bulletin* 4, no. 3 (April 1948).
Ruxton, George Frederick. "Adventures in Mexico and the Rocky Mountains." *Blackwoods' Magazine*, 1848.
Sage, Rufus. *Scenes in the Rocky Mountains*. Philadelphia, 1846.
Shackford, James A. *David Crockett, the Man and the Legend*. Edited by John B. Shackford. Chapel Hill: University of North Carolina Press, 1956.
Sonnichsen, C. L. *Roy Bean, Law West of the Pecos*. Old Greenwich, Conn.: Devin Adair Co., 1935.
Stevens, James. *The Saginaw Paul Bunyan*. New York: Alfred A. Knopf, 1932.

Thorpe, Howard. *Songs of the Cowboy.* Boston: Houghton Mifflin Co., 1908.

Triplett, Colonel Frank. *Conquering the Wilderness.* New York: N. D. Thompson & Co., 1883.

Vestal, Stanley. *Mountain Men.* Boston: Houghton Mifflin, 1937.

Weigle, Marta. *Two Guadalupes: Legends and Magic Tales from New Mexico.* Santa Fe, N.M.: Ancient City Press, 1987.

Wells, Frank Evarts. *Story of Old Bill Williams.* A collection of stories about Old Bill printed and sold at Williams, Arizona, in pamphlet form.

About the Author

Richard Erdoes was born in Frankfurt, Germany, and educated in Vienna, Berlin, and Paris. His many books on the American West include *Lame Deer, Seeker of Visions; Saloons of the West; The Rain Dance People; The Sun Dance People;* and *The Sound of Flutes.* With Alfonso Ortiz he edited and selected *American Indian Myths and Legends,* and with Mary Crow Dog he wrote *Lakota Woman.* His photographs have been published in *National Geographic, Life,* and other magazines, and he created the illustrations that appear in this volume. He now lives in Santa Fe, New Mexico.

DATE DUE	
DEC 2 3 1993	
SEP 2 5 1996	
MAR 1 9 1997	
MAR 3 0 1998	
APR 2 1 1998	

GAYLORD   PRINTED IN U.S.A.